SUMMARY OF PARADOX OPERATIONS

KU-306-071

OPERATIONS	MENU OPTIONS OR KEY	PAGE
Forms (borders)	Forms/Border	190
Forms (calculated fields)	Forms/Field/Place/Calculated	292
Forms (changing)	Forms/Change	197
Forms (copying)	Tools/Copy/Form	199
Forms (creating)	Forms/Design	183
Forms (displaying)	Image/PickForm	196
Forms (enhancing)	Forms/Style	185
Forms (moving items)	Forms/Area/Move	192
Forms (multiple tables)	Modify/MultiEntry/Entry	344
Forms (placing fields)	Forms/Field/Place	186
Forms (Removing borders)	Forms/Border/Erase	195
Forms (removing fields)	Forms/Field/Erase	194
Forms (saving)	Forms/DO-IT!	195
Global deletions	Ask delete option	126
Global edits	Ask changeto option	124
Go to a field	Image/GoTo/Field	58
Go to a record	Image/GoTo/Record	58
Go to a value	Image/GoTo/Value	59
Go to a value	Zoom key (Ctrl-Z)	59
Help	Help *or* F1 key	17
Import data	Tools/ExportImport/Import	383
Insert a new record	Ins key	45
Locate a record	Ask find option	122
Locate a record	Zoom key (Ctrl-Z)	59
Locate next record	Zoom Next (Alt-Z)	59
Move a column	Image/Move	60
Number formats	Image/Format	56
Open a table	View	51
PAL program (create)	Scripts/Editor/Write	417
PAL program (modify)	Scripts/Editor/Edit	421
PAL program (run)	Scripts/Play	419
Print data	Instant Report key (Alt-F7)	64
Print a report	Report/Output	149
Protect data	Tools/More/Protect	375

ALAN W FOSTER

MASTERING
PARADOX™

Third Editon

ALAN SIMPSON

San Francisco • Paris • Düsseldorf • London

Cover design by Thomas Ingalls + Associates
Cover photography by Casey Cartwright
Series design by Julie Bilski

Paradox is a trademark of Ansa Software.
Symphony and **1-2-3** are trademarks of Lotus Development Corporation.
dBASE II and **dBASE III** are trademarks of Ashton-Tate.
WordStar and **MailMerge** are trademarks of MicroPro International.
IBM and **IBM Personal Computer** are registered trademarks of International Business Machines Corporation.
VisiCalc is a trademark of VisiCorp.
Pfs is a registered trademark of Software Publishing Corporation.

SYBEX is a registered trademark of SYBEX, Inc.

SYBEX is not affiliated with any manufacturer.

Every effort has been made to supply complete and accurate information. However, SYBEX assumes no responsibility for its use, nor for any infringements of patents or other rights of third parties which would result.

Copyright ©1986 SYBEX Inc., 2021 Challenger Drive #100, Alameda, CA 94501. World rights reserved. No part of this publication may be stored in a retrieval system, transmitted, or reproduced in any way, including but not limited to photocopy, photograph, magnetic or other record, without the prior agreement and written permission of the publisher.

Third edition copyright ©1988 by SYBEX, Inc.

Library of Congress Card Number: **87-83564**
ISBN **0-89588-490-9**
Manufactured in the United States of America
10 9 8 7 6 5 4 3 2 1

To the "women" in my life—Susan and Ashley

ACKNOWLEDGMENTS

Many thanks to all the people at SYBEX who helped carry this book from the idea stage into your hands: Barbara Gordon, managing editor; Jon Strickland, editor; Bob Campbell, technical reviewer; John Kadyk, word processor; Charles Cowens, typesetter; Maria Mart, proofreader; Michelle Hoffman, screen-shot reproducer; and Debbie Burnham-Kidwell, indexer.

Also, many thanks to Bill and Cynthia Gladstone, my literary agents, for keeping my writing career alive and well. And of course, many thanks to Susan, my wife, for being patient through my long hours at the keyboard, and our daughter Ashley, for keeping me company in the office.

TABLE OF CONTENTS

P   A   R   T   2   *MULTIPLE TABLES IN A DATABASE* ___

INTRODUCTION

Quite simply, Paradox is a powerful database-management system that anyone can use. Historically, database-management systems have been "programming-language" oriented and thus best used as tools by programmers and sophisticated computer users. The need to remember numerous commands, functions, data types, syntax rules, file structures, and so on made the older database-management systems unwieldy for the neophyte and occasional computer user.

Enter Paradox—a new approach to database management that frees the user from having to memorize complex commands. With Paradox, even the occasional user can effectively manage large amounts of data with no programming whatsoever. You can store, retrieve, sort, print, change, and ask questions about your data by selecting options from menus and filling in standardized forms.

So what is so paradoxical about Paradox? The paradox is that even though the program is so easy to use, it does not compromise on power or flexibility. You can ask complex questions about several interrelated tables of data without any programming. On the other hand, if you like to program or you want to develop sophisticated custom applications, Paradox allows you to do so, using a sophisticated programming language named PAL.

WHO THIS BOOK IS FOR

This book is designed for a true database novice—one who has never used Paradox or any other database-management system. In fact, if you can turn a computer on and off, you're off to a good start. If you don't know what a database-management system is, don't worry about it—you will after the first chapter.

This book will also help those who already have experience with Paradox or some other database-management system. By working through the basics using common, practical examples and then building on acquired skills, this book can help anyone gain full mastery over Paradox's more advanced features, including techniques for designing and managing systems with multiple tables.

Those who are already accomplished Paradox users and want to learn programming techniques in PAL may find that this book is too introductory. While this book does touch on the subject and presents examples of more common programming techniques, a complete tutorial on advanced database-management techniques is simply beyond its scope.

This book is designed to be a tutorial, not a reference guide. Of course, you can use the book as a reference simply by referring to the index, but the book is designed to be read from beginning to end. Concepts are taught in order of complexity, from the simple to the more abstract. Such an approach facilitates learning and understanding. Once you've learned how to use Paradox effectively and understand what Paradox is all about, you'll find more technical information, in a form that is easier to assimilate, in the *Paradox User's Guide* that comes with the program.

HELPFUL TOOLS

Before embarking on your work with Paradox, you should familiarize yourself with some helpful tools included in the Paradox package. To begin with, there is a plastic template that shows the effects of the various function keys on your keyboard. Put this template over the function keys for quick reference. These keys and their Paradox names are summarized in Table I.1.

In Chapter 2 of the *Paradox User's Guide*, there is a fold-out diagram of special keys you can use while working in various modes of Paradox. Appendices A–D of this book also show keys that you can use in Paradox's various modes.

The other manuals that come with the Paradox package are, of course, also valuable tools. These manuals, though difficult to learn from, present all the capabilities of Paradox and are useful reference books. This book does not duplicate all of the material found in those

FUNCTION KEY	PARADOX FUNCTION NAME
F1	Help
F2	DO-IT!
F3	Up Image
Alt-F3	Instant Script Record
F4	Down Image
Alt-F4	Instant Script Play
F5	Example
Alt-F5	Field View
F6	Check Mark
Alt-F6	Check Plus
F7	Form Toggle
Alt-F7	Instant Report
F8	Clear Image
Alt-F8	Clear All
F9	Edit

Table I.1: The Paradox function key names

manuals, so you should refer to them for more technical information when necessary.

STRUCTURE OF THE BOOK

This book starts with the basics and builds on acquired skills to help you gain total mastery. In the first ten chapters you will learn how to create, edit, store, retrieve, sort, search, print, and restructure a database. Chapter 11 touches on the concept of *scripts*, which allow you to record and play back long keystroke sequences.

Chapters 12 through 15 deal with more advanced techniques involving multiple tables of information. Chapter 16 discusses general techniques that you can use to manage information, as well as techniques for interfacing with other software systems such as Lotus 1-2-3, Symphony, dBASE II and III, WordStar, and WordPerfect.

Chapter 17 introduces PAL, the Paradox Applications Language, and demonstrates numerous PAL commands and programming techniques that you can use in developing custom applications. Chapter 18 presents a complete application, written with PAL, to manage a mailing list or customer list. Chapter 20 demonstrates the Paradox Personal Programmer, a tool that comes with your Paradox package to help you develop custom applications, even if you have little or no programming experience.

Chapter 21 discusses the Data Entry Toolkit, which also comes with your Paradox package. This Toolkit lets you create sophisticated forms for entering data into a table, and is used primarily by advanced PAL programmers.

Appendices A through D present illustrations of keys used in various Paradox modes.

WHICH VERSION OF PARADOX?

This book is written entirely for version 2.0 of Paradox. For those of you who are already familiar with the earlier versions of Paradox, the following list describes the major features that are new to version 2:

- Multi-user capabilities: Version 2 of Paradox can run on most of the networks currently available for microcomputers, allowing multiple users to manipulate tables simultaneously.

- Bigger tables: The original 65,000 record limit on tables has been increased to a maximum of 2 billion records.

- Memory Management: Version 2 supports EMS and EEMS to prevent you from running out of memory.

- Zoom: You can look up information quickly in any field in a table using the new Zoom key.

- LookUpHelp and Automatic FillIn: You can quickly look up information in a related table, and copy similar fields to the current table with a single keystroke.

- Extended Field view: Field view is no longer limited to table edits, and can be used at anytime.

- Word-wrap: Long alphanumeric fields can be word-wrapped—that is, broken between words rather than between characters—on printed reports.

- Mailing labels: You can print single or double columns of mailing labels without resorting to a PAL script.

- More forms and reports: A single table can have up to 15 forms and reports associated with it, rather than the previous 10.

- Range output: When printing reports you can specify a particular range of pages to print, which is particularly handy when your printer makes a mess of just a few pages.

- Summary functions: Besides the Calculated and Summary fields already available in earlier versions of Paradox, you can now use summary functions to perform calculations on the sum, average, highest value, lowest value, or count of records in a report group.

- Personal Programmer enhancements: The new Personal Programmer offers many new features over the previous ApGen, including Table view and Form Toggle for editing, entering, and viewing data; automatic generation of high-speed procedure libraries, automatic documentation generation, outer joins, and tools for copying, deleting, and renaming entire applications.

- The Data Entry Toolkit: This new feature lets experienced PAL programmers develop highly sophisticated data-entry and editing forms.

- New PAL commands and functions: PAL offers new commands and functions for networking, error trapping, form management, and more.

PARADOX 386

Those of you with microcomputers that use the Intel 80386 microprocessor may want to use the Paradox 386 package, which allows you to build larger, faster, and more sophisticated applications than Paradox version 2.0. Paradox 386 takes full advantage of the 80386 microprocessor and add-in boards that emulate the 80386 processor, by breaking through the 640K memory barrier and using up to 16 megabytes of RAM. Paradox 386 also uses the 80386 32-bit instruction set to speed performance.

Even though Paradox 386 takes advantage of the increased capabilities of the 80386 processor, it still remains compatible with other processors and microcomputer environments. This is a big benefit to large corporations with many different hardware and software configurations on their computers, because network systems using a variety of hardware and operating systems can still share Paradox database files and applications. In addition, corporations that are gradually upgrading to more powerful systems will be able to take advantage of Paradox 386 compatibility with the DOS 3.X and OS/2 operating systems.

—— *CONVENTIONS USED IN THIS BOOK* ——

Several typographical conventions used throughout this book are summarized here:

Crtl-, Alt-, Shift-	Indicates that you must hold down the Ctrl, Alt, or Shift key (respectively) while typing the character that follows. For example, Ctrl-Z means, "Hold down the Ctrl key and press the letter Z."
F keys	Function keys labeled F1 through F10 (or F12) on your keyboard are displayed in text as they are on the keyboard. For example, "Press F1" means, "Press the F1 key", *not* "Press the two separate keys F and 1."
Ins	The Ins key is labeled Insert on some keyboards.
Del	The Del key is labeled Delete on some keyboards.
Enter	The Enter key is labeled ⏎ on some keyboards and Return on others.
Esc	The Escape key is labeled Esc, Escape, or Cancel on different keyboards.

A GOOD TIP FOR TYROS

If you are an absolute beginner on computers, a simple saying to keep in mind is

If in doubt...
Escape key out!

This means that if you ever find yourself lost in the Paradox menus, and want to get back to more familiar territory, you can usually press the Esc key (labeled Esc, Escape, or Cancel on your keyboard) to move back up the menu system until you are in more familiar territory. The key is named "Escape" because it usually lets you do just that!

A DISK TO ACCOMPANY THIS BOOK

All of the sample tables, custom forms, report formats, scripts, and PAL applications in this book can be purchased on disk, ready to use on your computer. See the coupon at the end of this book for ordering instructions.

P A R T   I

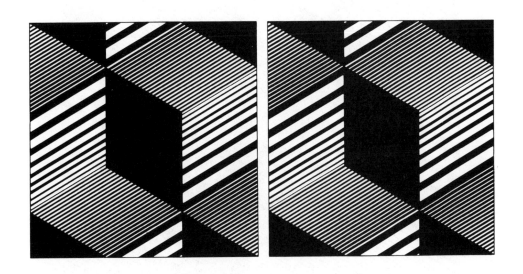

THE BASICS

DATABASES

IF YOU ARE NEW TO THE DATABASE-MANAGEMENT game, you'll need to understand a few basic concepts, as well as the buzzwords that go along with them. In this chapter, we'll discuss all the basics to get you started in the direction of total mastery, beginning with a definition of the term *database management.*

WHAT IS A DATABASE?

A database is simply a collection of information or *data,* like a Rolodex file, file cabinet, or shoe box filled with names and addresses on index cards. Whenever you access a database, whether it be to add new information, get information, change information, or sort the information into some meaningful order, you are *managing* your database.

A computer *database-management system,* like Paradox, performs these same types of operations on a database that is stored on a computer disk. It allows you to add, change, delete, look up, and sort information. However, tasks that may take several minutes, hours, or even days to perform manually usually take the computer only a few seconds to perform.

We often refer to our paper databases as files. A computer database is also called a *file,* or a *table.* The term table stems from the unique structure that all databases use. Every file, or table, in a database is neatly organized into *columns* and *rows.* Let's look at an example.

Suppose you have a Rolodex file, and each card in the Rolodex file contains the name and address of an individual, as in Figure 1.1. The Rolodex card has four lines of information on it: (1) name, (2) address, (3) city, state, zip, and (4) phone number.

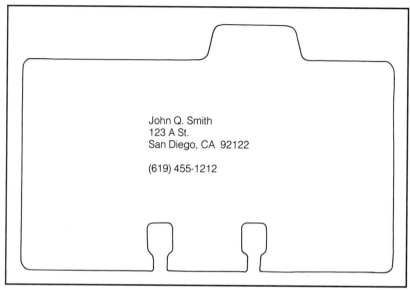

Figure 1.1: A sample Rolodex card

This one Rolodex card represents 1 row, or *record,* on a database table. Each unique item of information (name, address, city, state, zip code) represents roughly 1 column, or *field,* of information on a table. Figure 1.2 shows how information from a Rolodex file might look on a database table.

```
Last Name    First Name   Address     City      State  Zip Code    Phone
======================================================================
Smith        John Q.      123 A St.   San Diego  CA    92122     (619)455-1212
Jones        Alma         234 B St.   Berkeley   CA    94710     (415)555-4141
Zeepers      Zeke         Box 1234    Ashland    OR    98765     (123)555-1010
```

Figure 1.2: A sample database table with three records

Note in Figure 1.2 that the table consists of three records (rows): one each for Smith, Jones, and Zeepers. Each record contains seven fields (columns): Last Name, First Name, Address, City, State, Zip Code, and Phone. As you've probably guessed by now, the terms *record* and *row* are synonymous, as are the terms *fields* and *column.*

Do keep in mind that this is only a simple example. A table can be used to store and manage any kind of information—inventory, book-keeping, accounts payable, receivables . . . just about anything that comes to mind. However, regardless of the *type* of information you plan on managing, that information will be stored in tables consisting of rows and columns (that is, records and fields). Some types of information might be spread across several tables, but we need not concern ourselves with that issue just yet.

FIELD NAMES

One important difference between human database managers and computers is the issue of *context*. Humans can often tell what a piece of information is just by its context. For example, it does not take a genius to figure out that on a Rolodex card, Smith is probably someone's last name, and (619) 455-1212 is probably a phone number. This seems pretty obvious.

Nothing is obvious to a computer. Therefore, each column in a database must have a name. Notice that in Figure 1.2, field names were listed across the top of the table, as below:

<u>Last Name</u> <u>First Name</u> <u>Address</u> <u>City</u> <u>State</u> <u>Zip Code</u> <u>Phone</u>

When storing data on a database table, each unique item of information must have a unique *field name* associated with it. With that in mind, we need to discuss just what constitutes a *unique* item of information.

In the sample Rolodex card we discussed a while ago, each card contained the following information:

Name
Address
City, State   Zip code
Phone number

Hastily, one might set up a table with four fields of information to resemble the format of the Rolodex card, as below:

<u>Name</u>   <u>Address</u>   CityStateZip   <u>Phone</u>

But to set up a database table in this way would be a mistake, simply because the table is not broken down into enough unique items of information. For example, if you wanted to sort the data in this table into zip code order to do a bulk mailing, you would not be able to. Because the zip code is embedded in the same field as the city and state, there is no way to tell Paradox to sort by zip code. Zip code would have to be a unique field in order to sort on it.

And what about the Name field? Suppose you had a list of names as below:

Andy Zeepers
Melba Miller
Zanda Adams

If you asked Paradox to sort these names into alphabetical order, they would stay in their current order, rather than being ordered alphabetically by last name. To properly sort by last name, the Name field would need to be divided into at least two fields—Last Name and First Name. That way, you could tell Paradox specifically to sort into last name order.

Finally, suppose you wanted a listing of only California residents. Again, the hasty table structure would not allow you to obtain such a list, because the state is embedded in the same field as the city and zip code.

With a bit of experience (which you'll gain while using this book) and forethought, you would probably structure a table of names and addresses for the Rolodex data with at least seven fields, as below:

Last Name   First Name   Address   City   State   Zip Code   Phone

Now, each *meaningful* item of data is placed in a separate field, which will give you complete freedom in managing your data. (If you've never used a computer before, don't worry. You'll find out soon enough what I mean by "complete freedom" in managing your data.)

Once you've broken your information down into meaningful units of information (which we've just done) and structured a database table with Paradox (which we'll do in the next chapter), you can begin *managing* your data. Let's discuss this term in more detail.

MANAGING A DATABASE

Managing a database primarily involves the following tasks:

- *Adding* new data to the database
- *Sorting* the database into some meaningful order
- *Searching* the database for types of information
- *Printing* data from the database onto formatted reports
- *Editing* data in the database
- *Deleting* data from the database

Looking back at our Rolodex example, occasionally we may need to *add* some new cards. We may want to *sort* the cards into some meaningful order (say, alphabetically or by zip code) for easy access. We might want to *search* through them and find all the people who live in Los Angeles, or all the people in the 92123 zip code area, or perhaps just find out where Clark Kenney lives. If Clark Kenney moves, we may want to change (*edit*) his card to reflect his new address and phone number. Then again, if Clark Kenney stops paying his dues, we may want to *delete* him altogether from the Rolodex. We might want to use these data to *print* various other documents, such as mailing labels, form letters, or a directory.

Paradox can easily handle all of these basic database-management tasks. In fact, these tasks represent only a small sample of Paradox's full capabilities. Paradox can do all kinds of additional tasks, such as calculate totals and subtotals, access and combine data from multiple tables, and import and export data from other software systems. However, the big difference between managing a database by hand and doing so with Paradox is speed. As mentioned earlier, what might take hours with a typewriter and Rolodex cards will probably take only seconds or minutes with Paradox.

PARADOX LIMITATIONS

Now that you know what records and fields are, you may be curious about just how much information Paradox can handle. Paradox limitations are listed below. Keep in mind that one *character* of information is equal to one alphabetic letter. For example, "Dog" consists of three characters, and "My House" consists of eight characters (spaces count as characters). Furthermore, the term *byte* also refers to one character, hence "My House" contains eight bytes. In Paradox, a single table can contain the following quantities of information, in these combinations:

- 2 billion rows (records)
- 4,000 characters on a single record
- 255 fields in a single record
- 255 characters within a single field

There is no limit to the number of tables that you can manage with Paradox, other than the sheer amount of disk storage capacity that you have.

SYSTEM REQUIREMENTS

In order to use Paradox, you need the following hardware and software:

- An IBM PC, XT, AT, or PS/2 computer, or a computer that is 100% compatible with one of the IBM models
- At least 512K bytes of main memory (RAM)
- DOS 2.0 or higher as your operating system
- Either one hard disk and one floppy disk, or two floppy disks

Let's review the basics of database management with Paradox before we move on to Chapter 2 and start putting Paradox to work.

SUMMARY

- A *database* is a collection of information, like a file cabinet or a Rolodex file.

- Paradox stores information in *tables*.

- A *table* consists of *rows* (*records*) and *columns* (*fields*).

- Each *column* or *field* in a database contains a unique item of information, such as a last name, address, or zip code.

- Each field in a table must have a unique *field name*.

CREATING A TABLE

CHAPTER 2 _____

IN THIS CHAPTER WE'LL USE PARADOX TO CREATE A table. Before you can actually begin using Paradox, however, you'll have to tailor the program to run on your computer, which is what we'll discuss now.

Note that in the discussions below, the Enter key refers to the key marked ◄─┘ on most IBM keyboards. This same key is also referred to as the Return key, or the Carriage Return key.

INSTALLATION _____

The procedures you use to install Paradox on your computer will depend on the particular computer configuration that you are using. This section discusses techniques for installing *single-user* Paradox on a computer with a hard disk or a computer with two floppy disks. If you plan to use *multiuser* Paradox on a network, you should refer to the appropriate installation procedures that came with your Paradox package in the booklet entitled *Network Administrator's Guide*.

Keep in mind that you need only install Paradox once on your computer. If you (or somebody else) has already installed Paradox, you can skip this section altogether and move right to the next section entitled *Starting Paradox*.

INSTALLING PARADOX ON A HARD DISK

Before you install Paradox on your hard disk, use the DOS DIR or CHKDSK command to make sure that you have at least 1 megabyte

(1,000,000 bytes) of space available. Then follow these steps to perform the installation procedure:

1. Make sure your hard disk is the current drive (on most computers you'll see the DOS C> prompt on the screen when logged onto the hard drive). If you are not logged onto the hard disk, enter the hard disk drive letter and a colon at the DOS prompt and press Enter (for example, type

    C:

    and press Enter to log onto drive C).

2. If your computer uses 5¹/₄-inch floppy disks, insert the disk labeled "Installation Disk" that came with your Paradox package into drive A (label side up and facing you). If your computer uses 3¹/₂-inch disks, insert the disk labeled "Installation/Sample Tables Disk" instead.

3. Type in the command A:INSTALL followed by the drive letter of your hard disk and a colon. For example, if your hard disk is C, type in the command

    A: INSTALL C:

    and then press Enter.

4. Follow the instructions as they appear on the screen. When asked to specify a country group, select the country group that best suits your needs from the options presented on the screen and summarized in Table 2.1. Type in the appropriate number and then press the key labeled F2 to enter your selection and continue. (Even though you select a country group here, you can always change your mind later for a particular situation.)

5. Paradox will copy a few files onto your hard disk and then ask that you insert System Disk I (if you are using 5¹/₄-inch disks) or System Disk I/II (if you are using 3¹/₂-inch disks) into drive A. First, remove the installation disk from drive A and then insert the appropriate disk as instructed. Press any key to continue.

6. A *sign in* screen will appear in which you must enter your name, company name (if any), and Paradox serial number

OPTION	COUNTRY GROUP	APPROPRIATE FOR...
1	United States	United States
2	English International	English-speaking countries outside the U.S.
3	European	Non-Scandinavian European countries
4	Swedish/Finnish	Sweden and Finland
5	Norwegian/Danish	Norway and Denmark

Table 2.1: Country groups for installing Paradox

(which is inside your Paradox package). Fill in the appropriate information, pressing Enter after completing each item. The last question on the screen,

Access data on a network? [Y,N]:

should be answered by typing Y only if you are using Paradox on a network. (Again, refer to the Paradox *Network Administrator's Guide* for network installation techniques if it is appropriate.) Press the F2 key after filling in all the questions.

7. Insert the various disks as Paradox requests to complete the installation procedure. When the installation is complete, you'll see the message

Paradox has been successfully installed

and instructions for starting Paradox. At that point, remove the floppy disk from drive A and reboot by simultaneously holding down the Ctrl and Alt keys on your keyboard and pressing the Del key.

INSTALLING PARADOX ON A COMPUTER WITH FLOPPY DISKS ONLY

If your computer has two floppy disk drives rather than a hard disk, follow the instructions in this section to install Paradox. If you are using a computer with 5¹/₄-inch disks, you'll need to use a copy of your DOS disk and a bootable disk during the installation procedure. If you have never done so, make a copy of your DOS disk by placing the DOS disk in drive A and a blank, unformatted disk in drive B of your computer. From the A> prompt, enter the command

FORMAT B:/S

and press Enter. When the format is complete, enter the command

COPY *.* B:

and press Enter. When the copy is complete, remove the disk from drive B and label it "DOS disk for booting Paradox."

To make a blank, bootable disk, place a new, unused disk (not a Paradox disk or any other disk containing information) in drive B, enter the command

FORMAT B:/S

at the DOS A> prompt, and press Enter. Then follow these steps to install Paradox:

1. Start your computer with the copy of the DOS disk in drive A so that the DOS A> prompt appears. If the A> prompt does not appear, enter the command

    A:

    and press Enter to log onto drive A.

2. If you are using 5¹/₄-inch floppy disks, insert the Paradox Installation Disk in drive A and the DOS copy in drive B. If you are using a computer with 3¹/₂-inch disk drives, insert the Installation/Sample Tables Disk in drive A instead of the Installation Disk.

3. Type the command

    FINSTALL

    and press Enter.

4. The program will ask you to select a country group for organizing data, as summarized in Table 2.1. Enter the number corresponding to the appropriate country, then press the key labeled F2. (Even though you select a country group here, you can always change your mind later for a particular situation.)

5. Copy a file named Config.SYS to your DOS copy, and, when instructed, remove the DOS copy from drive B and replace it with Paradox System Disk I. (If you are using 3½-inch disks, insert the Paradox System Disk I/II disk in drive B instead.)

6. A *sign in* screen will appear in which you must enter your name, company name (if any), and Paradox serial number (which is inside your Paradox package). Fill in the appropriate information, pressing Enter after completing each item. The last question on the screen,

   Access data on a network? [Y,N]:

   should be answered by typing Y only if you are using Paradox on a network. (Again, refer to the Paradox *Network Administrator's Guide* for network installation techniques if it is appropriate.) Press the F2 key after filling in all the questions.

7. The screen will instruct you to remove and insert other disks as the installation procedure progresses. Follow the instructions as they appear on the screen.

8. As a safety precaution, make backup copies of all your Paradox disks. To do so, place any Paradox disk in drive A of your computer, place a blank disk in drive B, and type the command

   DISKCOPY A: B:

   at the A > prompt. (As usual, press Enter after typing in the command.)

STARTING PARADOX

Once you've successfully installed Paradox on your computer, you can begin to use it. To do so, you'll need to first get it up and running, using the appropriate instructions for your computer as discussed below.

STARTING PARADOX ON A HARD DISK

If your computer has a hard disk, you can follow the steps below to run Paradox. (Note: To see which directory you are logged onto on your hard disk you can enter the command

PROMPT PG

at the DOS C> prompt. As you change directories, the directory name will appear next to the C> prompt.)

1. Log onto the Paradox2 directory by typing the command

   CD\PARADOX2

   at the DOS prompt, followed by the Enter key.

2. To start Paradox, type in the command

   PARADOX2

   and press Enter. The Paradox opening screen and copyright notice will appear, followed by the Paradox Main menu.

STARTING PARADOX
ON A FLOPPY DISK SYSTEM

To start Paradox on a computer with only floppy disks, first insert the DOS disk for booting Paradox (the DOS copy you made during the installation procedure discussed previously) into drive A. Then follow these steps:

1. Turn on the computer if it is not already on, or reboot by holding down the Ctrl and Alt keys while pressing the Del key.

2. After the DOS A> prompt appears, remove your DOS disk for booting Paradox from drive A and insert your Paradox System Disk I disk in its place.

3. Next to the A> prompt, type the command

   PARADOX2

   and press the Enter key.

4. When so instructed, remove System Disk I from drive A, insert Paradox System Disk II, and press any key to continue. A copyright notice will appear, followed by the Paradox Main menu.

THE MAIN MENU

Once you've started Paradox, you'll see the Main menu as shown in Figure 2.1. The top two lines of the screen represent the *menu area.* The empty space below the menu area is called the *workspace.* The first menu item, View, is highlighted with the *menu highlight.* In addition, some messages will occasionally be displayed in the lower-right corner of the screen in an area called the *message window.*

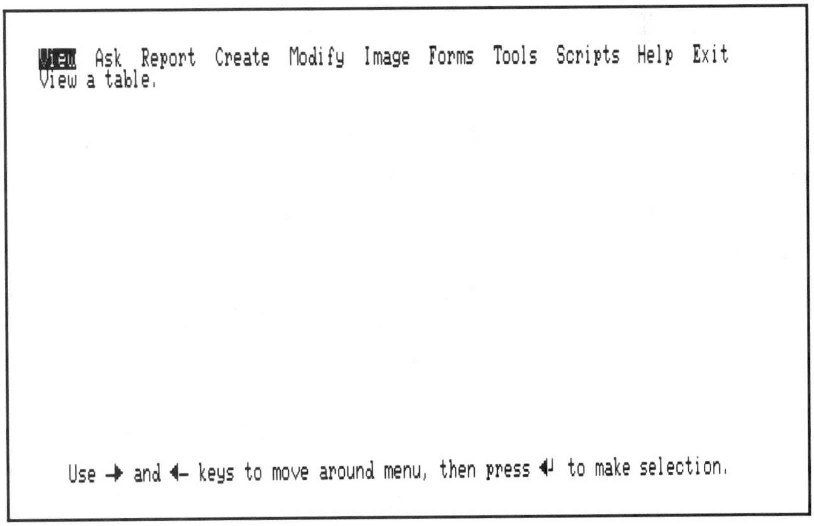

```
View Ask Report Create Modify Image Forms Tools Scripts Help Exit
View a table.



















    Use → and ← keys to move around menu, then press ↵ to make selection.
```

Figure 2.1: The Paradox Main menu

You can move the menu highlight from one menu item to the next using these keys:

KEY	*EFFECT*
←	Move highlight to the left one item
→	Move highlight to the right one item
Home	Move highlight to the first menu item
End	Move highlight to the last menu item
Enter	Select the currently highlighted item
Esc	Unselect an item: return to previous menu

To try out the keys, try pressing the ← and → keys a few times. (Notice that if you hold one of these keys down, the highlight moves quickly through the options.) As you highlight each menu option, a brief description of what the menu option does appears below the menu. For example, when the View option is highlighted, the message

View a table.

appears just below the menu.

Pressing the Home key moves the highlight to the first menu item; pressing End moves the highlight to the last menu item. If these arrow keys do not work, and instead produce only beeps, press the NumLock key above the number pad on your keyboard. This will switch from "Numbers" to "Arrow" mode.

SELECTING MENU ITEMS

There are two ways to select items from the menu:

1. Highlight the option you wish to select, using the arrow keys, then press Enter.

2. Type the first letter of the menu option. For example, to select View, type V.

UNSELECTING MENU ITEMS

Occasionally, particularly as a beginner, you might get lost in the series of menus that Paradox will display. In that case, simply press the Escape key (labeled Esc or CANCEL on most keyboards) to return to the previous menu. The rule of thumb on navigating menus is

> If in doubt . . .
> Escape key out

To try out the Escape key, select the Tools option, either by moving the highlight to the option and pressing Enter or by typing the letter T. The Tools menu will appear, as below:

> Rename QuerySpeedup ExportImport Copy Delete
> Info Net More

Since probably none of these items means much to you right now, you can "back out" of this menu by pressing the Escape key. Do so now to return to the Main menu.

CALLING UP THE MENU

In some situations the Paradox Main menu will disappear, to be replaced by other information. To bring the menu back to the screen, simply press the Menu (F10) key. This is an important key to remember, because most Paradox operations begin by selecting an item from a menu.

GETTING HELP

Paradox has an elaborate system of help screens, which you can access at any time by pressing the Help (F1) key. For example, if you press the Help (F1) key while the View option on the Main menu is highlighted, you'll see the help screen shown in Figure 2.2.

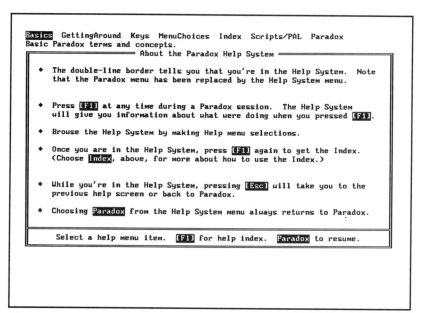

Figure 2.2: A Paradox help screen

Notice that there is a menu above the help screen. Like all menus in Paradox, you can move the highlight with the arrow keys. You select an option either by pressing Enter when the option is highlighted or by typing in the first letter of the menu option.

You might want to take a moment now to explore the help screens. Paradox's help system is *context sensitive,* which means that if you press Help while creating a table, you'll receive help in creating a table. If you press Help while sorting a table, you'll see a help screen with information about sorting.

Pressing the Help key while you are viewing any help screen brings you to the highest-level help screen (the one shown in Figure 2.2). Selecting the Paradox option (or typing P) while you are viewing a help screen always returns you to the place where you left off before pressing the Help key. Take a moment to read the contents of the help screen in Figure 2.2 and experiment with some of its options. When you are done, select the Paradox option to return to the Main menu, so we can create our first table.

CREATING A TABLE

For our first example, we'll create a table to manage a basic mailing list, or customer list. We'll put the following fields of information on it:

FIELD NAME	*CONTENTS*
Mr/Mrs	A title such as Mr., Mrs., Ms., or Dr.
Last Name	An individual's last name
First Name	An individual's first name
M.I.	A middle initial and period (for example, M.)
Company	A company name
Department	A department name
Address	A street address or mailing address
City	A city name
State	A two-letter state abbreviation
Zip	A zip code up to 10 digits (for example, 12345-1234)
Start Date	The date the record was entered into the computer
Credit Limit	A dollar amount

I've included the Credit Limit field only to demonstrate techniques used in managing numbers. A basic mailing-list system might not need such a field, but we will need it for examples and exercises later in the book.

In later chapters, we'll develop some more complex, interrelated tables. But to get a good foundation in the basics, we'll start with this fairly simple example.

The first step in creating a table is to select the Create option from the Main menu. Do so now. Paradox will ask for the name of the new table, as shown below:

Table:
Enter new table name

A table name must adhere to a few simple rules, listed below:

- It can be no more than eight characters in length.
- It can contain letters, numbers, and underline characters (_), but the name must begin with a letter or number.
- It should not contain any blank spaces—that is, it must be a single word.
- Though not essential, the table name should describe its contents, such as "Mail" for a mailing-list table, or "Invoices" for an invoice table.

For this example, enter the table name Custlist by typing in the name Custlist and pressing Enter. This brings up a screen for entering the table structure, as shown in Figure 2.3. Notice that the word "STRUCT" appears in the upper-left corner of the box on the screen. This is short for "structure."

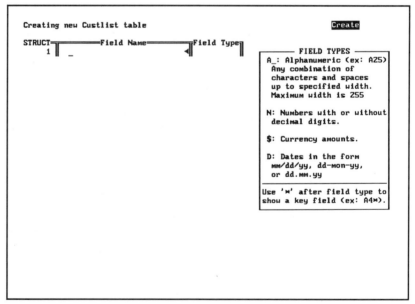

Figure 2.3: A screen for creating a new table

FIELD NAMES

The Field Name area on the screen is where you enter the name of each field to be used in the table. Rules for entering field names are listed below:

- Each can be no more than 25 characters in length.

- Each field name can contain letters, numbers, spaces, and other symbols, but it must begin with a letter.

- Each must be unique within the table: a single table cannot have two fields with the same name.

Now, keep in mind that you may assign any name you like to a field. For example, you could actually assign the field names "hamburger" or "termite lips" to a field that contains zip codes. Neither Paradox, nor your computer, would object, since neither knows the difference between a zip code, a hamburger, or a pair of termite lips. However, for the sake of convenience it is best to assign field names that describe the contents of the fields. Therefore, you should use descriptive field names, such as Zip or Zip Code, when creating table structures for a field containing zip codes.

DATA TYPES

The Field Type column is where you define the type of data to be stored in a field. Your options, as displayed on the screen, are listed below:

SYMBOL   DATA TYPE

A   Alphanumeric data: These fields can contain letters, numeric characters, spaces, and other symbols. Alphanumeric data consists of "textual" information such as names, addresses, titles, or any other information for which you will not be performing math. A field length must be included with this data type. For example, A25 defines an alphanumeric field with a fixed length of 25 characters. The maximum length you can define is 255 characters.

N Numeric data: These fields store "real" numbers, such as quantities, and allow for mathematical operations such as addition, subtraction, multiplication, and division. They can accept only numeric characters (0–9), decimal points, commas, and negative signs. Alphabetic characters are not allowed.

$ Currency data: These fields store numeric data representing dollar amounts. Currency data is like numeric data, except that all numbers are automatically rounded to two decimal places of accuracy, and negative values are enclosed in parentheses.

D Date: This data type is used to store dates in either MM/DD/YY or DD-Mon-YY format. Paradox automatically validates any entry, rejecting a date like 02/31/88, and allows for "date arithmetic."

Armed with this knowledge of data types, we can begin structuring our table.

ENTERING THE TABLE STRUCTURE

To enter a table structure, simply type in field names and data types. Finish each entry by pressing the Enter key. For example, to enter the first field, "Mr/Mrs", type Mr/Mrs and press Enter. This field will contain alphanumeric data, with a maximum (fixed) length of four characters, so enter the data type as A4 (by typing A4), then press the Enter key. Your screen should now look like Figure 2.4.

Before entering any more field definitions, take a look at the key commands listed in Table 2.2. These keys, as you'll discover later, are almost universal in Paradox. That is, they are used in the same manner to perform several different tasks. Take a moment to study them now. Be advised that the Backspace key is the one with the large, dark, left arrow, which is usually on the upper-right corner of the main typing keys on your keyboard.

Enter the remaining field definitions as shown in Figure 2.5. If you make a mistake while entering the table structure, try using the key commands shown in Table 2.2 to make corrections.

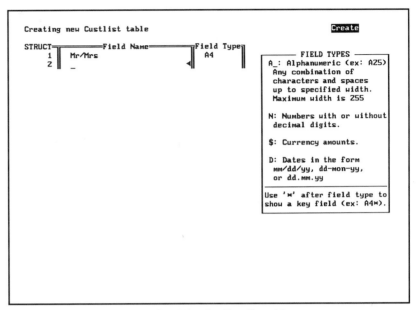

Figure 2.4: The first field defined for the Custlist table

KEY	EFFECT
Backspace	Moves cursor to the left, and erase as moving
→	Moves cursor to the right
←	Moves cursor to the left
↑	Moves cursor up a row
↓	Moves cursor down a row
Enter	Completes entry of a field definition
Ins	Inserts a blank at this field position
Del	Deletes this field definition
DO-IT! (F2)	Saves table structure
Help (F1)	Provides help defining a table structure

Table 2.2: Keys used when defining a table structure

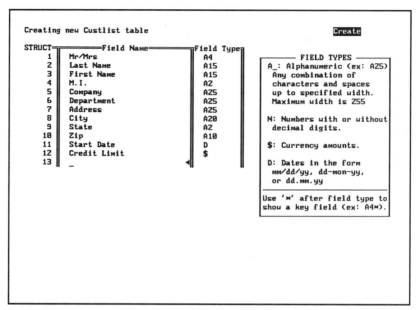

Figure 2.5: The structure for the Custlist table

Let's discuss the rationale for the structure for our table. First of all, the customer name is actually divided into four separate fields: a title (Mr/Mrs), last name, first name, and middle initial (M.I.). As we'll see later, it is easier to manage the database when the name is broken into this many meaningful pieces of information. We've made each of these fields the alphanumeric data type, since none has any numeric value. The fixed (maximum) length for the title is four characters ("Miss" is the longest title), both Last Name and First Name have maximum lengths of 15 characters, and M.I. (middle initial) has a length of two characters.

When determining a length for a field, keep in mind that the longer the maximum length assigned, the more memory will be required to store the information. (For example, even the last name "Nye" will be stored as 15 characters of information if the field definition allows 15 characters.) Therefore, be conservative, though realistic, when defining lengths.

The Company, Department, Address, City, State, and Zip Code fields are also alphanumeric data. They have lengths of 25, 25, 25, 20, 2, and 10, respectively.

Now you may be wondering why the zip code is not stored as a number. After all, isn't 92122 a number? The answer to that is both yes and no. While it is true that 92122 is a number, some zip codes, such as 92038-2802, or 00341, or A0341J11, are not. If the Zip Code field were defined as a real number (N), the following problems would occur with the "oddball" zip codes:

1. Hyphenated zip codes might eventually be treated as equations. For instance, 92038-2802 might result in 89236, which is the difference of 92,038 minus 2,802.

2. Leading zeroes are always eliminated from real numbers; hence the zip code 00341 would appear as 341 on a mailing label or envelope.

3. A foreign zip code such as A0341J11 would not be allowed in the table, since real numbers cannot contain alphabetic characters.

In view of these constraints, a zip code is clearly not a real number. (The same holds true for phone numbers, for similar reasons.) Hence we've defined Zip Code as alphanumeric data. (Don't worry, they will still sort into proper order later.)

The Start Date field is defined as the date data type. No length is specified, because only alphanumeric fields require a length specification. The Credit Limit field is defined as the currency data type, since it reflects a dollar amount.

SAVING THE TABLE STRUCTURE

Once you've defined your table structure as shown in Figure 2.5, save it by pressing the DO-IT! (F2) key. You will see the message

Creating Custlist

momentarily on the screen, and then you will be returned to the Main menu.

At this point you could begin entering data into the table. But first let's discuss the important aspect of exiting Paradox.

EXITING PARADOX

Before you turn off your computer, or even before you remove any disks from their drives (except in special cases when the screen tells you to do so), you should *always* exit Paradox first. This ensures that any new data or changes to existing data will be properly stored on disk.

To exit Paradox, select the Exit option from the Main menu. Remember, if the Main menu is not displayed, press the Menu (F10) key to bring up the menu. Selecting the Exit option displays this prompt:

```
No   Yes
Do not leave Paradox
```

Because the highlight is already on the No option, if you change your mind and decide to stay in Paradox, just press Enter. Otherwise, type the letter Y to answer Yes, and you'll be returned to the DOS prompt. All of your work will be saved on either the floppy disk in drive B or your hard disk. When the DOS prompt is on the screen, it is safe to remove the floppy disks and turn off the computer.

CHANGING A TABLE STRUCTURE

Don't worry too much about getting your table structure exactly right the first time. Just try to break the information into as many meaningful fields as possible. If you decide to add new fields later, or delete fields, you can do so using the Modify option from the Main menu (as we'll discuss later). Paradox is very flexible, so corrections and changes are easy to make.

KEY FIELDS

You may have noticed this message near the bottom of the screen when creating your first table:

```
Use "*" after field type to
show a key field (ex: A4*).
```

Key fields are not relevant to this table, so don't worry about this. We'll use this option in a later example.

In the next chapter, we'll call our Custlist table back into Paradox and add some data to it. But first, we'll take a moment to review some of the basic commands and techniques discussed in this chapter.

SUMMARY

- Before you can use Paradox, it needs to be installed on your computer.

- To start Paradox, enter the command PARADOX2 at the DOS A> or C> prompt. If you are using a computer with two floppy disk drives, be sure to put a data disk in drive B.

- To perform operations in Paradox, select options from the Main menu. You can select menu options by highlighting the option and pressing the Enter key, or by typing in the first letter of the menu option.

- To unselect previous menu selections, press the Escape key to move back to the previous menu.

- To call up a menu at any time, press the Menu (F10) key.

- To get help at any time, press the Help (F1) key.

- To create a new table, select the Create option from the Main menu.

- Table names can contain a maximum of eight characters, with no spaces.

- Field names can be up to 25 characters in length.

- Fields can be any one of four data types: alphanumeric (A), numeric (N), currency ($), or date (D).

- To save a table structure, press the DO-IT! (F2) key.

- To exit Paradox before removing disks or turning off the computer, select the Exit option from the Main menu.

ADDING DATA TO A TABLE

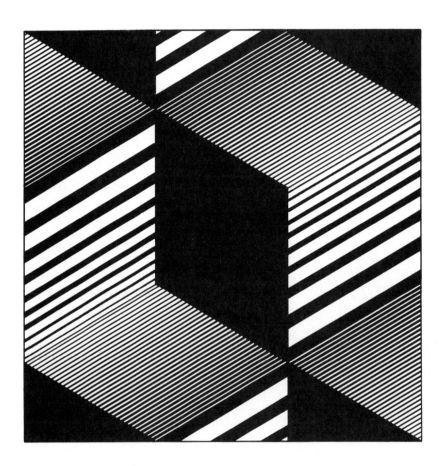

NOW THAT YOU'VE CREATED A TABLE, YOU NEED TO learn how to add data to it. In the last chapter, we left off by exiting Paradox back to the DOS prompt. So in this chapter, you first need to get Paradox "up and running" on your computer, as we discussed in the last chapter.

PARADOX DATA ENTRY

There are several techniques that you can use to add data to a table. In most situations, you'll want to use the DataEntry option from the Modify option on the Main menu. Let's try it now.

Select the Modify option from the Main menu. This will bring up a submenu, as below:

Sort   Edit   CoEdit   DataEntry   MultiEntry   Restructure

Select the DataEntry option. The screen will then ask for the name of the table to add data to, as below:

Table:
Enter name of table to add records to, or press ←┘ for a list

You can either type in the table name, Custlist, or press Enter to see a list of table names. Press the Enter key now. You'll see the Custlist table (and perhaps some other tables), as below:

Customer   Products   Orders   Custlist   Oldjunk

If there are more table names than will fit across the screen, some will run off the right edge of the screen. The following keys will help you find a table name:

End	Move to end of table name list
Home	Move to beginning of table name list
→	Move highlighter right one table name
←	Move highlighter left one table name
Ctrl-→	Move right one "screen"
Ctrl-←	Move left one "screen"
Any letter	Display tables starting with that letter

If there are many table names on your screen, you can narrow down the display by typing the first letter of the table name you are interested in. In this example, you would type the letter C to view table names that begin with C. (Note: If only one table name begins with the letter you enter, that table will be selected automatically.)

Now, move the highlighter to the CustList table name (if necessary) and press Enter, just as you would select a menu item. A screen for entering data will appear, as in Figure 3.1.

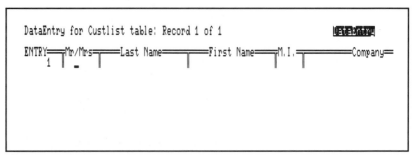

Figure 3.1: Screen for entering data

Notice that only a portion of the table appears on the screen—as much as will fit. As you enter data, the screen will scroll to the left, so you can fill in other fields.

Let's enter the following data into our first record:

Ms. Janet J. Jackson
Zeerox, Inc.
Accounts Payable
1234 Corporate Hwy.
Los Angeles, CA   91234

Start Date: January 1, 1988
Credit Limit: 10,000.00

The cursor is in the Mr/Mrs field, so type

Ms.

and press Enter. (Remember, you can use the Backspace and ← keys to correct errors.) The cursor moves to the Last Name field. Type

Jackson

and press Enter. Then type

Janet

and press Enter; then type

J.

and press Enter. At this point, the screen scrolls to the left so that you can enter data into the Company field. Type

Zeerox, Inc.

and press Enter. For the Department field, type

Accounts Payable

and press Enter. For the Address field, type

1234 Corporate Hwy.

and press Enter. For the City field, type

Los Angeles

and press Enter. Type

CA

as the state and press Enter. Type

91234

as the zip code and press Enter.

When entering dates, you can use either a MM/DD/YY format or a DD-Mon-YY format. So you can enter January 1, 1988 as either

1/1/88

or

1-Jan-88

If you enter an invalid date, such as 2/29/87, Paradox will reject the entry and ask that you reenter it (Paradox knows all about leap years and leap centuries). Press the Backspace key, reenter the date, and then press Enter.

Finally, enter the credit limit. When entering dollar amounts, you need not type ".00" at the end if you are entering an even dollar amount. You can enter commas between thousands (such as 10,000), or you can leave them out (like 10000). For this example, type

10,000

At this point, you've entered data for one record. Your screen will look like Figure 3.2.

When you press the Enter key, the screen will scroll to the right so that you can enter another record, as shown in Figure 3.3. Note that the display resembles a table, with rows and columns. For this reason, this type of display is called the *Table View* in Paradox. (Later, we'll look at another way of displaying data.)

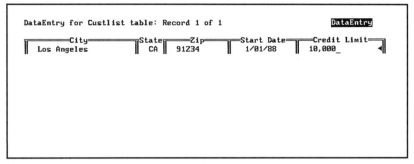

Figure 3.2: One record added to the Custlist table

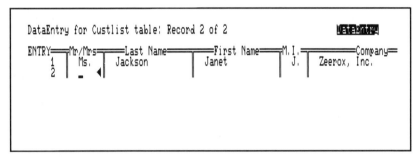

Figure 3.3: Paradox ready to accept a second record

When entering new data into a table, you can use the keys shown in Table 3.1 to help you make changes and corrections as you type. (See Appendix B for a chart of keys used when entering and editing data in Table View.) Note that Ctrl-Backspace (hold down the Ctrl key and press the Backspace key) deletes the entire contents of a field. (Throughout the book, we'll use a hyphen to indicate when two keys should be held down together. For example, Ctrl-Y will mean "hold down the Ctrl key and type Y.")

Now we want to enter the following data for the second record:

Mr. Andy A. Adams
23 Ocean View Dr.
San Diego, CA   92038

Start Date: January 15, 1988
Credit Limit: $2,500.00

KEY	EFFECT
←	Moves cursor to the left one field
→	Moves cursor to the right one field
↑	Moves up one record
↓	Moves down one record
Backspace	Moves back one character and erases
Ctrl-Backspace	Deletes entire field entry
Home	Moves to first record
Ctrl-Home	Moves to first field
End	Moves to last record
Ctrl-End	Moves to last field
Ins	Inserts a new record
Del	Deletes a record
Ctrl-→	Moves to the right one screen
Ctrl-←	Moves to the left one screen

Table 3.1: Basic keys for entering and editing data

Before you type in these data, read along to learn a few new tricks. Begin by typing

> Mr.

into the Mr/Mrs field, and press Enter. Then type

> Adams

in the Last Name field, and press Enter. Then type

> Andy

into the First Name field and press Enter; then type

> A.

into the M.I. field and press Enter.

Since Andy has no company affiliation, press Enter to leave the Company field empty. Press Enter again to leave the Department field empty. This brings you to the Address field. Type in the address

23 Ocean View Dr.

and press Enter.

Now let's try a little experiment. Suppose you suddenly realize that Andy's address should have been 234 Ocean View Dr. Press the ← key to move back to the Address field. You have two options for making the correction. The more laborious option is to press the Backspace key and erase everything but the "23", then type "4 Ocean View Dr." Let's look at an alternative.

FIELD VIEW EDITING

A more elegant way to make this correction is to enter the *Field View* mode by typing Alt-F5 (hold down the Alt key while pressing the F5 key). (The term Field View is based upon the fact that the arrow keys are reduced to operating within a single field. For example, pressing ← moves the cursor to the left one character within the field, rather than all the way to the next field.) The cursor will change from an underline to a block (and turn grey on a color screen). Now press the ← key until the cursor is between "23" and "Ocean", as below:

23_Ocean View Dr.

Type the number 4. You'll see it inserted into the current position, as below:

234_Ocean View Dr.

Press Enter when you're done editing. The cursor will shrink back to an underline, and you'll be in normal Edit mode.

Table 3.2 shows the keys that you can use to perform edits in the Field View mode. (See Appendix C for a chart of the keys used in Field View.) Also, pressing Help (the F1 key) provides some helpful information.

KEY	EFFECT
Alt-F5	Enters Field View mode
←	Moves cursor one character to the left
→	Moves cursor one character to the right
Home	Moves cursor to first character in the field
End	Moves cursor to last character in the field
Del	Deletes character at cursor
Backspace	Moves back one character and erases
Ctrl-Backspace	Deletes entire field entry
Ins	Turns Insert mode on/off
Enter	Ends Field View mode

Table 3.2: Keys used in Field View

You can enter Field View at any time, so it is possible to move the cursor to any field, in any record, and make changes using Field View. Pressing Enter always indicates that you are done editing, and returns you to the normal cursor and editing mode.

Now press Enter to put the cursor in the City field and type

San Diego

Press Enter.

THE DITTO KEY

Now we can learn another trick to simplify data entry. Since both this record and the record above have "CA" as the state, you can use the Ditto command to copy the contents of the field in the previous record to this field. The Ditto command is Ctrl-D (hold down the Ctrl key while typing D). You'll see CA inserted into the State field. The Ditto command works at any time, in any field, so you might want to use it later as you add more records. Keep in mind that it always duplicates the field from the record directly above.

To finish Andy's data, press Enter and type 92038 into the Zip Code field, 1/15/88 into the Start Date field, and 2,500 into the Credit Limit field. Press Enter and you're ready to enter data for the third record.

Before continuing, let's discuss another technique for entering data which you may (or may not) prefer.

USING FORM VIEW

There is another technique that you can use to enter records into a table. By simply pressing the Form Toggle (F7) key, you can switch from the current Table View, where the data are displayed in a tabular format, to a *Form View,* where only one record at a time is displayed on a screen resembling a paper form. If you press Form Toggle (F7) now, you'll see the Form View for the Custlist table, as in Figure 3.4.

The same basic editing keys are used for making changes as you type in the Form View as in the Table View. That is, the arrow keys,

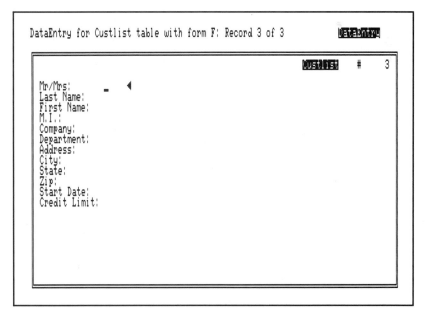

Figure 3.4: The Custlist table in Form View

Backspace, Enter, and Field View (Alt-F5) all perform the same tasks as before except that PgUp and PgDn move up and down through records, and ↑ and ↓ move up and down through fields.

Now enter another record into the table, as below, by typing the data into the form. As usual, be sure to get the right data in the right field, and press Enter after entering data into each field:

Dr. Ruth Zastrow
Scripts Clinic
Internal Medicine
4331 La Jolla Scenic Dr.
La Jolla, CA   92037

Start Date: 1/1/88
Credit Limit: 10,000

When you have entered this record, your screen should look like Figure 3.5.

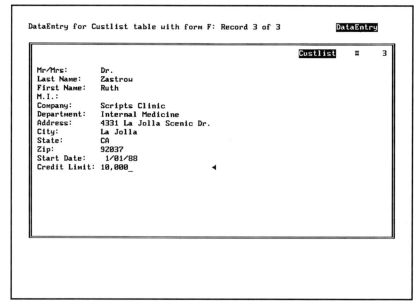

Figure 3.5: A new record added through a form

KEY	EFFECT
←	Previous field (left or up)
→	Next field (right or down)
↑	Up one field
↓	Down one field
PgUp	Up one record (or screen)
Ctrl-PgUp	Same field of previous record
PgDn	Down one record (or screen)
Ctrl-PgDn	Same field of next record
Home	First record of table
Ctrl-Home	First field of current record
End	Last record of table
Ctrl-End	Last field of record
Del	Deletes record
Backspace	Erases character to left
Ctrl-Backspace	Erases field contents
Alt-F5	Switches to Field View

Table 3.3: Keys used in Form View

In Form View, several other keys can be used to scroll through records in a table. You might want to try some of these out. Table 3.3 shows additional keys that work in the Form View. (See Appendix B for a chart of the keys used in Form View.)

To switch back and forth between Table View and Form View, just press the F7 key. Try it—you'll see that it is very easy to do.

DATA ENTRY SHORTCUTS

There are a few shortcuts that you can use when entering data into Numeric, Currency, or Date fields. These are summarized below.

NUMERIC FIELDS

When entering data into Currency or Numeric fields, the following shortcuts might help speed your work:

- You can press the Space bar in lieu of the period (or comma in international format) to enter a decimal point.

- Negative numbers may be entered with either a leading minus sign (hyphen) or enclosed in parentheses.

- If you omit the ".00" portion of a currency amount, Paradox will automatically fill it in for you.

- You may separate thousands places with a comma (or period in international format) when entering large numbers, so long as the punctuators are in the correct places. For example, you may enter 7654321 or 7,654,321 or 7.654.321 but not 76,543,21, because the punctuators (commas in this case) are in the wrong place.

DATE FIELDS

When entering dates into a field of the Date data type, use the following shortcuts to speed your work:

- As mentioned earlier, you may enter dates in the MM/DD/YY or DD-Mon-YY format, and you may also use the international format, DD.MM.YY. For example, you may enter January 31, 1988 as 1/31/88, 31-Jan-88, or 31.1.88. Regardless of the format you enter dates in, you can later select any format for displaying those dates using the Image Format options from the Main menu (discussed in the next chapter).

- To place the current month, day, or year into a date, just press the Space bar. (You must make sure, of course, that DOS knows what the correct date is.) For example, if the current date is March 31, 1988, pressing the space bar three times will enter the date 03/31/88. You can enter any individual component into the date field by pressing the Space bar once. In the example above, you could type 5, Space bar, 87 to have Paradox enter the date 5/31/87.

- To enter the month name in a date, you can enter the first letter only, followed by a couple of presses on the space bar. In cases where more than one month begins with a given letter (such as January, June, and July), Paradox enters the earlier date. Hence, typing 31, then J, then the Space bar twice, enters 31-Jan into the Date field.

Remember that Paradox will reject invalid dates such as June 31 (June has only 30 days). In your zeal to use shortcuts, you might occasionally enter an invalid date and have to reenter without using a shortcut technique.

You may want to experiment with some of these shortcut techniques while entering new data. To build up this database to help with future exercises, add the following records to the table. Use whichever method you prefer, Form View or Table View. Be sure to put the right data in the right field. For example, don't put "Richard" in the Last Name field when entering the data below:

Dr. Richard L. Rosiello
Raydontic Labs
Accounts Payable
P.O. Box 77112
Newark, NJ   00123

Start Date: 3/15/88
Credit Limit: 7,500

On the record below, enter "Tara Rose" as the first name, and leave the M.I. field blank.

Miss Tara Rose Gladstone
Waterside, Inc.
Acquisitions
P.O. Box 121
New York, NY   12345

Start Date: 2/28/88
Credit Limit: 15,000

Mrs. Susita M. Simpson
SMS Publishing
Software Division
P.O. Box 2802
Philadelphia, PA   23456

Start Date: 1/1/88
Credit Limit: 15,000

Careful, the next one has a Company field, but no Department field:

Mr. Clark E. Kenney
Legal Aid
371 Ave. of the Americas
New York, NY   12345

Start Date: 1/31/88
Credit Limit: 5,000

This next record has no Middle Initial, Company, or Department fields:

Ms. Randi Davis
371 Oceanic Way
Manhattan Beach, CA   90001

Start Date: 3/1/88
Credit Limit: 7,500

SAVING YOUR WORK

Once you've finished adding new records to your table, you need to save them by pressing the DO-IT! (F2) key. Don't worry about getting everything perfect before pressing DO-IT!. It's simple to make changes later. When you press the DO-IT! key, all the data you entered will be stored on disk under the file name Custlist.DB (DB stands for database). Paradox automatically assigns the ".DB" file name extension whenever you save the data with the DO-IT! key. Then you'll be returned to the Main menu, and the new records will appear on the workspace, as in Figure 3.6.

```
Viewing Custlist table: Record 1 of 8                        Main

CUSTLIST═Mr/Mrs═══════Last Name═══════First Name═══M.I.═══════Company═══
    1        Ms.      Jackson         Janet         J.    Zeerox, Inc.
    2        Mr.      Adams           Andy          A.
    3        Dr.      Zastrow         Ruth                Scripts Clinic
    4        Dr.      Rosiello        Richard       L.    Raydontic Labs
    5        Miss     Gladstone       Tara Rose           Waterside, Inc.
    6        Mrs.     Simpson         Susita        M.    SMS Publishing
    7        Mr.      Kenney          Clark         E.    Legal Aid
    8        Ms.      Davis           Randi
```

Figure 3.6: New records displayed in the workspace

You can always tell when you are in the "Viewing" mode because the top of the screen displays

Viewing (table name) table: Record X of Y

Let's take a look at an alternative method of adding new records to a table.

ENTERING NEW RECORDS IN THE EDIT MODE

You can also add new records to a table in the Paradox Edit mode. To enter the Edit mode, just press the Edit (F9) key while viewing records. The message at the top of the screen will change to

Editing Custlist table: Record 1 of 8   EDIT

To add new records in this Edit mode, press the End key to move the cursor to the last record in the table. Then press ↓. The screen will make room for record number 9, as shown in Figure 3.7.

Type in the data below as record number 9, using the same techniques you used for entering the previous records in this chapter.

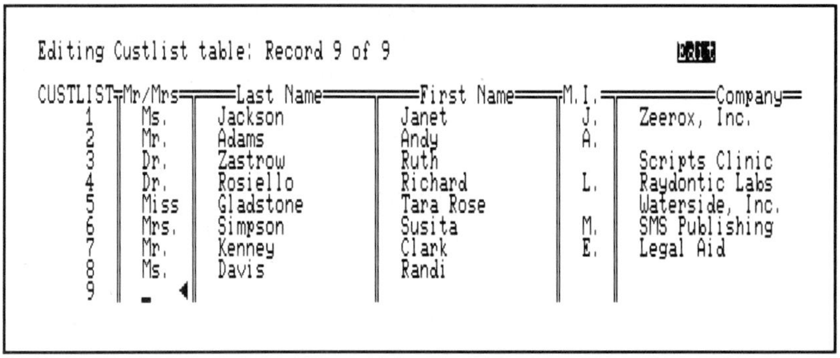

```
Editing Custlist table: Record 9 of 9                        EDIT
CUSTLIST┬Mr/Mrs═══════Last Name═══════┬First Name═══┬M.I.┬═══════Company═══
   1  │  Ms.  │ Jackson          │ Janet       │ J. │ Zeerox, Inc.
   2  │  Mr.  │ Adams            │ Andy        │ A. │
   3  │  Dr.  │ Zastrow          │ Ruth        │    │ Scripts Clinic
   4  │  Dr.  │ Rosiello         │ Richard     │ L. │ Raydontic Labs
   5  │  Miss │ Gladstone        │ Tara Rose   │    │ Waterside, Inc.
   6  │  Mrs. │ Simpson          │ Susita      │ M. │ SMS Publishing
   7  │  Mr.  │ Kenney           │ Clark       │ E. │ Legal Aid
   8  │  Ms.  │ Davis            │ Randi       │    │
   9  │  ▄   ◄│
```

Figure 3.7: Space for a new record in the Edit mode

(The arrow keys, Backspace, and Field View options all work the same as they do when entering data through the DataEntry mode.)

> Mr. Mark S. Macallister
> BBC Publishing
> Foreign Sales
> 121 Revelation Dr.
> Bangor, ME   00001
>
> Start Date: 3/15/88
> Credit Limit: 7,500

When you are done, press Enter. The screen will make room for another new record. Enter the information below, which you will note includes no Company or Department fields:

> Miss Ann Z. Abzug
> 301 Crest Dr.
> Encinitas, CA   92024
>
> Start Date: 3/1/88
> Credit Limit: 7,500

Press Enter after typing in the new record.

INSERTING RECORDS

Any time that you are in the Edit mode, you can add new records to the table by inserting them between existing records. Try this example: press the ↑ key six times to move the cursor to "Gladstone". To insert a blank record, press the Ins (or Insert) key. The screen will make space for the new record, as shown in Figure 3.8.

At this point, you could type in a new record. Or you could change your mind and press the Del (or Delete) key to delete the record. Press the Del key now and watch the table "close up" again. The table will appear as it did before you entered the new, blank record.

(*Note:* Though you can insert records, it is not necessary to do so just to maintain a sorted order. Paradox can quickly and easily re-sort your table into any order you wish, as we'll discuss later.)

When done entering new records in the Edit mode, press DO-IT! (F2) to save your changes. You'll be returned to the View mode, and will see your new records at the bottom of the table, as in Figure 3.9.

We'll discuss the Edit mode and editing techniques in more detail in a later chapter.

```
Editing Custlist table: Record 5 of 12                    EDIT

CUSTLIST═Mr/Mrs══════Last Name══════First Name══M.I.══════════Company═
    1     Ms.     Jackson          Janet         J.    Zeerox, Inc.
    2     Mr.     Adams            Andy          A.
    3     Dr.     Zastrow          Ruth                Scripts Clinic
    4     Dr.     Rosiello         Richard       L.    Raydontic Labs
    5                    ◄
    6     Miss    Gladstone        Tara Rose           Waterside, Inc.
    7     Mrs.    Simpson          Susita        M.    SMS Publishing
    8     Mr.     Kenney           Clark         E.    Legal Aid
    9     Ms.     Davis            Randi
   10     Mr.     Macallister      Mark          S.    BBC Publishing
   11     Miss    Abzug            Ann           Z.
   12
```

Figure 3.8: Room for new record inserted into the table

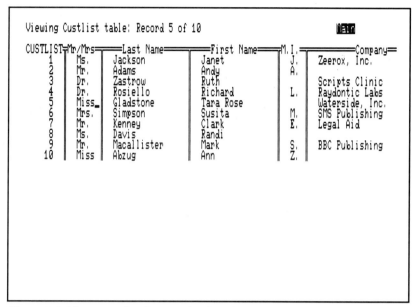

Figure 3.9: New records added to the Custlist table

━━━ *A FEW CAUTIONS* ━━━

Keep in mind that whenever you add new records to a table through DataEntry, the first record is always number 1, even though there may already be other records in the table. Don't worry about this. DataEntry always starts adding new records at record number 1, then adds the new records to the existing table after you press the DO-IT! key.

Whenever you enter or change data in a table, the changes are not permanent until you press the DO-IT! (F2) key. Therefore, if you are adding a great deal of data to a table, you should occasionally press the DO-IT! key to save your work. Then you can select the Modify and DataEntry options from the menu or press the Edit (F9) key to continue adding new records.

Only an accidental cancellation, a power failure, or some other unlikely hazard will destroy your work, so you need not press DO-IT! after every new record or modification. However, if you plan on entering hundreds of records to a table, you might want to press DO-IT! after every 25 or so new records. It would be a real pity to be on your 999th record and have a friendly cohort trip over a wire and unplug your computer by accident. You could lose quite a bit of your work (as well as a friendly cohort).

You may be ready to take a break now, so you can just exit Paradox in the usual fashion. Select Exit from the Main menu. Remember, if the Main menu is not displayed, press Menu (F10) to call up the Main menu. If you are in the middle of some other task, such as data entry, press DO-IT! (F2) to finish that task, then select Exit from the Main menu.

SUMMARY

In this chapter, you've learned a great deal about adding new records to a table. However, you've also learned a number of techniques for managing the cursor and making corrections, which will come in handy in future chapters. Take a moment now to review some of the basic techniques we've discussed in this chapter.

- To add new data to a table, select the Modify option from the Main menu and the DataEntry option from the submenu.

- Enter dates in either MM/DD/YY format or DD-Mon-YY format. Invalid dates will be rejected, and you'll need to reenter using the Backspace key.

- When entering dollar amounts it is not necessary to type in ".00" if you are entering a whole dollar amount.

- To make a simple change when entering data in a table, use the arrow and Backspace keys.

- To make a more refined change while entering data, change to Field View (press Alt-F5) while the cursor is in the field that you want to edit. Press Enter when you are done editing.

- To duplicate data from the previous record in a field, use the Ditto command (Ctrl-D).

- To switch from Table View to Form View when entering records, press the Form Toggle (F7) key.

- To save all new records added to a table, press the DO-IT! (F2) key.

- As an alternative, you can add records to a table through the Edit mode. When viewing a table, just press the Edit (F9) key. Use the arrow, Backspace, Field View, Ins, and Del keys to help with data entry. Press DO-IT! (F2) when you are done entering new records.

- If you are entering large amounts of data into a table, press the DO-IT! (F2) key occasionally to save your work. Then select the Modify and DataEntry options from the menus, or press the Edit (F9) key, to continue entering new records.

VIEWING TABLE DATA

BECAUSE THE DATA YOU ENTER INTO A TABLE ARE always stored on disk, the copy of the records that you see on the screen is often referred to as an *image*. In this chapter, we'll discuss basic techniques for calling up an image of the data, as well as techniques for modifying the image on the screen. In later chapters, we'll discuss techniques for developing formatted reports, such as a directory, mailing labels, and form letters.

VIEWING A TABLE

To see a portion of the data stored in a table, first get Paradox up and running, of course, and select the View option from the Main menu. Paradox will ask for the name of the table to view. As before, you can type in the table name, Custlist, and press Enter. Or you can press Enter to view the names of existing tables, then highlight the name of the Custlist table and press Enter. A portion of the table data will appear on the screen, in Table View format, as in Figure 4.1.

You can use the same keys we discussed in the last chapter to move the cursor and scroll the screen. You can exaggerate the movements of the arrow keys by holding down the Ctrl key while pressing an arrow key. (The Paradox manual sometimes refers to the Ctrl key as the *Turbo* key, because it exaggerates movements.) For example, pressing Ctrl-→ moves the cursor an entire screen to the right, displaying fields that were previously hidden. Since the current table is about three screens wide, pressing Ctrl-→ three times will scroll all the way to the right end of the table. Pressing Ctrl-← three times will scroll all the way back to the first field.

The ↑ and ↓ keys do not work in the same way with the Ctrl key. Instead, you use the PgUp key to scroll up a page and PgDn to scroll

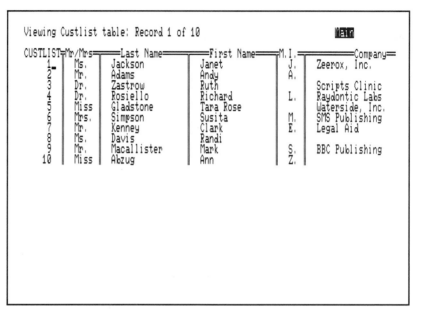

Figure 4.1: Viewing data on the workspace

down a page. (The Custlist table is too small to fully demonstrate these keys, but trying them will give you an idea of how they work.)

The Home key always takes you to the first record in a table. Ctrl-Home takes you to the first field in a record. The End key moves the cursor to the last record in a table, and Ctrl-End to the last field in a record. Table 4.1 lists these keys, and Appendix A shows them on a chart.

THE IMAGE MENU

There are a number of things you can do to alter the image you see on the screen without affecting the actual contents of the table. All of these options are under the Image selection on the Main menu. (If the Main menu is not displayed, just press the Menu (F10) key.) When you highlight the Image option, this sentence appears below the menu:

Resize or reformat an image, move to a field, record, or value;
pick a form

KEY	EFFECT
↑	Up one record
PgUp	Up one screen
↓	Down one record
PgDn	Down one screen
←	Left one field
Ctrl-←	Left one screen
→	Right one field
Ctrl-→	Right one screen
Home	First record in table
Ctrl-Home	First field in record
End	Last record in table
Ctrl-End	Last field in record

Table 4.1: Keys used when viewing records in Table View

Selecting the Image option displays the following submenu:

> TableSize ColumnSize Format Goto Move
> PickForm KeepSettings

We'll discuss each of these options in the remaining sections.

CHANGING THE TABLE SIZE

When several tables are displayed simultaneously on the screen, you may want to alter the sizes of some of them. Though it is not necessary to do so with the small Custlist table, we'll discuss this option now for use later in the book.

To alter the table size, select the TableSize option. The screen will display these instructions:

> Use ↑ to decrease the table by one row; ↓ to increase by one row . . .
> then press ⏎ when finished.

Pressing the ↑ key shortens the table display; pressing the ↓ key lengthens it. Increasing or decreasing the table display does not affect the number of records in the table. For example, if you shorten the display to two records, only two records at a time will appear on the screen. However, you can still use the arrow or PgUp and PgDn keys to scroll through all the records in the table. After altering the table size with the arrow keys, press Enter.

═══ CHANGING THE COLUMN WIDTH ═══

You can change the width of any column on the screen by selecting the Image option from the Main menu and the ColumnSize option from the submenu. Doing so brings up these instructions:

> Use ← and → to move to the column you want to resize . . . then press ↵ to select it.

For this example, press the → key twice to move the cursor to the Last Name field, then press the Enter key. The instructions on the screen will then read

> Now use → to increase column width, ← to decrease . . . press ↵ when finished.

You can narrow the Last Name field by pressing the ← key four times. Press Enter when you're done.

Let's do the same for the First Name field. Call up the Main menu, and select the Image and then the ColumnSize options. Move the cursor to the First Name field and press Enter. Press the ← key six times, and press Enter. Now both the Last Name and First Name field are smaller, leaving more room for the Company field, as shown in Figure 4.2.

Besides the ← and → keys, you can use the following keys when changing the column size:

KEY	EFFECT
Home	Quickly resizes to the minimum width of 1 character
End	Quickly resizes to the maximum width as set in the table structure

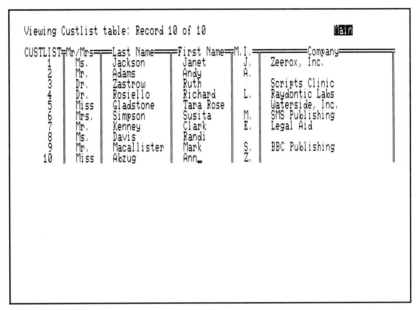

Figure 4.2: The Last Name and First Name columns narrowed

KEY	EFFECT
Escape	Cancels the resizing for the current column
Enter	Finishes the resizing for the current column

Keep in mind that these changes affect only the image on the screen; they have no effect on the structure of the table. Also, unless you specifically save these changed sizes (as discussed in a moment), they will last only during your current work section; they will be reset back to their original value as soon as you exit Paradox.

There are a few limitations to changing column sizes, as listed below:

- The minimum width of a column is one character.

- A numeric or currency field can be no more than 25 characters wide, or slightly wider than the field name, whichever is less.

- A date field can be no more than 14 characters wide, unless the field name is longer.

- An alphanumeric field can be no wider than the width defined in the table structure, or 76 characters, whichever is less.

When resizing a field, Paradox will beep when you reach the maximum width.

FORMATTING NUMERIC AND DATE FIELDS

You can modify the way in which numeric and date data are displayed in the image by selecting the Image and Format options from the Main menu. Let's give it a whirl. Choose the Image and Format options from the Main menu. The screen will display these instructions:

Use → and ← to move to the field you want to reformat . . .
then press ←┘ to select it.

Move the cursor to the Start Date field and press Enter.
Next, the screen displays the following options:

MM/DD/YY   DD-Mon-YY   DD.MM.YY

Move the cursor to the right to select the DD-Mon-YY option, and press Enter. The dates convert to the new format, as shown in Figure 4.3.

If, during the formatting process, you select a numeric field to reformat, you'll be given the following menu of choices:

General   Fixed   Comma   Scientific

When you select an option, the screen will display this prompt:

Number of decimal places: 2
Enter the number of digits to show after the decimal point
(Range: 0–15)

Type in a number between 0 and 15 (inclusive) to specify the number of decimal places to display. (In most situations, 2 is adequate.)

```
Viewing Custlist table: Record 1 of 10                          Main
╓═══════City═══════╥═State╥══Zip══╥═Start Date══╥═Credit Limit═╖
║    Los Angeles   ║  CA  ║ 91234 ║   1-Jan-88_ ║    10,000.00 ║
║    San Diego     ║  CA  ║ 92038 ║  15-Jan-88  ║     2,500.00 ║
║    La Jolla      ║  CA  ║ 92037 ║   1-Jan-88  ║    10,000.00 ║
║    Newark        ║  NJ  ║ 00123 ║  15-Mar-88  ║     7,500.00 ║
║    New York      ║  NY  ║ 12345 ║  28-Feb-88  ║    15,000.00 ║
║    Philadelphia  ║  PA  ║ 23456 ║   1-Jan-88  ║    15,000.00 ║
║    New York      ║  NY  ║ 12345 ║  31-Jan-88  ║     5,000.00 ║
║    Manhattan Beach║ CA  ║ 90001 ║   1-Mar-88  ║     7,500.00 ║
║    Bangor        ║  ME  ║ 00001 ║  15-Mar-88  ║     7,500.00 ║
║    Encinitas     ║  CA  ║ 92024 ║   1-Mar-88  ║     7,500.00 ║
```

Figure 4.3: Dates converted to DD-Mon-YY format

The various formats for displaying numbers are discussed below:

FORMAT	*DISPLAY*
General	Each number in the column is displayed with as many decimal places as accuracy requires, within the limits you specified in the first prompt. Hence, 1234.00 is displayed as 1234, and 1234.567000 is displayed as 1234.567.
Fixed	Sets a fixed number of decimal places for the numbers in the column. If you specify 3 decimal places of accuracy, the number 1234 is displayed as 1234.000. The number 1234.123456789 is displayed as 1234.123.
Comma	Commas separate thousands, and negative numbers are displayed in parentheses. Hence, the value 1234 is displayed as 1,234.00, and the number –1234.56 is displayed as (1,234.56).

FORMAT	DISPLAY
Scientific	Generally used only in scientific applications where very large numbers are involved, this option displays numbers in exponential format. Hence, 123456 is displayed as 1.23E + 05.

Paradox can store very large numbers in the range of 10^{-307} to 10^{308}, with up to 15 significant digits. Note that if a column is too narrow to display a number, the number will appear as a series of asterisks (for example, *****). To remedy this, select the Image and ColumnSize options from the Main menu, and widen the column. A number might also be displayed as asterisks if a portion of it is off the edge of the screen. Scrolling the screen will remedy that situation.

Numbers that are too large to display in Paradox's General format will automatically be converted to Scientific format.

LARGE MOVES THROUGH THE IMAGE

When a table becomes very large, it is unwieldy to move through records and fields by scrolling. The GoTo option under the Image menu allows you to jump directly to a particular record or field.

To try this out, call up the Main menu and select the Image option, then select the GoTo option. The screen will display three options:

Field   Record   Value

If you select the Field option, the screen displays a menu of possible fields to jump to, as below:

Mr/Mrs   Last Name   First Name   M.I.   Company
Department   Address

Use the arrow keys to highlight the name of the field you want to jump to, then press Enter. The cursor will jump to the appropriate field within the current record.

Selecting the Record option from the GoTo submenu displays this prompt:

Record Number:
Enter record number you want.

You type in the record number and press Enter. For example, if you type in 6 and press ENTER, the cursor will jump to record number 6.

The Value option from the GoTo submenu lets you locate a particular value within a field. For example, if you select Image from the Main menu, GoTo from the submenu, and Value from the GoTo submenu, the screen displays the prompt

> **Use → and ← to move to the column you want to search in...then press ← to select it.**

Use the → key to move the cursor to the Zip field, and press Enter to select this field. Next the screen prompts:

> **Value: Enter value or pattern to search for.**

Type in a zip code to look for (such as 12345) and press Enter. The cursor will immediately jump to the first record that has 12345 in the zip-code field.

A shortcut technique for accessing the Value option on the GoTo menu is to use the Zoom (Ctrl-Z) keys. To use Zoom, first position the cursor in the field (column) you wish to search. Then press Ctrl-Z, and you'll immediately be presented with the prompt to enter a value to search for. Fill in a value and press Enter. The cursor will move to the first record that contains that value. To move the cursor to the *next* record that has the same value, press the Zoom Next keys (Alt-Z). You can continue using Zoom Next to locate the next matching record until there are no more records in the database that match the search value.

When you're accessing the Value option under GoTo or through Zoom, character strings must match in case in order for the search to be successful. For example, if you attempt to locate the string *adams*, the screen will display the message

> **Match not found**

and the cursor will stay at its current position. The reason for the unsuccessful search is that the name is stored as *Adams*, not *adams*.

You may use the *wild-card characters*

..

and

@

in search values using GoTo Value or Zoom. The @ wild-card character matches any other character, and .. matches any group of characters. For example, a search for the value

Sm@th

will match Smith, Smyth, Smath, and so forth. A search for a value such as

J..n

would match Johnson, Jan, Jordan, Jackson, and any other word beginning with *J* and ending with *n*. These wild-card characters are discussed in more detail in Chapter 7.

Note that when you use GoTo Value or Zoom a second time, it displays the value entered from the previous search. To remove this old value quickly, press Ctrl-Backspace. To modify the displayed value quickly, you can use Field View (Alt-F5).

The GoTo selection and Zoom key offer only a rudimentary technique for positioning the cursor in a particular field or record. In larger databases you'll need more advanced search, or *query*, techniques to look up information quickly. These powerful techniques are discussed in Chapter 7.

MOVING COLUMNS

You can also rearrange the order of the columns displayed on the screen. Let's give it a try by moving the Last Name field to the right of the M.I. field. Call up the Main menu (F10), and select the Image option. From the submenu, select the Move option. Paradox displays this prompt:

Name of field to move:
Mr/Mrs   Last Name   First Name   M.I.   Company
     Department   Address

Use the → key to highlight the Last Name field, then press Enter to select that field. Paradox displays this message:

> Now use → and ← to show the new position for the field . . .
> then press ←⏎ to move it.

Press the → key to move the cursor to the M.I. field, then press Enter. The Last Name field is inserted in the position indicated by the cursor, as shown in Figure 4.4.

Keep in mind that this affects only the current display, not the structure of the table. Also, unless you specifically save these changes to the image (through a procedure we'll discuss in a moment), they will be lost when you exit Paradox.

QUICK MOVES WITH THE ROTATE COMMAND

You can move a field quickly from any position on the image to the far-right column position by moving the cursor to that field, using

```
Viewing Custlist table: Record 6 of 10                    Main

CUSTLIST═Mr/Mrs══First Name═M.I.══Last Name════════Company═══════
     1  │ Ms.   │ Janet     │ J. │ Jackson     │ Zeerox, Inc.     │
     2  │ Mr.   │ Andy      │ A. │ Adams       │                  │
     3  │ Dr.   │ Ruth      │    │ Zastrow     │ Scripts Clinic   │
     4  │ Dr.   │ Richard   │ L. │ Rosiello    │ Raydontic Labs   │
     5  │ Miss  │ Tara Rose │    │ Gladstone   │ Waterside, Inc.  │
     6  │ Mrs.  │ Susita    │ M. │ Simpson_    │ SMS Publishing   │
     7  │ Mr.   │ Clark     │ E. │ Kenney      │ Legal Aid        │
     8  │ Ms.   │ Randi     │    │ Davis       │                  │
     9  │ Mr.   │ Mark      │ S. │ Macallister │ BBC Publishing   │
    10  │ Miss  │ Ann       │ Z. │ Abzug       │                  │
```

Figure 4.4: The Last Name field moved to a new position

the usual arrow keys, and issuing the Rotate command (Ctrl-R). For example, if you place the cursor in the Mr/Mrs field and press Ctrl-R, the Mr/Mrs field will disappear off the right edge of the screen, and all fields to the right will rotate to the left. Each time you press Ctrl-R, the fields will rotate to the left. If you press Ctrl-R a total of 12 times (once for each field in the table), the Mr/Mrs field will rotate back to its original position.

——— *SWITCHING TO FORM VIEW* ———

As we have already learned, you can switch quickly from Table View to Form View, and vice versa, by pressing the Form Toggle (F7) key. Figure 4.5 shows a record from the Custlist table in Form View.

You can also switch to Form View by selecting the PickForm option from the Image menu and F from the submenu. As we'll see in later chapters, Paradox allows you to develop your own custom forms in addition to this standard form. The PickForm option, in

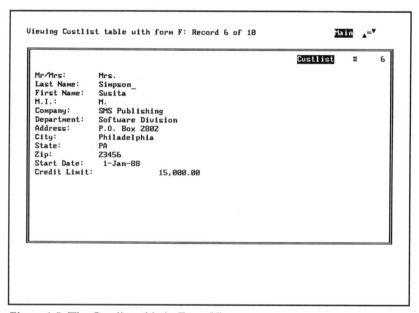

Figure 4.5: The Custlist table in Form View

turn, will allow you to select the particular form (standard or one of your custom forms) you want to display. The Form Toggle (F7) key switches back to Table View, even if you used the PickForm option to switch to Form View.

SAVING IMAGE SETTINGS

As mentioned throughout this chapter, any changes that you make to the image are only active during the current session. There is no need to save the image settings we used in this chapter. But for general information, in order to save image settings, you select the Image option from the Main menu, and then select the KeepSettings option from the submenu.

If you change image settings and select the KeepSettings option, the new settings will overwrite the old settings. (The actual table structure, of course, remains unchanged.)

To erase previously saved settings and return to the original image display, call up the Main menu and select the Tools option. From the submenu select the Delete option and then the KeepSettings option. Specify the name of the table (Custlist in this example), and press Enter. If the current image does not change, clear the screen by pressing the Clear Image (F8) key, and select the View option from the Main menu. Then specify the name of the table to view.

Those of you familiar with file names and DOS commands might be interested to know that the image settings are stored on a file with the same name as the table, but with the extension .SET (for instance, Custlist.SET). Therefore, you can also erase settings by using the command

    ERASE Custlist.SET

from the DOS prompt, outside of Paradox.

PRINTING AN IMAGE QUICKLY

If you want a quick printed copy of your table, make sure your printer is on and on-line, ready to accept the output. Then just press the Instant Report (Alt-F7) key combination. The data will be displayed in Table Format, as on the screen. (This printed display is indeed a rudimentary one. I'll discuss techniques for printing much fancier, formatted reports in Chapter 8.)

If you wish to stop printing before the entire table is printed, press Ctrl-Break (hold down the Ctrl key and press the ScrollLock key). You'll be returned to the View mode.

Now, let me digress for a moment and give you a little lesson on managing pages in a printer. Before you turn on your printer, you should always make sure there is a page perforation just above the print head. That way, Paradox "knows" where the top of a page is and can properly place margins at the top and bottom of each page. If you "hand crank" the paper in the printer, Paradox will no longer "know" where page breaks are, and you'll likely get future reports spread randomly across page perforations.

If at any time you are not sure that the pages are properly aligned in the printer, first turn the printer off, manually crank the paper through to the top of the next page, then turn the printer back on. Many printers have a Form Feed button to move the paper to the top of the next page. If you have such a printer, use the Form Feed button, rather than hand cranking, to move pages through the printer.

CLEARING AN IMAGE

If you wish to remove an image from the screen (for example, if you want to clear one image to view another), just press the Clear Image (F8) key. The workspace will clear and you'll see only the Main menu. To view another table, select the View option and enter the name of the table.

SUMMARY

- To view a table, call up the Main menu (F10) and select the View option. Specify the name of the table to view when requested.

- To change the size of the table on the screen, select the Image option from the Main menu and the TableSize option from the submenu.

- To change the width of a column on the screen, select the Image option from the Main menu and the ColumnSize option from the submenu.

- To change the format of numbers or dates, select the Image option from the Main menu and the Format option from the submenu.

- To jump the cursor to a particular field or record, select the Image option from the Main menu and the GoTo option from the submenu. You can also press the Zoom key (Ctrl-Z) to enter a value to search for.

- To change the order of columns on the screen, select the Image option from the Main menu and the Move option from the submenu. To move a column quickly to the far right of the table, move the cursor to the column and issue the Rotate command (Ctrl-R).

- To switch between Table View and Form View, press the Form Toggle (F7) key.

- To save image settings, select the Image option from the Main menu and the KeepSettings option from the submenu.

- For a printed copy of your data, press the Instant Report (Alt-F7) key combination.

- To clear an image from the screen, press the Clear Image (F8) key.

EDITING AND VALIDATING DATA

WHEN WORKING WITH COMPUTERS, THE TERM *EDIT* refers to any type of modification to the data on a table, whether it is a change of address, correction of a misspelling, deletion of a record, or any other change. Editing data with Paradox is easy. In fact, you already know quite a bit about it, as you'll see.

Before you can edit a table, it needs to be on the workspace. If the workspace on your screen is empty, select the View option from the Main menu, and specify Custlist as the table to use.

THE EDIT MODE

To begin editing the Custlist table, just press the Edit (F9) key. The top portion of the screen will read as follows:

Editing Custlist table: Record 1 of 10   Edit

You can edit data in Table View, Form View (by pressing the Form Toggle (F7) key), or Field View (by pressing Alt-F5). In any of these cases, the arrow keys have their usual effects as described earlier. Appendices A, B, and C illustrate these keys.

SIMPLE EDITS

Simple edits in the Edit mode are identical to those discussed when we were adding new data to the table. The following keys have the following effects:

- Any character typed into a field will just be added to the field. For example, if the cursor is in the Last Name field for

Adams and you type the letters "on", the Last Name field will contain "Adamson".

- Backspace: Pressing the Backspace key erases the character to the left of the cursor and moves the cursor to the left one space.

- Ctrl-Backspace: Pressing Ctrl-Backspace erases the entire current contents of the field.

- Typing Ctrl-U "undoes" an edit.

- Arrow keys: The arrow keys move the cursor up, down, left, and right, without changing any data.

FIELD VIEW EDITING

As we discussed in Chapter 3, pressing Field View (Alt-F5) narrows the effects of the arrow keys to the current field. Review Table 3.2 or see Appendix C if you need to be reminded of the effects of the editing keys in Field View.

SAVING EDITS

You can move the cursor around the table and make whatever changes you wish as long as you are in the Edit mode. To save your changes and return to the View mode, press the DO-IT! (F2) key. To reenter the Edit mode, just press the Edit (F9) key again.

You can also save your edits by calling up the Edit menu while in the Edit mode. To do so, press F10 and select the DO-IT! option from the menu that appears on the screen. All of your changes will be saved, and you'll be returned to the View mode.

UNDOING EDITS

Occasionally, you may feel a little lost while editing records in a table and want to *undo* some of your changes. There are a few techniques that you can use to undo recent changes to a table. The quickest method is simply to press Ctrl-U. Doing so undoes the most recent edit *transaction* that occurred. (A single edit *transaction* is all changes made to a single record while the cursor was still within the record.) Hence, if you were to move the cursor to record 2 and change the name Adams to Adamson and the zip code to 99999, then pressing Ctrl-U would undo both of those edits.

Ctrl-U works in a reverse, incremental order. If you repeatedly press Ctrl-U, Paradox will undo edit transactions in the reverse order of that in which they occurred. For example, suppose you make two changes to record number 2 in a table and three changes to record number 6. The first time you press Ctrl-U, Paradox will undo the three changes made to record number 6. If you press Ctrl-U again right away, Paradox will undo both changes made to record number 2.

You can also use the Edit menu to undo changes made to a table. To call up the Edit menu while in the Edit mode, just press the F10 key. You'll be given the options

> Image   Undo   ValCheck   Help   DO-IT!   Cancel

The Undo option under the Edit menu works in exactly the same manner that the Ctrl-U keys do, except that the menu option gives you a second chance to change your mind. When you select UnDo from the Edit menu, you'll be presented with the options

> No   Yes
> Do not undo the last change made to current image.

Selecting Yes undoes the most recent edit transaction and returns you to the Edit mode. Selecting No retains the most recent edit and returns to the Edit submenu. (To resume editing from this point, just press the Esc key.)

To abandon *all* the edits made in the current editing session, select Cancel from the Edit menu. You'll see the submenu

> No   Yes
> Do not undo changes made to the current image.

If you select Yes, Paradox will undo *all* recent edits (since the last DO-IT! command) and return to the View mode. (To edit more records, you'll need to press the F9 key again.) If you select No, Paradox will not undo recent edits and will return to the previous menu.

To continue editing, press the Esc key.

We'll experiment with edits and undos in a moment. However, you may want to experiment now with some of these editing features to get a feel for how they operate. When you are done experimenting, call up the Edit menu (by pressing F10) and select Cancel and Yes to undo all your experimental edits and bring the table back to its previous form.

DELETING A RECORD

To delete a record while in Edit mode, move the cursor to the record and press the Del key. All the records following the deleted record will move up one notch. For example, press F9 now to begin editing, then move the cursor to the record for Clark Kenney in the Custlist table and press the Del key. The record will disappear, and all those beneath will move up a row, as in Figure 5.1.

```
Editing Custlist table: Record 7 of 9                    EDIT

CUSTLIST═Mr/Mrs══════Last Name══════First Name══M.I.═══════════Company═══
     1 ║  Ms. ║ Jackson        ║ Janet        ║ J. ║ Zeerox, Inc.
     2 ║  Mr. ║ Adams          ║ Andy         ║ A. ║
     3 ║  Dr. ║ Zastrow        ║ Ruth         ║    ║ Scripts Clinic
     4 ║  Dr. ║ Rosiello       ║ Richard      ║ L. ║ Raydontic Labs
     5 ║  Miss║ Gladstone      ║ Tara Rose    ║    ║ Waterside, Inc.
     6 ║  Mrs.║ Simpson        ║ Susita       ║ M. ║ SMS Publishing
     7 ║  Ms. ║ Davis          ║ Randi        ║    ║
     8 ║  Mr. ║ Macallister    ║ Mark         ║ S. ║ BBC Publishing
     9 ║  Miss║ Abzug          ║ Ann          ║ Z. ║
```

Figure 5.1: Kenney deleted from the Custlist table

UNDELETING A RECORD

If you delete a record by accident, or change your mind, you can retrieve the record by pressing Ctrl-U or by calling up the menu (press F10) and selecting the Undo and Yes options. The record will reappear, as in Figure 5.2.

```
 Editing Custlist table: Record 1 of 10                        Edit
 CUSTLIST═Mr/Mrs═════════Last Name═════════First Name═════M.I.═════════Company═══
      1     Ms.     Jackson            Janet           J.    Zeerox, Inc.
      2     Mr.     Adams              Andy            A.
      3     Dr.     Zastrow            Ruth                  Scripts Clinic
      4     Dr.     Rosiello           Richard         L.    Raydontic Labs
      5     Miss    Gladstone          Tara Rose             Waterside, Inc.
      6     Mrs.    Simpson            Susita          M.    SMS Publishing
      7     Mr.     Kenney             Clark           E.    Legal Aid
      8     Ms.     Davis              Randi
      9     Mr.     Macallister        Mark            S.    BBC Publishing
     10     Miss    Abzug              Ann             Z.
```

Figure 5.2: A record recalled from deletion

LOCATING THE RECORD TO EDIT

As discussed in the previous chapter, you can use Zoom (Ctrl-Z) to locate a particular record quickly for editing, based on a value in a field. For example, if you wanted to edit the record for a person named Smith in a large table, you would move the cursor to the Last Name field, press Ctrl-Z, and enter **Smith** as the name to search for. If the first Smith that the cursor located was not the correct Smith, you could press Zoom Next (Alt-Z) to locate the next Smith until the cursor was positioned at the appropriate record.

AN EXERCISE IN EDITING

To test some of the editing techniques discussed so far, you might want to try the following rather simple exercise. Suppose you wish to change the name Susita to Susan in the sixth record. One way to do so would be to put the cursor in the First Name field, press Ctrl-Z, and enter **Susita** as the value to search for. (Then, of course, press Enter.)

Press F9 to go into the Edit mode. With the cursor to the right of Susita, you can enter Field View by pressing Alt-F5. As usual, the cursor changes from an underline to a box. Next, press the ← key three times so that the box is over the letter *i*, as in the example below (which shows an underline where the box would be located):

Sus<u>i</u>ta

Type the letters

an

so the name now reads

Susan<u>i</u>ta

To delete the unnecessary *ita* press the Del key three times, leaving only the name *Susan:*

Susan_

Press Enter to finish the edit and leave Field View. The cursor once again appears as an underline, and you are back in normal editing.

Now, suppose you also wish to delete the record for Rosiello. You could either position the cursor to the Last Name field and use Zoom to locate the record, or just press ↑ twice (in this simple example) to get the cursor to the appropriate record. Press the Del key, and the entire record will disappear, as shown in Figure 5.3.

For the sake of example, suppose you change your mind about the record you just deleted. To recall the record, just press Ctrl-U.

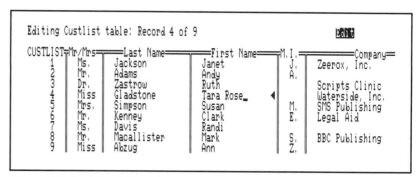

Figure 5.3: Rosiello deleted from the table

Rosiello's record instantly reappears on the screen. If you now wish to go ahead and save the change to Susan Simpson's name, press DO-IT!. Note that Paradox returns to the View mode (as indicated in the upper-left corner of the screen), and the change to Susan's name remains. (To resume editing, press F9 again.)

INSERTING A RECORD

As discussed in Chapter 3, you can insert a new record into the table at any time while in Edit mode. Just move the cursor to the place where you want the new record to appear and press Ins. (Optionally, move the cursor to the last record and press ↓.) A blank record will be added to the table, and you can fill in the fields with new data.

WHEN THE DATA DOESN'T FIT

Occasionally, the data in a field won't fit into a column on the screen (most likely because the column was narrowed manually using the Image and ColumnSize options). You will see either a group of asterisks (∗∗∗) or only a portion of a field with the rest off the screen.

When that situation occurs, the cursor will land at the start of the field, rather than at the end, when editing. To view the entire field so you can see what you're editing, switch to Field View (press Alt-F5).

THE EDIT MENU

As discussed earlier, pressing the Menu (F10) key when in the Edit mode brings up the following menu:

Image Undo ValCheck Help DO-IT! Cancel

The Image option allows you to perform the same tasks as the Image option from the Main menu. You can resize a column or a table, format numeric and date fields, move a field, switch to Form View, or go to a specified field or record.

The Undo option, as discussed earlier, undoes edit transactions incrementally in reverse order.

The Help option displays help screens, as does pressing the Help (F1) key.

The DO-IT! option saves all edits and returns to the View mode, as does pressing the DO-IT! (F2) key.

The Cancel command, as discussed, undoes all edits since the last DO-IT! command and returns to the View mode.

The ValCheck command allows you to set up "validity checks" that limit the types of data entered into fields. We'll discuss this menu option in more detail in the next section.

CHECKING THE VALIDITY OF DATA

Paradox automatically makes some checks on data that you enter into a table, such as ensuring that dates are proper and that numeric fields contain only numeric values. The ValCheck option from the Edit menu (as well as under the DataEntry option from the Modify menu) lets you set up additional checks on data entered into a table. This helps keep erroneous data from being stored in the table, which in turn reduces the need to edit and make corrections later on.

To enter validity checks, first make sure you are in the Edit mode and then press F10 to call up the Edit menu. Select Valcheck, and you'll see the submenu below:

Define   Clear

Selecting the Define option displays these instructions:

Use → and ← to move to field for which you want to set check . . .
then press ↵ to select.

Once you select the field for which you want to define validity checks and press Enter, the following submenu of options appears on the screen:

LowValue   HighValue   Default   TableLookup   Picture
Required

Each of these options is discussed below in general terms. We'll try out some later in the chapter.

DEFINING THE LOWEST ACCEPTABLE VALUE

Selecting the LowValue option from the Define submenu allows you to set the minimum acceptable value for a field. When selected, this option displays the following instructions:

Value:
Enter the lowest acceptable value for this field.

This option is most often used with numeric or currency fields. For example, if you wanted the minimum credit limit entered into the Custlist table to be $500, typing in 500 and pressing Enter would ensure that values smaller than $500 are rejected from entry when adding or editing data.

The LowValue option can also ensure that numbers are not inadvertently added to alphanumeric fields. For example, if you define the letter A as the LowValue for the Last Name and First Name fields, it would be impossible to inadvertently enter a number into either of these fields.

DEFINING THE HIGHEST ACCEPTABLE VALUE

The HighValue option allows you to define the highest acceptable value for a field. The HighValue option displays these instructions:

Value:
Enter the highest acceptable value for this field.

For example, if you wanted to ensure that nobody on the Custlist table was assigned a credit limit greater than $15,000, you would enter 15000 as the HighValue and press Enter.

ENTERING DEFAULT VALUES

Default values are those that will automatically appear in a field if the field is left blank. For example, suppose that the vast majority of entries on the Custlist table were California residents. You could set up a default value that automatically filled in the State field with the letters CA. Simply highlight the State field and select the Default option from the menu. The screen displays the following instructions:

Value:
Enter the value to insert if field is left blank.

Type in CA and press Enter. And that's all there is to it!

ENTERING PICTURE FORMATS

A Picture format is a template that ensures a consistency in the format of the data being entered. The most common uses of Picture formats are for social security numbers and telephone numbers. For example, the Picture format ###-##-#### ensures that a social security number will be entered with hyphens in the appropriate places. The Picture format (###)###-#### is good for telephone numbers with area codes.

Other characters used in Picture formats act as default values that are automatically added to typed-in data. For example, the Picture template (###)###-#### accepts only numeric digits and automatically inserts the parentheses and the hyphen.

SYMBOL	ACCEPTS
#	Numeric digits
?	Any letter A–Z or a–z
&	Any letter, but automatically converts it to uppercase
@	Any character (no exclusions)
!	Any character, converting all letters to uppercase
*	Repeats the next symbol either indefinitely or the number of times specified by the number following the *
;	Take following symbol as a literal character
[ ]	Optional item, but must be complete

Symbol	*Accepts*
{}	Specifies a group of acceptable entries
,	Separates acceptable values within a group

Paradox provides a number of symbols that you can use in Picture formats to restrict data entry in different parts of the format in different ways.

When you select the Picture option, the screen displays the following prompt:

Picture:
Enter a PAL picture format, (e.g. ###-##-####)

(PAL stands for Paradox Application Language; but don't worry about this just yet.) Type in your Picture template and press Enter.

Let's look at some sample picture formats and the types of data that they allow (and exclude). Later, we'll create some examples that can be used within the sample Custlist table.

The template #####-#### would allow only a 9-digit numeric value (such as an extended zip code) into a field. However, if you used the picture format #####[-####], the last four digits would be optional, so either a 5-digit zip code or extended 9-digit zip code would be acceptable.

The picture format &????????????????????? would require a 20-character string to be entered into the field. Every character entered must be a letter. The first character would be converted to uppercase.

The picture format &*@ would allow an entry of any length and convert the first letter to uppercase. The picture format &*19? would convert the first letter to uppercase and require 19 additional letters to be entered into the field.

If you want to include a symbol as a *literal* character in a field, use the semicolon character to change the symbol to a literal. For example, suppose you have an inventory system that uses the # symbol in part codes, as in the part number ABC-#1234. If you tried using the picture &&&-#@@@@, then an entry such as ABC-1234 would be considered incomplete, because Paradox interprets =# @@@@ as requiring five characters to the right of the hyphen.

However, if you enter the picture as &&&-;#@@@@, Paradox "knows" that the # symbol is to be placed into the entry, so when you typed in ABC-1234 Paradox would display

ABC-#1234

The template

{Yes,No,Maybe}

would allow only the letter *Y*, *N*, or *M* to be entered into an alphanumeric field, and would immediately convert the entry to Yes, No, or Maybe. Note the use of the curly braces to enclose the alternative acceptable entries and the use of commas to separate them within the curly braces.

The pictures that support alternative choices can be *nested* to allow multiple choices with the same first letter. For example, if you wanted to present the alternatives

{Mon,Tue,Wed,Thu,Fri}

entering the letter *T* would automatically fill in the field as *Tue* because *Tue* comes before *Thu* in the list of alternatives. To provide the choice *ue* or *hu* within the common *T* entry, nest these choices within the T alternative:

{Mon,T{ue,hu},Wed,Fri}

In English, the above picture reads, "Accept M, T, W, or F entries. If a T is entered, accept either *u* or *h* before filling in the rest of the field."

From the above example, you see how the following example would allow Saturday or Sunday to be entered into the field as well, again allowing the letter *S*, but asking for *at* or *un* before completing the entry:

{Mon,T{ue,hu},Wed,Fri,S{at,un}}

Notice in the above example that there are exactly as many open curly braces as closed curly braces. Make sure when entering your own pictures that yours also have an equal number of open and closed curly braces.

Note that curly braces can also be used to force entry of a particular character instead of automatically filling in the character. For example, if you use the picture ###-##-#### for a social security field, Paradox will automatically fill in the two hyphens when you later enter the number. If you prefer to type in the hyphens yourself (but still want Paradox to reject any other character), you can enter the picture in the format ###{-}##{-}####. In a sense, {-} means, "The only option allowed here is a hyphen."

When experimenting with pictures of your own, remember to avoid using symbols that conflict with the data type of the field. For example, you would not want to use the ? or @ symbol in a Numeric or Currency field since these symbols require alphabetic characters and Numeric and Currency fields allow only numbers! Also keep in mind that for *formatting* the display of numbers and dates (rather than performing validity checks), you can use the Image Format options from the Main menu.

DEFINING REQUIRED VALUES

A field that is assigned the Required validity check *must* have data entered into it; it cannot be left blank. For example, you could ensure that no record in the Custlist table is inadvertently entered without a last name by assigning the Required validity check to the Last Name field.

When you select this option, the screen displays these options:

No   Yes
Field may be left blank.

Select the Yes option to disallow blank entries into the field.

TABLELOOKUP

TableLookup is a special type of validity check, by which the value entered into a table is compared against that in another table. We'll discuss this option when we get to the chapters on managing multiple tables.

CLEARING VALIDITY CHECKS

The Clear option from the ValCheck submenu lets you eliminate previously defined validity checks. When selected, this option displays the submenu below:

Field   All
Remove Validity checks from one field.

If you select the Field option, you are given the opportunity to move the cursor to the field from which you want to clear validity check(s). Do so, and then press Enter to clear the validity check(s). If you select the All option, validity checks are removed from all fields in the table.

SAVING VALIDITY CHECKS

When you've defined validity checks for a table, you must select DO-IT! from the Edit menu (or press F2) to save those validity checks. Otherwise, the validity checks you defined will be erased when you exit Paradox and will not be activated the next time that you use the table. (Those of you who are familiar with DOS might be interested to know that Paradox stores all validity checks on disk in a file with the same name as the table combined with the extension .VAL.)

SAMPLE VALIDITY CHECKS

If you'd like to try some validity checks, first make sure the Custlist table is on the screen and you are in Edit mode. (Press the Edit (F9) key if you are in View mode.)

Let's first add an upper limit of $15,000 to the Credit Limit field. Press the Menu (F10) key, and select the ValCheck option. From the submenu, select Define. Then use → or ← to move the cursor to the Credit Limit field, and press Enter to select the field. Select the HighValue option, and type in 15000 when the screen asks for a value. Then press Enter. A brief message informs you that the entry has been recorded.

Let's now make CA the default value for the State field. Call up the menu (F10), and select the ValCheck option. Select the Define option, move the cursor to the State field, and press Enter. Select the Default option. Enter CA as the Default value, and press Enter.

Let's now make Last Name a required field. Call up the menu and select the ValCheck and Define options. Move the cursor to the Last Name field and press Enter. Select the Required option, and answer Yes to the prompt.

Here's a tricky one. Let's add a Picture template to the Last Name field that ensures that the last name always begins with a capital letter. Call up the menu and select the ValCheck and Define options. Move the cursor to the Last Name field (if it isn't already there), and press Enter. Select the Picture option. Enter the picture as

&*@

and press Enter. This picture translates as "capitalize the first letter and accept any character in the rest of the field." The asterisk indicates that the @ symbol should be repeated an indefinite number of times. That is, the name can be any length. If you had entered the picture as

&*4@

the last name could contain only five characters—the first letter and four others. Now let's try out the validity checks we've made.

Press the End key to move to the last record in the table, then the ↓ key to add a new blank record. Type in "Mrs." in the Mr/Mrs field and press Enter.

Now try leaving the Last Name field blank by just pressing Enter. Note that Paradox displays this message:

A value must be provided in this field; press [F1] for help.

Now try typing in the last name "smith" (no capitals), then press Enter. Notice that the first letter is automatically capitalized because of the Picture format.

Type in "Stan" as the first name, and press Enter several times to skip over the Company, Department, Address, and City fields. Notice that the State field is empty. If you press Enter to skip over this field, it is automatically filled with CA as the state.

Press Enter twice to move over to the Credit Limit field. Try entering a limit of 100,000. Notice that Paradox displays the message

Value no greater than 15000.00 is expected.

Use the Backspace key to change the entry to 15,000, and press Enter again. Paradox will accept the new value.

For now, delete the new record but save the validity checks. To do so, press Ctrl-U and then press F2.

GETTING UNSTUCK

If you ever get stuck in a field and can't get out because of an error message, there are several techniques you can use to get unstuck. First, try using the Backspace key to edit the value to an acceptable value. If you have trouble with that, use Ctrl-Backspace to delete the entire entry. Then either leave the field by pressing Enter or enter a new value.

If all else fails, press the Del key or Ctrl-U to delete the entire record. If it is necessary to delete an entire record, there may be something wrong with your validity check. Call up the menu, select ValCheck, and either clear or replace the validity check with a new one.

SUMMARY

Thus far in this book, you've learned techniques for creating a table, adding data to it, and changing those data. In addition, you've learned some valuable techniques for validating data as they are entered into the table, which will help prevent mistakes from being entered in the first place. By now you're probably ready to learn features of Paradox with more power, such as sorting, querying, formatting reports, custom screens, and more. These are discussed in the next few chapters. But before moving ahead, take a moment to review the rich array of editing features we've discussed in this chapter.

- To edit data in a table, press the Edit (F9) key.

- To switch between Table View and Form View, press the Form Toggle (F7) key.

- To switch to Field View for editing, press Alt-F5. Press Enter when you are done editing in Field View to return to normal Edit mode.

- To save edits, press the DO-IT! (F2) key or call up the menu (F10) and select the DO-IT! option.

- To delete a record, move the cursor to the record and press the Del key.

- To undo current edits, call up the menu (F10) and select the Undo or Cancel option or just press Ctrl-U.

- To set validity checks for a table while in Edit mode, call up the menu and select the ValCheck option.

- There are six types of validity checks: HighValue (highest acceptable value), LowValue (lowest acceptable value), Default (automatic values), TableLookup, Picture (format templates), and Required (fields for which data *must* be entered).

- To clear validity checks, select the Clear option from the Val-Check menu.

SORTING

CHAPTER *6*

SORTING INVOLVES PUTTING ALL THE DATA IN A table into some kind of order, such as zip code order for producing bulk mailings or alphabetical order by last name for a printed directory. Sorting is very easy in Paradox, and quite fast. For example, on an IBM XT, it takes only about a minute to sort a table with 1,000 records on it. Sorting is handled by the Sort option under the Modify option from the Main menu.

SORTING BY A SINGLE FIELD

To sort a table, you need merely specify the field (or fields) you wish to sort by, using a simple form that Paradox displays. Let's try sorting the Custlist table. First, make sure the Custlist table is on the screen. (If not, select the View option from the Main menu and specify the Custlist table.) You'll see it in its original, unsorted order, as in Figure 6.1.

```
Viewing Custlist table: Record 1 of 10                    Main

CUSTLIST═Mr/Mrs═══════Last Name═══════First Name═══M.I.═══════════Company═
    1      Ms.     Jackson          Janet          J.    Zeerox, Inc.
    2      Mr.     Adams            Andy           A.
    3      Dr.     Zastrow          Ruth                 Scripts Clinic
    4      Dr.     Rosiello         Richard        L.    Raydontic Labs
    5      Miss    Gladstone        Tara Rose            Waterside, Inc.
    6      Mrs.    Simpson          Susan          M.    SMS Publishing
    7      Mr.     Kenney           Clark          E.    Legal Aid
    8      Ms.     Davis            Randi
    9      Mr.     Macallister      Mark           S.    BBC Publishing
   10      Miss    Abzug            Ann            Z.
```

Figure 6.1: The Custlist table in its original order

To sort this table, call up the Main menu (F10) and select the Modify option. This brings up the following submenu:

Sort   Edit   CoEdit   DataEntry   MultiEntry   Restructure

Select the Sort option. The screen displays this prompt:

Table:
Enter name of table to sort, or press ◄─┘ to see a list of tables.

Either type in or highlight the table name Custlist and press Enter. Next, Paradox displays two more options:

Same   New
Place results of sort in the same table.

If you select the Same option, the data will be reordered in the Cust-list table. If you select the New option, the sorted records will be placed in a new table with the name you specify, and the records in the Custlist table will remain in their original order. Unless there is some reason why you want to retain the original unsorted order in the Custlist table, select the Same option. (Do so now.) Paradox then displays a screen for specifying fields to sort by (which we'll refer to hereafter as the sort form), as shown in Figure 6.2.

To sort by a single field, simply type the number 1 in front of the field name, press Enter, and then press the DO-IT! key. In this example, we'll sort by last name. So use the arrow keys to move the cursor to the Last Name field. Type 1 and press Enter, so your screen looks like Figure 6.3.

Press the DO-IT! (F2) key and wait a couple of seconds. In a moment you'll see the Custlist table sorted by last name, as in Figure 6.4.

You can sort on any field in a table, regardless of the type of information the field contains.

DESCENDING SORTS

Unless you specify otherwise, Paradox always sorts data in ascending (smallest to largest) order. To specify descending order, simply

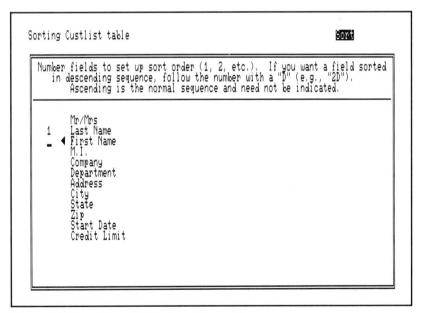

```
Sorting Custlist table                                          Sort

  Number fields to set up sort order (1, 2, etc.).  If you want a field sorted
     in descending sequence, follow the number with a "D" (e.g., "2D").
             Ascending is the normal sequence and need not be indicated.
  ─────────────────────────────────────────────────────────────────────────

   _     Mr/Mrs
         Last Name
         First Name
         M.I.
         Company
         Department
         Address
         City
         State
         Zip
         Start Date
         Credit Limit
```

Figure 6.2: Screen for specifying sort orders

```
Sorting Custlist table                                          Sort

  Number fields to set up sort order (1, 2, etc.).  If you want a field sorted
     in descending sequence, follow the number with a "D" (e.g., "2D").
             Ascending is the normal sequence and need not be indicated.
  ─────────────────────────────────────────────────────────────────────────

         Mr/Mrs
   1     Last Name
   _   ◄ First Name
         M.I.
         Company
         Department
         Address
         City
         State
         Zip
         Start Date
         Credit Limit
```

Figure 6.3: Last Name field selected for sorting

```
Viewing Custlist table: Record 1 of 10                        Main
CUSTLIST╤Mr/Mrs═══════Last Name═══════╤═══First Name═══╤M.I.╤══════════Company══
   1▂    Miss    Abzug              Ann             Z.
   2      Mr.     Adams              Andy            A.
   3      Ms.     Davis              Randi
   4      Miss    Gladstone          Tara Rose              Waterside, Inc.
   5      Ms.     Jackson            Janet           J.     Zeerox, Inc.
   6      Mr.     Kenney             Clark           E.     Legal Aid
   7      Mr.     Macallister        Mark            S.     BBC Publishing
   8      Dr.     Rosiello           Richard         L.     Raydontic Labs
   9      Mrs.    Simpson            Susan           M.     SMS Publishing
  10      Dr.     Zastrow            Ruth                   Scripts Clinic
```

Figure 6.4: Custlist table sorted by last name

place the letter D next to the number when specifying a field. Let's try it out.

Call up the Main menu, and select the Modify and Sort options once again. Enter Custlist as the name of the table, and select the Same option from the submenu. When the menu of fields appears, move the cursor to the Zip field and type in 1D, then press Enter. Your screen should look like Figure 6.5.

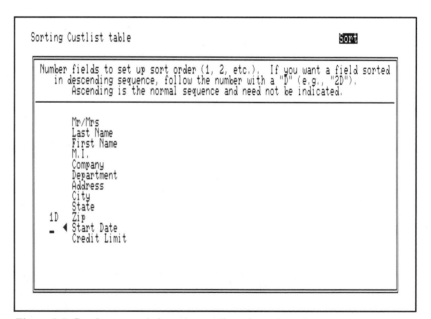

Figure 6.5: Sorting records into descending zip code order

Press the DO-IT! key and wait a couple of seconds. When the table reappears, you'll need to scroll over to the Zip field to see the results. (Press Ctrl-→ twice.) You'll see that the table has been sorted into descending zip code order, as shown in Figure 6.6.

```
Viewing Custlist table: Record 1 of 10                           Main

    ═══Address═══            ═══City═══      ═State═  ═══Zip═  ══Star
   234 Ocean View Dr._       San Diego        CA       92038    1/1
   4331 La Jolla Scenic Dr.  La Jolla         CA       92037    1/0
   301 Crest Dr.             Encinitas        CA       92024    3/0
   1234 Corporate Hwy.       Los Angeles      CA       91234    1/0
   371 Oceanic Way           Manhattan Beach  CA       90001    3/0
   P.O. Box 2802             Philadelphia     PA       23456    1/0
   P.O. Box 121              New York         NY       12345    2/2
   371 Ave. of the Americas  New York         NY       12345    1/3
   P.O. Box 77112            Newark           NJ       00123    3/1
   121 Revelation Dr.        Bangor           ME       00001    3/1
```

Figure 6.6: Table sorted into descending order by zip code

SORTING BY SEVERAL FIELDS

On a large table, sorting by a single field may be inadequate. Though our Custlist table is much too small to demonstrate the full power of sorting by several fields, a general example will demonstrate the usefulness of this capability.

Suppose you had a table with 10,000 names and addresses. On that table, there happened to be about 200 Smiths. If you sorted the table by last name, all the Smiths would be grouped together, but they would be in random order by first name, as shown below:

Smith   Michael   K.

Smith   Anton   A.

Smith   Jennifer   J.

Smith   Wally   P.

Smith   Anita   R.

Smith   Michael   D.

Smith   Antonio   L.

Smith   Vera

Smith   Susan   M.

.

.

.

However, if you specified Last Name as the first (1) sort field and First Name as the second (2) sort field, the records would be sorted alphabetically by first name within a common last name, as below:

Smith   Anita   R.

Smith   Anton   A.

Smith   Antonio   L.

Smith   Jennifer   J.

Smith   Michael   K.

Smith   Michael   D.

Smith   Susan   M.

Smith   Vera

Smith   Wally   P.

.

.

.

This order makes it much easier to look up a particular Smith in a printed copy of the table.

Notice that the second sort field acts as a "tie breaker." That is, when two individuals have the same last name, the secondary sort order is used to break the tie, enforcing a sort order within the major sort order.

You can specify as many fields as you wish when sorting. For example, if you made Last Name the first sort field, First Name the second sort field, and Middle Initial the third sort field, the order would be refined even more. (Notice, in the list below, that Michael D. is now listed before Michael K.)

Smith	Anita	R.
Smith	Anton	A.
Smith	Antonio	L.
Smith	Jennifer	J.
Smith	Michael	D.
Smith	Michael	K.
Smith	Susan	M.
Smith	Vera	
Smith	Wally	P.

.

.

.

Now let's try out an example on our small Custlist table. Call up the Main menu, and select the Modify and Sort options. Enter Custlist as the table name, and select Same from the submenu. On the sort form, specify Last Name as the second sort field and Start Date as the first sort field, as in Figure 6.7.

Press the DO-IT! (F2) key to perform the sort. The records in the table will be sorted into chronological order by start date. Within common start dates, the records will be in alphabetical order by last name. You can see this better if you move the Start Date column over to the left. (To do so, call up the menu, and select the Image and Move options. Highlight the Start Date field and press Enter. Move the cursor to the Last Name field, and press Enter.)

With the Start Date field placed next to the Last Name field, you can see that within identical dates the records are sorted by last name, as in Figure 6.8.

You can even combine ascending and descending sort orders. Let's try an example, and at the same time we'll try sorting records to a new table. Call up the Main menu and select the Modify and Sort

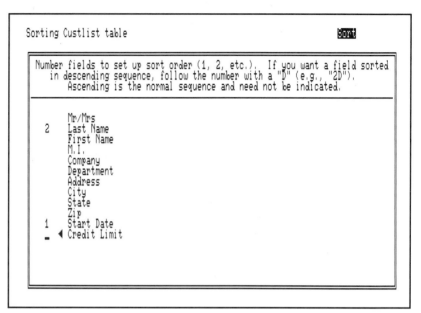

Figure 6.7: Sorting by date and last name

```
Viewing Custlist table: Record 1 of 10                    Main

CUSTLIST   Start Date      Last Name        First Name    M.I.          Co
   1        1/01/88        Jackson          Janet         J.     Zeerox, In
   2        1/01/88        Simpson          Susan         M.     SMS Publis
   3        1/01/88        Zastrou          Ruth                 Scripts Cl
   4        1/15/88        Adams            Andy          A.
   5        1/31/88        Kenney           Clark         E.     Legal Aid
   6        2/28/88        Gladstone        Tara Rose            Waterside,
   7        3/01/88        Abzug            Ann           Z.
   8        3/01/88        Davis            Randi
   9        3/15/88        Macallister      Mark          S.     BBC Publis
  10        3/15/88        Rosiello         Richard       L.     Raydontic
```

Figure 6.8: Records in chronological and alphabetical order

options. Specify Custlist as the table to sort, and select the New option when Paradox asks whether you want to sort to the same or a new table. Paradox displays this prompt:

Table:
Enter name for new sorted table.

You can enter any valid table name (remember, no spaces or punctuation). In this example, enter the name Tempsort as the table to store the sorted records in. (If the Cancel/Replace options appear, select Replace.)

On the sort form, specify Start Date as the first sort field, in descending order (1D), and Last Name as the second sort field (2), as shown in Figure 6.9.

Press the DO-IT! key. The records will be sorted in a new table named Tempsort and displayed on the screen, as in Figure 6.10. Notice that in the Tempsort table the dates are in descending order, and last names within common dates are in ascending alphabetical order.

You'll notice that both the Custlist table and the new Tempsort table are displayed on the screen. Tempsort contains the records in their latest sort order. (Once again, I've moved the Start Date column to the left of the Last Name column to better display the sort order.) The Custlist table still has records in the previous sort order.

We don't really need this Tempsort table for anything just now, so you can press Clear Image (F8) to erase it from the screen.

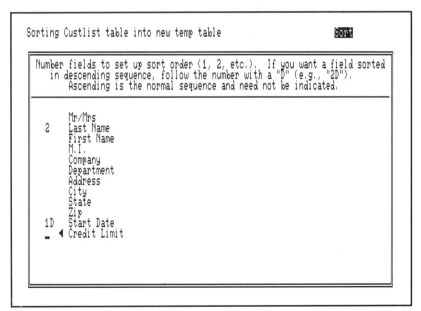

Figure 6.9: Sorting by descending date and ascending last name

```
Viewing Tempsort table: Record 1 of 10                    Main  ▲═

CUSTLIST═┯═Start Date═┯═════Last Name═════┯═════First Name═════┯M.I.═┯═══════Co
       2 ┃  1/01/88   ┃ Simpson           ┃ Susan              ┃ M.  ┃ SMS Publis
       3 ┃  1/01/88   ┃ Zastrow           ┃ Ruth               ┃     ┃ Scripts Cl
       4 ┃  1/15/88   ┃ Adams             ┃ Andy               ┃ A.  ┃
       5 ┃  1/31/88   ┃ Kenney            ┃ Clark              ┃ E.  ┃ Legal Aid
       6 ┃  2/28/88   ┃ Gladstone         ┃ Tara Rose          ┃     ┃ Waterside,
       7 ┃  3/01/88   ┃ Abzug             ┃ Ann                ┃ Z.  ┃
       8 ┃  3/01/88   ┃ Davis             ┃ Randi              ┃     ┃
       9 ┃  3/15/88   ┃ Macallister       ┃ Mark               ┃ S.  ┃ BBC Publis
      10 ┃  3/15/88   ┃ Rosiello          ┃ Richard            ┃ L.  ┃ Raydontic

TEMPSORT═┯═Start Date═┯═════Last Name═════┯═════First Name═════┯M.I.═┯═══════Co
       1 ┃  3/15/88   ┃ Macallister_      ┃ Mark               ┃ S.  ┃ BBC Publis
       2 ┃  3/15/88   ┃ Rosiello          ┃ Richard            ┃ L.  ┃ Raydontic
       3 ┃  3/01/88   ┃ Abzug             ┃ Ann                ┃ Z.  ┃
       4 ┃  3/01/88   ┃ Davis             ┃ Randi              ┃     ┃
       5 ┃  2/28/88   ┃ Gladstone         ┃ Tara Rose          ┃     ┃ Waterside,
       6 ┃  1/31/88   ┃ Kenney            ┃ Clark              ┃ E.  ┃ Legal Aid
       7 ┃  1/15/88   ┃ Adams             ┃ Andy               ┃ A.  ┃
       8 ┃  1/01/88   ┃ Jackson           ┃ Janet              ┃ J.  ┃ Zeerox, In
       9 ┃  1/01/88   ┃ Simpson           ┃ Susan              ┃ M.  ┃ SMS Publis
      10 ┃  1/01/88   ┃ Zastrow           ┃ Ruth               ┃     ┃ Scripts Cl
```

Figure 6.10: Records in descending date and ascending last name order

EXAMPLES

Sorting is very easy in Paradox, and with a little practice you'll be able to sort any table into any order you wish. As mentioned, our small Custlist table cannot demonstrate the full potential of Paradox's sorting abilities. But take a look at the examples below to see how various sorting options would affect the order of a Custlist table with many records on it.

The sort form in Figure 6.11 specifies that records be sorted in ascending Credit Limit order (1). Within identical credit limits, records are sorted by last name (2), first name (3), and middle initial (4).

On a very large table, a portion of this sort order might appear as below:

5,000	Adams	Andy	A.
5,000	Adams	Andy	Z.
5,000	Adams	Barbara	Z.
5,000	Miller	Mike	M.

```
Sorting Custlist table                                          Sort

┌──────────────────────────────────────────────────────────────────┐
│ Number fields to set up sort order (1, 2, etc.).  If you want a field sorted │
│    in descending sequence, follow the number with a "D" (e.g., "2D").       │
│              Ascending is the normal sequence and need not be indicated.    │
├──────────────────────────────────────────────────────────────────┤
│                                                                    │
│          Mr/Mrs                                                    │
│     2    Last Name                                                 │
│     3    First Name                                                │
│     4    M.I.                                                      │
│          Company                                                   │
│          Department                                                │
│          Address                                                   │
│          City                                                      │
│          State                                                     │
│          Zip                                                       │
│          Start Date                                                │
│     1_ ◄ Credit Limit                                              │
│                                                                    │
└──────────────────────────────────────────────────────────────────┘
```

Figure 6.11: Sorting by credit limit and name

5,000	Zastrow	Ruth	R.
7,500	Aardvark	Annie	A.
7,500	Smith	Bob	
7,500	Smith	Sandy	S.
7,500	Zeepers	Zeppo	Z.
10,000	Baker	Babs	T.
10,000	Baker	Mary	J.
10,000	Miller	Andy	A.

.

.

.

Figure 6.12 shows a similar order specified on the sort form, but here the Credit Limit field is specified as descending order. The other sort fields are still in ascending order.

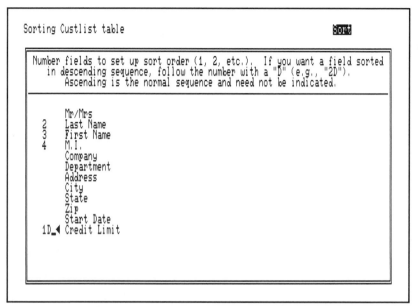

Figure 6.12: Sorting by descending credit limit and ascending name

The resulting sort on a hypothetical table might appear as below:

15,000	Aronson	Aaron	A.
15,000	Aronson	Aaron	T.
15,000	Baker	Billy	
15,000	Miller	Mary	M.
15,000	Miller	Mary	N.
15,000	Miller	Nancy	A.
15,000	Young	Yolanda	Z.
10,000	Abraham	Arthur	T.
10,000	Carlson	Carla	J.
10,000	Carlson	Manny	
10,000	Mason	Tara	
10,000	Watson	Wilbur	A.
7,500	Askey	Albert	J.

| 7,500 | Byte | Robert | B. |
| 7,500 | Miller | Mandy | L. |

.

.

.

Figure 6.13 displays a request to sort records alphabetically by company name (1) and, within each company, alphabetically by department (2).

The resulting sort order on a hypothetical table might appear as below. Notice that the names are in random order within the departments. Had we specified Last Name as the third sort field and First Name as the fourth sort field, the names would have been alphabetized within each department in each company.

ABC Co.	Accounts Payable	Albertson	Steve
ABC Co.	Accounts Receivable	Miller	Mikey
ABC Co.	Accounts Receivable	Brookes	Alvin
ABC Co.	Accounts Receivable	Peterson	Anne
ABC Co.	Insurance Division	Root	Quincy
ABC Co.	Insurance Division	Parker	Carl
ABC Co.	Training Division	Davies	Tina
Baker Int.	Bookkeeping	Starlight	Stella
Baker Int.	Training Division	Adams	Arthur
Cable View	Installation Dep't	Mason	Maggie
Cable View	Installation Dep't	Andrews	Mick
Cable View	Special Projects	Targa	Ferry

.

.

.

Figure 6.14 shows a sort form with State specified as the first sort field, City as the second sort field, and Address as the third sort field.

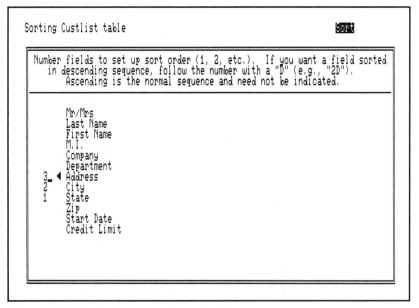

```
Sorting Custlist table                                         Sort

 Number fields to set up sort order (1, 2, etc.).  If you want a field sorted
   in descending sequence, follow the number with a "D" (e.g., "2D").
          Ascending is the normal sequence and need not be indicated.

        Mr/Mrs
        Last Name
        First Name
        M.I.
    1   Company
    2_ ◄ Department
        Address
        City
        State
        Zip
        Start Date
        Credit Limit
```

Figure 6.13: Sorting by company and department

```
Sorting Custlist table                                         Sort

 Number fields to set up sort order (1, 2, etc.).  If you want a field sorted
   in descending sequence, follow the number with a "D" (e.g., "2D").
          Ascending is the normal sequence and need not be indicated.

        Mr/Mrs
        Last Name
        First Name
        M.I.
        Company
        Department
    3_ ◄ Address
    2   City
    1   State
        Zip
        Start Date
        Credit Limit
```

Figure 6.14: Sorting by state, city, and address

The resulting sort would put all records in alphabetical order by state. Within each state, cities would be in alphabetical order. Within each city, addresses would be in order, as below:

Alabama	Arken	455 Elm Rd.
Alabama	Bakerville	999 Oak St.
Alaska	Akron	100 A St.
Alaska	Akron	100 B St.
Alaska	Akron	101 Grape Drive
Alaska	Akron	102 Village Square
Alaska	Akron	200 A St.
Alaska	Akron	201 B St.
Alaska	Briton	999 First St.
Alaska	Cavern City	344 Ashton Way

.

.

.

Learning to master Paradox's sorting capabilities is basically a matter of trying things out and practicing. Experiment freely; you cannot possibly do any harm to Paradox or your computer.

THE SORT MENU

While the sort form is displayed on the screen, you can press the Menu (F10) key to bring up the menu shown below:

Help   DO-IT!   Cancel

The Help option displays a help screen for sorting (as does pressing the F1 key). The DO-IT! option performs the requested sort, as does pressing the F2 key. The Cancel option terminates the sort request and returns you to View mode without sorting the records.

—— *SUMMARY* ————————————

- To sort a database on a single field, select the Modify and Sort options from the menus. You can sort the existing table by selecting Same, or you can make a sorted copy of the existing table by selecting New from the submenu.

- To specify a field to sort by, place a 1 next to the field name on the sort form that Paradox displays.

- To sort in descending (largest to smallest) order, place a D next to the number on the sort menu (for example, 1D).

- To perform sorts within sorts, specify fields in order of importance (1, 2, 3, and so forth) on the sort form.

SEARCHING THE DATABASE

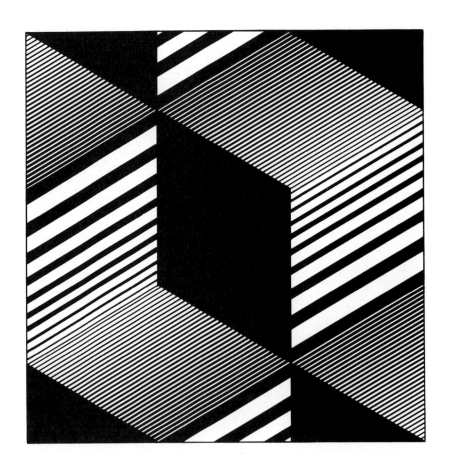

CHAPTER 7

TO SEARCH (OR *QUERY*) A DATABASE MEANS TO PULL
out all records that meet some criterion. For example, you might
want to view only New York residents, or individuals in California
with credit limits over $10,000. Perhaps you'll want to send a form
letter to individuals whose starting date was one year ago, or maybe
you just want to look up Clark Kenney's address. In this chapter,
we'll discuss several techniques for searching a database through
query forms.

QUERY FORMS

You can call up the query form at any time by selecting the Ask
option from the Main menu. It's a little easier to work with query
forms if the workspace is clear on the screen. If you are currently
viewing the Custlist table, press Clear Image (F8) to clear the screen.
Then select the Ask option from the Main menu. When prompted,
specify Custlist as the table to ask about. You'll see a query form as in
Figure 7.1.

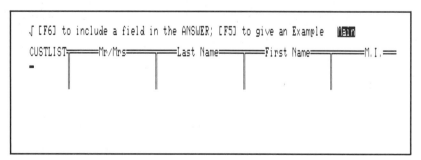

Figure 7.1: The query form for the Custlist table

You can enter and change data on the query form as you do with tables. That is, the arrow keys move the cursor, the Backspace key erases characters that you've typed, and Field View (Alt-F5) allows you to make more refined edits.

SELECTING FIELDS TO VIEW

You may not want to see all the fields in a table when querying. You can specify which fields to display by putting check marks in those fields. Pressing the Checkmark (F6) key toggles the check-mark symbol. That is, pressing Checkmark once puts a check mark into a field. If you change your mind, just press Checkmark again to erase the check mark.

You can quickly enter check marks into all the fields on the query form by pressing the Checkmark (F6) key while the cursor is in the leftmost column. Pressing the Checkmark key a second time erases all the check marks.

Suppose you wish to view only the names from the Custlist table. Using the arrow keys and Checkmark (F6) key, place a check mark in the Last Name, First Name, and M.I. fields, as shown in the top half of Figure 7.2. Press DO-IT! (F2) after entering the check marks, and you'll see the three fields from the Custlist table displayed on the screen, as in the bottom half of Figure 7.2.

Notice that the table displaying the data is named Answer. This is NOT the same table as Custlist; it is only an image of the data from the Custlist table, displaying the fields that you requested. Note also that the record numbers on the Answer table may not correspond to those on the Custlist table. You shouldn't do any editing on the Answer table because it will not be reflected in the original Custlist table. (However, we'll see a way around this later in the chapter.)

PRINTING THE ANSWER

To create a printed copy of the answer to your query, make sure the printer is ready, then press Instant Report (Alt-F7).

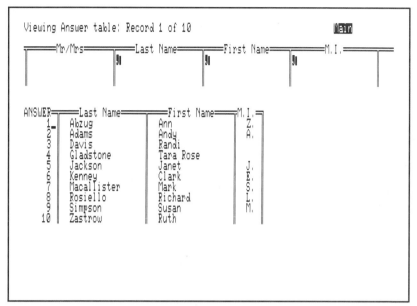

Figure 7.2: Selecting three fields from the Custlist table

CLEARING THE ANSWER TABLE

Once you've viewed your answer, simply press the Clear Image (F8) key. This will bring you back to the query form. You can change the query form and perform another query, or press Clear Image (F8) to clear the query form and return to the Main menu.

SEEING UNIQUE ITEMS

Normally, Paradox will not display duplicates when you select fields to display. Duplicate entries are those whose fields are identical as far as the terms of the query are concerned. For example, if you place a check mark in only the Start Date field on the query form and press DO-IT!, you'll see only the unique dates, as in Figure 7.3.

If you prefer that all records including duplicates be displayed, use the check-plus symbol in the query form. Do this by pressing Check Plus (Alt-F6). Placing a check plus in the Start Date field on the query form and pressing DO-IT! displays all the dates, as in Figure 7.4.

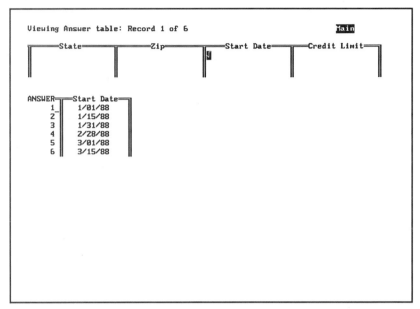

Figure 7.3: Viewing unique dates from the Custlist table

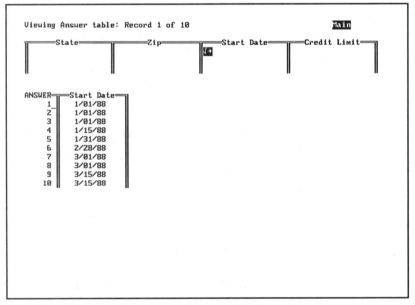

Figure 7.4: Viewing all start dates from the Custlist table

If several fields are selected with check marks, records that have identical data in all fields will be listed only once. For example, if you place check marks in the Zip and State fields, all records with unique zip codes and states will be displayed. If you place check-plus symbols in the Zip and State fields, all zip codes and dates will be displayed, including those that duplicate one another.

FINDING A PARTICULAR GROUP OF RECORDS

Besides placing check marks in the query form, you can enter *criteria* that define the types of records you want to display. For example, let's say that you want to see the name and city of all individuals who live in California. First, let's start with a fresh query screen. Press Clear Image (F8) until only the Main menu appears on the screen. Select the Ask option, and then specify Custlist as the table to query.

Place a check mark in the Last Name, First Name, City, and State fields, using the usual arrow and Checkmark (F6) keys. Now, to specify that only California residents be displayed, type the letters CA next to the check mark in the State field, as shown at the top of Figure 7.5. (*Note:* I've used the Rotate keys [Ctrl-R] in several examples in this chapter to better fit the query form on the screen and page. You need not rearrange or alter your own query form to perform these queries. Just be sure to place the check marks and search criteria in the appropriate fields.)

Press DO-IT! to perform the search. The Answer table will display only California residents, and only those fields you've checked, as shown in the bottom half of Figure 7.5.

This same technique will work with any field. To see only people whose last name is Jackson, first press Clear Image (F8) twice to clear the screen and the query form. Then select the Ask option from the Main menu and Custlist as the table. Enter Jackson into the Last Name field on the query form. Use check marks to mark the fields you want to see in the image, and then press DO-IT! to see the records. The screen will display only people with the last name Jackson, as shown in Figure 7.6.

When searching for letters and words, you must match the case you used in the original table. For example, a search for "ca" or

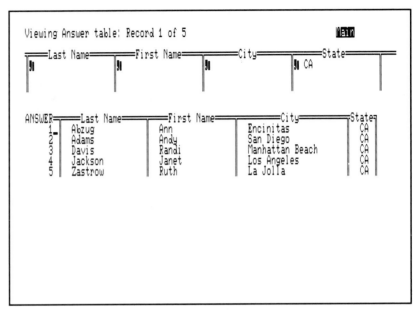

Figure 7.5: A search for California residents

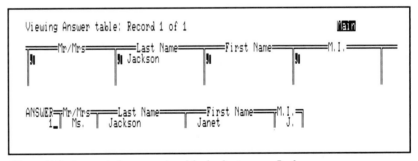

Figure 7.6: A search for records with the last name Jackson

"jackson" (instead of "CA" or "Jackson") would produce nothing, because the cases don't match. (However, we'll see a way around this later in the chapter.)

To see the records of customers whose Start Date is 3/1/88, call up the query form, check-mark the fields you want to see displayed in the answer, type 3/1/88 into the Start Date field of the query form, and press DO-IT!. The records containing the date March 1, 1988, will be displayed, as in Figure 7.7.

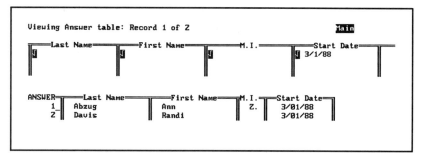

Figure 7.7: A search for records with start dates of 3/1/88

—— *SEARCHING FOR VALUES* ——

Often, you'll want to view records that have some value that is less than or greater than some constant. For example, you might want to view records for people who have credit limits of $10,000 or more. You can use *range operators* to perform such searches. Paradox's range operators are listed below:

OPERATOR	MEANING
=	Equal to (=)
<	Less than
>	Greater than
< =	Less than or equal to
> =	Greater than or equal to

To try this, start with a blank query screen and put check marks in the Last Name, First Name, and Credit Limit fields. Next to the check mark in the Credit Limit field, type

>= 10000

(*Note:* You cannot use commas in numbers on the query form. That is, 10000 cannot be entered as 10,000. Commas are used for something else in query forms, as we'll see.) Press the DO-IT! key to see the answer, which is shown in Figure 7.8.

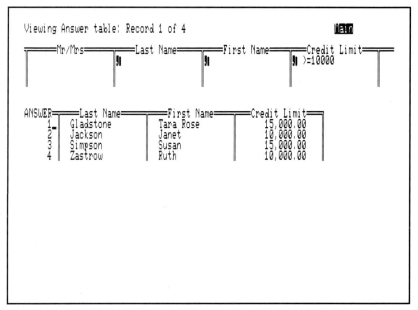

Figure 7.8: Records with credit limits of $10,000 or more

You can use range operators with date and alphanumeric data as well. For example, if you type

> M

in the Last Name field of the query form, the Answer table will display records for individuals with last names beginning with the second half of the alphabet (letters N–Z), as shown in Figure 7.9. (Don't forget to erase the > = 10000 in the Credit Limit field before pressing F2!)

If you wanted to see all individuals whose start dates were on or before March 1, 1988, you would enter the following criterion into the Start Date field of the query form:

< = 3/1/88

The resulting Answer table would display records for individuals whose Start Date field contained a date on or before March 1, 1988, as shown in Figure 7.10. (Again, you'll need to erase any previous query conditions before pressing F2 to perform the query.)

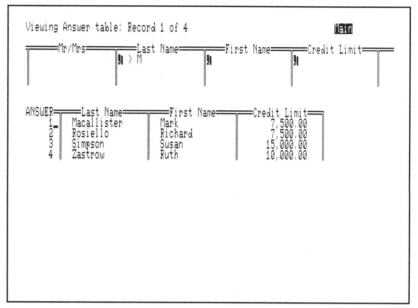

Figure 7.9: A display of individuals whose last names begin with letters N–Z

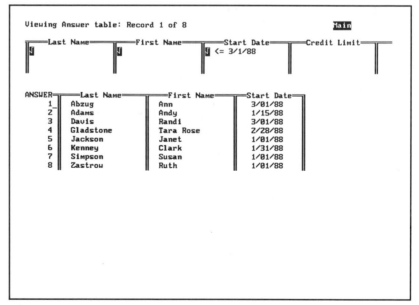

Figure 7.10: A search for records with start dates on or before 3/1/88

═══ SEARCHING FOR NONMATCHES ═══

Suppose you wanted to view records for everyone in the table except California residents. You would use the *not* operator in that case. For example, placing the criterion

> not CA

in the State field, as shown in the top portion of Figure 7.11, results in an Answer table of non-California residents, as shown in the bottom half of the figure.

═══ SEARCHING FOR RANGES ═══

You can pull out records based on a range of values, for example all records with start dates between 1/1/88 and 3/1/88, or records with credit limits from $7,500 to $10,000. To do so, you need to place two search criteria, separated by a comma, in the appropriate field of the query form. For example, Figure 7.12 shows a search for records

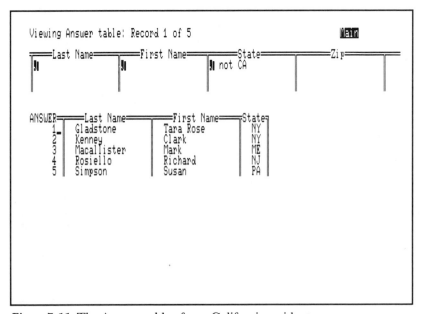

Figure 7.11: The Answer table of non-California residents

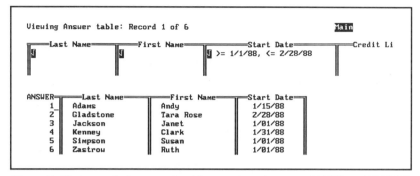

Figure 7.12: A search for records with start dates between 1/1/88 and 2/28/88

with dates between 1/1/88 and 2/28/88 on the query form, and the results of the query. Figure 7.13 shows a query for records with credit limits from $7,500 to $10,000, and the results of the query.

Range searches also work with alphanumeric data. For example, the criteria

$$> = M, < = S$$

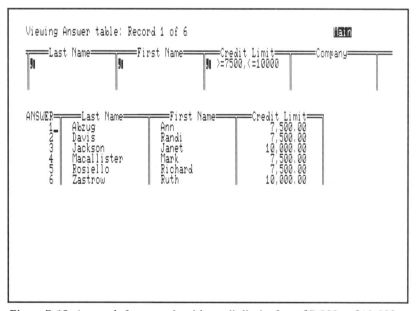

Figure 7.13: A search for records with credit limits from $7,500 to $10,000

in the Last Name field of the query form would display individuals whose last names begin with the letters M through S, as shown in Figure 7.14. Note that two search criteria are used, separated by a comma, which translate to "greater than or equal to M, *and* less than or equal to S." Using multiple criteria allows you to perform interesting And and Or searches, as we'll see in the next section.

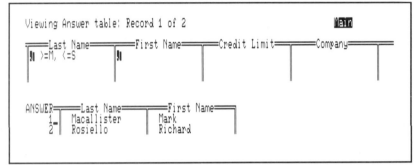

Figure 7.14: A search for individuals whose last names begin with letters M–S

PERFORMING AND/OR SEARCHES

Some of your queries might become a little more complicated than those we've discussed so far. For example, you might want to see a list of all California residents whose credit limits are over $10,000 and whose start dates are in January, or you might want a list consisting only of residents of New York or California. For these kinds of searches, you need to specify *And* or *Or* relationships in your queries.

And relationships are specified by simply filling in more than one criterion on a single line of the query form. Figure 7.15 shows a query for California residents whose start dates are in the month of January and whose credit limits are equal to or greater than $10,000. The Answer table shows the results of the query.

Notice that the criteria in the State, Start Date, and Credit Limit fields are on the same line of the query form. Placing the criteria on the same line specifies that an And relationship is to be used with the criteria. In an And query, only records that meet *all* criteria will be displayed.

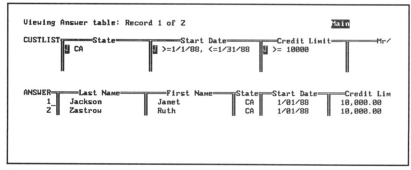

Figure 7.15: A search for California residents with start dates in 1/88 and credit limits of $10,000 or more

For an Or search, you need to place the criteria on separate lines of the query form. Furthermore, be sure to place check marks in the fields on both lines. Figure 7.16 shows a search for all people who live in either California or New York. Notice that check marks for displaying last name and first name are also specified in both lines of the

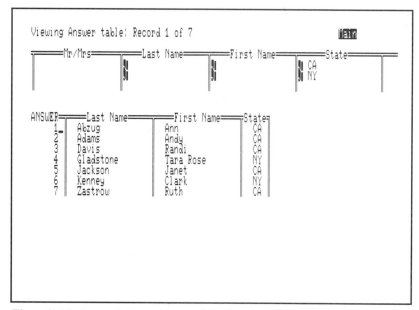

Figure 7.16: A search for residents of California or New York

query form. The resulting Answer table is also displayed in the figure. In answer to an Or query, a record will be displayed if it matches any one or all criteria.

When filling out query forms, remember that Paradox compares values in the table with what you enter into the query form. It does not attempt to guess at what you mean in English. For example, take a look at the query in Figure 7.17. Notice that no records were selected as matching the search criterion, so the Answer table is empty. That's because it is impossible for any record in the Custlist table to have both CA and NY in the State field at the same time.

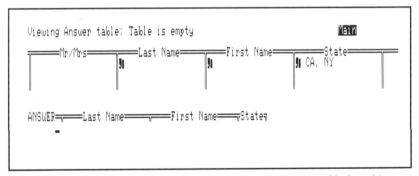

Figure 7.17: An incorrect attempt to list California and New York residents

The query we performed in Figure 7.16 showed the correct form for displaying all residents of either California and New York by placing the criteria on separate lines, thereby specifying records that have CA in the State field *or* have NY in the state field.

Or searches can be a little tricky and usually require a little thought. For example, look at the query and results shown in Figure 7.18.

Notice that California and New York residents are displayed, as well as a Pennsylvania resident with a credit of $10,000 or more. Furthermore, several California and New York residents whose credit limits are below $10,000 are displayed. That's because the query criteria ask for "records with CA in the State field, *or* NY in the State field, *or* credit limits of $10,000 or more." (In other words, people with credit limits over $10,000 are displayed, regardless of what state they live in.)

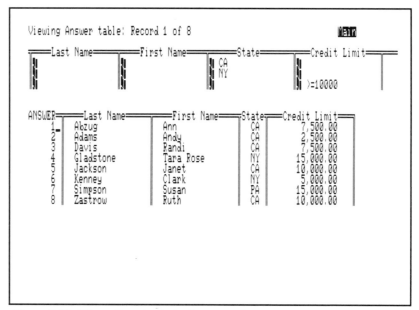

Figure 7.18: Three Or criteria in the query form

Now take a look at the query criteria and results in Figure 7.19. Notice that only California and New York residents with credit limits of $10,000 or more are displayed.

The results are different, because these criteria translate as "Display records that have CA in the State field *and* a credit limit of at least $10,000, *or* NY in the State field *and* a credit limit of at least $10,000."

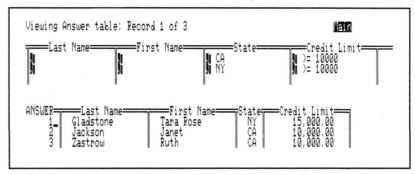

Figure 7.19: A search for California and New York residents with credit limits of $10,000 or more

_____ *PATTERN-MATCHING SEARCHES* _____

Sometimes, you might want to view records that match some pattern or contain a certain sequence of characters. For example, in an inventory system, you might want to view all records that have the letter J2 embedded in the part number (assuming this is some meaningful code). If you want to look up an individual named Smith but are not sure of the spelling, you might wish to view records that are spelled like Smith (though not exactly). The operators that you can use for these types of searches are listed below:

OPERATOR	*MEANING*
..	Stands for any series of characters, numbers, spaces, and so on
@	Stands for any single character
like	Matches items similar to the criterion
blank	Matches items that have no data in the field
today	Used to compare items against today's date

Let's look at some examples. Suppose you want to list all individuals who live on a particular street. You can't ask for all records that contain a street name, such as Ocean, because the word Ocean will be embedded somewhere in the middle of the address (for example, 1234 Ocean St.). However, you could use the .. operator to indicate the numbers preceding the street name, followed by the word Ocean, followed by .. again to indicate any other characters. Figure 7.20

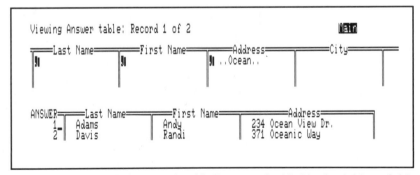

Figure 7.20: A search for records with Ocean embedded in the Address field

shows such a query and its results. Notice that records with the word Ocean embedded in the Address field are displayed.

You could, of course, be more specific in your query for residents on Ocean. For example, a query such as

..Ocean Blvd

would list any records with addresses that start with any characters and end with Ocean Blvd (thereby excluding Ocean View, Ocean Ave, Ocean Way, and so forth). In addition, you could set up an And condition on the search to find only residents on Ocean Blvd in a certain city, by specifying

..Ocean Blvd

in the Address field and a particular city name (Malibu, for instance) in the City field.

You can also use the .. operator to pull out records for a particular month. Notice the query and results in Figure 7.21. Since a particular day was not specified in the 1/../88 query, all records with start dates in the month of January are listed.

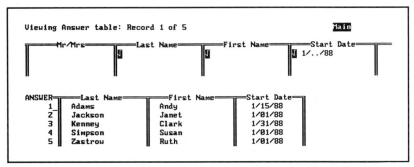

Figure 7.21: Search for records with start dates in January

The @ operator is used to match a single character, as opposed to any series of characters. For example, a search for Sm@th would find names such as Smith and Smyth. A search for Sm@th.. would find Smith, Smythe, Smithsonian, Smathers, and others that have a single letter embedded between the m and the t, with or without any characters following the h.

The use of upper- and lowercase letters will sometimes mislead a query. As mentioned earlier in the chapter, a query for all "ca" residents would display nothing, since CA is stored in uppercase in all records. This could be a problem if you were not absolutely certain of the case in all records. But using the *like* operator takes care of the problem. Notice that the query in Figure 7.22 asks for all records that have states like ca. Paradox displays all California residents. (Had there been some records with the state stored as CA or Ca, these too would have been displayed.)

You should use the like operator liberally, since it may find records with slight misspellings that might otherwise have gone unnoticed. Similarly, if you are not absolutely sure of the spelling of something you are trying to find, try using the like operator. Note the query in Figure 7.23, which asks for records with last names like Abzig. The results display a record for Abzug, which would not have been found without the like operator.

The *blank* operator finds records that have no data in a field. For example, the query in Figure 7.24 asks to see the last name and first

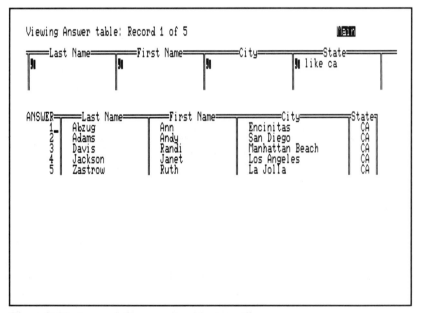

Figure 7.22: A search for records with states like ca

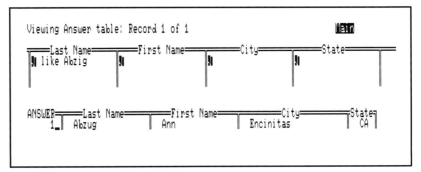

Figure 7.23: A search for records with last names like Abzig

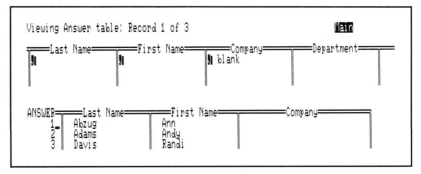

Figure 7.24: Records with blank Company fields

name of individuals who do not have a company affiliation (that is, the Company field is blank). The results of the query show the appropriate records.

The opposite of the blank operator is the *not blank* operator. A search for records with

not blank

in the Company field will show only individuals who have company affiliations.

Records can be compared against the current date (the date you type in when you first boot up your computer) by using the *today* operator. For example, if the current date were 3/1/88 and you entered the query shown in Figure 7.25, you'd see records whose start dates match today's date.

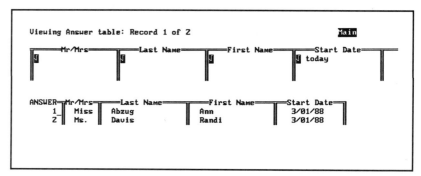

Figure 7.25: Records that match today's date

You can use the usual <, >, < =, > =, and the arithmetic operators listed below when working with dates:

OPERATOR   MEANS

\+   Add a number of days to the date

\-   Subtract a number of days from the date

Once again, assuming today's date is 3/1/88, the query in Figure
7.26 requests all records with start dates that are 30 or more days earlier than today's date.

QUERIES AS AN EDITING TOOL

On a very large table, editing can become laborious. You might
spend a good deal more time looking for items that you want to
change than you spend making the changes. With the use of the *find*
operator, you can make the query form into a great tool for looking
up and editing quickly. When you use the word *find* in the leftmost
column of the query form, Paradox displays the actual table, which
you can edit, rather than the Answer table. (Since the find operator
always displays the actual table, you cannot use check marks to display only certain fields.) Let's try an example.

First, let's pretend that there are 1,000 records on the database,
and you need to make a change to Kenney's record. To make matters

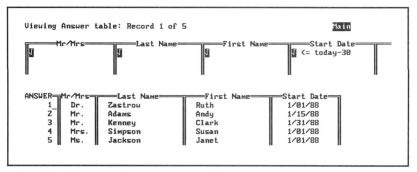

Figure 7.26: Records that were entered 30 or more days ago

a little more interesting, let's assume that you're not even sure how to spell Kenney.

Rather than using the arrow keys to scroll around searching, you can call up the query screen and enter the word *find* into the leftmost column. In the Last Name column, enter the criterion

like Kenny

Press the DO-IT! (F2) key and, lo and behold, the cursor is right on Kenney's record in the Custlist table, as shown in Figure 7.27. To edit, just press the Edit (F9) key as usual, and the DO-IT! key when finished editing.

GLOBAL EDITS

Here is a technique that may someday save you many hours of tedious work. Through a process known as *global editing,* you can automatically change the contents of a field to a new value in records that meet a certain criterion. For example, suppose you have two different people entering data into your database. One types in *Los Angeles* for all Los Angeles residents, and the other types in *L.A.*. This ends up creating problems, because queries that search for Los Angeles records miss those with L.A. and vice versa. (Even though an Or search could take care of this, it would still be better to have a consistent entry.)

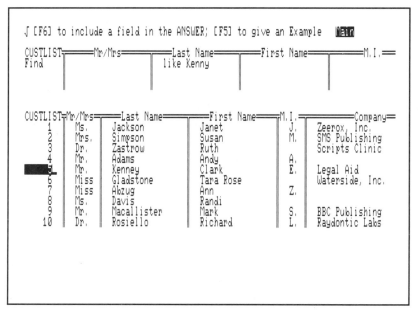

```
√ [F6] to include a field in the ANSWER; [F5] to give an Example   Main

CUSTLIST╤══Mr/Mrs═══╤════Last Name═══╤═════First Name═══╤═════M.I.══
Find     │          │    like Kenny  │                  │
         │          │                │                  │


CUSTLIST╤Mr/Mrs═╤════Last Name═══╤════First Name══╤M.I.═╤══════Company═══
     1   │ Ms.   │ Jackson        │ Janet          │ J.  │ Zeerox, Inc.
     2   │ Mrs.  │ Simpson        │ Susan          │ M.  │ SMS Publishing
     3   │ Dr.   │ Zastrow        │ Ruth           │     │ Scripts Clinic
     4   │ Mr.   │ Adams          │ Andy           │ A.  │
     5   │ Mr.   │ Kenney         │ Clark          │ E.  │ Legal Aid
     6   │ Miss  │ Gladstone      │ Tara Rose      │     │ Waterside, Inc.
     7   │ Miss  │ Abzug          │ Ann            │ Z.  │
     8   │ Ms.   │ Davis          │ Randi          │     │
     9   │ Mr.   │ Macallister    │ Mark           │ S.  │ BBC Publishing
    10   │ Dr.   │ Rosiello       │ Richard        │ L.  │ Raydontic Labs
```

Figure 7.27: A query to find and edit a record for Kenney

Another use of global editing would be to increase credit limits. For instance, you might want to raise all credit limits by 25 percent, as long as the current limit is less than $10,000.

You use the *changeto* operator in your queries to perform such global changes. We can try a global change with even the small Custlist table. We'll make a simple global edit of changing all records that have CA in the state field to ca. First, clear any images from the screen with the Clear Image (F8) key, so only the Main menu is displayed. Then select the Ask option and specify the Custlist table. Fill in the query screen as shown at the top of Figure 7.28.

Notice how the query is set up. CA in the State field indicates that CA is the value we're searching for. The comma separates the query (CA) from the command

    changeto ca

When you press DO-IT! (F2), Paradox displays the records that have been changed in a special table called Changed, as shown in the

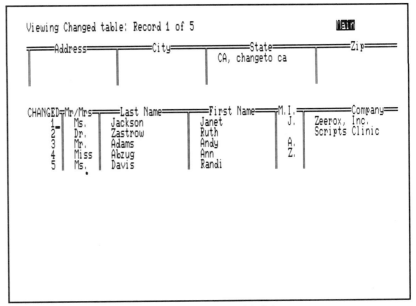

Figure 7.28: A query to change all records with CA to ca

bottom half of Figure 7.28. (Like the find operator, changeto always displays all the fields in a table. Hence, check marks cannot be used on the query form.)

The changes themselves do not actually show up in the Changed table. To see the new values in the Custlist table, first clear the Changed image and the query form from the screen by pressing Clear Image (F8) twice. Then select the View option from the Main menu and specify Custlist as the table to work with. Scroll over to the State field to view the changes. Notice all the ca entries are in lowercase, as Figure 7.29 shows.

To restore the original values, clear the image (press F8). Select the Ask option from the menu and specify the Custlist table. Enter the criterion

ca, changeto CA

in the State field, and press DO-IT!. Press Clear All (Alt-F8) to clear the screen. Select the View option and specify the Custlist table.

```
┌─────────────────────────────────────────────────────────────────────┐
│ Viewing Custlist table: Record 1 of 10                        Main    │
│                                                                       │
│ CUSTLIST┌─────────City══════╤State╤═════Zip═══╤═════Start Date═╤════Credit Lim │
│    1    ║ Los Angeles_      │ CA  │ 91234     │ 1/01/88        │ 10,000.00     │
│    2    ║ Philadelphia      │ PA  │ 23456     │ 1/01/88        │ 15,000.00     │
│    3    ║ La Jolla          │ CA  │ 92037     │ 1/01/88        │ 10,000.00     │
│    4    ║ San Diego         │ CA  │ 92038     │ 1/15/88        │ 2,500.00      │
│    5    ║ New York          │ NY  │ 12345     │ 1/31/88        │ 5,000.00      │
│    6    ║ New York          │ NY  │ 12345     │ 2/28/88        │ 15,000.00     │
│    7    ║ Encinitas         │ CA  │ 92024     │ 3/01/88        │ 7,500.00      │
│    8    ║ Manhattan Beach    │ CA  │ 90001     │ 3/01/88        │ 7,500.00      │
│    9    ║ Bangor            │ ME  │ 00001     │ 3/15/88        │ 7,500.00      │
│   10    ║ Newark            │ NJ  │ 00123     │ 3/15/88        │ 7,500.00      │
│                                                                       │
└─────────────────────────────────────────────────────────────────────┘
```

Figure 7.29: The results of a global edit to the State field in the Custlist table

Scroll over to the State field to see that all CA entries are back in uppercase.

In our hypothetical example of changing the L.A. entries to Los Angeles, you would enter the following criterion into the City field of the query form:

L.A., changeto Los Angeles

This would globally change the L.A. entries to Los Angeles.

We'll discuss global changes that increase or decrease numbers in a later chapter on managing numbers. For now, just keep in mind that you can use the changeto operator to alter records in a table globally. We'll see more uses for this type of query throughout this book.

GLOBAL DELETIONS

By placing the word *delete* in the leftmost column of the query form, you can globally delete a group of records that meet a certain criterion. This is not a particularly safe technique to try out right now, because we do not have enough skill to undo a global deletion. However, we can try a hypothetical and safe example with our Custlist table.

Select the Ask option from the Main menu and specify the Custlist table. In the leftmost column of the query form, type in the word *delete*. In the State column, enter the letters TX and press DO-IT! (F2). The effect of this query is to delete all records that have TX in the State field.

The records that have been deleted will be displayed in a table named Deleted, as shown in Figure 7.30. In this example, there were no records with TX in the State field, so no records were deleted. This is just as well, since the table need not be any smaller. Nonetheless, this little example should give you an idea of how this capability works.

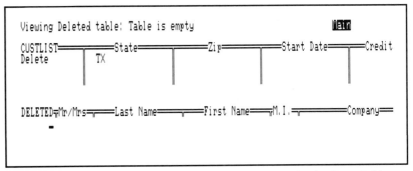

Figure 7.30: The global deletion of all records with TX in the State field

LIMITATIONS

Basically, there is no limit to the number of ways in which you can combine the various searching techniques we've discussed here. The only limitation is that the query form can contain only 22 rows of information (22 Or conditions), which are probably far more than you'll ever need.

However, one must exercise caution in the use of certain keywords and symbols in queries. For example, suppose you wish to find a record for someone with the last name Davis, Jr. If you enter the query by typing

Davis, Jr.

into the Last Name field, Paradox will separate Davis and Jr. as two separate queries (as in an And search). Hence, the query will attempt to find records that contain only the name Davis, and only the name Jr. No records will meet such a criterion. Therefore, to state that you literally are looking for the name *Davis, Jr.,* enclose the query in quotation marks, as below:

"Davis, Jr."

Similarly, suppose there were a city named Blank, and you wished to view records of everyone who lived there. If you enter the query

Blank

in the city field, you'll get all the records that have no data in the City field (since Blank has special meaning in Paradox queries). To specify that you literally are looking for a city named Blank, enclose the name in quotation marks, as below:

"Blank"

Using quotation marks in queries keeps Paradox from converting special symbols and words (such as the comma and the words *blank, not,* and *today*) into commands, and instead treats them as items to look up.

SAMPLE QUERIES

Before ending this chapter, let's look at a few more examples that combine the many techniques we've discussed. Since the Custlist table is too small to demonstrate the full query capability of Paradox, we'll just present some examples and the types of data they would display.

The query in Figure 7.31 requests all records of individuals who live in Red Rock, Arizona (that is, records with Red Rock in the City field and AZ in the State field).

The query in Figure 7.32 would locate all individuals whose title is Dr. and whose zip code is in the 90000 to 99999 area.

The query in Figure 7.33 requests all records that have the letter *s* embedded in either the Last Name, First Name, or M.I. (middle initial) field. This may seem a bit odd as a query, but you may be surprised. Someday you may have a database with three different part numbers per record, and you need to find records that have some

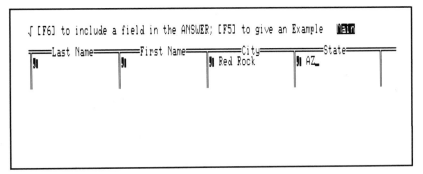

Figure 7.31: A search for residents of Red Rock, Arizona

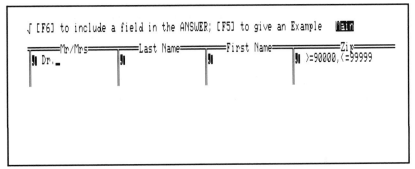

Figure 7.32: A search for doctors in the 90000 to 99999 zip code area

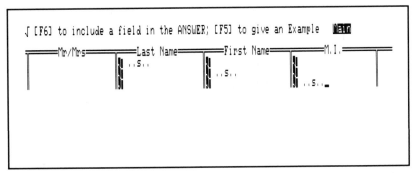

Figure 7.33: A query for records with the letter s in the Last Name, First Name, or M.I. fields

code embedded in any of the three part numbers. It would be the same type of query, but with different fields.

The query in Figure 7.34 would display all San Diego residents whose credit limits were in the range of 5,000 to 10,000. Note the three And conditions. In English, this query finds "all records that have San Diego in the City field, *and* have Credit Limits greater than or equal to $-5000, *and* Credit Limits less than or equal to $10000."

The query in Figure 7.35 asks for the records of all people who have credit limits in the range of $5,000 to $10,000 and who have zip codes in the range of 80000 to 85000.

The best way to fully master the query form is to experiment. Again, don't be worried about doing any harm. You cannot possibly

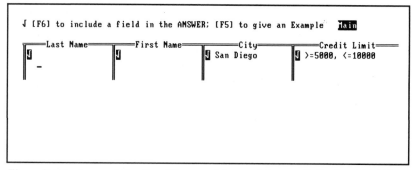

Figure 7.34: A search for San Diego residents with a credit limit of $5,000 to $10,000

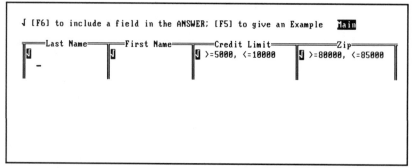

Figure 7.35: A search for residents in the 80000–85000 zip code area with credit limits of $5,000 to $10,000

damage anything by using queries. Experiment and enjoy. Later, we'll do more queries with bigger tables, as well as with several tables simultaneously.

SUMMARY

- To search (or query) a table, select the Ask option from the Main menu and specify a table name.

- Press Checkmark (F6) to place a check mark in each field of the query form that you want to see displayed.

- Place a check plus (press Alt-F6) in each field if you wish to include duplicates in a display.

- To search for particular records, put the data that you want to search for in the appropriate field in the query form.

- To search for values, use the <, >, < =, and > = operators in your query forms.

- To search for nonmatches, use the not operator in your criterion.

- To search for ranges, place two values (with < or < =, and > or > = operators) in a single field, separated by a comma.

- To specify an And relationship among several criteria, place all items in the same row on the query form.

- To specify an Or relationship among criteria in the query form, place the criteria on different rows.

- For trickier searches, you can use the .., @, *like, blank,* and *today* operators.

- To edit data using queries, use the *find* operator in the leftmost column of the query form and the criteria you wish to search for in the appropriate column(s).

- To globally change a table, use the *changeto* operator in your criterion.

- To globally delete records on a table, use the *delete* operator in the leftmost column of the query form.

PRINTING FORMATTED REPORTS

IN COMPUTER JARGON, A *REPORT* IS ANY FORMATTED display of data. In this chapter we'll explore techniques for displaying table data in a variety of formats, including a printed directory, mailing labels, and form letters. We'll use the Paradox *report generator* to design and develop these reports.

The Paradox report generator is very powerful, very flexible, and also a bit overwhelming at first glance. In this chapter, we'll cover the basics and develop some reports for our Custlist table. Later, we'll deal with more complicated issues such as subtotals and grouping.

Now let's jump right in and develop a printed directory that displays data from the Custlist table in the format shown in Figure 8.1. Notice that the report is formatted, as well as sorted into alphabetical order.

```
3/31/88              Directory of Customers            Page    1


Abzug, Miss Ann Z.
         301 Crest Dr.
         Encinitas, CA    92024    (1)
         Start Date: 3/01/88       Credit Limit:7,500.00

Adams, Mr. Andy A.
         234 Ocean View Dr.
         San Diego, CA    92038    (2)
         Start Date: 1/15/88       Credit Limit:2,500.00

Davis, Ms. Randi
         371 Oceanic Way
         Manhattan Beach, CA    90001    (3)
         Start Date: 3/01/88       Credit Limit:7,500.00

Gladstone, Miss Tara Rose
         Waterside, Inc.
         Acquisitions
         P.O. Box 121
         New York, NY    12345    (4)
         Start Date: 2/28/88       Credit Limit:15,000.00
```

Figure 8.1: A printed directory from the Custlist table

══ *DESIGNING A REPORT* ══

To design a report format for the directory shown in Figure 8.1, select the Report option from the Main menu. You'll be given five options:

> Output   Design   Change   RangeOutput   SetPrinter

To create a new report, select the Design option. When Paradox asks for the name of the table to use, enter Custlist as the table name. Paradox will show another menu:

> R   1   2   3   4   5   6   7   8   9

"R" is the standard report format Paradox automatically creates for every table; it is the format used when you press Instant Report (Alt-F7) to print a report. Additional reports used with a table can be assigned to the numbers 1 through 14. Select option 1 to assign report number 1 to the directory report. Paradox then displays all report options that begin with the number 1, as below:

> <u>1</u>   10   11   12   13   14
> Unused report

Note that option 1 is highlighted, and the prompt *Unused report* informs you that no report format has been assigned to this number yet. Press Enter to select number 1. (Optionally, you can use the arrow keys to highlight another number, and then press Enter to select that number. However, for simplicity, it makes sense to number our first report as 1.)

Paradox will now ask for a description of the report:

> Report description:
> Enter report description.

You can enter any description up to 40 characters long. For this example, type

> Directory of Customers

and press Enter. (This description can also be used as a title in the report, as we'll see in a moment.)

Next, Paradox asks which type of report you want, as below:

Tabular   Free-form

The Tabular option displays data in much the same way that Table View does on the screen. Each field of information is placed in a single column. The Free-form option allows you to display data in any format you wish. All the sample reports in this chapter will use the Free-form option, so go ahead and select Free-form now.

A suggested report format will appear on the screen, which looks like the standard form you see on the screen when you display data in Form View. This screen, shown in Figure 8.2, is called the *report specification*, because it allows you to specify a format for the report.

Notice that the report specification shows lines for a *page band* and a *form band* (indicated by down-pointing triangles next to the words *page* and *form*). The page band shows what will appear at the top and bottom

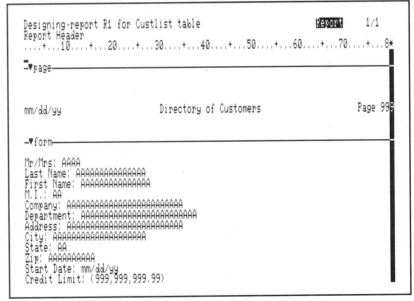

Figure 8.2: A free-form report specification

of each printed page of the report. In this example, the current date (mm/dd/yy), title (Directory of Customers), and page number will be displayed at the top of each page (unless we make changes).

Within the page band is the form band. The form band shows what will be printed for each record in the table. The contents of the form band will be printed as many times as necessary to fill a single page. In other words, while the heading will appear only at the top of each page, the contents of the form band may be repeated several times on a page.

To get the exact format we want for the directory, we'll need to modify this suggested format on the report specification. As usual, you can use the arrow keys to move the cursor up, down, left, and right, and Backspace and Ctrl-Backspace to delete items and make corrections. In addition, you can use the keys listed in Table 8.1 to help design a report format.

Key	Effect
Ctrl-←	Moves left half a screen
Ctrl-→	Moves right half a screen
PgUp	Moves up one screen
PgDn	Moves down one screen
Home	Moves to first line of screen
Ctrl-Home	Moves to beginning of line
End	Moves to last line
Ctrl-End	Moves to last character of line
Ins	Turns Insert mode on/off
Del	Deletes character at cursor
Ctrl-Y	Deletes all characters to right of cursor
Ctrl-V	Turns vertical ruler line on/off
Enter	If Insert mode is on, inserts a blank line

Table 8.1: Keys used for designing report formats

Note that the Ctrl-Y key combination deletes all characters to the right of the cursor. If the cursor is in the leftmost column, Ctrl-Y deletes the entire line.

The Ins key toggles the Insert mode on and off. When Insert mode is on, newly typed characters are inserted between existing characters, and pressing the Enter key inserts a whole new line. When Insert mode is off, newly typed characters overwrite existing characters, and pressing Enter merely moves the cursor to the next line. We'll get a little practice with these keys in this chapter.

Now let's get to work. Use the arrow keys to move the cursor to the start of the Mr/Mrs field, as below:

<u>Mr</u>/Mrs: AAAA

Type Ctrl-Y to delete the entire line.

Next, press the Del key 10 times to erase the words *Last Name* and the colon, so that the form band looks like this:

```
AAAAAAAAAAAAAAA
First Name: AAAAAAAAAAAAAAA
M.I.: AA
Company: AAAAAAAAAAAAAAAAAAAAAAAAA
Address: AAAAAAAAAAAAAAAAAAAAAAAAAA
City: AAAAAAAAAAAAAAAAAAAA
State: AA
Zip: AAAAAAAAAA
Start Date: mm/dd/yy
Credit Limit: (999,999,999.99)
```

Notice that most fields have *templates,* consisting of the letter A or the number 9, next to them. These act as markers that tell you where a field's contents will appear on the printed report and how much room they'll take up. (The size and configuration come from the original table structure.) You can tell which template goes with which field by moving the cursor into the template and looking at the upper-right corner of the screen. For example, when the cursor is in the current template, the upper-right corner of the screen shows the words *Last Name.*

Now type Ctrl-End to move the cursor to the last character of this template, and type in a comma. Then press the Space bar, so the top line looks like this:

AAAAAAAAAAAAAAA, _

PLACING FIELDS

Now let's put the Mr/Mrs title next to the last name, after the comma. With the cursor in its current position, press Menu (F10) to call up the Report menu. Note that you are given several new options, as below:

Field   Group   Output   Setting   Help   DO-IT!   Cancel

To place a field on the report specification, select the Field option. Another submenu appears, as below:

Place   Erase   Reformat   Justify   CalcEdit   WordWrap

We want to place a field, so select the Place option. Now another submenu appears:

Regular   Summary   Calculated   Date   Time   Page   #Record

Mr/Mrs is a regular table field, so select the Regular option.

At this point Paradox displays a menu of field names. Press Enter to select the Mr/Mrs option. The screen displays these instructions:

Use ↑ ↓ → ← to indicate where field should begin . . .
then press ↵ to place it . . .

The cursor is already at the position we want to display the Mr/Mrs field, so just press Enter.

Next, Paradox instructs you as follows:

Now use → and ← to indicate how many characters to show . . .
press ↵ when finished.

We want to show all the characters in the Mr/Mrs field, so just press the Enter key.

You'll notice that when the cursor is in the new AAAA template, the upper-right corner of the screen displays the name of the field, Mr/Mrs. Again, this is just to help you keep track of which template goes with which field.

Now let's place the First Name field next to the Mr/Mrs field. Press the → key twice so there is a space between the last A in the Mr/Mrs template and the cursor, as below:

AAAAAAAAAAAAAAA, AAAA   _

Place the First Name field here by following these steps:

1. Press the Menu (F10) key.

2. Select Field.

3. Select Place.

4. Select Regular.

5. Select First Name.

Once again, Paradox will ask that you place the cursor and then specify a size. Just press Enter in response to both these prompts.

Now, to place the middle initial, press the → key twice to move the cursor to the right. Again, call up the menu (press F10) and select the Field, Place, and Regular options; then select the M.I. option from the menu. Press Enter twice to bypass the two questions about placement and size.

Now the report specification has the entire name in a single row, with a comma after the last name:

Last Name, Mr/Mrs First Name M.I.

(For example, *Smith, Dr. Albert T.*) We no longer need the First Name and M.I. fields from the lines below, so use ↓ and Ctrl-← to move the cursor down a line and to the leftmost column. Then type Ctrl-Y twice to erase the original suggested First Name and M.I. rows. Your screen should look like Figure 8.3.

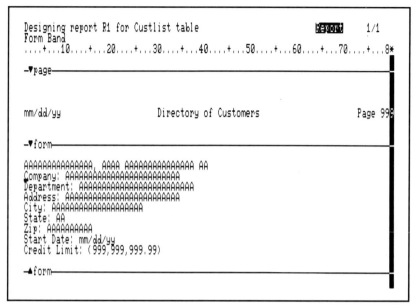

Figure 8.3: The name portion of the directory defined

Now let's erase the title *Company:* but leave the contents of the field indented. First, make sure the Insert mode is off. (Press the Ins key repeatedly, and watch for the Ins message to appear and disappear at the upper-right corner of the screen. Stop pressing when the Ins message does *not* appear on the screen.) Now, overwrite *Company:* with spaces by pressing the Space bar eight times. Your form band should now look something like this:

```
AAAAAAAAAAAAAAA, AAAA AAAAAAAAAAAAAAA AA
          AAAAAAAAAAAAAAAAAAAAAAAAAA
Department: AAAAAAAAAAAAAAAAAAAAAAAAAA
Address: AAAAAAAAAAAAAAAAAAAAAAAAAA
City: AAAAAAAAAAAAAAAAAAAA
State: AA
Zip: AAAAAAAAAA
Start Date: mm/dd/yy
Credit Limit: (999,999,999.99)
```

Let's take care of the Department field now. Press ↓, then Ctrl-←. Press the Space bar nine times to overwrite most of the word *Department:*, then press Del three times to delete the rest of the word and line up the Department template with the Company template, as follows:

```
AAAAAAAAAAAAAAA, AAAA AAAAAAAAAAAAAAA AA
        AAAAAAAAAAAAAAAAAAAAAAAAAA
        AAAAAAAAAAAAAAAAAAAAAAAAAA
Address: AAAAAAAAAAAAAAAAAAAAAAAAAA
City: AAAAAAAAAAAAAAAAAAA
State: AA
Zip: AAAAAAAAAA
Start Date: mm/dd/yy
Credit Limit: (999,999,999.99)
```

For the Address field, press ↓, then Ctrl-←. Press the Space bar eight times to erase the *Address:* heading.

For the City field, press ↓, Ctrl-←, and then the Space bar five times to erase the *City:* heading. To get the City template aligned with the others, press the Ins key so that the Insert mode is on. (The word Ins appears in the upper-right corner of the screen.) Press the Space bar three times to move the template to the right. Your screen should look like this:

```
AAAAAAAAAAAAAAA, AAAA AAAAAAAAAAAAAAA AA
        AAAAAAAAAAAAAAAAAAAAAAAAAA
        AAAAAAAAAAAAAAAAAAAAAAAAAA
        AAAAAAAAAAAAAAAAAAAAAAAAAA
        AAAAAAAAAAAAAAAAAAA
State: AA
Zip: AAAAAAAAAA
Start Date: mm/dd/yy
Credit Limit: (999,999,999.99)
```

Now we want to place a comma after the city and tack on the State and Zip fields. Press Ctrl-End to move the cursor to the last character of the City template. Then type in a comma and press the Space bar, so the line looks like this:

```
AAAAAAAAAAAAAAAAAAA,  _
```

Call up the menu and select the Field, Place, and Regular options. Select State from the menu of field names, and press Enter twice to bypass the prompts about position and size.

Now press the → key four times. Place the Zip field by pressing Menu (F10) and selecting the usual Field, Place, and Regular options. Select Zip from the menu of field names, and press Enter twice to bypass the position and size prompts.

We don't need the original suggested City and State fields anymore, so press ↓, Ctrl-←, then Ctrl-Y twice to erase the original fields. Now your screen should look like Figure 8.4.

Let's take care of the Start Date and Credit Limit fields now. First, press the Space bar nine times (the Insert mode is still on) to move the Start Date field to the right nine places. Next, press Ctrl-End, then the → key seven times so that the cursor is to the right of the Start Date template, aligned with the Zip template, as below:

```
AAAAAAAAAAAAAA, AAAA AAAAAAAAAAAAAA AA
AAAAAAAAAAAAAAAAAAAAAAAAA
AAAAAAAAAAAAAAAAAAAAAAAAA
AAAAAAAAAAAAAAAAAAAAAAAAA
AAAAAAAAAAAAAAAAAA,  AA  AAAAAAAAA
Start Date: mm/dd/yy    _
```

Now, type

```
Credit Limit:
```

(including the colon and a space). Place the Credit Limit field by using the usual method. (Press Menu (F10), select the Field, Place, and Regular options, and select the Credit Limit field.) Because Credit Limit is a currency field, Paradox will ask about the position, size, and number of decimal places to display. Once again, you can just press Enter in response to these prompts, because the default values are adequate.

We don't need the Credit Limit field down below anymore, so press ↓ and Ctrl-←, then Ctrl-Y to delete the line. Now your screen should look like Figure 8.5.

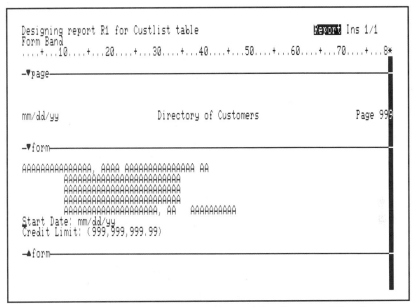

Figure 8.4: The Name and Address portions of the directory defined

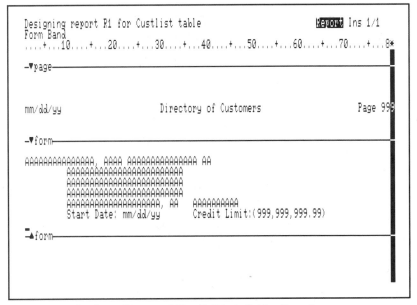

Figure 8.5: The Start Date and Credit Limit fields aligned

ADDING THE RECORD NUMBER

It's always nice (though not necessary) to have a record number on a printed report to simplify looking up table data from a printed directory. We can add the record number to the directory by following these steps. First, press ↑ twice to move the cursor to the City-State-Zip line. Position the cursor somewhere to the right of the Zip template, and type an open parenthesis, as below:

AAAAAAAAAAAAAAAAAAAA, AA   AAAAAAAAAA   (

To the right of this parenthesis, we'll put the record number. Call up the menu (press F10) and select the Field and Place options. From the submenu, select the #Record option (which always displays the current record number). Next, select the Overall option (since this report uses no grouping), and press Enter twice to bypass the position and size prompts. (Grouping is a technique used most often in reports that contain subtotals. We'll discuss such reports in a later chapter.)

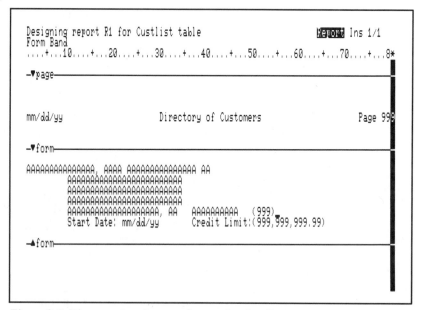

Figure 8.6: The completed report format for the directory

Press → until the cursor is to the right of the last 9 on the 999 template. Type a closing parenthesis to surround the record-number template. That should just about do it. Your screen should now look like Figure 8.6.

You might want to take a moment now to compare the report format that appears on the screen (and in Figure 8.6) to the actual printed report shown in Figure 8.1. Notice how the A's show the placement of various alphanumeric fields on the report, the 9's show the placement of numbers (including Currency values), and the mm/dd/yy shows where the date is displayed. In addition, the actual words Start Date and Credit Limit, and the parentheses surrounding the record number, appear directly on the report format.

Note also that we've used the basic editing keys listed in Table 8.1 to move, insert, and delete information from the original "suggested" format to create the format we want. In addition, we've used a few basic menu selections to place fields directly on the report format. (If you're feeling like this went a bit too quickly, don't worry. You'll get more practice in this chapter.)

A TRIAL RUN

Before we save this report format, let's take a look at an actual report that it will produce. To do so, call up the menu (press F10) and select Output. For our trial run, we'll just take a look at the report on the screen, so select the Screen option from the displayed submenu. You'll see the report go by on the screen in pages, as in Figure 8.7.

The basic format is right, but as you can see, the report is not quite in tip-top shape. As you press any key to scroll from page to page, you'll see that the fields include the blank spaces allocated for the field in the table structure. Also, people who have no company or department data have blank lines in their records. It looks like the directory still needs a little work.

To finish viewing the report, keep pressing any key until you see the prompt

End of Report
Press any key to continue...

```
Now Viewing Page 1 of Page Width 1
Press any key to continue..._


    10/31/87   6:28 pm      Directory of Customers            Page   1


    Abzug          , Miss Ann           Z.


               301 Crest Dr.
               Encinitas          , CA  92024        (  1)
               Start Date:  3/01/88      Credit Limit:          7,500.00


    Adams          , Mr. Andy            A.


               234 Ocean View Dr.
               San Diego          , CA  92038        (  2)
               Start Date:  1/15/88      Credit Limit:          2,500.00


                          paradox fig8-7
```

Figure 8.7: The directory report still in need of a little work

Then press any key to view the report format once again. Now let's get to work on taking out all those extraneous blank spaces and blank lines.

SQUEEZING OUT THE BLANKS

To delete extraneous blanks from the printed report format, press F10 while the report format is displayed on the screen to call up the Report menu. Select the Setting option, which displays the following submenu of options:

RemoveBlanks   PageLayout   Margin   Setup   Wait

Right now, we'll be concerned only with the RemoveBlanks option. Select it, and you'll see this submenu:

LineSqueeze   FieldSqueeze

To squeeze out blank lines (like empty Company and Department fields on some records), select the LineSqueeze option, and answer Yes to the ensuing prompt. Do so now.

The next submenu displays the options and prompt

Fixed   Variable
Forms are the same length; blank lines moved to the bottom.

If you select Fixed, blank lines will be squeezed out of individual records, but added to the bottom of each page so that the same number of records appear on each page. If you highlight the Variable option (by pressing →), the prompt displays

Forms are variable length; blank lines deleted.

which means that any blank lines will be deleted entirely, and thus not carried to the bottom of the page. Since it is not necessary to include exactly the same number of records on each page in this report format, press Enter while the Variable option is highlighted to select that option.

We also need to squeeze out all those blank spaces from people's names. So call up the menu (F10) again and select the Setting and RemoveBlanks options. Then select FieldSqueeze and answer Yes to the next prompt to squeeze out trailing blanks from individual fields.

Let's take another look at the report. Call up the menu (press F10) and select the Output and Screen options. You'll see a much-improved version of the directory, as shown in Figure 8.8. Keep pressing any key to scroll through the pages of the report, until you see the report specification again.

SAVING A REPORT FORMAT

We certainly do not want to go through all these steps each time we want to print a directory, so let's save this format for future use. To do so, just press the DO-IT! (F2) key. You'll be returned to the Main menu.

CANCELING A REPORT FORMAT

If by some chance you really make a mess of your report and want to start all over from scratch, you can cancel and abandon your work by calling up the Report menu (F10) and selecting the Cancel option. Paradox will double-check for permission before abandoning the

```
Now Viewing Page 1 of Page Width 1
Press any key to continue..._


      10/31/87   6:29 pm       Directory of Customers              Page   1


      Abzug, Miss Ann Z.
             301 Crest Dr.
             Encinitas, CA   92024      (1)
             Start Date: 3/01/88       Credit Limit: 7,500.00



      Adams, Mr. Andy A.
             234 Ocean View Dr.
             San Diego, CA   92038      (2)
             Start Date: 1/15/88       Credit Limit: 2,500.00
```

Figure 8.8: The directory report with extra blanks removed

report format. (*Note:* You can always change a report format after it is saved, so you need not cancel every time you make a small mistake.) You'll be returned to the Main menu.

PRINTING THE SORTED DIRECTORY

Let's now make a nice printed copy of our directory. If you haven't saved the report format yet, do so now by pressing DO-IT!.

PRESORTING THE TABLE

Before you print the directory, you might as well sort it into alphabetical order by name. Select the Modify option from the Main menu and the Sort option from the submenu. Specify the Custlist table, and select Same when asked how to sort the table. Make Last

Name the first sort field, First Name the second sort field, and M.I. the third sort field on the sort form, as shown below:

```
  Mr/Mrs
1 Last Name
2 First Name
3 M.I.
  Company
  Address
  City
  State
  Zip
  Start Date
  Credit Limit
```

Press the DO-IT! (F2) key. After a brief delay, the data will appear on the screen in the appropriate sort order.

PRINTING A REPORT FROM THE MAIN MENU

To print a report from the Main menu (F10), select the Report option. This will bring up the submenu

Output   Design   Change   RangeOutput   SetPrinter

Select the Output option to print the report. When Paradox asks for the name of the table to use, enter or select Custlist. Next, Paradox asks which report you want to print, as below:

R   1

R is the standard tabular report that Paradox prints by default. If you move the highlight to the 1, you'll see the description associated with report #1, as shown below:

R   <u>1</u>
Directory of Customers

Press Enter to select this report.

Finally, Paradox gives you three options for displaying the report, as below:

Printer   Screen   File

Selecting the Printer option will print the report. Selecting Screen displays the report on the screen only. Selecting File allows you to assign a file name, and then the report is stored on disk under the file name you assign. (This option is sometimes used to pass reports to word processed documents, as we'll discuss in Chapter 16.)

For now, select the Printer option. (Make sure your printer is hooked up, turned on, and on line.) You'll see the printed report, with the first page looking something like Figure 8.9.

FINE-TUNING YOUR REPORT

After printing your report, you may find that some more changes are needed in the general format, such as a change in page length, width, or margins. Let's discuss general techniques for formatting a report on the printed page.

CHANGING AN EXISTING REPORT FORMAT

To modify an existing report, select the Report option from the Main menu and the Change option from the submenu. Paradox will prompt you for the name of the associated table (enter Custlist in this example) and then display a menu of existing reports, as below:

R   1

Select the 1 option to modify the Directory of Customers report. Paradox will display the report description and allow you to modify it. To retain the original report description, just press Enter. The report format appears on the screen, ready for editing.

The keys you use to modify the report at this point are identical to those used when creating it. So you can easily move the cursor around, place fields, and so forth, just as we did when first creating the report. Now we'll look at other ways to change the appearance of the report.

```
3/31/88          Directory of Customers        Page   1


Abzug, Miss Ann Z.
        301 Crest Dr.
        Encinitas, CA    92024    (1)
        Start Date: 3/01/88        Credit Limit:7,500.00



Adams, Mr. Andy A.
        234 Ocean View Dr.
        San Diego, CA    92038    (2)
        Start Date: 1/15/88        Credit Limit:2,500.00


Davis, Ms. Randi
        371 Oceanic Way
        Manhattan Beach, CA   90001   (3)
        Start Date: 3/01/88        Credit Limit:7,500.00




Gladstone, Miss Tara Rose
        Waterside, Inc.
        Acquisitions
        P.O. Box 121
        New York, NY   12345    (4)
        Start Date: 2/28/88        Credit Limit:15,000.00

Jackson, Ms. Janet J.
        Zeerox, Inc.
        Accounts Payable
        1234 Corporate Hwy.
        Los Angeles, CA    91234    (5)
        Start Date: 1/01/88        Credit Limit:10,000.00

Kenney, Mr. Clark E.
        Legal Aid
        371 Ave. of the Americas
        New York, NY   12345    (6)
        Start Date: 1/31/88        Credit Limit:5,000.00
```

Figure 8.9: The first page of the printed Directory of Customers

CHANGING HEADING AND FOOTING MARGINS

You can change the size of the margins at the top and bottom of each printed page by changing the gap between the page band and the form band. For example, if you move the cursor down to near the bottom of the screen (under the bottom form band marker and above the bottom page band marker), you can type Ctrl-Y a few times to narrow the gap between the two bands. Figure 8.10 shows the directory report format with a smaller margin at the bottom of each page. Note how close the bottom form band and page band are.

```
Changing report R1 for Custlist table                    Report    1/1
Page Footer
....+...10....+...20....+...30....+...40....+...50....+...60....+...70....+...8*

-▼page────────────────────────────────────────────────────────────────────


mm/dd/yy                    Directory of Customers                  Page 999

-▼form────────────────────────────────────────────────────────────────────

AAAAAAAAAAAAAAA, AAAA AAAAAAAAAAAAAAA AA
          AAAAAAAAAAAAAAAAAAAAAAAAAA
          AAAAAAAAAAAAAAAAAAAAAAAAAA
          AAAAAAAAAAAAAAAAAAAAAAAAAA
          AAAAAAAAAAAAAAAAAAAA, AA   AAAAAAAAA  (999)
          Start Date: mm/dd/yy       Credit Limit:(999,999,999.99)

-▲form────────────────────────────────────────────────────────────────────
-▲page────────────────────────────────────────────────────────────────────

═══════════════════════════════════════════════════════════════════════════
```

Figure 8.10: The page footer size reduced on the Directory report

You can change the size of the heading margin in the same manner. Put the cursor between the page band and form band lines near the top of the screen, and use Ctrl-Y to delete blank lines. To increase the size of the margin, make sure Insert mode is on and press Enter a few times.

Deleting blank lines between the form bands and page bands reduces the white space at the top and bottom of each printed page. You may want to experiment with this on your own.

ADJUSTING PAGE LENGTH

Most often, you will probably be using 8½ by 11-inch paper in your printer, so there won't be any need to change the page length. However, if you do need to adjust the page length, simply call up the Report menu, select the Setting option, and then select the PageLayout option. The PageLayout submenu will appear as follows:

    Length   Width   Insert   Delete

Select the Length option. The screen will display

> New page length: 66
> Enter number of lines per page.

To leave the setting at the usual 66 lines per page, just press Enter. Otherwise, enter a new page length and then press Enter. (For now, 66 lines per page is fine.)

ADJUSTING PAGE WIDTH

The default page width for reports is 80 characters, which is good for the screen but leaves little room for margins on an 8½ by 11-inch sheet of paper. To change the page width, select Setting from the Report menu, and PageLayout and then Width from the submenus. Paradox will display

> Enter new page width: 80
> Enter the new width for report pages, or press ⏎ to leave unchanged.

Press the Backspace key twice to erase the 80, then type in 75 and press Enter. You'll notice that the bar marking the right edge of the page moves to the left five spaces on the report specification. This causes the page number to extend beyond the right margin, which we'll have to rectify. But before doing so, let's add a left margin. First, so you can better see the report specification, press Ctrl-Home to scroll to the left.

CHANGING THE MARGIN SETTING

To change or add a margin, select the Setting option from the Report menu and the Margin setting from the submenu. Paradox displays this prompt:

> Margin size: 0
> Enter the new width for the left margin, or press ⏎ to leave unchanged.

For now, enter the number 5 and press Enter.

When the report specification reappears, you'll see that everything has been shifted to the right. Now the heading extends well beyond the right margin (which will cause part of it to be displayed on a separate page). To rectify this situation, simply move the cursor to the heading line, somewhere between the date and the title (with spaces to the right of the cursor). Press the Del key to delete a few blank spaces so that the title moves in closer to the center of the report.

Next, move the cursor to the right of the title, but leave space in front of the page number. Again, press the Del key to pull the page number in from the right. You may have to experiment a little bit to get everything within the margins and reasonably centered, as in Figure 8.11.

When you've made these changes in the format, save them by pressing the DO-IT! (F2) key. You may want to print a copy of the report again by selecting the Report and Output options from the Main and Report menus.

As you can see from this exercise, designing a report is an iterative process. You can "rough out" a report by placing fields within the

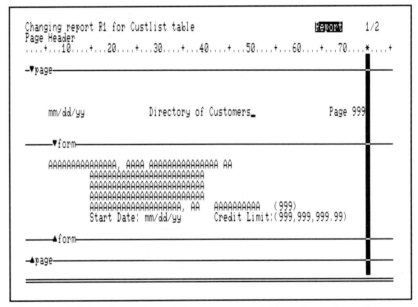

Figure 8.11: A heading adjusted for new page width and margin setting

form band and printing a copy. If what you get is not quite what you had in mind, simply return to the report specification and make changes. Just remember to press the DO-IT! key after creating or modifying a report format to save your work.

MAILING LABELS

The same techniques we used to develop a report format for printing a directory will help us print mailing labels. In fact, rather than develop a report format from scratch, we'll borrow the report format from our Directory of Customers report, since its format already resembles the address portion of a letter and will therefore require relatively little modification.

COPYING A REPORT FORMAT

Paradox has the ability to copy anything, although we will not discuss this topic in depth until a later chapter. For now, we need to make a copy of the Directory report format to simplify the development of a mailing-labels report format. Select the Tools option from the Main menu and the Copy option from the submenu. Next, select the Report option and specify the Custlist table when Paradox asks for the table name.

Paradox will display a list of existing report formats, as below:

```
R   1
```

To copy the Directory format, select option 1. Paradox will then display a list of other report formats that you can copy to. Select 2 in this example, since it is the next unused option in the list. You'll see this message:

```
Copying R1 report for Custlist to R2
```

indicating that copying is in progress.

Now, we need to change report 2 from an identical copy of the Directory report into a format for mailing labels. Select the Report option from the Main menu and the Change option from the sub-menu. Specify the Custlist table and report 2 (select 2 from the submenu).

Paradox will display the description of the report as Directory of Customers. Type Ctrl-Backspace to erase this description, and enter the description

Mailing Labels

FORMATTING LABELS

Now you'll see the report specification on the screen. First of all, it's pretty obvious that mailing labels do not need a report heading. So delete the heading by placing the cursor just below and inside the page band (press ↓ twice). Then type Ctrl-Y until there is no heading at all, as in Figure 8.12.

Next, we need to reorganize the name portion of the label. Move the cursor to the line where the name currently appears. Make sure the cursor is in the leftmost column (type Ctrl-← if it is not). Make sure you are

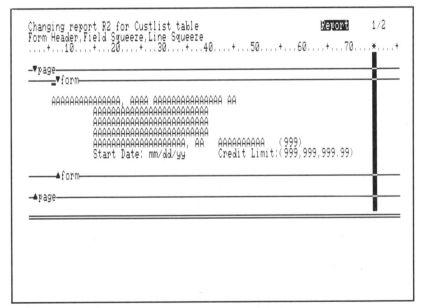

Figure 8.12: The heading removed for mailing labels

in the Insert mode (press the Ins key if not), then press the Space bar about 15 times to make room for the data we will be moving. Type Ctrl-← once again to move the cursor to the left column.

Place the Mr/Mrs field in the leftmost column by calling up the menu and selecting the Field, Place, and Regular options. Select the Mr/Mrs field from the menu, and press Enter twice to use the suggested position and size provided. Press → twice to make some space. Now place the First Name field by selecting the Field, Place, and Regular options from the menus provided and the First Name field from the menu of field names, and pressing Enter twice. Place the M.I. field by pressing → twice, then selecting the usual Field, Place, and Regular options from the menus, and M.I. from the field-name menu. Again, press Enter twice.

Now press → twice, and the Del key 12 times to bring the Last Name field template over to the M.I. field, leaving a blank space between. Move the cursor to the comma trailing the Last Name template, and type Ctrl-Y to delete everything to the right of the cursor. Your screen should now look something like Figure 8.13.

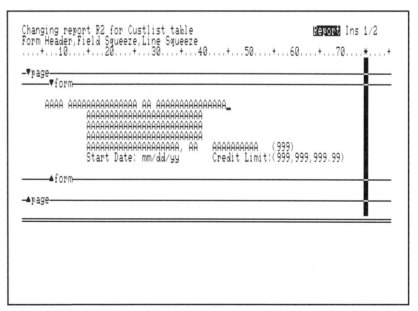

Figure 8.13: The Name portion of mailing label modified

We no longer want the remaining fields to be indented. So press ↓ and Ctrl-← to move the cursor to the leftmost position on the screen. Press the Del key nine times to align the Company field template with the name field. Do the same for the Department, Address, and City-state-zip lines, so the screen looks like Figure 8.14.

DELETING A FIELD FROM A REPORT

We might as well get rid of the record number, since it won't do much good on a mailing label. To remove a field from a report specification, call up the Report menu and select the Field and the Erase options. As instructed, use the arrow keys to move the cursor to the field you wish to delete (999 on this screen), and press Enter. After removing the field, you can get rid of the parentheses by using the Del key.

We won't need the Start Date and Credit Limit fields on mailing labels, so press ↓, Ctrl-←, and Ctrl-Y to delete this line from the screen.

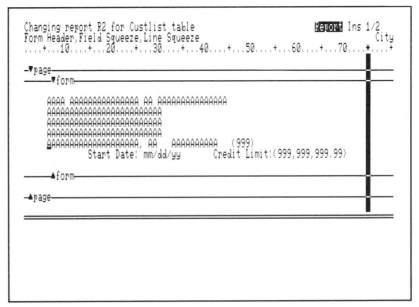

Figure 8.14: The mailing-labels specification with name and address aligned

Now we have to think a little about the way the address will fit on the labels. Most mailing labels are one inch tall, and most printers print six lines to the inch. Because the addresses are five lines long, we need to ensure that six lines are printed for each label so that each address will be placed on a separate label. To do this, leave one blank line inside the form band on the screen, and no blank lines between the form bands and page bands. Use Ctrl-Y to delete the blank line just above the bottom form band. Figure 8.15 shows how the screen looks when set up like this.

CONTINUOUS-FEED PAPER

Now all we need to do is tell Paradox to exclude *form feeds* between pages when printing labels. (Form feeds leave margins at the top and bottom of each printed page.) You do so by setting the page length to C (for continuous). Call up the Report menu and select the Setting, PageLayout, and Length options. Type Ctrl-Backspace to erase the

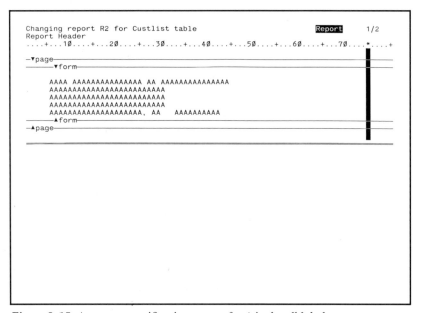

Figure 8.15: A report specification set up for 1-inch-tall labels

current page length, type in the letter **C** as the new page length, and press Enter.

To ensure that each label prints with an identical height, you'll need to use a fixed line-squeeze setting. To do so, press F10 to call up the Report menu, select Setting, RemoveBlanks, LineSqueeze, and then Fixed to ensure that any blank lines that are squeezed out of a label are printed at the bottom of the label.

MULTIPLE LABEL COLUMNS

In its current configuration, the report format will print a single column of mailing labels. If you wish to print two columns of labels, press F10 to call up the Report menu, and select the Setting, Page-Layout and Width options. Type Ctrl-Backspace to erase the original setting, and enter 40 as the new page width.

To print labels in the second column, press Menu (F10) and select the Setting, Labels, and Yes options. Doing so tells Paradox to repeat the label specification on the left of the highlighted menu line (now down the middle of your screen) on the right side of the menu line.

FINE-TUNING THE LABELS

To print a test run of labels, call up the Report Menu and select Output and either the Printer or Screen option. (If you are using a laser printer, you might need to print labels twice in order to see them. Optionally, you can use the "form feed" script presented in Chapter 19 to eject a page from a laser printer directly from the keyboard.)

If your labels look OK, press DO-IT (F2) to save the label format specification. If the format still needs work, you can continue making adjustments until you get the format you want. Note that if your labels are taller than one inch, you'll need to insert more blank lines within the form band, above the name template. (To do so, move the cursor to the blank line, make sure the Insert mode is on, and press Enter. To delete blank lines, make sure the cursor is in the leftmost column and type Ctrl-Y.)

If the left margin is incorrect on your label, you can use the Margin option under Setting on the Report menu to adjust the left margin setting. If the printed labels are too wide, you'll need to reduce their widths. There are two ways to do so. Either delete fields from the format (such as Mr/Mrs or M.I.), using the Field and Erase options from the Report menu, or decrease the widths of fields using the Field and Reformat options under the Report menu. Both of these options provide simple instructions at the top left corner of the screen for deleting and narrowing fields.

(If your mailing label format is particularly tricky, you might want to use the custom script provided in Chapter 19 of this book to print them. However, you'll probably need to learn a few things about creating PAL scripts, as discussed in Chapter 17, before you can use the script.)

PRINTING THE MAILING LABELS

Once you are satisfied with your mailing-label format, save it either by pressing DO-IT! or by calling up the report menu and selecting the DO-IT! option. At any time in the future, you can print mailing labels simply by calling up the Paradox main menu and selecting the Report and Output options. Specify Custlist as the table to print from, and select the options 2 (for the mailing-labels report format) and Printer from the submenus.

Of course, if you wish to print labels in zip code order, use the usual Modify and Sort options from the main menu to sort by zip code, then use the Report and Output options to print the mailing labels.

FORM LETTERS

Our Mailing Labels report format is a good first step in getting a form letter started, so once again we'll make a copy of an existing report to help generate a new one. To copy the Mailing Labels report format, select the Tools option from the Main menu. Then select the Copy and Report options from the submenus. Specify the Custlist table. Select 2 (Mailing Labels) as the report to copy. Select 3 as the report to copy to. You'll briefly see this message as Paradox makes the copy:

Copying R2 report for Custlist to R3

When the menu reappears, you can begin creating your form letter. Select Report from the Main menu and Change from the submenu. Once again, specify the Custlist table when requested, and select report 3. When Paradox displays the report description, type Ctrl-Backspace to erase *Mailing Labels,* and enter

Form Letter

as the description. You'll then see the report specification appear with the mailing labels format.

Most letters start with a date at the top of the page. To put in the date, press ↓ three times so the cursor moves inside the form band. Type the current date the way you want it to appear on the letter. Then, put Insert mode on and press the Enter key once or twice. This will insert a blank line or two between the date and the address heading, as in Figure 8.16.

Use the arrow keys to move the cursor to below the city, state, and zip code, and press the Enter key to add some blank lines. (Remember, the Enter key only adds blank lines if the Insert mode is on.)

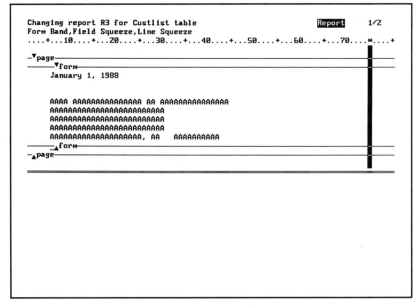

Figure 8.16: The date added to the top of the form letter

Press ↑, then Ctrl-←, and type in the word **Dear.** Use the → key to put a space after the word *Dear,* then place either the First Name or Mr/Mrs and Last Name fields (depending on which style you prefer) after the word *Dear.* In this example, I've chosen First Name by calling up the Report menu, selecting the usual Field, Place, and Regular options, and then the First Name field choice. Press Enter twice, as usual, to accept the suggested placement and size. You can also type a colon after the template, as shown in Figure 8.17.

Press the Enter key a few times to make room, then just type in your letter. Be sure to press Enter at the end of each line, before your text extends beyond the right margin.

You can place fields into the body of your letter at any time using the usual Report, Field, Place, and Regular menu options. In Figure 8.18, I've placed the First Name field into the first paragraph of the letter.

When typing your letter, be sure to stay within the form band and the right margin. You can use the usual Backspace and arrow keys to make changes and corrections.

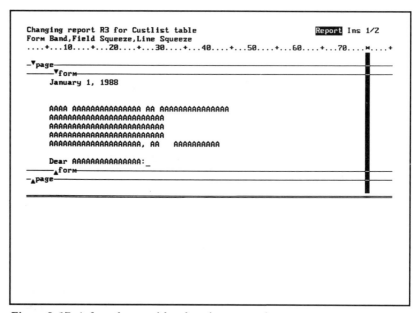

Figure 8.17: A form letter with salutation entered

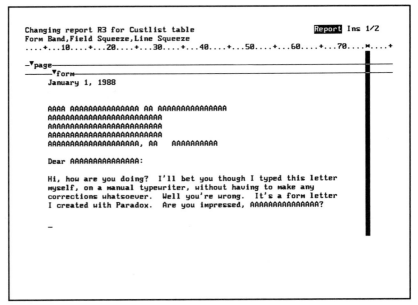

Figure 8.18: The first paragraph of the form letter typed in

PAGE BREAKS

To ensure that each letter is printed on a separate page, you need to tell Paradox where the page break belongs. You do so by simply typing the word PAGEBREAK right into the letter, making sure that it starts in the leftmost column and is the only word on the line. Figure 8.19 shows the complete sample form letter, with the page break properly placed at the bottom.

SINGLE-SHEET PRINTING

If you are to be printing your letter on single sheets rather than continuous-feed paper, you'll want the printer to pause between each printed page to give you a chance to load a new page. To do so, select the Setting option from the Report menu. Select Wait from the Setting menu, and Paradox will display the following prompt:

No   Yes
Do not pause after each page.

Select the Yes option for single-sheet printing.

```
Changing report R3 for Custlist table                    Report Ins 1/2
Report Footer
....+...10....+...20....+...30....+...40....+...50....+...60....+...70....*....+

       Dear AAAAAAAAAAAAAAA:

       Hi, how are you doing?  I'll bet you thought I typed this letter
       myself, on a manual typewriter, without having to make any
       corrections whatsoever.  Well you're wrong.  It's a form letter
       I created with Paradox!  Are you impressed, AAAAAAAAAAAAAAA?

       Well, gotta run because there is lots more to learn.  Take
       care, and write soon.

       Best Regards,

       Ellsworth P. Wonka

       PAGEBREAK
—————————▲form————————————————————————————————————————————————
—▲page—————————————————————————————————————————————————————————
       ▪
```

Figure 8.19: A completed form letter with page break

FORMATTING THE LETTER

For the finishing touches on the format of the form letter, you'll want to make the following menu selections while the mailing label format still appears on the screen. To ensure blank lines and fields are removed, press F10 to call up the Report menu, and select the options Setting, RemoveBlanks, LineSqueeze, Yes, and Fixed. To squeeze out blank fields, call up the Report menu and select Setting, RemoveBlanks, FieldSqueeze, Yes.

To set margins for 8½-by-11-inch paper, call up the Report menu and select Setting, PageLayout, and Length; then type Ctrl-Backspace to erase the current setting, type in **66**, and press Enter. (Given that most printers print six lines to the inch, 66 lines will print on an 11-inch page.)

You may need to experiment with the best margins for your printer. To set a left margin of 5, call up the Report menu, select Setting and Margin, press Ctrl-Backspace to erase the current setting, type in **5**, and press Enter. To set a right margin of 75, call up the menu, select Setting, select PageLayout and Width, and enter a new value of **75**. Press Enter.

To cancel the Labels setting that was originally copied over from the mailing-label format, press F10 and select Setting, Labels, and No.

A TRIAL RUN WITH YOUR FORM LETTER

To test your form letter, just call up the menu and select the Output option as usual. If you select the Printer option, you can use the Break command (Ctrl-ScrollLock) to stop printing.

Remember to press DO-IT! to save the form letter. To print form letters from the Main menu, first remember to sort the table, if necessary, using the Modify and Sort options from the Main and Modify menus. (If mailing labels are printed for the letters, in zip code order, you'll want to print the letters in the same order so that you can match them up easily.) Then select the Report and Output options from the Main and Report menus, and select report 3.

For new form letters, you can erase the body of the letter we've just created (using the Report and Change options) and type in your new letter. If you wish to save the existing form letter, use the Copy option under the Tools menu, as we've done in the past, and make a copy of the letter. Then use the Report and Change options to modify the new form letter.

PRINTING GROUPS OF PAGES

Occasionally, you may need to stop printing a report in the middle (by pressing Ctrl-Break), because the printer runs out of ribbon, or for some other reason. To resume printing where you left off, call up the Paradox Main menu and select Report, as usual. From the submenu, select the RangeOutput option. The screen will display the options

Beginning page number: 1
Enter first page number to be printed.

To select another starting page, press Backspace, type in the new starting page number, and press Enter. The screen will then display the prompt

> Ending page number:
> Enter last page number to be printed, or press ◄─┘ for
> last page of report.

Here, you can enter any page number at which to stop printing. Optionally, just press Enter to print all remaining pages in the report.

Note that if you've set the page length option to C (continuous), as when printing mailing labels, Paradox will assume that your entries refer to *records*, rather than pages. For example, if you are printing mailing labels and enter 22 as the starting page, and 500 as the ending page, Paradox will print labels starting at the 22nd record and ending at the 500th record.

USING QUERY FORMS WITH REPORTS

So far we've developed some useful reports for the Custlist table, and have seen techniques for presorting and printing a directory, mailing labels, and form letters. In each case, we printed data for every record in the Custlist table. But suppose we want to send letters to just California residents, or people whose start dates were a year ago, or some other group of individuals. Well, we've already seen how query forms can pull out records that match a certain criterion, so all we have to do now is somehow link these selected records with a report from the Custlist table.

Recall that the query form always stores the results of its searches in a table named Answer. This being the case, we need to perform a query on the Custlist table, then copy the report formats to the Answer table to display data from that table. Let's give it a try, by printing form letters and mailing labels for New York residents only.

Start with only the Main menu showing on the screen (use Clear Image (F8) and Menu (F10) if necessary). Select the Ask option, and specify Custlist as the table to query.

When the query form appears, press Checkmark (F6) while the cursor is still in the leftmost column to put check marks in all the fields on the query form.

Using the → key, move the cursor to the State field and type in NY. Press the DO-IT! (F2) key to perform the query. The two New York residents will appear in the Answer table on the screen, as in Figure 8.20.

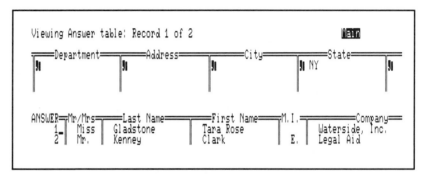

Figure 8.20: New York residents on the Answer table

Now you can sort the Answer table, if you wish, using the Modify and Sort options, being sure to specify Answer as the name of the table to sort, and Same when asked whether to sort to the same table or a new one.

Now you need to copy the report formats from the Custlist table to the Answer table. Here's how:

1. Call up the Main menu (press F10).

2. Select the Tools option from the Main menu.

3. Select the Copy option from the submenu.

4. Select the JustFamily option.

5. Specify Custlist as the table to copy from (the *source* table).

6. Specify Answer as the table to copy to (the *target* table).

When you use JustFamily to copy from one table to another, all report formats and other related items (such as custom forms) are copied from one table's "family" of reports to another. The tables themselves, however, are not altered. Therefore, in this example, we've copied the various report formats from the Custlist table to the Answer table, and used them to print data from the Answer table.

If you've previously performed a copy similar to the one we're performing now, Paradox will double-check before it erases the contents of the previous copy. The screen will display these options:

Cancel   Replace
Do not continue with the family copy

To proceed, select the Replace option. If you've made an error, select Cancel. (When copying JustFamily to the Answer table, you can always safely select the Replace option.)

When the copy is finished, you can print the reports as you normally would, except that you specify the Answer rather than Custlist table when Paradox asks for a table name. In this example, select the Report option from the Main menu and the Output option from the submenu. Specify Answer when prompted for a table name. To print mailing labels, select report 2 and the Printer option. To print form letters, select report 3 and the Printer option.

When you are done printing, use Clear Image (F8) to clear the Answer table and the query form. Of course, you can query for any records you wish, using the techniques we discussed in Chapter 8. The procedure for copying the reports to the Answer table will always be the same, regardless of the query you perform.

OTHER REPORT OPTIONS

Though the options we've discussed in this chapter are adequate for our needs at this time, the report generator has a few other easy, though useful, capabilities you should know about.

DATES AND TIMES

In our Directory of Customers, the date was automatically printed in the report heading. You can actually place both the current date and the current time any place in your report. Furthermore, you can specify formats for these special fields.

To place the date into a report, put the cursor at the place where you want the date to appear, then call up the Report menu. Select the Field and Place options from the submenus, which bring up the following submenu:

Regular   Summary   Calculated   Date   Time   Page   #Record

Select the Date option, and Paradox will display a menu of eleven format options. Examples of the various date formats are listed below:

DATE FORMAT	*EXAMPLE*
1) mm/dd/yy	3/31/88
2) M o n t h dd, yyyy	March 31, 1988
3) mm/dd	3/31
4) mm/yy	3/88
5) dd-Mon-yy	3-Mar-88
6) Mon yy	Mar 88
7) dd-Mon-yyyy	3-Mar-1988
8) mm/dd/yyyy	3/31/1988
9) dd.mm.yy	31.03.88
10) dd/mm/yy	31/03/88
11) yy-mm-dd	88-03-31

Use the arrow keys to highlight the date format you want, then press Enter. Paradox will ask you to position the cursor at the place you want the date to appear. Use the arrow keys to position the cursor, if necessary, then press Enter to place the field in the report format.

To place the current time on a report, select the Time option from the submenu. Paradox displays these two formatting options:

Enter the time format to use:
1) hh:mm pm   2) hh:mm:ss (military)

The first option displays the time based on a 12-hour clock, such as 2:55 pm. The second option displays the time based on a 24-hour clock, such as 14:55:00. Select your option and place the field.

If you change your mind about a Date or Time format, call up the Report menu and select the Field and Reformat options. Move the cursor to the field you wish to reformat and press Enter. Depending on the type of the field you specify, Paradox will display a menu of formatting options identical to the menu used when initially placing the field. Select the new format and press Enter.

PAGE NUMBERS

When you first create a report, Paradox automatically displays the page number in the heading. You can, however, display the page number anywhere you wish. First, you might want to remove the suggested placement for the page number. To do this, place the cursor in the page number template on the report specification (shown as 999 on the screen) and select the Field and Erase options from the Report menu. Also, erase the word Page from the heading.

In this example, we'll move the page number to the bottom of each page and center it. Remember, whatever is inside the form band is printed repeatedly on a page. Whatever is outside the form band but inside the page band is printed once on each page. So to display the page number centered on the bottom of each page, you need to place the cursor above the bottom page-band marker, but below the bottom form-band marker. Center the cursor, then call up the menu and select the Field and Place options. Then select the Page option from the submenu, and use the arrow keys to place the page number. (The page number is initially displayed as 999. You can use the ← and → keys to change the size of the page-number template.) Figure 8.21 shows the page number in the Directory report relocated to the bottom of the page.

FORMATTED NUMBERS

You can change the way numbers are displayed in the report as well. Simply move the cursor to some numeric field (such as Credit Limit in the Directory report), call up the menu, and select the Field and Reformat options. Press Enter when the cursor is inside the numeric field, and Paradox will display a list of options, as below:

Digits   Sign-Convention   Commas   International

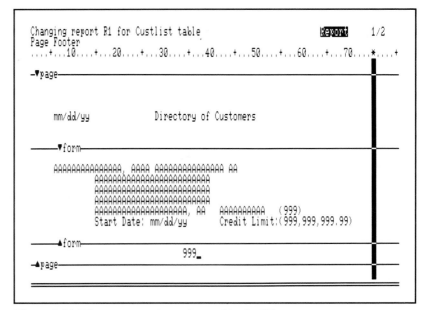

Figure 8.21: The page number relocated in the Directory report

The Digits option lets you specify the maximum number of whole or decimal digits to display. Just as when you first place a numeric field in a report column, this option will let you use the ← and → keys to increase or decrease the number of digits and decimal places shown in the report column.

The Sign-Convention option displays this submenu:

Unsigned   ParenNegative   AlwaysSign

The Unsigned option places a minus sign in front of negative numbers and no sign in front of positive numbers. (This is the default display for N (numeric) fields.) The ParenNegative option displays negative numbers in parentheses and positive numbers with no sign. (Currency data are always displayed in this format.) The AlwaysSign option displays plus signs in front of positive numbers and minus signs in front of negative numbers.

Selecting the Commas option displays this submenu:

NoCommas   Commas

The NoCommas option does not punctuate the thousands place in numbers (the default setting for N (numeric) fields). The Commas option does punctuate thousands with commas (the default setting for currency data).

The International option displays the submenu shown below:

U.S.Convention   InternationalConvention

If you select U.S.Convention, Paradox uses a period for the decimal separator, and a comma as a digit separator to display numbers (12,345.67). If you select InternationalConvention, Paradox will display numbers with a comma as a decimal separator and a period as the digit separator (12.345,67).

CONDENSED AND EXPANDED PRINT

Most dot matrix and laser printers allow you to use a variety of print sizes, particularly condensed and expanded print. Some printers also allow you to use a variety of fonts. These are activated by sending the printer a special code or *setup string.*

Paradox includes an option that allows you to send these special codes at the beginning of a report. For example, you can send a code for condensed print that will allow you to print up to 132 characters (80 characters is the usual setting) across an 8½-by-11-inch sheet of paper.

Paradox provides setup strings for several IBM-compatible printers, including (at the time of writing) the following:

- IBM PC Graphics Printer and compatibles
- Epson MX and FX series
- Okidata 82, 83, 92, 93, and 192
- HP LaserJet

You can also define codes for other printers.

To send a setup string to the printer, you need to call up the Report menu and select the Setting and Setup options from the submenus. Paradox will display these options:

Predefined   Custom

Selecting the Predefined option displays a menu of ready-to-go printer options, as listed below:

MENU OPTION	*EFFECT*
StandardPrinter*	Standard print
Small-IBMgraphics	Condensed print on IBM Graphics printer
Reg-IBMgraphics	Regular print on IBM Graphics printer
Small-Epson-MX/FX	Condensed print on Epson MX or FX printer
Small-Oki-92/93	Condensed print on Okidata 92 or 93 printer
Small-Oki-82/83	Condensed print on Okidata 82 or 83 printer
Small-Oki-192	Condensed print on Okidata 192 printer
HPLaserJet	Normal print on HP LaserJet printer
HP-Landscape-Normal	Normal print size in LaserJet Landscape mode
HP-Portrait-66lines	HP LaserJet Portrait mode
Intl-IBMcompatible	Normal size international print on IBM compatible
Intl-IBMcondensed	Condensed print on international IBM

StandardPrinter*, the default option, does not send any special codes to the printer. The other options will send codes, as predefined by the Paradox Custom Configuration program (CCP), discussed in Chapter 16 of the *Paradox User's Guide.* To experiment with the current settings, use the ← and ↓ to highlight an option that matches your current printer, and press Return to select that option.

To test the effects of your selection quickly on a printed report, just press the Instant Report (Alt-F7) key. If you wish to save the printer setup you've selected for future report output, press DO-IT! (F2).

If your printer does not fall into the predefined category, you can select the Custom option to create your own setup string. Paradox will display this prompt:

Printer port:
LPT1   LPT2   LPT3   COM1   COM2   AUX

Most likely, your printer is hooked up to the LPT1 port, so you can just press Enter to select that default value. (If you know for a fact that your printer is connected to some other port, highlight the appropriate port name on the menu and press Enter to select it).

The next prompt to appear on the screen lets you enter a custom printer setup string:

Setup string:
Enter the setup string to be sent to the printer before printing the report.

The trick here is knowing what code to send. Every printer uses different setup strings, and the only place to find this information is in your printer manual. Furthermore, the code may need some translation. Your custom string can be up to 175 characters long, though most codes are only one or two characters in length.

Many printers use *escape sequences* for setup strings—that is, a press on the Esc key followed by another character. In your printer manual, the escape sequence might be displayed as ESC-A, Esc = , or something similar. The code for the Esc key is 027. So if your printer required the escape sequence ESC 6 to switch to, say, expanded print mode, you would enter

\0276

as your custom setup string. Note that the setup string always begins with a backslash (\).

Some printers use a number, usually in the range of 0 to 31, to put special printer attributes into effect. For example, the Okidata 83A uses code 31 to enter expanded print mode. To put this into effect, you would enter the code

\031

as your custom setup string. (Note that the setup code must contain three digits—hence the leading zero.)

Appendix C of the *PAL User's Guide,* which comes with your Paradox package, shows an ASCII chart that may help you translate a code. ASCII stands for *American Standard Code for Information Interchange* and includes 256 characters used by most microcomputers.

Keep in mind that once a setup string is sent to the printer, it stays in effect until either the printer is turned off or another code is sent. Therefore, if you print mailing labels in condensed print and then immediately print form letters, your form letters may also come out in condensed print. To avoid this situation, just select the Setting, Setup, Predefined, and StandardPrinter* options from the Report menu to cancel the previous printer setup before printing the next report. (This, of course, assumes that you have not used the Paradox Custom Configuration Program to change the StandardPrinter* code.)

TEMPORARY PRINTER REDIRECTION

If you have several printers hooked up to your computer, or a printer that can switch to different fonts or typefaces easily, you can alter the selected port and setup string without modifying the report format. To do so, press F10 to call up the Paradox Main menu (not the Report menu), select Report, and then select SetPrinter.

Under the SetPrinter option, you will be given two choices:

Regular   Override

Selecting Regular specifies the default printer port and print-setup string defined in the report format (under the Report menu Setting option). Selecting Override lets you temporarily bypass the printer port and setup string defined in the report format, and lets you redefine those on the spot.

When you first select Override, you'll be given the options

PrinterPort   Setup

To change the printer port (for example, to use the printer connected to your COM1 port), select PrinterPort. You'll be given the options

Printer port:
LPT1   LPT2   LPT3   COM1   COM2   AUX

As usual, highlight the port of your choice, and press Enter to select it.

Under the Override menu, you can also select the Setup option, which presents the prompt

Setup String:
Enter a setup string to be sent to the printer before printing
the report.

As discussed previously, you must enter the setup string as an ASCII number preceded by a backslash. For example, to send ASCII codes 27 (Esc key), 54, and 15 to the printer, enter the setup string as \027\054\015.

ADDITIONAL REPORT CAPABILITIES

The basic report-formatting techniques discussed in this chapter will be enough to get you started in developing neatly formatted printed reports. Chapter 14 picks up where this chapter leaves off, and discusses more advanced features of the Paradox report generator, including tabular reports, totals and subtotals, calculated fields, and printing reports from multiple tables. However, before dealing with those topics, we'll look at techniques for developing custom forms for displaying, entering, and editing data on the screen.

SUMMARY

- To create a report format, select the Report and Design options from the Main and Report menus.

- To place a field on a report format, call up the Report menu (F10) and select the Field and Place options from the submenus.

- To squeeze out extraneous lines and blank spaces from a report, select Setting from the Report menu and Remove-Blanks from the submenu. Then select the LineSqueeze and/or FieldSqueeze options.

- To print a trial copy of a report format, select the Output option from the Report menu.

- To save a report format, press the DO-IT! (F2) key.

- To abandon a report format, call up the Report menu and select the Cancel option.

- To presort data before printing a report, use the usual Modify and Sort options from the Main and Modify menus, and sort a table to the same table (not a new table).

- To change page length, page width, or left margin settings, use options under the Report menu Setting option.

- To print continuous data without page breaks, set the Page-Length option to C (for continuous).

- To force a page break into a report, type the word PAGE-BREAK, starting in the leftmost column, where you want the new page to begin.

- To pause between pages for a paper change, set the Wait option to Yes under the Setting option on the Report menu.

- To print a selected group of pages or records in a report, use the Range Output and change the beginning and ending page (record) numbers.

- To use query with reports, query your table in the usual fashion. While the Answer table is showing the results of the query, use the Tools, Copy, and JustFamily options to copy reports from the original table to the Answer table.

- To add dates, times, record numbers, and page numbers to reports, select the appropriate options under the Field and Place options from the Report submenu.

- To use special printer attributes like condensed print or special fonts, select the Setting and Setup options from the Report menu, and either select a predefined code or enter a custom code. See your printer manual for custom codes.

CUSTOM FORMS

CHAPTER 9

WHENEVER YOU SWITCH FROM TABLE VIEW TO FORM
View by pressing the Form Toggle (F7) key, Paradox allows you to enter
or edit data a single record at a time. Unless you develop your own custom forms, Paradox will display a standard form that it automatically
generates for your table, similar to the one shown in Figure 9.1.

You can easily design and develop your own forms for a table,
using commands under the Forms option of the Main menu. Like
the Report option, the Forms option allows you to draw a basic format for a form on the screen, as well as make changes to improve the

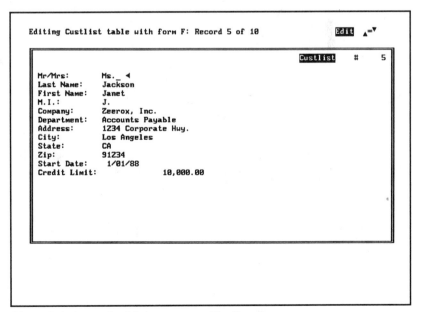

Figure 9.1: A standard form generated by Paradox

appearance of your form. Some of the keys and menu options work differently with Forms, however. In this chapter, we'll develop a custom form for the Custlist table, shown in Figure 9.2.

Notice that the custom form has certain attributes that make it preferable to the standard form. Boxes and highlights improve the appearance of the form. Some field prompts, such as Starting Date and Zip Code, are spelled out, rather than abbreviated as in the field names. The box at the bottom of the screen displays useful reminders about managing the cursor.

———— *CREATING A CUSTOM FORM* ————

To create a custom form, select the Forms option from the Main menu. Paradox will display the following submenu:

Design   Change

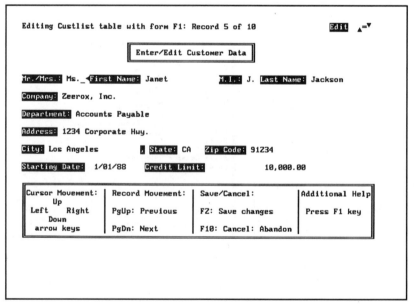

Figure 9.2: The custom form for the Custlist table

Select the Design option to create a new form. Paradox will ask for the name of the table for which the form is being designed. In this example enter Custlist as the table name. Then Paradox displays a menu of form options, as below:

F   1   2   3   4   5   6   7   8   9   10   11   12   13   14

F is the standard form that Paradox creates automatically for the table. You can change this form or select one of the other options, 1–14, for your new form name. In this example, select option 1.

Next, Paradox asks for a description of the form, as below:

Form description:
Enter description of the new form.

Enter any description, up to 40 characters long. As with reports, the description will be displayed later when you select a form to use. For this example, enter the form name

Customer Entry

Then press Enter.

Once you've entered the description, Paradox gives you a blank screen on which to design your form. At the top-left corner of the screen, the prompt

Designing new F1 form for Custlist

reminds you that you are designing form number 1 (F1) for the Cust-List table. Beneath that, the prompt

< 1, 1>

tells you that the cursor is currently on row 1, column 1, of the form. On the right edge of the screen, the prompt

1/1

tells you that you are on the first page of a one-page form (Page 1 of 1). Let's now discuss techniques for managing the cursor on the form.

MANAGING THE FORM CURSOR

As usual, the ↑, ↓, ←, and → keys move the cursor freely about the screen. In addition, the Ins key toggles the Insert mode on and off. To move text to the right, you can put the Insert mode on and press the Space bar. The Del and Backspace keys erase any text that you've already entered onto the form.

Table 9.1 summarizes the keys to design and edit a form. The Forms menu offers additional techniques for placing, moving, deleting, and copying fields and text on the screen, as later examples will demonstrate.

DISPLAY ENHANCEMENTS

Before you actually type anything onto the form, you should know about some options you have for enhancing the appearance of your

KEY	EFFECT
F10	Displays the Report menu
↑	Moves cursor up a line
↓	Moves cursor down a line
→	Moves cursor right a column
←	Moves cursor left a column
Backspace	Moves cursor left, and delete one character
Home	Moves cursor to top of screen
End	Moves to bottom of screen
Ins	Turns Insert mode on/off
Del	Deletes character at cursor
Ctrl-Home	Moves cursor to start of line
Ctrl-End	Moves cursor to end of line

Table 9.1: Keys for designing and editing forms

form. To view these options, press Menu (F10) to call up the Forms menu. This menu displays the following options:

Field   Area   Border   Page   Style   Form   Help   DO-IT!
Cancel

Selecting the Style option shows you a variety of enhancement options. After selecting an enhancement option, any text that you type on the screen is given the enhancement quality you select. Your options, as displayed on the Style menu, are

Intensity   Blink   Reversal   Fieldnames   Default

These options are summarized below:

OPTION	*EFFECT*
Intensity	Displays text or borders in bright intensity or color
Blink	Makes text or borders blink on and off
Reversal	Highlights text or borders in reverse video (dark on light)
Fieldnames	Field names appear on the screen where they were placed
Default	Removes previous enhancements and restores standard display

You can combine style options however you wish. Let's give one a try. (If the menu is currently showing, press the Esc key until it disappears.) Press the ↓ key to move the cursor down a line. Then press → about 25 times to move the cursor near the center of the screen so that the row/column indicator shows <2,26>. Call up the menu (press F10) and select the Style and Intensity options. From the Intensity submenu, select High for high intensity.

Notice that Paradox displays the current settings for screen enhancements at the bottom of the screen, as below:

Intensity: high;   Blink: off;   Reversal: off;   Fieldnames: off

A quick glance lets you see the current status of the enhancement options. Also, the arrow next to the word Form at the top of the screen will reflect your current enhancements. In this case, the arrow will be in red on a color screen or high intensity on a monochrome screen.

Now type in this title:

Enter/Edit Customer Data

On a monochrome screen the text will be in high intensity. On a color screen the text will be in red. To switch back to normal intensity, call up the menu (F10) and select the Style and Intensity options. Then select the Regular option from the submenu.

━━━ *PLACING FIELDS ON THE SCREEN* ━━━

The form we are creating will be used to enter or edit data on the Custlist table, so we need to specify positions on the form for entering and changing field data. This is very easy to do; we'll quickly review the basic steps before we actually try it.

To place a field, call up the Form menu (F10) and select the Field option. This brings up the following submenu:

Place   Erase   Reformat   CalcEdit   WordWrap

To place fields from an existing table, select the Place and Regular options.

When you select the Regular option, Paradox will display a menu of existing field names. When you select the field name, Paradox asks where you want to place the field, as below:

Use ↑ ↓ → ← to move to where you want the field to begin . . .
then press ↵ to place it . . .

You use the arrow keys to position the cursor where you want the field to begin, then press Enter. Next, Paradox will ask you to adjust the width of the field:

Now use → and ← to adjust the width of the field . . .
press ↵ when finished.

Usually, you'll want the full field size, so you'll just press Enter to use the suggested size. Let's give it a try.

First, if necessary, press Esc until the top menu disappears. Then press ↓ three times, and use the ← key (or Ctrl-Home) to place the cursor in the leftmost column, a couple of lines beneath the screen title, so the cursor is at <5,1>.

To enhance our screen, we'll put field prompts in reverse video. Call up the menu (F10) and select the Style and Reversal options. The screen will display these options:

ReverseVideo   Normal

Select the ReverseVideo option.

Now type in the prompt

Mr./Mrs.:

Notice that the display is in reverse video as you type. Press → to put a space after the colon. When you place prompts on a custom form, you should use words that describe the contents of the data to be entered on the form. The prompt, however, does not need to be the same as the field name.

Now, place the Mr/Mrs field next to this prompt. To do so, call up the Forms menu (F10) and select the Field, Place, and Regular options. Select Mr/Mrs as the field to place by pressing Enter. Then press Enter to place the field. Press Enter again to define the size. You'll notice that the field position is displayed as hyphens, equal to the size of the field, as in Figure 9.3.

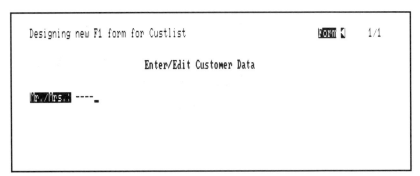

Figure 9.3: The field prompt and field placed on the screen

Now, to enter a prompt and field for First Name, press → once. Type

First Name:

Press → to make a space. Now call up the menu and select Field, Place, and Regular. Press → to highlight the First Name option and press Enter. Press Enter twice in response to the position and size prompts. Now two prompts and two field locations appear on the screen, as below:

Mr./Mrs.: – – First Name: – – – – – – –

Keep in mind that pressing the Space bar will move the cursor, but it will also extend the reverse video. To move the cursor without extending the reverse video, use the arrow keys rather than the Space bar.

Try entering the rest of the field prompts and appropriate field values, so your screen looks like Figure 9.4.

To design the form exactly as shown in Figure 9.4, use the cursor coordinates listed below. Remember, to place prompts, simply move the cursor to the coordinates shown below, and type in the prompt

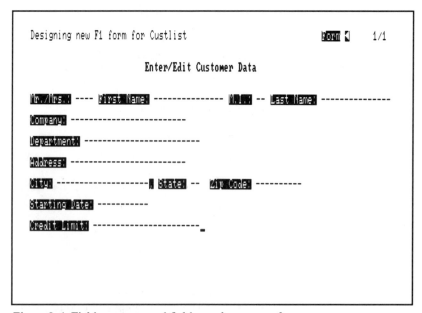

Figure 9.4: Field prompts and fields on the custom form

exactly as shown. To place fields on the screen, move the cursor to the cursor coordinates shown below, press F10, and select the Field, Place, and Regular options, followed by the appropriate field name.

PROMPT/FIELD	*STARTING CURSOR POSITION*
Mr./Mrs.: prompt	< 5, 1>
Mr./Mrs. field	< 5,11>
First Name: prompt	< 5,16>
First Name field	< 5,28>
M.I.: prompt	< 5,44>
M.I. field	< 5,50>
Last Name: prompt	< 5,53>
Last Name field	< 5,64>
Company: prompt	< 7,1>
Company field	< 7,10>
Department: prompt	< 9, 1>
Department field	< 9,13>
Address: prompt	<11, 1>
Address field	<11,10>
City: prompt	<13, 1>
City field	<13, 7>
, prompt	<13,27>
State: prompt	<13,29>
State field	<13,26>
Zip Code: prompt	<13,39>
Zip field	<13,49>
Starting Date: prompt	<15, 1>
Start Date field	<15,16>
Credit Limit: prompt	<17,1>
Credit Limit field	<17,15>

To correct mistakes in prompts, use the usual Backspace and arrow keys. To remove a field that was placed accidentally, move the cursor to the hyphens that represent the field on the screen. (Even though you can only see the hyphens, you can identify the field by viewing the upper-right corner of the screen when the cursor is within the hyphens.) Then, call up the Forms menu (F10), and select the Field and Erase options. Press Enter to erase the field that the cursor is presently on.

After you have entered all of the prompts and fields, and your screen looks like Figure 9.4, you've finished the basic work of placing the prompts and fields. To enhance the form, you can also add borders, as discussed next. Before doing so, however, you'll want to turn off the reverse video mode (so the borders do not appear in reverse video). To do so, call up the menu (F10), and select the Style, Reversal, and Normal options.

BORDERS

Borders are another way to enhance a custom form. To draw borders, call up the menu (F10) and select the Border option. The options

Place   Erase

appear. Select Place to begin drawing a border. A submenu of options will appear, as below:

Single-line   Double-line   Other

You can draw borders with either a single thin line, double thin lines, or any other character you specify with the Other option. For this example, select the Double-line option. Paradox will display these instructions:

Use ↑ ↓ → ← to move to a corner of the box or border . . .
then press ← to select it . . .

Use the arrow keys to move the cursor just slightly above and to the left of the title (centered at the top of the screen). Press Enter when you get the cursor to that position. Paradox then displays these instructions:

> Now use ↑ ↓ → ← to move to the diagonal corner of the area . . .
> press ↩ to place it.

Now use the ↓ and → keys to start drawing a box around the title. As you move the cursor, you'll see the box appear as a ghost image on the screen. Move the cursor to a point where the title is enclosed by the box, and then press Enter. You'll see a box of double lines around the screen title, as in Figure 9.5.

If you select Other rather than the Double-line or Single-line options, before drawing a border Paradox will display the following prompt:

> Character:
> Enter the character you want to use for the border.

If you wish to use a character from the keyboard for your border, such as an asterisk, type in the character and press Enter. When you draw your box or border, the character you entered will form the border.

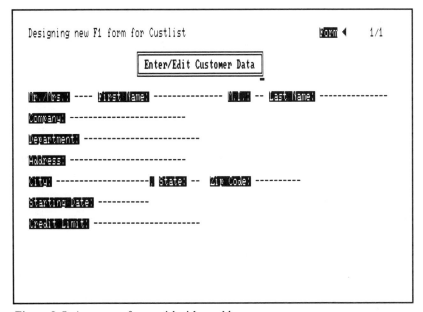

Figure 9.5: A custom form with title and box

If you wish to use a graphic character that is not available from the keyboard, you can type in the ASCII code from your terminal's extended ASCII character set. (Appendix C of the *PAL User's Guide*, which comes with Paradox, shows these graphics characters.) To enter a special character, hold down the Alt key and type in the appropriate code number using the numeric keypad. For example, to use ASCII character 219 (a solid block) in your border, hold down the Alt key and type 219 using the numbers on the numeric keypad. When you release the Alt key, the character you chose will be displayed. Press the Enter key to select it. Note that you can only use characters in the range of 128–254.

If, while drawing a box, you move off the edge of the screen, the ghost border will wrap around the screen. If you do so by accident, just move the border back in the opposite direction to unwrap the border.

MOVING ITEMS ON THE FORM

You may find that you want to make a change to a screen after initially entering data. For example, suppose you want to move the Credit Limit field up next to the Starting Date field. Use the Move option from the Forms menu. Let's give it a try.

Call up the menu and select the Area and Move options. Paradox displays this prompt:

> Use ↑ ↓ → ← to move cursor to a corner of the area to be moved . . .
> then press ⏎ to select it . . .

Use the arrow keys to move the cursor to the starting C in Credit Limit. Press Enter to mark the corner. Paradox then displays the following instructions:

> Now use ↑ ↓ → ← to move to the diagonal corner . . .
> press ⏎ to define the area . . .

Use the → key to highlight the area to be moved, as in Figure 9.6. (You can, of course, highlight an area of any size to move.) Press Enter when both the prompt and the field area are highlighted.

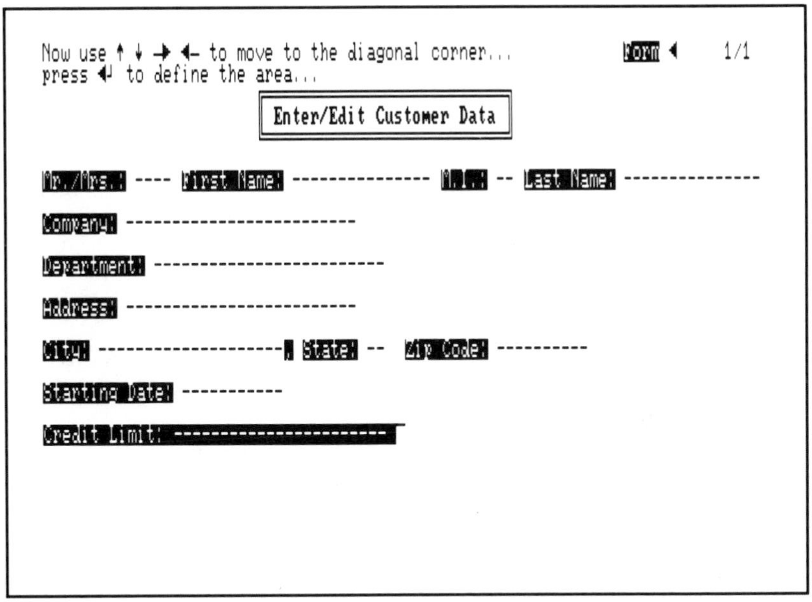

Figure 9.6: Highlighting the area to move

Paradox then prompts you to drag the highlighted area to its new location on the screen. As you press the ↑ and → keys, the highlight will move on the screen. Keep pressing the arrow keys until the highlight is a few spaces to the right of the Starting Date field, as in Figure 9.7. Then press Enter to complete the move. The highlight will disappear, and the Credit Limit prompt and field will jump to the new location.

REFORMATTING FIELDS ON THE FORM

To change the width of a field on the form, call up the Forms menu and select the Field and Reformat options. The screen will prompt you to use the arrow keys to move the cursor to the field you wish to reformat, then press Enter to select that field. You can then use the ← and → keys to increase or decrease the width of the field. As instructed on the screen, press Enter when you are done changing the size of the field.

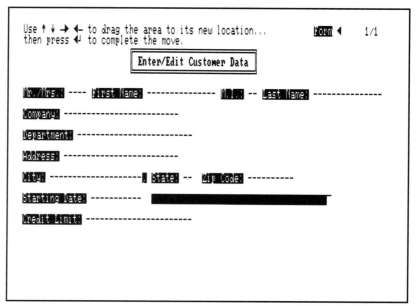

Figure 9.7: The highlighted area moved to a new location

ERASING PARTS OF THE FORM

To erase the general text placed on a form, use the usual Backspace and Del keys on your keyboard. To remove larger portions of the screen, use one of the techniques listed below. (Because there is no need to remove anything from the current sample form, you may not want to try any of these techniques at the moment.)

ERASING A FIELD

To remove a field from the screen, first move the cursor to the appropriate field hyphens. (Look to the upper-right corner of the screen for the name of the field that the cursor is currently in.) Then, call up the menu and select the Field and Erase options. The screen will ask you to move the cursor to the field you want to erase. If the cursor is already in the field you wish to erase, you can simply press Enter. (Optionally, you can use the arrow keys to highlight a different field to erase, or press Esc to cancel the command and not erase any fields.)

ERASING A BORDER

To erase a border from the screen, call up the Forms menu and select the Border and Erase options. As instructed on the screen, move the cursor to a corner of the box to be erased, and press Enter. Then, as instructed, use the arrow keys again to move the cursor to the opposite (diagonal) corner of the box, and press Enter once again to erase the box.

ERASING AN AREA

To erase a larger area of the screen, call up the menu and select the Area option. From the submenu, select the Erase option. The screen will display the prompt

> Use ↑ ↓ → ← to move to a corner of the area to be removed...
> then press ← to select it...

Use the arrow keys to move the cursor as instructed, then press Enter. The screen will ask that you

> Now use ↑ ↓ → ← to move to the diagonal corner of the area to be removed...then press ← to erase the area.

As instructed, move the cursor to a diagonal corner. Note that the area you define cannot contain only a portion of a field; if there is a field (or fields) within the area to be erased, *all* of the hyphens that represent that field must be enclosed within the area to be erased. After highlighting the area to erase, press Enter (or Esc to cancel the erasure).

SAVING A FORM

When you've finished entering your form, save it by pressing the DO-IT! (F2) key.

CANCELING A FORM

If you somehow manage to make a mess of a form and wish to abandon it altogether, call up the menu (F10) and select the Cancel option. Paradox will double-check to make sure you want to abandon the form. Answer Yes to abandon the form and return to the Main menu, or No to continue working on the form.

USING A FORM

Generally, you'll want to use a form while entering or editing data. For example, select the View option from the Main menu to view the Custlist table. Press the Edit key (F9) to switch to Edit mode. Then, to use the new form, call up the menu (F10) and select the Image option. From the submenu, select the PickForm option. You'll be given a menu of existing form options, as below:

    F 1

To use the new form, select option 1 (or whatever number you have assigned to it). You'll see the custom screen, as in Figure 9.8. Once selected, you can still use the Form Toggle key (F7) to switch back and forth from Form View to Table View.

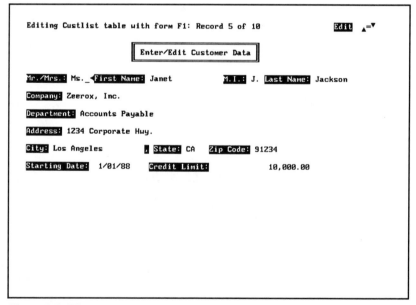

Figure 9.8: The custom screen used for editing

All keys work the same way on a custom form as they do on the standard form. PgUp and PgDn scroll up and down through records. The arrow keys move the cursor up, down, left, and right, and Backspace and Ctrl-Backspace erase data. Pressing Field View (Alt-F5) allows for more refined editing. As usual, you must press DO-IT! when done editing (if you wish to save your edits), and Clear Image (F8) to clear the screen.

CHANGING A FORM

To modify an existing form, call up the Main menu and select the Forms option. Select Change from the submenu and specify the name of the table with which the form is associated. Paradox will display a menu of existing forms, as below:

F   1

Select the appropriate number for your custom form. You'll have an opportunity to change the description of the form; then the form will appear on the screen, ready for editing. Use the same keys and commands we've already discussed in this chapter to make changes. Remember to press the DO-IT! key to save your work.

ADDING HELP TO A FORM

If you wish to make your form easier for a novice to use, you can develop your own "help box," like the one at the bottom of the screen shown in Figure 9.9. To develop one like that shown in the Figure, call up the Paradox Main menu, and select the Forms and Change options. Specify CustList as the table, 1 as the form, and press Enter to keep the existing description. Then follow these steps to draw the box:

1. Move the cursor to <17, 1>.

2. Call up the Forms menu (F10), and select the Border, Place, and Double-line options.

3. Press Enter to specify the current cursor position as the first corner of the box.

4. Press ↓ six times and → enough times to extend the ghosted border to the right edge of the screen.

5. Press Enter to complete the border.

Within the box, type in the text as shown in Figure 9.9. The individual vertical lines can be entered as single-line borders. For example, to fill in the first vertical line, move the cursor to <18,19> (or thereabouts, depending on how you've typed in the text), and call up the menu. Select Border, Place, and Single-line, and press Enter to mark the top of the line. Press ↓ four times to extend the ghosted line down four lines, then press Enter. The single line will appear within the box. Use this same technique to draw other vertical lines inside the box.

After adding the small help box to the bottom of your screen, remember to press DO-IT! (F2) to save your work.

COPYING A FORM

You can copy forms in the same way that we copied report formats in the previous chapter. Call up the Main menu and select the Tools

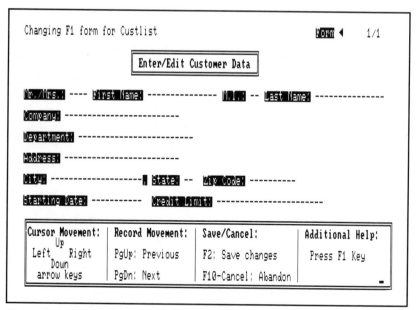

Figure 9.9: Some help text added to a custom form

option. Then select the Copy and Form options. Paradox will ask about the table name and form names as in the last chapter. Follow the instructions as they appear on the screen.

SUMMARY

- To create a custom form, select the Forms option from the Main menu and the Design option from the submenu.

- To use video enhancements on a form, call up the Forms menu and select the Style option.

- To place fields on a form, call up the Forms menu and select the Field and Place options.

- To place borders around text on a form, select the Border and Place options from the Forms menu.

- To move items on the form, select the Area and Move options from the Forms menu.

- To erase parts of a form, select the Area and Erase options from the Forms menu.

- To save a form, press the DO-IT! (F2) key after designing the form.

- To abandon an edited form, select the Cancel option from the Forms menu.

- To use a form for entering or editing data, select the Pick-Form option under the Main menu Image option, and choose a form by number. Use the Form Toggle (F7) key to switch from Table View to Form View.

- To modify an existing form, select Forms from the Main menu and the Change option from the submenu.

- To copy forms, use the Copy and Form options under the Tools option from the Main menu.

RESTRUCTURING A TABLE

CHAPTER 10

ONCE YOU'VE CREATED A TABLE, ADDED SOME DATA
to it, and used it for a while, you may find that you want to change
something about its basic structure. For example, you might want to
add a field for storing the phone number to the Custlist table. Or you
may need to lengthen a field such as Company or Address. In this
chapter, we'll add a phone number field to the Custlist table, and discuss general techniques for restructuring a table.

ADDING A NEW FIELD

To modify the structure of a table, first select the Modify option
from the Main menu, which brings up this familiar submenu:

    Sort   Edit   CoEdit   DataEntry   MultiEntry   **Restructure**

Then select the Restructure option. Paradox will ask for the name
of the table to restructure. In this example, enter Custlist. The current table structure appears on the screen, ready for editing, as in
Figure 10.1.

You can use the arrow keys, as usual, to move the cursor around
and make changes. The Ins and Del keys allow you to insert and
delete fields.

To add the Phone field to the Custlist table, first move the cursor
down to the Start Date field by pressing ↓ ten times and → once. Press
the Ins key. You'll see a blank line appear between the Zip and Start
Date fields. Enter the new field name and field type, as below:

    Phone   **A13**

When done, your screen should look like Figure 10.2.

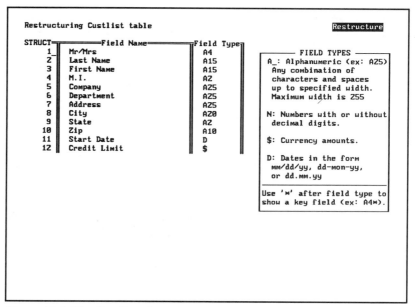

Figure 10.1: The Custlist table structure

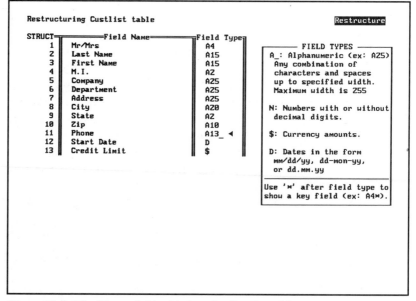

Figure 10.2: The Phone field added to the Custlist table

SAVING THE NEW STRUCTURE

When you're satisfied with your new table structure, just press the DO-IT! (F2) key to save it. Paradox will display some messages as it updates the standard form and report formats, then return to the Main menu.

CHANGING YOUR MIND

If you make a mistake while restructuring a table and want to go back to the original structure, do *not* press the DO-IT! key. Instead, call up the menu (F10) and select the Undo option. Paradox will ask for confirmation before canceling your current change. (Optionally, select the Cancel option to cancel the current changes and return to the Main menu.)

DELETING A FIELD

To delete a field while the table structure is displayed, simply move the cursor to that field and press the Del key. Because doing so automatically erases all the data stored in the deleted field, Paradox will ask for confirmation before deleting the field, after you press DO-IT! (F2). You'll see the options

Delete   Oops!

Select the Delete option to delete the field and all data stored in it. Optionally, select Oops! to cancel the deletion. At that point, you need to reinsert the deleted field, or call up the menu and select Cancel to recover the original table structure.

RENAMING A FIELD

To change the name of a field, simply move the cursor to the appropriate field name in the structure and type in the new name.

REARRANGING FIELDS

You can rearrange the order of fields in a table structure (though you can achieve a similar effect by just modifying the image on the screen in View or Edit mode). To move a field to a new position, place the cursor in the new position for the field and press the Ins key to insert a blank line. Type in the field name exactly as it is spelled in the original position. When you press the Enter key, Paradox will move the field from its original position to its new position.

CHANGING THE LENGTH OF A FIELD

Lengthening an alphanumeric field (for instance, from A20 to A25) will generally not cause any problems, though you might have to change the format of a custom form or report later to accommodate the new width (as discussed later in this chapter).

Shortening an alphanumeric field (for example, from A25 to A20) may cause some data loss if there are existing data longer than the new width. When you shorten an alphanumeric field, and press DO-IT! Paradox will warn you if there is a potential data loss, then give you these three options for handling the potential loss:

Trimming   No-Trimming   Oops!

Selecting the Trimming option will simply truncate all data that are too long, so that they fit into the new width. Selecting the No-Trimming option will place all data that do not fit into a temporary table named Problems. You can then change the data in the Problems table and add them to the original table using the Tools option (see Chapter 16). The Oops! option allows you to bow out gracefully and either re-enter the field width, or call up the menu and select Cancel to retain the original table structure.

CHANGING THE TYPE OF A FIELD

You can change field types (alphanumeric, numeric, currency, date), though the results may be similar to shortening an alphanumeric field (as discussed above). If there is a potential data loss, Paradox will warn you and give you the Trimming, No-Trimming, and Oops! options discussed above.

Generally, you won't want to change the type of data in a field. But in case you've made an error at the outset, it's easy enough to do. If you remember to put numeric values in either numeric or currency fields, dates in date fields, and everything else in alphanumeric fields, you probably will never have to change a field type.

Note: Paradox also offers the S field type for *short numbers*. A short field can contain whole numbers (no decimal places) in the range of − 32,767 to 32,767. Until you are an experienced Paradox user, you should avoid using this field type. It has the advantage of conserving memory, but the small range of acceptable numbers makes it very restrictive. For example, the number 1.1 is not acceptable because it has a decimal place, and the zip code 40001 is too large.

LONG-RANGE EFFECTS OF RESTRUCTURING A TABLE

When you delete a field from a table or change a field type, the field will automatically be deleted from the forms and reports associated with the table. If you've simply changed a field type, you may wish to place the field back into a form or report, using the techniques we'll discuss momentarily. If you've changed a field name, that name will be changed in all the associated report and form specifications.

If you add a new field to a table, your custom forms and reports will not be modified in any way. Of course, you can place the new field into the existing reports and forms if you wish, which we'll do right now.

UPDATING A REPORT FORMAT

To add the new Phone field to the Directory of Customers report format, call up the Main menu and select the Report and Change options. Specify Custlist as the table, and select report 1. Press Enter to retain the report description.

Next, move the cursor to the Start Date field, press Ins to go into Insert mode, and press Enter to add a new blank line. (You may have to realign the Start Date field by pressing the Space bar nine times.)

Next, press ↑ to move the cursor up a line, type

Phone:

and press the Space bar again. Place the Phone field next to the prompt by calling up the menu (F10) and selecting the Field, Place, Regular, and Phone options. Press Enter twice to place the field. Your new report format will look like Figure 10.3. Press the DO-IT! key to save the new report format.

Since the Phone field has no data in it yet, printing the report will not show phone numbers. Before filling in the Phone field, let's modify the custom form for entering and editing data.

UPDATING A CUSTOM FORM

To add the new Phone field to the custom form for entering and editing data, call up the Main menu and select the Forms and Change options. Specify Custlist as the table, and select form 1. Press Enter to retain the original form description. The existing form will appear as in Figure 10.4.

We'll first move the City and State fields up next to the Address field to make more room for the zip code and phone number. First, move the cursor to the C in the prompt

City:

Call up the menu (F10) and select the Area and Move options. Press Enter, then highlight the City and State prompts and fields (using →), which appear on the screen as

City: ---------------, State: --

Once highlighted, press Enter. Move the cursor up and to the right of the Address field, using ↑ and →. Press Enter when done.

Now move the Zip Code field over to the left column. Place the cursor on the Z in Zip, call up the menu, and select the Area and

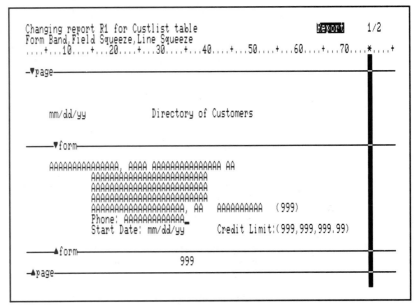

```
Changing report R1 for Custlist table                    Report   1/2
Form Band,Field Squeeze,Line Squeeze
....+...10....+...20....+...30....+...40....+...50....+...60....+...70....*....+
  ─▼page─────────────────────────────────────────────────────────────


      mm/dd/yy              Directory of Customers


   ─────▼form───────────────────────────────────────────────────────

      AAAAAAAAAAAAAAAA, AAAA AAAAAAAAAAAAAAAA AA
              AAAAAAAAAAAAAAAAAAAAAAAAAA
              AAAAAAAAAAAAAAAAAAAAAAAAAA
              AAAAAAAAAAAAAAAAAAAAAAAAAA
              AAAAAAAAAAAAAAAAAAAA, AA    AAAAAAAAAA   (999)
              Phone: AAAAAAAAAAAAAA_
              Start Date: mm/dd/yy       Credit Limit:(999,999,999.99)
   ─────▲form───────────────────────────────────────────────────────
                                  999
  ─▲page─────────────────────────────────────────────────────────────
```

Figure 10.3: The Phone field placed into the Directory report format

```
Changing F1 form for Custlist                          Form ◄   1/1

                   ┌───────────────────────────┐
                   │   Enter/Edit Customer Data │
                   └───────────────────────────┘

   Mr./Mrs. ---- First Name -------------- MI -- Last Name ----------------

   Company: -------------------------

   Department: ---------------------

   Address: -------------------------

   City: -------------------- State -- Zip Code ----------

   Starting Date: ----------     Credit Limit: -----------------------

  ┌─────────────────┬──────────────────┬──────────────────┬─────────────────┐
  │ Cursor Movement: │ Record Movement: │ Save/Cancel:     │ Additional Help: │
  │        Up        │                  │                  │                  │
  │   Left    Right  │ PgUp: Previous   │ F2: Save changes │  Press F1 Key    │
  │       Down       │                  │                  │                  │
  │    arrow keys    │ PgDn: Next       │ F10-Cancel: Abandon │              _ │
  └─────────────────┴──────────────────┴──────────────────┴─────────────────┘
```

Figure 10.4: The custom form ready for editing

Move options. Press Enter to start highlighting, then use the → key to highlight the Zip prompt and field (the portion shown below):

Zip Code: -----------

Press Enter after highlighting, and use ← to move the highlight to the left column. Press Enter to finish the move.

Now we'll put the Phone field next to the Zip Code field. Move the cursor to the right of the Zip Code field (<13,23>), and switch to reverse video by calling up the menu and selecting the Style, Reversal, and ReverseVideo options. Type

Phone:

Turn off reverse video by calling up the menu and selecting the Style, Reversal, and Normal options. Place the Phone field by pressing →, then calling up the menu and selecting the Field, Place, Regular, and Phone options. Press Enter twice to place and size the field. Your new form should look like Figure 10.5. Press DO-IT! (F2) to save the form.

We should also add a Picture template to the form, to simplify entering phone numbers. To do so, first make sure the Custlist table appears on the screen. (If not, select the View option and specify the Custlist table.) Then press Edit (F9). Call up the custom form by pressing Menu (F10) and selecting the Image, Pickform, and 1 options. Your new form will appear on the screen.

To add the template, call up the menu. Select the ValCheck and Define options. Move the cursor (if necessary) to the Phone field by pressing → a few times, and press Enter. Next, select the Picture option from the menu and type in this Picture template:

(###)###-####

This will ensure that all phone numbers entered use this format. Press Enter after typing in the Picture template. To make this template permanent, press DO-IT!.

To fill in phone numbers, press Edit (F9) to enter the Edit mode, put the cursor in the Phone field and press the Space bar to automatically fill in the open parenthesis. Then just type in the area code and phone number (Paradox will fill in the closing parenthesis and hyphen as you type). Figure 10.6 shows the new custom form

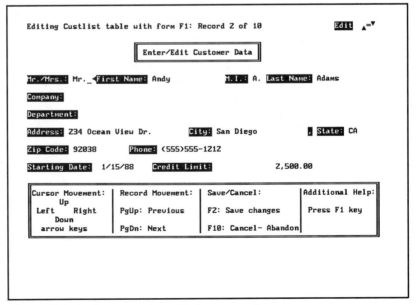

```
Changing F1 form for Custlist                          Form ◀   1/1

                    ┌─────────────────────────┐
                    │  Enter/Edit Customer Data │
                    └─────────────────────────┘

Mr./Mrs. ---- First Name: -------------- M.I. -- Last Name: --------------

Company: -----------------------

Department: -----------------------

Address: -----------------------    City: --------------------- State --

Zip Code: ----------         Phone: -------------_

Starting Date: ----------  Credit Limit: ---------------------

┌───────────────┬─────────────────┬──────────────────┬──────────────────┐
│Cursor Movement:│ Record Movement: │ Save/Cancel:     │ Additional Help: │
│       Up       │                  │                  │                  │
│ Left   Right   │ PgUp: Previous   │ F2: Save changes │ Press F1 Key     │
│      Down      │                  │                  │                  │
│  arrow keys    │ PgDn: Next       │ F10-Cancel: Abandon │               │
└───────────────┴─────────────────┴──────────────────┴──────────────────┘
```

Figure 10.5: The custom form modified to accommodate the Phone field

```
Editing Custlist table with form F1: Record 2 of 10          Edit ▲=▼

                    ┌─────────────────────────┐
                    │  Enter/Edit Customer Data │
                    └─────────────────────────┘

Mr./Mrs.: Mr._ First Name: Andy        M.I.: A. Last Name: Adams

Company:

Department:

Address: 234 Ocean View Dr.      City: San Diego        State: CA

Zip Code: 92038       Phone: (555)555-1212

Starting Date: 1/15/88   Credit Limit:            2,500.00

┌───────────────┬─────────────────┬──────────────────┬──────────────────┐
│Cursor Movement:│ Record Movement: │ Save/Cancel:     │Additional Help:  │
│       Up       │                  │                  │                  │
│ Left   Right   │ PgUp: Previous   │ F2: Save changes │ Press F1 key     │
│      Down      │                  │                  │                  │
│  arrow keys    │ PgDn: Next       │ F10: Cancel- Abandon │               │
└───────────────┴─────────────────┴──────────────────┴──────────────────┘
```

Figure 10.6: A phone number added to a record

with a phone number typed in. Use PgUp and PgDn to move from record to record and fill in phone numbers. Press DO-IT! (F2) to save your work when done.

SUMMARY

- To change the structure of a table, select the Modify and Restructure options from the Main menu.

- To add a new field to a table, use the Ins key to make space and enter the new field name and field type.

- To delete a field from a table, move the cursor to the field and press the Del key.

- To move a field to a new location, use the Ins key to make room for a new field, then type in the field name exactly as it appears in its original position.

- To save a modified table structure, press the DO-IT! (F2) key.

- To cancel modifications to a table structure, call up the menu and select the Cancel option.

- To update forms or reports after modifying a table structure, use the Change option from the Forms or Reports Main-menu option.

SCRIPTS

SOME TASKS IN PARADOX NATURALLY REQUIRE several keystrokes to perform. A simple example is the printing of a customer directory in alphabetical order. You need to call up the Main menu, select the Modify and Sort options, fill out the sort form, then call up the menu again, select the Report option, and so on.

You don't have to repeat all these keystrokes every time you wish to perform the task, however. Instead, you can record the required keystrokes in a Paradox *script,* then play them all back by selecting only a few menu options. In other words, you can make your entire task a single menu item and access it as you would any other Paradox menu item. Let's create a script for printing a customer directory in alphabetical order, and then we'll discuss some general techniques that you can use with scripts.

YOUR FIRST SCRIPT

Though there are several ways you can begin recording a script, the easiest is to call up the Main menu (F10) and select the Scripts option. This brings up the following submenu:

Play BeginRecord QuerySave ShowPlay Editor

To begin recording a script, select the BeginRecord option. Paradox will ask for a name for the script, as below:

Script:
Enter name for new script.

The name you give to a script can be up to eight characters long and cannot contain spaces or punctuation. In this example, enter the script name as

Director

and press Enter. (*Note:* If you enter the name of an existing script, Paradox will double-check for permission before replacing the old script with the new one. Select the Cancel option to rename the new script, or the Replace option to replace the old script with the new one.)

From this point on, all of your keystrokes will be recorded and stored in a script named Director. When space permits, the letter R will appear in the upper-right corner of the screen to remind you that you are recording a script.

First, press Clear All (Alt-F8) to clear everything from the screen. (In general, it's a good idea to start every script by pressing Clear All, so that you begin with a blank workspace.) Now, sort the Custlist table into alphabetical order by selecting the Modify and Sort options from the Main menu. When Paradox asks for the name of the table, type in or select Custlist. Select the Same option from the submenu, then sort by last name, first name, and middle initial by filling out the sort form as in Figure 11.1. Press DO-IT! after specifying the sort order, and wait for Paradox to finish sorting.

When the sorted Custlist table appears on the screen, call up the menu (F10) and select the Report and Output options. Once again, type in or select Custlist. Select report 1, then select the Printer option. Paradox will print the Directory of Customers.

When the printing is done, stop recording the script by calling up the menu (F10) and selecting the Scripts and End-Record options. To play back the script, call up the menu (F10) and select the Scripts option. From the submenu, select the ShowPlay option. Paradox will ask for the name of the script to play, as below:

Script:
Enter name of script to play, or press ⏎ to see a list of scripts.

You can either type in the script name, Director, or press Enter to see a list of script names. As with table names, you can highlight the name of the script and press Enter to select it. When Paradox asks if you want the script played Fast or Slow, select Fast.

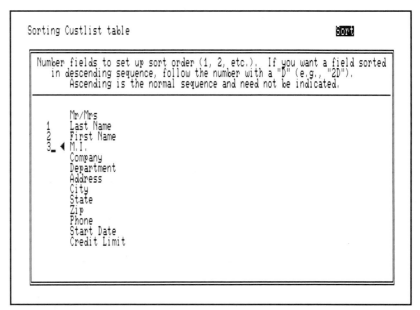

Figure 11.1: A sort form filled out for alphabetical sort

You'll now see Paradox play back all your keystrokes, exactly mimicking every step you used to print the sorted directory. Furthermore, the Director script will be saved automatically when you exit Paradox, so you can use it over and over again in the future.

This simple example does not demonstrate the full potential of scripts. But when you begin performing more complex tasks in Paradox, requiring perhaps hundreds of keystrokes, you'll really begin to appreciate the power of being able to record the steps taken in performing a task, and then repeat them at any time in the future by selecting a script name from the Scripts submenu.

VIEWING A RECORDED SCRIPT

You can look at the contents of a recorded script by calling up the Main menu and selecting the Scripts and Editor options. From the submenu, select Edit. Paradox will ask for the name of the script to edit. In this example, type in or highlight the name Director. You'll see the recorded script as in Figure 11.2.

```
 Changing script Director                                    Script
 ....+...10....+...20....+...30....+...40....+...50....+...60....+...70....+...80
 ClearAll {Modify} {Sort} {Custlist} {Same} Down  "1" Down
 "2" Down  "3" Do_It! Menu {Report} {Output} {Custlist} {1}
 {Printer} Menu {Scripts} {End-Record}
```

Figure 11.2: A recorded script ready for editing

Notice that the script contains all the keystrokes and menu options you selected during recording. You can change or modify the script, using the usual keys for moving the cursor, but don't do so now. We'll discuss techniques for customizing and enhancing scripts later in the book. For now, just call up the menu (F10) and select the Cancel and Yes options.

THE SCRIPTS MENU

Now let's briefly discuss what each option under Scripts provides. You will recall that the Scripts submenu consists of the following options:

Play   BeginRecord   QuerySave   ShowPlay   Editor

The Play option allows you to play back a previously recorded script, as does the ShowPlay option. The Play option, however, displays only the net results of the entire script (a printed directory in the Director example), without displaying the menus and keystrokes along the way as the script is being played.

The BeginRecord option, as we discussed, allows you to name a script and begin recording keystrokes. If you call up the menu (F10) after selecting BeginRecord, you'll see these options:

Cancel   End-Record   Play

The End-Record option stops recording your script. The Cancel option discards all recorded keystrokes since the last BeginRecord session and returns you to the workspace. The Play option selects another script and plays it *inside* the script currently being recorded. This advanced technique is discussed in later chapters.

The ShowPlay option plays back a script, showing menus and keystrokes along the way. Before playing back a script, ShowPlay presents these options:

> Fast   Slow

The Fast option plays the script rapidly, and the Slow option plays back the script very slowly. The Slow option is usually used when developing more complex scripts that need to be analyzed in slow motion for changes and enhancements.

The QuerySave option saves a query form set up through the Ask option. We'll see examples of the power of this option in later chapters. But for now, suffice it to say that queries involving multiple tables can become quite complicated. QuerySave lets you record a complex query and play it back at any time, just as a recorded script allows you to record and play back keystrokes.

The Editor option presents this submenu:

> Write   Edit

The Write option allows you to write your own PAL (Paradox Application Language) program. Until you become familiar with PAL you won't want to use this option. The Edit option allows you to change or modify existing scripts or PAL programs.

INSTANT SCRIPTS

Another way to record a script is simply to press Instant Script Record (Alt-F3). As with the BeginRecord option, an R will appear in the upper-right corner of the screen (when room permits), and all keystrokes will be recorded. To stop recording an instant script, press Alt-F3 again. To play back an instant script, press Instant Script Play

(Alt-F4). Paradox will instantly play back your keystrokes exactly as you recorded them.

Paradox stores the instant script in a file named Instant. To save an instant script, you'll need to change its name, because Paradox can save only one instant script at a time. To do so, call up the Tools option and select Rename. Then select the Script option and change the name of the instant script to some new, unique name.

Whenever you use Instant Script Record, Paradox automatically erases the existing instant script. Therefore, if you do not intentionally save your instant script after recording, it will be lost the next time you press Instant Script Record.

THE PAL MENU

If you are in the middle of an operation when you decide to begin recording a script, you may not be able to get to the Main menu to select the Scripts options. To get around this, you can call up the PAL menu by pressing Alt-F10. The PAL menu also provides the BeginRecord, End-Record, and Play options, which are identical to those options under the Scripts menu.

AUTOEXECUTE SCRIPTS

If you give the name *Init* to a script, it will be played automatically each time Paradox is started. Paradox always stores scripts with the name you assign followed by the extension .SC (for example, Director.SC). When Paradox first starts up, it looks on the program disk for a file named Init.SC. If it finds Init.SC, Paradox plays the script immediately before displaying the Main menu. If no Init.SC script is found, Paradox runs normally. (We'll discuss this in greater detail when we get to the PAL language.)

BEING CREATIVE

As with most Paradox functions, the best way to learn about scripts is simply to experiment with them. You certainly can't do any harm by recording keystrokes and playing them back. A good way to practice, however, might be to create a script called Labels that sorts Custlist data into zip code order, then prints mailing labels.

In later chapters we'll see how we can combine scripts with PAL to create very powerful customized systems. Before we get to that point, however, we need to enhance our present skills by learning to manage multiple tables. We'll get started on this topic in the next chapter.

SUMMARY

- To record a script, call up the Main menu (F10) and select the Scripts and BeginRecord options. Enter a name for the script, using a maximum of eight letters and no spaces or punctuation.

- To stop recording, call up the Main menu and select the Scripts and End-Record options.

- To play back a script, call the Main menu and select the Scripts option. Then select either the Play or ShowPlay options.

- To view a recorded script, select the Editor and Edit options from the Scripts and Editor menus.

- To record a script instantly, press Instant Script Record (Alt-F3) to begin recording keystrokes. To stop recording, press Alt-F3 again. To play back an instant script, press Instant Script Play (Alt-F4). To save an instant script, you must rename it by selecting the Rename and Script options from the Tools submenu.

P A R T   II

MULTIPLE TABLES IN
A DATABASE

DATABASE DESIGN WITH MULTIPLE TABLES

CHAPTER 12 _____

UP TO THIS POINT, ALL OF OUR WORK WITH PARADOX has used a single table, named Custlist, to teach and demonstrate the important "nuts-and-bolts" of managing data stored in a single table. With that important information under our belts, we can begin to move into some of the more sophisticated aspects of Paradox database management.

The techniques used to manage multiple tables are largely the same as the techniques used to manage a single table, so we certainly have not wasted any time in previous chapters. However, several new concepts come into play when managing multiple tables; those concepts are what this chapter is all about.

Many applications, such as those that manage a mailing list or customer list, require only a single table. Larger business applications typically require more complex designs, using several related tables. The task of determining how to divide data into separate, related tables is called *database design*.

THE ONE-TO-ONE DATABASE DESIGN

The *one-to-one* relationship is the simplest and perhaps most common database design. The customer list developed in previous chapters used a one-to-one design. The term *one-to-one* stems from the fact that for each field in the table, there is another related field. In the customer table, for each one customer name, there is one company affiliation, one address, one city, one state, and so forth. As a reminder, Figure 12.1 shows the structure of the Custlist table used in previous chapters.

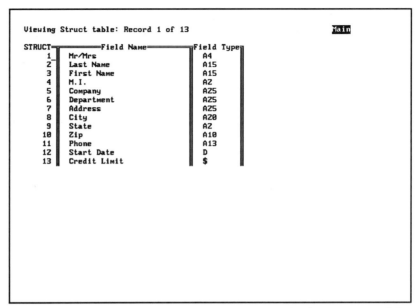

```
Viewing Struct table: Record 1 of 13                          Main

STRUCT          Field Name              Field Type
       1    Mr/Mrs                      A4
       2    Last Name                   A15
       3    First Name                  A15
       4    M.I.                        A2
       5    Company                     A25
       6    Department                  A25
       7    Address                     A25
       8    City                        A20
       9    State                       A2
      10    Zip                         A10
      11    Phone                       A13
      12    Start Date                  D
      13    Credit Limit                $
```

Figure 12.1: One-to-one database design illustrated in the structure of the Custlist table

THE ONE-TO-MANY DATABASE DESIGN

The *one-to-many* database design is used in situations where many (usually an unknown number) items of data are associated with another data item. For example, in an accounts-receivable system, each individual customer might charge several items during the course of the month. In other words, there could be many charge transactions placed by one customer.

If you attempt to design the database for an accounts-receivable system using a single table, you'll quickly see the problems inherent in the design. If the table has a single record for each charge transaction, where do you store the customer's name, address, city, state, zip code, and so forth? If you store this information with each charge transaction, there will be a great deal of redundant data.

For example, even though there are only three unique customers (Smith, Miller, and Jones) in the charge transactions listed in Figure 12.2, the table uses a lot of disk space because of all the redundant data in the name and address fields. A data-entry operator will waste a lot of time typing the name and address of each customer repeatedly. Furthermore, if one of the customers moves and changes their address, that address will have to be changed in many different records.

```
Last Name    First Name Address           City         Charge
Jones        Fred       345 Grape St.      Encinitas    6457.42
Smith        Albert     345 C St.          San Diego       5.10
Smith        Albert     345 C St.          San Diego    1000.00
Adams        Martha     P.O. Box 1107      Alameda        76.50
Smith        Albert     345 C St.          San Diego    4567.89
Adams        Martha     P.O. Box 1107      Alameda        99.00
Adams        Martha     P.O. Box 1107      Alameda       123.45
Adams        Martha     P.O. Box 1107      Alameda      3245.69
Jones        Fred       345 Grape St.      Encinitas     333.33
Smith        Albert     345 C St.          San Diego     596.43
Jones        Fred       345 Grape St.      Encinitas     764.32
```

Figure 12.2: Example of a poor accounts-receivable database design

One solution to the problems with this design is to store one record for each customer, and have several fields for charges. But such a design limits the number of transactions that can be assigned to a particular customer to the number of fields allocated for transactions in the table. It also makes it virtually impossible to answer questions such as, "How many charge transactions this month involved part number A-123?"

USING A COMMON FIELD TO RELATE TABLES

To resolve the inherent problems in trying to store accounts-receivable data in a single table, the data can be stored on two separate tables. Then a single *common field* (or *key field*) can be used to *relate* the two tables.

Figure 12.3 shows the structures of two tables named Customer and Charges. The Customer table contains a single record for each customer in the hypothetical accounts-receivable system. Each customer is assigned a unique customer number in the field named CustNo. The Charges table stores each individual charge transaction on a single record. The CustNo field in the Charges table identifies which customer in the Customer table the transaction belongs to.

Structure of the Customer table

Field	Field Name	Field Type	Description
1	CustNo	N*	Customer number
2	LName	A15	Last name
3	FName	A10	First name
4	Address	A25	Address
5	City	A20	City
6	State	A2	State
7	Zip	A10	Zip code
8	Phone	A13	Phone number
9	Last_Updat	D	Last updated
10	Start_Bal	$	Starting balance
11	Chg_Curr	$	Current charges
12	Pay_Curr	$	Current payments
13	Bal_30	$	Balance last month
14	Bal_60	$	Balance 2 months ago
15	Bal_90	$	Balance 3 months ago
16	Bal_90Plus	$	Balance over 3 months
17	Terms	A20	Credit terms

Structure of the Charges Table

Field	Field Name	Field Type	Description
1	CustNo	N	Customer number
2	Part_No	A5	Part number
3	Qty	N	Quantity purchased
4	Unit_Price	$	Unit price
5	Date	D	Date of purchase

Figure 12.3: The structures of the Customer and Charges tables

Note that the common field in the two tables, CustNo, has been given the exact same Field Name and Field Type in both table structures. This is essential to the success of relational database design. Notice also that the type of the CustNo field is marked with an asterisk, indicating that it is the key field. Paradox uses this field when sorting the table and when rejecting duplicate entries (a process we'll examine later in this chapter).

Figure 12.4 shows sample listings of the two tables. It is easy to see which charges belong to which customers, as the arrows linking customer number 1001 to his charges indicate.

Note that dividing the information into two separate tables minimizes the redundant data. Each customer and his address (and other related information) fills a single record on the Customer table. Each transaction for each customer requires one record on the Charges table. Only the customer number is repeated on both tables, and there is no limit to the number of transactions that can be assigned to each customer.

GUIDELINES FOR CREATING A COMMON FIELD

The common field that relates the two tables is an important one, and there are a couple of guidelines that you should follow when designing your own databases and choosing common fields.

Make Common Fields Unique

If there is a one-to-many relationship involved, the common field on the "one" side of the relationship must be unique to each record.

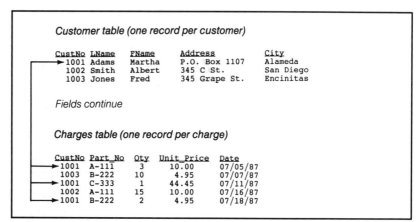

Figure 12.4: Sample data from the Customer and Charges tables

Otherwise, there will be no way of matching a given record with the appropriate record on the "many" side of the relationship. For example, suppose the last-name field (LName) rather than CustNo was the common field between the Customer and Charges tables discussed above.

Furthermore, suppose there are ten customers with the last name Smith on the Customer table. If one of the charges in the Charges table is charged to Smith, you have no way of knowing which Smith it refers to. You could refine the relationship a bit by trying to link the two tables by both last and first name, but if you have two customers with the same first and last name your problem will not be solved.

The customer number is the best way to set up the common field between the Customer and Charges tables, because you can then ensure that each customer has a unique customer number. That way, when a record on the Charges table refers to customer number 1005, there can be no ambiguity about which customer on the Customer table gets the bill (assuming, of course, that only one customer has been assigned the number 1005).

To make matters easier, a Paradox table can easily be set up to reject any duplicate entries in the common field on the "one" side of the one-to-many relationship. We'll see how this is accomplished a little later in this chapter.

Make Common Fields Arbitrary

A second guideline in creating common fields is to make them meaningless. A four-digit number (from 1001 to 9999) is a good choice, because it has no other meaning in the database.

If you decide to place encoded information into the customer number (for example, by assigning numbers such as SDC5112, where SD stands for San Diego, C5 stands for credit rating of 5, and 112 is the customer number), you might have some difficulty in ensuring that each customer has a unique number. Furthermore, if the encoded information changes (the customer moves away from San Diego or his credit rating changes), you'll have to change his customer number. As soon as you change the customer number on the Customer table, you have to make sure both that the new number is not already in use and that the same change is made to all the CustNo fields in any related tables.

To avoid this problem, put any meaningful information into a field of its own, and make the customer number a plain, arbitrarily (or sequentially) assigned number.

THE MASTER-TABLE/TRANSACTION-TABLE STRUCTURE

One of the most common applications of the one-to-many design is the master-table/transaction-table relationship. In this design, the master table keeps track of current, ongoing balances, while the transaction table records individual transactions that affect those balances. The master table tells us the status of things at the moment, while the transaction tables maintain a history, or audit trail, of the events that produced those current balances.

A retail-store inventory database provides a good example. The master table stores one record for each item that is kept in stock and the quantity currently in stock. Two other tables are used to keep track of individual sales transactions and individual purchases (items received into the stock room or warehouse).

Through a process called *updating*, Paradox can subtract the quantities of items sold from the appropriate in-stock quantity on the master table. The quantities of items received into the stock room can be added to the appropriate in-stock quantities. The net result is that the master table reflects the true quantity of each item in stock, while the tables recording individual sales and purchase transactions still retain their useful information.

The accounts-receivable system can be structured with a master-table/transaction-table relationship as well. The master table records the customer number, name, address, and current balance for each credit customer. Charges and payments can be stored in separate tables. Each charge and payment transaction can then be assigned to a customer, through the customer number, so there is no ambiguity about which customer each charge and payment transaction belongs to.

Through updating, the current charges can be added to each customer's balance, and his payments can be subtracted from his balance. Thus, current information is readily available (current balances), and historical information (the individual charges and payments that produced the balances) is maintained. Updating techniques are discussed in more detail in Chapter 15.

THE MANY-TO-MANY DATABASE DESIGN

The *many-to-many* relationship occurs in situations such as scheduling or exploded inventories. For example, when scheduling students for classes, there will be many students in each of many classes, and many classes each with many students. In an exploded inventory, a manufacturer might produce many products from many components. Likewise, each of many components might be used in many products. Let's discuss each example independently.

A SCHEDULING DATABASE

The class scheduling problem mentioned above is the classic example of the many-to-many relationship. To avoid redundancies in storing data, all of the necessary information is split into several tables. The Courses table contains information about each course or each section of each course. Each course has a unique number assigned to it, which is the common field that links specific students to specific courses. The structure and sample data for the Courses table are shown in Figure 12.5. (This table is simplified, because each course might really be offered in several different sections or time slots.)

The Students table contains one record for each student in the school. To identify students individually, each student is assigned a unique student number. The structure and sample data for the Students table are shown in Figure 12.6.

To link the many students to their appropriate courses, a third table—called a *linking* table—contains one record for each student enrolled in each class. For this example, the linking table is called SCLink and has the structure and sample data shown in Figure 12.7. From the contents of the SCLink table, you can clearly see that student number 10001 is enrolled in courses B-222 and C-333. Student number 10002 is enrolled in courses A-111, B-222, and C-333.

As Figure 12.8 shows, the SCLink table provides a sort of "map" as to which students are enrolled in which courses. There are no redundant data on either the Students or Courses tables; each contains a single record for a single student or course. The SCLink table does contain many redundant records, of course, but since there are

Structure of the Courses table

Field	Field Name	Field Type	Description
1	CourseID	A5*	Course number
2	CourseName	A20	Course name
3	Room_No	A5	Room number
4	Teacher	A20	Instructor name

Other relevant fields can be added

Sample Courses data

```
CourseID   CourseName   Room_No   Teacher
A-111      English      J-222     Watson
B-222      Spanish      E-345     Holmes
C-333      Greek        G-445     Moriarty
```

Figure 12.5: The structure and sample contents of the Courses table

Structure for the Students table

Field	Field Name	Field Type	Description
1	StudentID	N*	Student number
2	LastName	A10	Last name
3	FirstName	A10	First name
4	Address	A20	Address
5	City	A20	City
6	State	A2	State
7	Zip	A5	Zip code
8	Phone	A13	Phone number

Sample Students data

```
StudentID   LastName   FirstName   Address
10001       Adams      Angela      123 A St.
10002       Baker      Bobbi       345 B st.
10003       Carlson    Carla       345 C St.
```

Fields continue

Figure 12.6: The structure and sample contents of the Students table

Structure for the SCLink table

Field	Field Name	Field Type	Description
1	StudentID	N	Student number
2	CourseID	A5	Course number

Sample SCLink data

```
StudentID   CourseID
10001       B-222
10001       C-333

10002       A-111
10002       B-222
10002       C-333

10003       A-111
10003       C-333
```

Figure 12.7: The structure and sample contents of the SCLink table

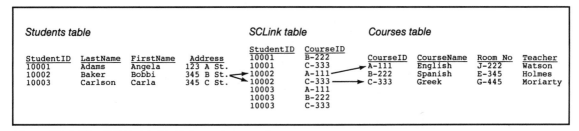

Figure 12.8: The SCLink table links students to the courses

only two fields on the table, little disk storage space is wasted. Furthermore, the Students and Courses tables are easy to maintain, because each contains only one record per student or per course, respectively.

In some situations, the linking table will contain more than two fields, as the next section demonstrates.

AN EXPLODED INVENTORY DATABASE

Another example of a many-to-many relationship among tables is the *exploded inventory* model. One table, named Product, stores one record for each type of product the company produces. The structure and sample data for the Product table are shown in Figure 12.9. (In Chapter 13, we'll see how the Needed field can be used to calculate the number of components needed to produce a certain number of products.) Of course, you can also include other fields, such as as the quantity in stock, selling price, and so forth, but this table just shows some basic fields to present the structure.

A second table, named Componen, contains one record for each type of component that the manufacturer purchases to create its products. Each component has a unique component number, stored in the field named Comp_No. The structure and sample data for the Componen table are shown in Figure 12.10. (Again, you might want to include other relevant information, such as purchase price, date of last shipment received, quantity on order, expected date of next shipment, vendor, and so forth.)

There is a many-to-many relationship between the Product and Componen tables, because each product uses many components, and each component is used in many products. A linking table, named Linker in this example, sets up the relation between these two tables, describing which products use which components.

Because some products use more than one of a particular component, the Linker table includes the quantity of each component

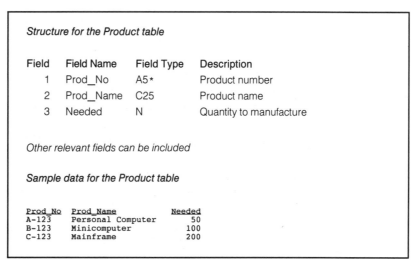

Figure 12.9: The structure and sample contents for the Product table

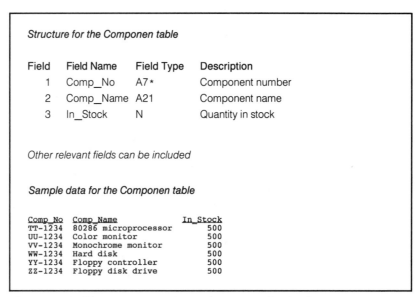

Figure 12.10: The structure and sample contents for the Componen table

required to produce each product. This information is stored in the Qty_Used field of the Linker table. The structure and sample contents of the Linker table for this example are shown in Figure 12.11.

Note that product number A-123 uses one component number TT-1234 and two component numbers ZZ-1234. You can see the relationships among the Product, Linker, and Componen tables in Figure 12.12, which uses arrows to show which components make up product number B-123.

Using standard Paradox query forms, you can use these three tables to answer questions such as, "If I plan to manufacture 75 personal computers and 50 business computers, how many of each component will I need?" or "Given that I've manufactured 22 personal computers and 17 business computers today, how many of each component are left in stock?" Chapter 13 provides examples of querying many-to-many tables.

NORMALIZING A DATABASE

The techniques for dividing data into separate, related tables have been formalized in database management literature into a theory

Structure of the Linker table

Field	Field Name	Field Type	Description
1	Prod_No	A5	Product number
2	Comp_No	A7	Component number
3	Qty_Used	N	Quantity used

Sample data for the Linker table

```
Prod_No Comp_No Qty_Used
A-123   TT-1234    1
A-123   VV-1234    1
A-123   YY-1234    2
A-123   ZZ-1234    2
B-123   TT-1234    1
B-123   UU-1234    1
B-123   YY-1234    2
B-123   ZZ-1234    2
C-123   TT-1234    1
C-123   UU-1234    1
C-123   WW-1234    1
C-123   YY-1234    1
C-123   ZZ-1234    1
```

Figure 12.11: The structure and sample contents of the Linker table

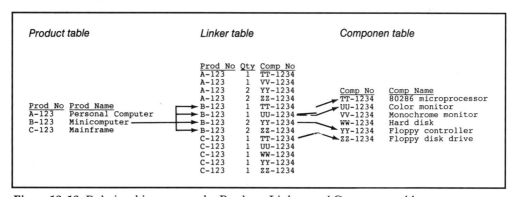

Figure 12.12: Relationships among the Product, Linker, and Componen tables

called *normalization*. The process of normalizing a database involves three rules:

1. Remove all redundant data.

2. Remove all partial dependencies.

3. Remove all transitive dependencies.

Each step in this process produces a database in one of what are called the *normal forms* of database design.

REMOVE REDUNDANT DATA

The first step in normalizing a database is to remove repeating data from the single table and place it in a separate table, using a common field to link the redundant information. When you've removed the redundant data from a single table by placing it into two separate related tables, the database is said to be in the *first normal form* of database design.

The sample accounts-receivable design discussed earlier in this chapter and illustrated in Figures 12.3 and 12.4 demonstrates a database in the first normal form; the redundant customer names and addresses have been removed from the Charges table and placed in a separate Customer table.

REMOVE ALL PARTIAL DEPENDENCIES

Partial dependencies may occur in a database that contains more than one common field. In that situation, any information that is not dependent on all common fields should be removed and placed in a separate table.

For example, the Linker table in the exploded inventory example contains two common fields: Prod_No, which acts as the link to the Products table, and Comp_No, which forms the link to the Componen table. This table also included the Qty_Used field, which is directly dependent on *both* the product number and component number (because it describes how many of each component each product requires).

Any other information stored on this database would be dependent on only one of the common fields (either Prod_No or Comp-_No). For example, the product name would be directly relevant only to the Prod_No field. To avoid any such partial dependencies, all information that is specific to individual products is stored on the separate Products table, and all information that is specific to individual components is stored in the Componen table. When only the data that are directly relevant to all common fields in a table record remain in the table, the database has reached the *second normal form*.

REMOVE TRANSITIVE DEPENDENCIES

The third step in normalizing a database design is to remove the *transitive dependencies*: those fields that are occasionally (though not always) dependent on some other non-common field in the same record. For example, in the Componen table, where information about components purchased by the manufacturer is listed, you might want to place the name and address of the vendor who supplies the component. However, if this were the only component purchased from that vendor and you later stopped using that component and deleted the record, you would lose the vendor's name and address. Hence, the dependence between the particular component and the vendor was a temporary, or transitive, one.

To avoid this situation, you could store a vendor code in the Componen table and use that to relate each component to a vendor in a separate table of vendors' names and addresses named Vendors. That way, your list of vendors would remain intact, regardless of the components you were using at a particular moment.

To use a bookkeeping example, you wouldn't want the chart of accounts to be dependent on (or derived from) the individual transactions that transpired within a given month, because some accounts might not be used in that particular month.

When all the transitive dependencies have been removed from the records, the database is said to be in the *third normal form.*

THE FULLY NORMALIZED DATABASE

Like most theories, perhaps this discussion tends to make abstract what is actually intuitively obvious. When you take away all the fancy terminology, a *fully normalized* database is one that is easy to manage because the data are grouped into tables of similar information. For example, in an inventory system, the data are simply divided into product information, component information, vendor information, and information that defines which components go into which products. If you think about it for a moment, it makes perfect sense to store information in such a manner.

Furthermore, if you look at most manual systems that are used to store and manage information, you'll often find that the information is already structured in the third normal form. So don't let a lot of theory confuse you. Strive to reduce the redundancies in your tables and make particular bodies of information independent and easy to work with, and you'll find that your databases will naturally fall into the desired third normal form.

A WORKING INVENTORY EXAMPLE

To demonstrate some hands-on techniques for creating and using multiple related tables, we'll work through the steps required to set up an inventory-management system. We'll also use this sample inventory system in examples in later chapters.

If you are using a computer without a hard disk, you might want to begin by formatting a new, blank disk for storing data. (You'll need to exit Paradox to do so.) Label this disk *Inventory System* and use it in drive B of your computer throughout the examples in the following chapters. If you are using a hard disk system, you need not, of course, do anything special to prepare for these examples.

MASTER INVENTORY TABLE

We'll name the master inventory table *Mastinv*. To create this table, first clear any data currently on the screen (Alt-F8). Then select the Create option and enter the table name Mastinv. Type in the table structure as shown in Figure 12.13, and press DO-IT! (F2) when you have finished.

REJECTING DUPLICATE ENTRIES

We can see in Figure 12.13 that the type of the Part No field is marked with an asterisk. As mentioned earlier, this informs Paradox that the field is a key field. Knowing this, Paradox will automatically reject any duplications in the field, and it will always keep the table in sorted order by this field. Let's now take a moment to see how Paradox handles duplicate entries in the Part No field of the Mastinv table.

From the Main menu, select the Modify and DataEntry options

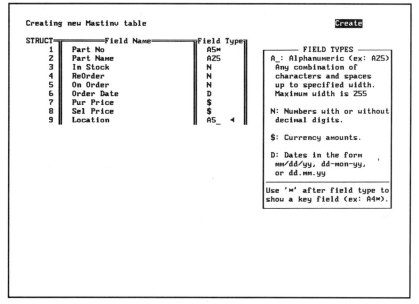

Figure 12.13: The structure for the Mastinv table

and specify the Mastinv table. Type in two records, using the information shown below:

Part No	Part Name	In Stock
A-100	Gershwin Bicycle	10
A-100	Nikono Bicycle	50

When you press the DO-IT! key, Paradox will show a new table named Keyviol, which displays the records with identical part numbers (see Figure 12.14).

To remedy this situation, you must first edit the Keyviol table so that there are no duplicate part numbers. Press Edit (F9) and change the second part number to A-101.

Next, add these records to the Mastinv table by following these steps:

1. Save the new Keyviol data (press DO-IT!).

2. Call up the Tools option from the Main menu.

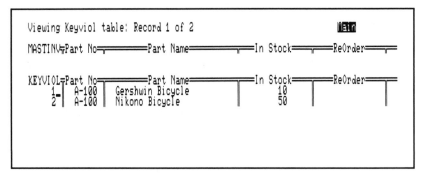

Figure 12.14: Keyviol table showing duplicate part numbers

3. Select the More and Add options.

4. Enter Keyviol as the name of the table from which to add records (the source table).

5. Enter Mastinv as the name of the table to which the records will be added (the target table).

6. Select New Entries.

Paradox will add the corrected records to the Mastinv file and return to viewing the Mastinv table.

Now, take a moment to complete these two records and to add some more data to the Mastinv file, as shown in Figure 12.15. (Use the Edit (F9) key to begin making changes.) When done, press the DO-IT! key to save the new data and then Clear Image (F8) to clear the screen.

Part No	Part Name	In Stock	ReOrder	On Order	Order Date	Pur Price	Sel Price	Location
A-100	Gershwin Bicycle	10	5	0	1/31/88	450.00	675.00	J-111
A-101	Nikono Bicycle	50	35	0	1/31/88	375.00	562.50	J-112
A-200	Racing Bicycle	2	3	1	2/01/88	600.00	900.00	M-991
B-100	Safety Helmet (Nikono)	50	10	0	2/15/88	20.00	30.00	L-111
B-111	Safety Helmet (Carrera)	2	10	0	1/31/88	40.00	60.00	J-333
B-112	Safety Helmet (Ozzy)	0	10	25	1/31/88	15.00	22.50	L-225
C-551	Hobie Skateboard	50	75	0	4/15/88	45.00	67.50	S-911
C-559	Flexie Skateboard	25	75	50	4/15/88	15.00	22.50	S-912

Figure 12.15: Sample data on the Mastinv table

An important point to keep in mind with the Mastinv table is that once initial values for the quantity in stock have been entered, they need not be modified manually. The In Stock, On Order, and Pur Price fields will all be maintained automatically through updating procedures, which we'll discuss in Chapter 15.

Notice also that Part No is the first (topmost) field defined in this table. This is intentional, because we can use the first field in a table to validate entries made in the related tables and to look up related information as well. We'll see how to perform these operations in a moment, when we create the related Sales table.

THE SALES TABLE

The Paradox sample tables include a table named Sales, which we will use in the following examples. If you have copied this table to your hard disk, and want to keep it for future use, you might want to change its name so that it does not conflict with the Sales table we'll create in this section. To do so, call up the Main menu (F10), select the Tools and Rename options, and select Sales as the name of the table to rename. When prompted, enter a new name for the table, such as OrigSales, and press Enter.

In our example, the Sales table will store individual sales transactions. Select the Create option from the Main menu, enter the table name Sales, and fill in the table structure as shown in Figure 12.16.

Notice that we did *not* specify Part No as a key field on this table. (That is, we did not put an asterisk next to the part-number field type.) In this table, we do not expect each transaction to have a unique part number. Only the Mastinv file needs to have a unique part number for every record. Since the Sales table might have any number of individual sales transactions for a given product, we do not want Paradox to reject duplicates in this field. When you've entered the table structure for the Sales table, press the DO-IT! key.

Notice also that we've used the field name Sel Price in this table, using the same field name and field type as the Sel Price field on the Mastinv table. By doing so, we can use the *automatic fill-in* feature that Paradox offers to copy the appropriate selling price automatically from the Mastinv table onto the Sales table during data entry and editing. We'll now discuss how to set up this automatic fill-in feature.

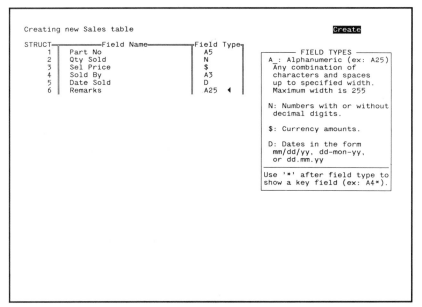

Figure 12.16: The structure of the Sales table

AUTOMATIC VALIDATION AND FILL-IN

Let's take a moment to think about entering data into the Sales table. Suppose whoever is typing sales transactions into this table accidentally enters an invalid part number (for example, a part number with no corresponding record on the Mastinv table). If that error is allowed into the Sales table, it may be very difficult to find and correct later. This error can be avoided altogether by asking Paradox to validate any entry into the Part No field against part numbers listed in the Mastinv table.

Suppose the person entering the data into the Sales table does not even *know* the correct part number or the correct selling price. How does the person go about getting the necessary information? By using Paradox's HelpAndFill feature, you can provide a quick and easy technique that allows the person entering data to look up part numbers quickly on the Mastinv table, and to automatically fill in the selling price stored on the Mastinv table as the selling price on the Sales table.

Your options for defining look-ups and validations across two related tables are shown in the TableLookup option under ValCheck in the Edit menu. Before actually trying them out, however, let's take a moment to discuss all the options in a general sense. The two main options for defining table look-ups are

JustCurrentField   AllCorrespondingFields

Let's discuss each of these options.

JustCurrentField

The JustCurrentField option checks any data entered into the common field against all existing entries in the look-up table. In this example, a part number entered into the Part No field in the Sales table will be compared against all entries in the Part No field. If you select JustCurrentField, you'll be given the options

PrivateLookup   HelpAndFill

The PrivateLookup option checks the entry in the current table against the first field in the look-up table, but does not provide any view of, or access to, the look-up table. Instead, invalid entries are simply rejected with the error message

Not one of the possible values for this field.

Like PrivateLookup, the HelpAndFill option also checks the entry in the current field against entries in the first field of the look-up table, but in addition allows you to view the look-up table, browse through it to find the information you need, and automatically copy that information to the current table. In the inventory system we've discussed, if you needed to enter a sales transaction for a Nikono Bicycle, but did not know the part number, HelpAndFill would let you locate the part name quickly on the Mastinv table, and press a key to copy the part number from the Mastinv table to the Sales table.

AllCorrespondingFields

The AllCorrespondingFields option under TableLookup works much like the JustCurrentField entry, but copies values in *all* fields with identical field names from the lookup table to the current table. (In this example, Sel Price exists on both Mastinv and Sales, so data can be copied from the Sel Price field in the Mastinv table to the Sel Price field in the Sales table).

When you select AllCorrespondingFields, you'll be given the options

FillNoHelp   HelpAndFill

The FillNoHelp option checks the entry in the current field against all entries in the first field of the look-up table. If the entry is valid, fields that have the same name as fields on the look-up table are automatically filled with the appropriate values from the look-up table. There is no way, however, to view the look-up table on the screen.

The HelpAndFill option checks the entry in the current field against all entries in the first field of the look-up table. If the entry is valid, fields that have the same name as fields on the look-up table are filled automatically with the appropriate values from the look-up table, just as with the FillNoHelp option above. However, you may optionally view the look-up table, select a value to fill in, which in turn also fills in all fields that have field names in common with the look-up table.

Using the Mastinv and Sales tables as an example, suppose you wish to enter a transaction into the Sales table for a Nikono bicycle, but do not know the part number. The HelpAndFill feature would allow you to look up the appropriate part number on the Mastinv table and copy both the part number and the selling price from the Mastinv table into the current record on the Sales table.

REFINING THE SALES TABLE

Now that we are familiar with these advanced database features, how can we use them to beef up the Sales table? As mentioned previously, we intentionally defined Part No as the first (topmost) field in the Mastinv table structure so that we could use the field for data validation and look-ups. Furthermore, we've used the field name Sel Price on both the Mastinv and Sales tables, so we could copy data from Mastinv into Sales during data entry and editing.

To add these features to the Sales table, make sure the Sales table is on the screen. (If not, select View from the Main menu, and specify Sales as the table to work with). Next, enter the Edit mode by pressing F9. Call up the Edit menu (F10), and select the ValCheck and Define options.

When Paradox asks you to select the field to validate, move the cursor to the Part No field and press Enter. You'll see the usual menu of Val-Check options. Select TableLookup. Paradox presents the prompt

> Table:Enter name of table to check values against,
> or press ◄─┘ for a list of tables.

Mastinv contains all the valid part numbers, so specify Mastinv as the look-up table. From the next menu to appear—

> JustCurrentField   AllCorrespondingFields

—select AllCorrespondingFields. (Since both Mastinv and Sales contain the Sel Price field, we might as well copy the selling price from the Mastinv table to the Sales table, which can only be done using the AllCorrespondingFields option.)

The next options to appear are

> FillNoHelp   HelpAndFill

There is no need to "hide" the Mastinv table from whoever is entering data in this example, so select the HelpAndFill option to provide both validation with help and automatic fill-in. When the process is done, press F2 to save the new ValCheck selections.

EXPERIMENTING WITH HELP AND FILL-IN

Now we can enter some sample data into the Sales table and experiment with the help and fill-in features we've added to this table. First, clear the screen clutter by pressing Clear All (Alt-F8). Then select View and specify the Sales table. Next, press Edit (F9) to begin entering data. The blank Sales table appears on the screen. Notice the message at the top of the screen:

> Press [F1] for help with fill-in

This prompt appears because we've assigned the HelpAndFill option to this field.

Testing the Table Look-up Validation

Enter the part number **K-456** into the Part No field, and press Enter. Since there is no corresponding value in the Mastinv table, the screen displays the error message

Not one of the possible values for this field.

Hence, the basic validation feature of the table look-up works fine—it rejects this invalid part number.

Testing the Table Look-up Help Feature

Now, let's get some help finding a *valid* part number. As instructed on the screen, press F1 to get some help. The Mastinv table appears on the screen, along with the prompt

Move to the record to be selected
Press [F2] to select the record; Esc to cancel; [F1] for help

Here is the basic help we've selected through our table look-up. By pressing F1, we've been presented with a list of parts in the Mastinv table, and we can now simply select a part number by positioning the cursor and pressing F2, as instructed on the screen. (Had we selected PrivateLookup rather than HelpAndFill under the TableLookup option, we would not have access to this table on the screen).

Now, just for the sake of exercise, suppose that the Mastinv table is very large, and we need to find the part number for a helmet. We can use the Zoom key, as with any other table. In this example, press → to move the cursor to the Part Name field, and type Ctrl-Z to start Zoom. When Paradox asks for a value to search for, enter **..Helmet..** and press Enter. The cursor drops to the first record with the word *Helmet* in the Part Name field. If this were not the correct record, you could use Zoom Next (Alt-Z) to find the next record with Helmet in the Part Name field. Now that we've located the proper record, let's try the automatic fill-in feature.

Testing the Automatic Fill-In

As the prompt at the top of the screen indicates, you can press F2 to select the current record. Note that the current record lists B-100 as the part number, and $30.00 as the selling price. Press F2 to select this record, and the Mastinv table will disappear from the screen. The Sales table appears on the screen with the part number B-100 in the Part no field, and $30.00 in the Sel Price field, as shown in Figure 12.17. (The image is in Form View, rather than Table View, in this example.)

Even though the Sel Price field is filled in automatically, you can still change it if you like when you move the cursor into that field. Use the usual Backspace key or Field View (Alt-F5) to do so.

As mentioned previously, when the Mastinv table is displayed on the screen to offer look-up help, it also displays the prompts

Move to the record to be selected
Press [F2] to select the record; Esc to cancel; [F1] for help

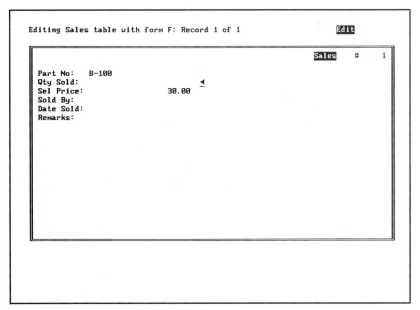

Figure 12.17: The Sel Price field automatically filled in from Mastinv table

As we have seen, pressing F2 copies data from the Mastinv table to the Part No and Sel Price fields on the Sales table. You can also press the F1 key to get additional help (the standard Paradox help screen). Optionally, you can press Esc to remove the Mastinv table image from the screen and return to the Sales table image without copying any data.

Take some time now to enter some more sample data into the Sales table to help with future examples. If you like, you can use Form View (F7) to enter records one at a time, rather than Table View. (The help and fill-in features will work the same in either view). Figure 12.18 shows some sample data that you can enter.

When done entering the sample data into the Sales table, save your work by pressing DO-IT! (F2). Then use Clear Image (F8) to clear the screen.

THE PURCHASE TABLE

Finally, we'll add another table for recording individual purchases (new stock) to the inventory system. Use the Create option from the Main menu to name the table Purchase, and give it the structure shown in Figure 12.19. Notice that once again, the Part No field is *not*

```
Editing Sales table: Record 12 of 12                        Edit

SALES═╤═Part No═╤═Qty Sold═╤═Sel Price═╤═Sold By═╤═Date Sold═╤═════════╤═Remarks═══
    1 ║ B-100  ║    1     ║    30.00  ║  JAK   ║  6/01/88  ║
    2 ║ C-551  ║    2     ║    67.50  ║  JAK   ║  6/01/88  ║
    3 ║ A-200  ║    1     ║   900.00  ║  JAK   ║  6/01/88  ║
    4 ║ C-559  ║    5     ║    22.50  ║  BBG   ║  6/05/88  ║
    5 ║ A-100  ║    5     ║   675.00  ║  BBG   ║  6/05/88  ║
    6 ║ B-112  ║    2     ║    22.50  ║  BBG   ║  6/05/88  ║
    7 ║ A-101  ║    1     ║   562.50  ║  JAK   ║  7/01/88  ║
    8 ║ B-111  ║    2     ║    60.00  ║  JAK   ║  7/01/88  ║
    9 ║ C-551  ║    1     ║    67.50  ║  JAK   ║  7/01/88  ║
   10 ║ A-100  ║    3     ║   675.00  ║  BBG   ║  7/15/88  ║
   11 ║ B-112  ║   -2     ║    22.50  ║  BBG   ║  8/01/88  ║ Return and Refund
   12 ║ A-100  ║    1     ║   675.00  ║  JAK   ║  8/01/88◀ ║
```

Figure 12.18: Sample data on the Sales tables

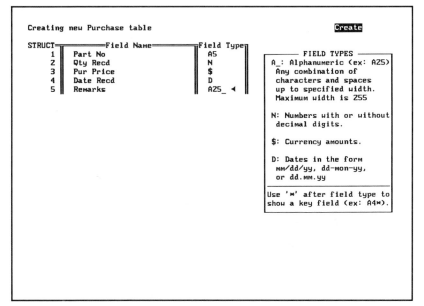

Figure 12.19: The structure of the inventory Purchase table

marked as a key field. Only the master file needs to reject duplicate part numbers. Press DO-IT! after entering the structure for the Purchase table.

Once again, we'll place a validity check on the Part No field. Call up the Main menu and select the Modify and Edit options, then specify the Purchase table. Call up the menu again and select the ValCheck and Define options. Specify the Part No field when requested. Select the TableLookup option and specify Mastinv as the table against which to validate part numbers. There is no need to use automatic fill-in on multiple fields in this example, so select JustCurrentField and HelpAndFill. Save the validity check by pressing DO-IT! when done.

Use Edit (F9) or the Modify and DataEntry options to add the data shown in Figure 12.20 to the Purchase table. Press DO-IT! when done entering data. Then press Clear (F8) to clear the screen.

Before we can really put the inventory system to work, we have to learn some specific techniques for managing numbers in a table, performing updates, querying multiple tables, and using advanced report techniques. These are the subjects of the next few chapters.

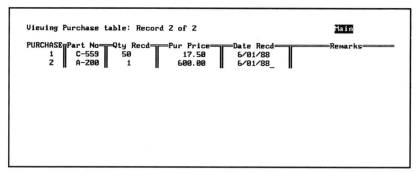

```
Viewing Purchase table: Record 2 of 2                        Main
PURCHASE Part No  Qty Recd   Pur Price   Date Recd             Remarks
    1    C-559    50          17.50      6/01/88
    2    A-200     1         600.00      6/01/88_
```

Figure 12.20: Sample data on the Purchase table

SUMMARY

- In larger business applications, data are usually stored in several separate tables. Multiple tables can save disk space by avoiding redundant data.

- Multiple tables allow easy access to both current and historical data, as in the example of master and transaction tables used in inventories.

- *Common fields* are used to relate data among multiple tables. Usually, the common field is a key field on one of the tables (for example, a customer-number or part-number field).

- A *key field* is one that contains a unique entry for each record in the table.

- To specify a key field in a table, mark it with an asterisk in the Field Type column when defining the structure.

- To validate entries in one table against values in another table, use the TableLookup option under the ValCheck menu.

- Only the first field in a table can be used as a look-up field.

- Any fields that have identical names in two related tables can be used for automatic fill-in.

ADVANCED QUERIES AND CALCULATIONS

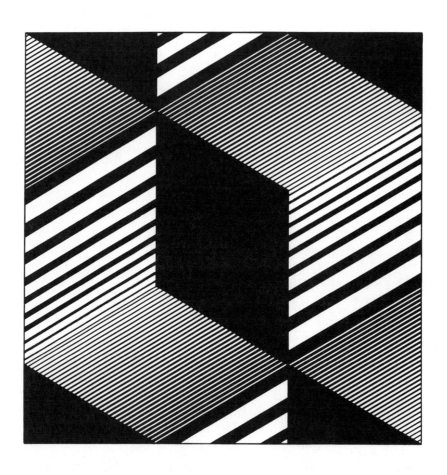

CHAPTER *13*

IN THIS CHAPTER WE'LL DISCUSS SOME MORE
advanced features of the Ask option, including querying multiple
tables and performing calculations. We'll use the inventory tables we
developed in the last chapter for our examples.

QUERYING MULTIPLE TABLES

When querying multiple tables, there are two points to keep in
mind:

1. You must fill out a query form for each table.

2. You must provide *examples* to link records from the two
   separate tables.

Other than these two items, the techniques for querying multiple
tables are the same as for querying a single table. Let's first work
through a somewhat simple example.

Suppose you wish to see the part number, quantity sold, and selling price for each item in the Sales table. To do so, you call up the
Main menu and select the Ask option. Specify the Sales table and
place check-plus symbols in the appropriate columns, as in the upper
part of Figure 13.1. (Remember, placing check-plus symbols by
pressing Alt-F6 displays duplicates, whereas placing check marks
alone (F6) does not.) When you press DO-IT!, Paradox shows the
appropriate data, as in the lower part of Figure 13.1.

Now suppose you also want to see the part names. Because these
are not stored on the Sales table, you'll have to get them from the
Mastinv table. To do so you'll first need to clear the Answer table

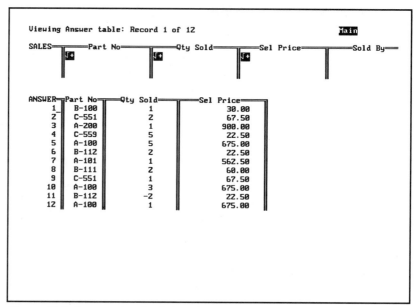

Figure 13.1: A query for the Sales table

(F8), then call up a query screen for the Mastinv table (press Menu (F10), select Ask, and specify the Mastinv table). Place a check mark in the Part Name field. Figure 13.2 shows how the screen looks with both query forms partially filled in (we're not ready to press DO-IT! yet, however).

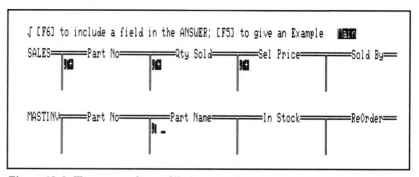

Figure 13.2: Two query forms filled out on the screen

ENTERING EXAMPLES

Now we need to find a way to tell Paradox that the two tables are linked by the Part No field. That is, when Paradox displays a sales transaction for part number A-100, we want to be sure it displays the appropriate part name from the Mastinv table. We define such a relationship with an *example*.

To enter an example, first move the cursor to the field on which the relationship is based. In this case, move the cursor to the Part No field of the Mastinv query form. Then press the Example (F5) key. Now you can type in any example that comes to mind. The actual content of the example is unimportant, because the example just acts as a place holder for performing comparisons. This time, type in **ABC** as the example, and press Enter. You'll notice that the example is highlighted, as in Figure 13.3.

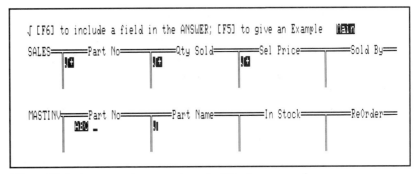

Figure 13.3: An example entered on the Mastinv query form

Now we need to enter the same example into the Part No field on the Sales query form. First, press Up Image (F3) to move the cursor up to the Sales query form. Then, with the cursor in the Part No field, press Example (F5) and type in the same example used in the Mastinv query form (ABC). Press Enter when done. Figure 13.4 shows how the two query forms look now, with examples in the Part No field of each query screen.

The query in Figure 13.4 tells Paradox to link the Mastinv and Sales tables by common Part No fields and to display the Part No,

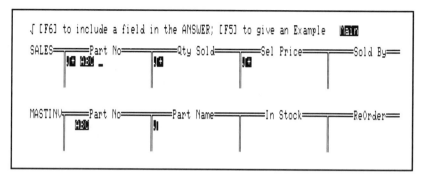

Figure 13.4: Examples in the Sales and Mastinv query forms

Part Name, Qty Sold, and Sel Price fields of these tables. Pressing DO-IT! performs the query and displays the result in the Answer table, as in Figure 13.5.

These are the important points to remember about examples:

- They are entered by first pressing the Example (F5) key.

- They must match exactly on the two query forms, telling Paradox to look for matching Part No fields when displaying data.

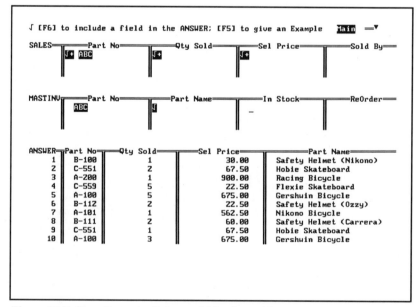

Figure 13.5: Data from the Sales and Mastinv tables

We could have used anything as the example—a single letter such as X, any number such as 9999, or a name such as Ronald. Again, the example only acts as a means of showing that we're looking for data that match between the two tables. Hence, had we used Ronald as the example on the Mastinv query form, we would have had to use Ronald as the example on the Sales query form as well. Keep in mind that examples may contain only letters and numbers. Punctuation marks and blank spaces cannot be used.

SEARCHES WITH MULTIPLE TABLES

Of course, you can perform all the usual types of searches with multiple tables. For example, to see only sales by salesperson JAK, fill in the Sales query form as you normally would for such a search. Once again, to view part names (available only on the Mastinv table), fill in a query form for the Mastinv table, and place a check mark in the Part Name field. Then place examples into the Part No fields on both the Mastinv and Sales query forms. (*Note:* The Up Image (F3) and Down Image (F4) keys let you move the cursor back and forth between query forms. Clear Image (F8) clears the Answer table or a query form from the screen, and Clear All (Alt-F8) clears everything from the screen.)

Figure 13.6 shows a query for all sales by salesperson JAK, with a check mark in the Part Name field of the Mastinv table and identical examples linking the two tables via the Part No field. The top query displays records from the Sales table that have JAK as the salesperson, and the bottom query adds part names to the display, based on matching part numbers in the two tables.

Let's try another query, phrasing it in English first. We want to tell Paradox to show the part number, date, part name, and purchase price of all items sold between July 1 and July 15. Let's take it one step at a time. First of all, the ''all items sold'' portion of the request immediately refers to the Sales table. The part name and purchase price data, however, are on the Mastinv table. So the first thing you need to do is call up query forms for the Sales and Mastinv tables. Then, for the ''show the part number, date, part name, and purchase price'' portion of the request, place check marks as in Figure 13.7. (Note that I've used the Rotate key to rearrange the columns.)

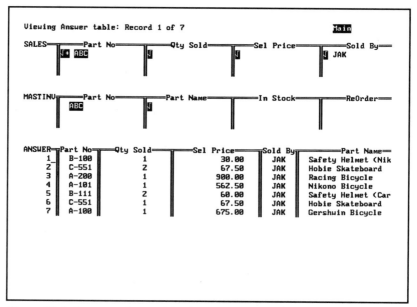

Figure 13.6: A query of two tables for sales by salesperson JAK

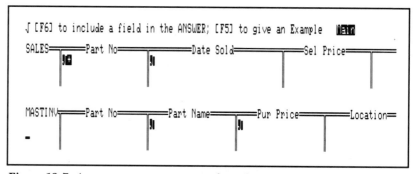

Figure 13.7: A request to see part number, date, part name, and purchase price

Now, for the "all items sold between July 1 and July 15" portion of the query, we need to fill in the appropriate search formula, as in Figure 13.8.

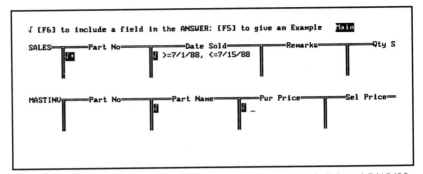

Figure 13.8: The query narrowed to items sold between 7/1/88 and 7/15/88

So far, so good. But now we need an example to link the two tables. Of course, this will be in the Part No field (since this is the only field that links the two tables). Put examples into the Part No field of each query form (don't forget to press F5 first), as shown in the upper portion of Figure 13.9. Press DO-IT!, and you'll see the results shown in the lower portion of the figure.

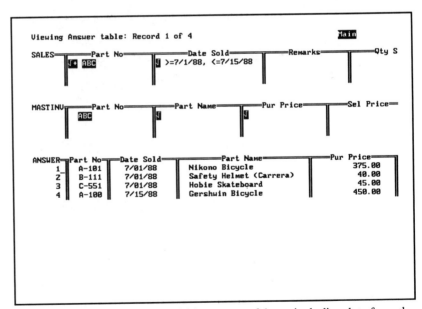

Figure 13.9: A query for sales within a range of dates, including data from the Mastinv table

AND *AND* OR *QUERIES*
WITH MULTIPLE TABLES

AND and OR queries with multiple tables are similar to AND and OR queries with a single table. For an AND query, place the search conditions on the same line. For instance, to display all sales of part number A-100 by salesman BBG, place the search criteria on the same line of the Sales query form. To pull in the part name from the Mastinv table, simply enter an example in each of the two Part No fields and check the Part Name field on the Mastinv query form, as shown in Figure 13.10.

Suppose you want to show sales for part numbers A-100, A-101, and A-200, and you want to use the Part Name and Pur Price fields from the Mastinv table. Well, you can set up the usual OR condition, as shown in the upper part of Figure 13.11. Notice that by placing the three requests on separate lines, you've specified that you want to see records that have either part number A-100, *or* part number A-101, *or* part number A-200.

Note that there are actually three distinct part numbers specified in the query form for the Sales table: A-100, A-101, and A-200. Each

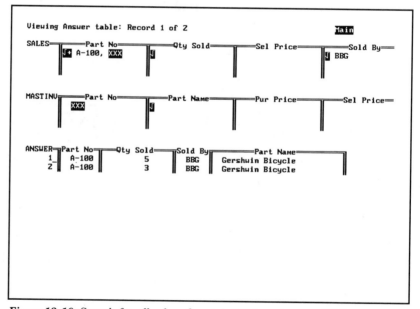

Figure 13.10: Search for all sales of part A-100 by salesman BBG

of these has its own unique part name stored in the Mastinv table. To keep Paradox from becoming "confused" about which part name belongs to which part number, each part number in the Sales query form is assigned a unique example. (e.g. A-100 uses the example ABC, A-101 uses XYZ, and A-200 uses 123). In the Mastinv table, all three examples are listed in the Part No field as well, and each example has a corresponding check mark in the Part Name field.

In English, we could interpret the query (shown in Figure 13.11) as follows: "Display those Part No and Qty Sold fields from the Sales table that have A-100 in the Part No field, and display the corresponding Part Name from the Mastinv table. Also display those Part No and Qty Sold fields from the Sales table that have A-101 in the Part No field, and display the corresponding Part Name from the Mastinv table. Also display those Part No and Qty Sold fields from the Sales table that have A-200 in the Part No field, and display the corresponding Part Name from the Mastinv table."

Note that the check-plus mark is used to ensure that duplicate records from the Sales table are displayed. Furthermore, note that the value to look up (for example, A-100) is separated from the

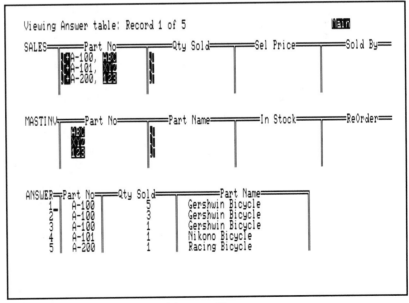

Figure 13.11: An OR query with two tables

example (ABC) by a comma. You must always separate an example from a search value in a single field with a comma, as shown.

Incidentally, since part numbers A-100, A-101, and A-200 represent all part numbers in the inventory tables beginning with the letter A, you could have entered this query as shown in Figure 13.12 and received the same results.

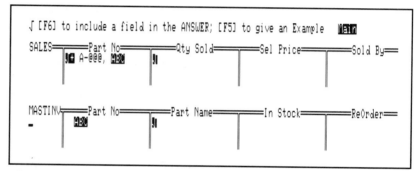

Figure 13.12: A query for part numbers starting with A-

USING EXAMPLES
TO FIND COMMON ELEMENTS

You can use examples in an OR query to find records that have some element in common. To do so, you need to stack identical examples next to each *or* condition. The example used in Figure 13.13 shows this operation.

Notice that the basic query, without the examples, asks for records that have either JAK or BBG in the Sold By field. The identical ABC examples in the Part No field add a condition which can be interpreted as "where Part Numbers are identical." The Answer table for this query is shown at the bottom of the screen in Figure 13.13.

We can interpret the result of the query as follows: "Only part number A-100 has been sold by both JAK and BBG." These two salespersons have no other part numbers in common. Notice that a couple of the field names in the Answer table are numbered. The Part No and Sold By field names refer to the first row in the query form—salesperson JAK. Part No-1 and Sold By-1 refer to the next row in the query form—salesperson BBG.

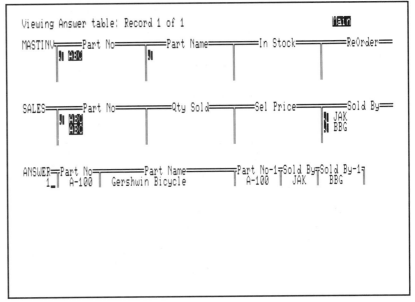

Figure 13.13: Matching examples in an OR query

USING QUERIES
TO CALCULATE RESULTS

To perform calculations, you can use the following arithmetic operators in your query forms:

OPERATOR	FUNCTION
+	Addition
−	Subtraction
*	Multiplication
/	Division
( )	Used for grouping

We've seen how to use arithmetic operators in queries before. For instance, if today's date were 9/1/88 and you performed the query shown in Figure 13.14, you'd see records with dates less than (earlier than) today's date minus 90 days (that is, transactions that are over 90 days old).

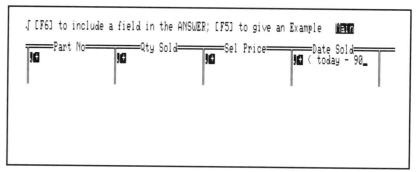

Figure 13.14: A query for transactions more than 90 days old

With the addition of the *Calc* option and examples, you can per-form more interesting calculations, such as sums, averages, fre-quency distributions, projections, and more. The Calc option can be used with the sum, average, max, min, and count operators listed in Table 13.1.

In its simplest form, the Calc option will calculate data on all records of a field. For example, the query in Figure 13.15 requests a sum of the Qty Sold field and returns the answer 22.

Had we used the Calc average option rather than Calc sum in the query form, Paradox would have displayed 1.83, the average of all the Qty Sold values. The query Calc max would display 5, the high-est value in the Qty Sold field. Calc min would have displayed − 2,

CALC OPERATOR	CALCULATES	WITH FIELD TYPES
sum	Total of values	N, $, S
average	Average of values	N, $, S, D
max	Highest value	A, N, $, S, D
min	Lowest value	A, N, $, S, D
count	Number of values	A, N, $, S, D

Table 13.1: Operators used with the Calc option

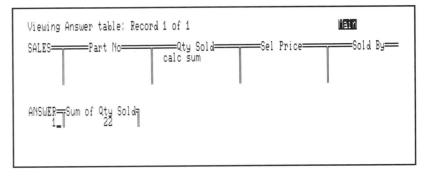

Figure 13.15: The sum of values in the Qty Sold field

the smallest value, and Calc count would have displayed 5, indicating that there are 5 different values in the Qty Sold field. (The request Calc count all would have displayed 12, the total number of records in the table.)

CALCULATIONS ON GROUPS OF RECORDS

Using check marks in fields of interest has a different effect on calculations than on normal queries. A checked field in the query form with a Calc option indicates a group of records on which to perform a calculation. For example, look at the query form in Figure 13.16. The check mark in the Part No field indicates that calculations should be based on groups of like part numbers. Calc sum in the Qty Sold field indicates that the sums should be calculated on this field for each unique part number. The results are shown in the Answer table.

The query in Figure 13.17 requests the sum of the quantity sold for each salesperson. In this instance, the Sold By field is checked for totaling, and the Calc sum operator is placed (as before) in the Qty Sold field.

Checking multiple fields in a Calc query will create even more groups. For example, in Figure 13.18, both the Part No and Sold By fields are checked. Calc sum again appears in the Qty Sold field. The end result is the quantity of each item sold by each salesperson.

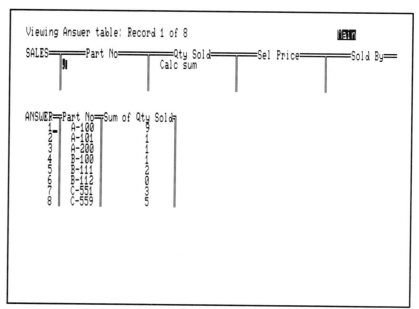

Figure 13.16: The sum of the Qty Sold field for each part number

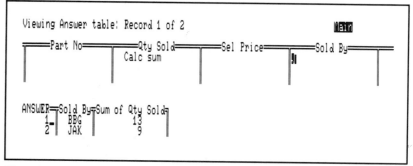

Figure 13.17: The sum of quantities for each salesperson

FREQUENCY DISTRIBUTIONS

The *Calc count all* operator combined with a checked field (or fields) provides a quick and easy frequency distribution. For example, suppose you select Ask and specify Custlist as the table to query. Then you place a check mark in the State field, along with the Calc count all operator, and you'll get a display counting the number of individuals residing in each state, as in Figure 13.19.

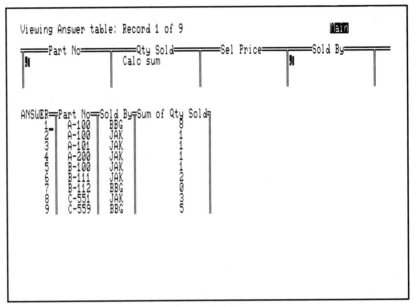

Figure 13.18: Sales of each part by each salesperson

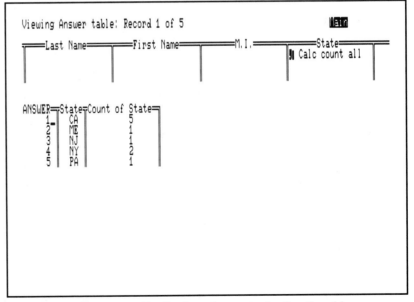

Figure 13.19: Frequency distribution of states in the Custlist table

CALCULATIONS WITH EXAMPLES

Using examples with calculations allows you to display the results of calculations of two or more fields, add a constant to a field, or project "what-if" situations. For instance, the Sales table has a field for quantity sold and a field for selling price. The actual dollar amount for the transaction, however, is the quantity sold times the selling price.

To calculate the actual dollar value of each transaction, you could set up a query screen for the Sales table as in Figure 13.20. Note that Qty and Price are *examples* of data found in the Qty Sold and Sel Price field. Next to the Price example (followed by a comma) is the instruction to multiply the quantity by the price. When Calc is used in this fashion, it will display the results of the calculation as a separate field, as shown in the Answer table in Figure 13.20.

If all the items in this table were taxable, you could add sales tax by multiplying the product of Qty times Price by 1.06 (assuming a 6 percent sales tax). Figure 13.21 shows such a calculation using the formula

(Qty * Price) * 1.06

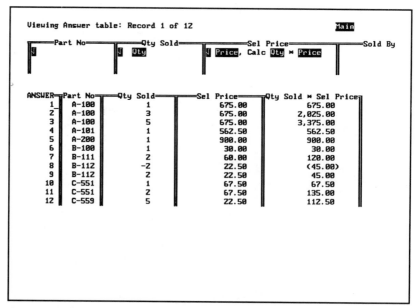

Figure 13.20: The total sales price calculated using examples

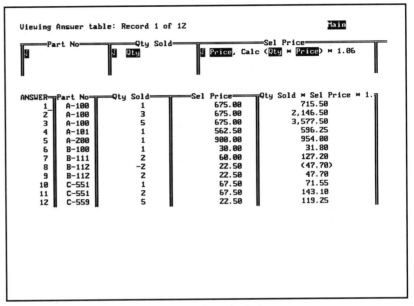

Figure 13.21: Sales tax included in sales calculations

You could display the total sales both with and without taxes by using two separate Calc instructions, as in Figure 13.22. Note that each Calc instruction is separated by a comma, and each displays its results in a separate new field.

When using examples, you can place the Calc instruction in any field. Because Calc will create a new field, it does not matter where you place it in the query form. Figure 13.23 shows calculations of the Qty Sold and Sel Price fields, with the Calc instruction arbitrarily placed in the Date Sold field. It is the examples that determine what will be calculated, not the location of the Calc instruction on the query form.

PERFORMING QUERIES IN A MANY-TO-MANY DESIGN

Back in Chapter 12, we discussed the *many-to-many* relationship, using the examples of students and courses, joined by a linking table, and an exploded inventory database, where products and components were joined by an example. It is quite easy to perform queries

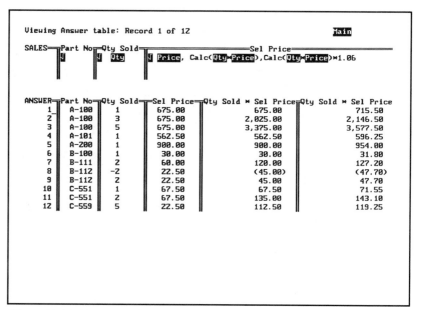

Figure 13.22: Two calculations in a field

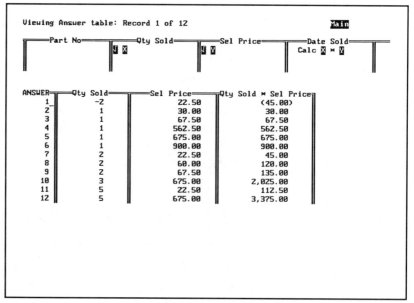

Figure 13.23: A calculation of quantity times selling price

on tables related in such a manner. To display data from all three tables, use one example to relate the linking table to one of the tables, and another example to relate the linking table to the other table. An example will demonstrate.

Figure 13.24 shows a sample query that will display a list of all students, with the names of the courses that they are enrolled in. Note that the example 9999 links the Students table to the SCLink table, and the example XXXXX links the Courses table to the SCLink table. Check marks in the fields specify which fields to display in the answer table. Figure 13.25 shows the results of the query in the Answer table.

As you can see in Figure 13.25, the Answer table lists every course that each student is enrolled in. The data are automatically placed in sorted order because of key field definitions placed in the StudentID field when the table was created (as discussed in Chapter 12). Of course, if you perform such a query without the use of key fields, you can still sort the Answer table using the usual Modify and Sort option from the Paradox Main menu.

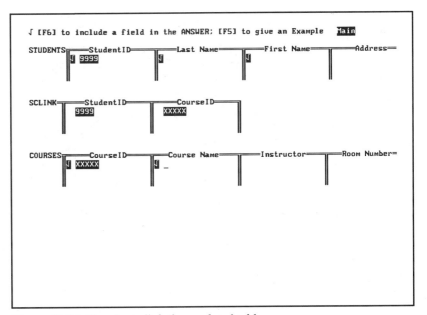

Figure 13.24: Queries to link three related tables

```
Viewing Answer table: Record 1 of 7                          Main
ANSWER═══StudentID═════════Last Name══════╦First Name╦CourseID╦═══════Course Name═
     1║  1001          Adams            ║  Andy  ║ A-111 ║ Algebra
     2║  1001          Adams            ║  Andy  ║ C-333 ║ Chemistry
     3║  1002          Black            ║  Sandra║ A-111 ║ Algebra
     4║  1002          Black            ║  Sandra║ B-222 ║ Botany
     5║  1002          Black            ║  Sandra║ C-333 ║ Chemistry
     6║  1003          Carlson          ║  Carla ║ B-222 ║ Botany
     7║  1003          Carlson          ║  Carla ║ C-333 ║ Chemistry
```

Figure 13.25: The results of the query shown in Figure 13.24

To look at the students and courses data from a different angle, listing courses with the names of the students enrolled in each course, place the Courses query form at the top and the Students query form at the bottom, and use the same technique of examples and check marks to define the relationships and the fields to display. Figure 13.26 shows an example query. Figure 13.27 shows the results of the query, wherein courses are listed in order, with students enrolled in each.

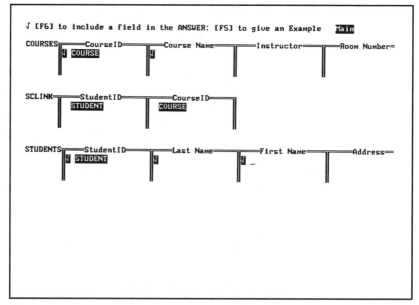

Figure 13.26: Another query for students and courses

```
┌─────────────────────────────────────────────────────────────┐
│  Viewing Answer table: Record 1 of 7                    Main │
│                                                              │
│  ANSWER═╤CourseID╤═Course Name═╤═StudentID═╤══Last Name══╤══First Name══╗ │
│      1  │  A-111 │  Algebra    │  1001     │  Adams      │  Andy        │ │
│      2  │  A-111 │  Algebra    │  1002     │  Black      │  Sandra      │ │
│      3  │  B-222 │  Botany     │  1002     │  Black      │  Sandra      │ │
│      4  │  B-222 │  Botany     │  1003     │  Carlson    │  Carla       │ │
│      5  │  C-333 │  Chemistry  │  1001     │  Adams      │  Andy        │ │
│      6  │  C-333 │  Chemistry  │  1002     │  Black      │  Sandra      │ │
│      7  │  C-333 │  Chemistry  │  1003     │  Carlson    │  Carla       │ │
│                                                              │
│                                                              │
│                                                              │
└─────────────────────────────────────────────────────────────┘
```

Figure 13.27: The results of the query shown in Figure 13.26

Again, the fact that the CourseID field in the Courses table is keyed (as discussed in Chapter 12) allows an automatic sort of the data in the Answer table into course-number order.

CALCULATIONS IN A MANY-TO-MANY DESIGN

Chapter 12 presented the basic model for an "exploded inventory" database, where a manufacturer keeps many different components in stock and produces several different products. The many-to-many relationship is based on the fact that each product manufactured consists of many components, and each component is used in many different products.

Suppose the user of this database wanted to know how many of each component is necessary to build 50 of product number A-123. The query shown in Figure 13.28 displays the answer. The top query, based on the Linker table, limits calculations to part number A-123. The CCCCCCC example links the component number in the Linker table to the Componen table, and check marks assure that the appropriate fields are displayed. The Y example holds the Qty Used value to aid in the calculation. The formula Calc Y * 50 multiplies the quantity required to produce the product by 50—the quantity to manufacture in this example.

As the Answer table in Figure 13.28 shows, the manufacturer would need 50 of component numbers TT-1234 and VV-1234 and 100 each of components YY-1234 and ZZ-1234 to manufacture 50

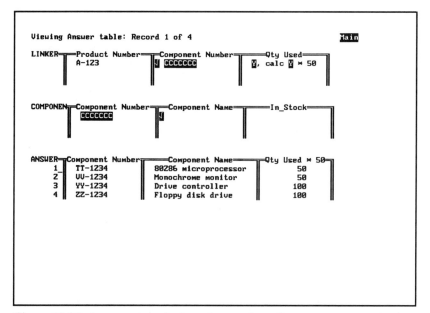

Figure 13.28: A query to calculate the number of components required to manufacture 50 of product A-123

personal computers (product number A-123). To calculate components needed for a different product, change the A-123 condition to the appropriate product name. To change the quantity of products being produced, change the 50 in the calculation to the number of products you wish to produce.

The simple query above is useful for calculating the number of components required to produce a single product. But suppose you wish to make a more "global" calculation to determine the number of each component required to manufacture several of each product? Such a calculation would require several steps.

First, you'd need to fill the Needed field on the Product table with the number of each product you wish to produce. Figure 13.29 shows an example in which the manufacturer wishes to produce 100 personal computers, 50 minicomputers, and 20 mainframe computers.

Next, you'll need to create a temporary table that holds all of the fields required to perform the calculation. Figure 13.30 shows just such a query. The top query, based on the Linker table, calculates the number of each component required to produce each product by

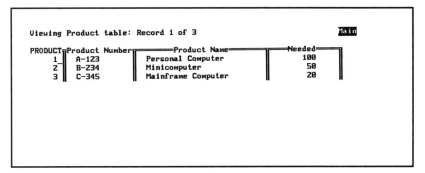

Figure 13.29: The Needed field filled in the Product table

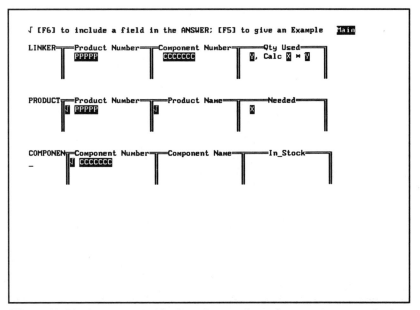

Figure 13.30: A query to calculate the number of components required to manufacture several products

multiplying the Qty Used field by the number of each item needed. (Y is the query example for the quantity of each component required, and X is the query example for the number of each product being manufactured.) The PPPPP example links the PC Link table to the Product table, and the CCCCCCC example links the Linker table to the Componen table. Check marks ensure that the appropriate fields will be displayed in the Answer table.

Figure 13.31 displays the Answer table that the query in Figure 13.30 produces. While the Answer table contains the appropriate data, it needs to be summarized a bit to be of real use.

To see the data in the Answer table in a better light, you'll want totals based on individual component numbers. To create such a table, copy the Answer table to a new table and use Calc sum to calculate the totals. In this example, you can copy the Answer table to a new table named Joined using the Main menu options Tools, Copy, Table. Specify Answer as the table to copy, and Joined as the name of the table to copy to. (If a table named Joined already exists, select Replace to replace its contents with the contents of the Answer table.)

Next, clear the screen to make some room (type Alt-F8), and select Ask from the Main menu. Specify Joined as the table to query, place a check mark in the Component number field (as this is the field we wish to group by), and Calc sum in the Needed * Qty Used field.

```
Viewing Answer table: Record 1 of 13                        Main

ANSWER┬─Product Number┬─────Product Name─────┬─Component Number┬Needed × Qty Used┬
    1 ║ A-123          ║ Personal  Computer    ║ TT-1234_         ║      100        ║
    2 ║ A-123          ║ Personal  Computer    ║ UU-1234          ║      100        ║
    3 ║ A-123          ║ Personal  Computer    ║ YY-1234          ║      200        ║
    4 ║ A-123          ║ Personal  Computer    ║ ZZ-1234          ║      200        ║
    5 ║ B-234          ║ Minicomputer          ║ TT-1234          ║       50        ║
    6 ║ B-234          ║ Minicomputer          ║ UU-1234          ║       50        ║
    7 ║ B-234          ║ Minicomputer          ║ YY-1234          ║      100        ║
    8 ║ B-234          ║ Minicomputer          ║ ZZ-1234          ║      100        ║
    9 ║ C-345          ║ Mainframe Computer    ║ TT-1234          ║       20        ║
   10 ║ C-345          ║ Mainframe Computer    ║ UU-1234          ║       20        ║
   11 ║ C-345          ║ Mainframe Computer    ║ UU-1234          ║       20        ║
   12 ║ C-345          ║ Mainframe Computer    ║ YY-1234          ║       20        ║
   13 ║ C-345          ║ Mainframe Computer    ║ ZZ-1234          ║       20        ║
```

Figure 13.31: The answer table produced by the query in Figure 13.30

Press F2, and the Answer table will display the results, as shown in Figure 13.32.

As the table shows, the manufacturer would need 170 of part number TT-1234 to produce the number of products specified in the Product table (Figure 13.29). You'll need 70 of part number UU-1234, and so forth.

This example shows how you can actually break a query into several steps to perform more complex tasks. Notice the basic steps we used. First, we created an Answer table containing the basic information we need, using one query. Then, we copied the Answer table to a new table, and performed a query on that new table. With a little practice, you should be able to perform similar complex queries of your own.

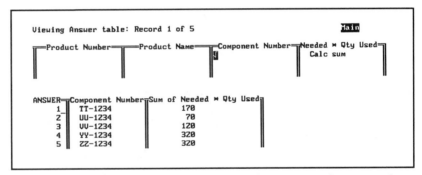

Figure 13.32: The totals of components required to manufacture products listed in Figure 13.29

HANDLING BLANKS IN QUERY CALCULATIONS

When you begin developing queries with more complex calculations, you may be alarmed to find that Paradox does not treat a blank field as zero. Instead, a calculation such as Calc X + Y + Z will display a blank if any of the fields referenced contains a blank (even if the other two fields contain numbers). No need to panic over this.

You can use the Paradox Custom Configuration program to reconfigure Paradox to treat empty fields as zeros when performing calculations. See Chapter 16 of the *Paradox User's Guide* for details.

SAVING QUERIES

As we've seen in this chapter, some queries can become quite complex, especially those involving two or more tables. (Even though we've used a maximum of three tables in our examples, Paradox can simultaneously query as many related tables as you wish.) To save yourself the trouble of retyping a query each time you want to use it, you can save a query for future use.

To do so, build the complete query on the screen in the usual manner, and test it (using the F2 key). If the query produces the results you want, press F8 to clear the Answer table, then save the query by calling up the Main menu (F10), and selecting the Scripts and QuerySave options. You'll be given the prompt

Query script name:
Enter name to be given to new query script.

Enter a name for the script (eight letters maximum, no spaces or punctuation), and press Enter.

To use the query in the future, you'll probably want to first clear the screen (Alt-F8), then select Scripts and Play from the main menu. You'll see the prompt

Move to the record to be selected
Press [F2] to select the record; Esc to cancel; [F1] for help

Type in the name of the saved query, or press Enter to see a list of saved queries (and scripts) and select the query name by highlighting and pressing Enter in the usual fashion.

The query will appear on the screen, in exactly the format you saved it. You can then press F2 to perform the query, or use the usual arrow keys to modify the query if you wish.

If the query actually involves several steps, as in the example of the exploded-inventory calculation above, you can store all the keystrokes needed to produce the query rather than the queries themselves. To do so, press Instant Script Record (Alt-F3), press Clear All (Alt-F8), and then type all the keystrokes necessary to perform the entire query. When you are done, press Alt-F3 again to stop recording keystrokes.

Paradox will save the script under the name Instant. To assign a more descriptive name to the script, call up the Main menu and select the Tools, Rename, and Script options. Enter Instant as the name of the script to rename, and enter a new name for the script (as usual, eight letters maximum length, no spaces or punctuation).

To perform the query steps at a later moment, call up the menu and select Scripts and either Play or ShowPlay. Enter the name of the script and press Return as usual. All of the necessary steps to perform the query will take place on the screen.

QUERY SPEED-UP

Large queries that do not use key fields can sometimes take a long time to complete. The QuerySpeedup option under the Tools menu can help speed up most queries. See the section "Speeding Up Queries" in Chapter 16 for more information on this option.

SUMMARY

- To link multiple tables in a query, you enter *examples* of matching data in the field that links the two tables.

- To enter an example on a query form, first press the Example (F5) key, then type in an example.

- To display fields from two tables, just place check-mark or check-plus symbols in the appropriate fields of the query forms, and use an example to relate the two tables.

- To perform calculations on numeric fields, you can use the Calc command with the average, sum, max, min, or count operators.

- To calculate subtotals of unique items in a field, use a check mark with the Calc sum command.

- To determine frequency distributions, use the Calc count all command.

- To display a new field based on the calculations of two or more existing fields, use examples to define fields in the calculation, and place the fields in a formula.

- To break complex queries into several steps, perform a part of the overall query; then query the resulting Answer table.

ADVANCED REPORT
AND FORM TECHNIQUES

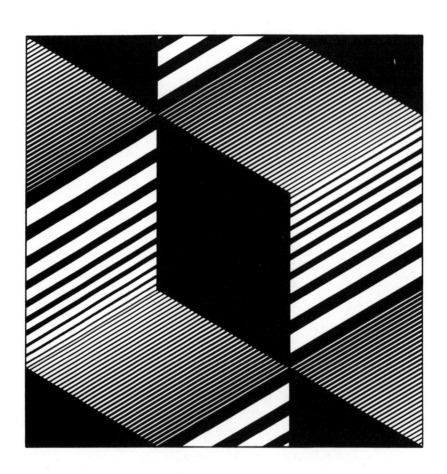

CHAPTER 14 _____

THIS CHAPTER DISCUSSES ADVANCED TECHNIQUES
that you can use to create custom reports and forms. The more
advanced report techniques we'll discuss include tabular reports;
totals, subtotals, and grouping; calculated fields; and techniques for
printing reports using data from multiple tables. Advanced techniques for forms include forms that access multiple tables, multiple-
page forms, and calculated fields.

   To begin with, we'll take a look at some of the basic options available for tabular reports. We'll assume that you are already adept at
selecting menu items and moving the cursor at this point. Rather
than spend time demonstrating all of these techniques with hands-on
examples, we'll present the tabular-report capabilities in a more general form, which you should be able to incorporate into your own
reports with a little practice.

──── TABULAR REPORTS ────────

   As you may recall from Chapter 8, when you select the Report
option from the Main menu, one of the submenus that appears
presents the options

   Tabular Free-form

When you select Free-form, Paradox displays a suggested free-form
report format on the screen. Similarly, the Tabular option presents
a suggested tabular report format on the screen. Figure 14.1 shows
the suggested report format that Paradox would display for a tabular
report of the Sales table.

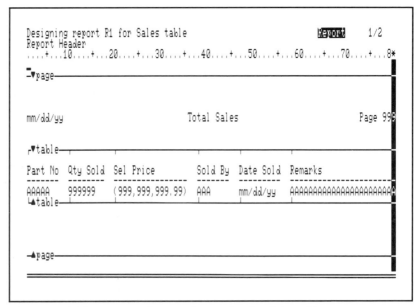

Figure 14.1: The suggested report format for the Sales table

Looking at the sample tabular report format in Figure 14.1, you can see that the field names and column titles are enclosed within the *table band*. (The word *table* appears on the line marking the table band, next to the upward and downward pointing triangles.) Generally speaking, the fields within the table band are printed once for each record in the table. The column titles and underlines are printed at the top of each page.

THE TABULAR REPORT MENU

When designing a tabular report, you can press Menu (F10) at any time to call up the Report menu. Doing so will present the options

Field   TableBand   Group   Output   Setting   Help   DO-IT!
Cancel

These options can be summarized as follows:

Field   Places, deletes, or formats a field on the report

TableBand   Copies, resizes, deletes, or inserts a field

Group	Specifies groups, either for general format or for subtotals
Output	Prints the report
Setting	Formats the printed page, prints single sheets, and specifies printer-setup strings.
Help	Provides help while formatting the report
DO-IT!	Saves the current report format
Cancel	Abandons the current report format

The Help, DO-IT!, and Cancel options above should all be obvious to you by now. The other options need some additional explanation.

MANAGING REPORT COLUMNS

One of the first steps in formatting a tabular report will probably be to get the report columns formatted to your liking. Options for managing the individual columns are available in the TableBand menu. The following sections briefly discuss these basic options. Each is very easy to use, and when you use them, you'll be given simple instructions on the screen to help you out.

INSERTING COLUMNS

To insert a new column into the report, call up the menu, select TableBand, and then select Insert. The screen will ask that you

USE ↑ ↓ → ← to show where the new column should be placed...
then press ◄─┘ to insert it.

Move the cursor to the report column to the right of the position where you want the new report column to appear. When you press Enter, Paradox will attempt to insert a new, empty, report column to the left of the cursor position. If there is not enough room in the report format for the new column, an error message will tell you so. You can make more room by deleting another report column (using the TableBand and Erase options from the menu), resizing a different column (using the TableBand and Resize menu options), or increasing the width of the printed report (using the Setting and PageLayout options).

Once inserted, the new report column will be 15 characters wide. You can define a field for the column using the Field and Place menu options. You can also resize the column using the TableBand and Resize menu options.

ERASING COLUMNS

To remove a column from the report format, select Tableband from the report menu, and Erase from the submenu. When you do so, Paradox will instruct you to move the cursor to the column to erase and then press Enter. (To change your mind, and not erase any columns, press Esc.)

When you press Enter, the column, its heading, and the underline under the heading will disappear. All columns to the right will shift to the left to fill in the gap left by the erased column.

RESIZING COLUMNS

To expand or contract the width of a report column, select the Resize option from the TableBand menu. As instructed, move the cursor to the column you want to resize. If you plan to shrink the column width, be sure to place the cursor on the same line as the field template (for example, the AAA or 999 or mm/dd/yy portion of the table band), either to the left or right of the template. That way, you won't erase anything as you narrow the column width. If you plan to expand the column width, you can place the cursor in the field template, within the underline, or in the column heading.

After positioning the cursor, press Enter. The screen displays the instructions

> Now use ← to contract the column, → to expand it...
> press ←┘ when finished.

Use the arrow keys to widen or narrow the column, then press Enter when done.

Note that you can expand the width of a column only as far as the margins in the report allow. If you do not have enough room to widen the column to your liking, make more room by either deleting another report column (using the TableBand and Erase options from the menu), resizing a different column (using the TableBand and Resize menu options), or by increasing the width of the printed report (using the Setting and PageLayout options).

If you make a numeric field too narrow to display the values in that field, the numbers will appear as asterisks in the printed report. If that happens, use the Report and Change options to bring the report format back onto the screen. Then select the TableBand and Resize options once again, and widen the field as necessary. Press F2 to save the new report format.

MOVING COLUMNS

There are two ways to move columns on the report format. If you simply want to rotate the fields, use the Rotate (Ctrl-R) key. This key works in the same fashion on the table band as it does on table images on the screen.

A second technique for moving a column is to select the Move option on the TableBand menu. When you select Move, the screen displays the instructions

> Use ↑ ↓ → ← to indicate the column to be moved...
> then press ← to select it.

Move the cursor into the report column that you wish to move, then press Enter. Next, the screen asks that you

> Now use → and ← to show the new location for the column...
> press ← to move it.

Move the cursor to the new location for the column, and press Enter. The column will move to the new location, and all other columns will shift accordingly to make room.

COPYING COLUMNS

If you want a column to appear in more than one place on the report, use the TableBand and Copy options from the Report menu to copy the column. When you select TableBand and Copy from the menu, the screen will ask that you

> Use ↑ ↓ → ← to indicate the column to be copied...
> then press ←┘ to select it.

Move the cursor to within the report column to be copied, then press Enter. The screen then asks that you

> Now use → and ← to show the location for the copy...
> press ←┘ to place it.

Move the cursor to the right of the position that you want to place the copy, and press Enter. The copy will appear to the left of the cursor position, and all other fields will shift to make room for the copy. As mentioned in the discussion of moving columns above, you can resize or erase another field, if necessary, to make room for the new column. Optionally, you can change the report width to make room for the copy.

MANAGING FIELDS

In tabular reports, you have at your disposal many options for placing and formatting report columns. All of these options appear under the Field option on the Report menu. When you select Field, the following submenu appears on the screen:

> Place   Erase   Reformat   Justify   CalcEdit   WordWrap

These options can be summarized as follows:

OPTION	*FUNCTION*
Place	Adds a new field to the report format
Erase	Removes a field from the report format
Reformat	Formats the field display
Justify	Aligns the data within the report column
WordWrap	Wraps long alphanumeric fields within a report column

These options are discussed in more detail in the sections that follow.

GENERAL TECHNIQUES FOR PLACING AND FORMATTING FIELDS

When you select Place from the Field menu, the following submenu is displayed on the screen:

Regular Summary Calculated Date Time Page
#Record

These options can be summarized as follows:

OPTION	FUNCTION
Regular	Places a field from the table on the report
Summary	Places a subtotal, total, average, count, lowest value, or highest value calculation on the report
Calculated	Calculates and displays the results of arithmetic operations on two or more fields
Date	Places the current date on the report
Time	Places the current time on the report
Page	Places the current page number on the report
#Record	Places the record number on the report

Each of these options uses the same general techniques for placing and formatting the field. Once you determine what you want to place on the report, the screen will display the instructions

Use ↑ ↓ → ← to indicate where the field should begin...
then press ⏎ to place it.

Use the arrow keys to move the cursor to the exact location where you want the field to appear. (If the field is to appear as a report column, you would need to use the TableBand and Insert options first to create a new, empty column for the field.)

You can place a field anywhere on the report format. How and when it is displayed on the printed report will be determined by its position within the various report bands, as discussed later. For now, suffice it to say that you may move the cursor to any position on the report format, and press Enter to place the field. When you press Enter, the field template will appear to the right of the cursor (assuming there is enough room for the field).

If there is not enough room to place the field where you want it, Paradox will present a warning message. You can either move the cursor to a new position to place the field or press Esc to cancel the field placement.

If you cancel the operation, you may be able to move things around on the report format to make more room. For example, you can use the Insert option under the TableBand menu to insert a new field, and the Resize option to widen that field. You can use the Erase or Resize option under the TableBand menu to resize or erase an existing field. You can also erase or move any literals (such as headings) that might be in the way, to make more room for the field.

Once you do get the field placed on the report, the screen will ask you to format the field. The way you format the field will depend on the data type of that field, as discussed below.

Formatting Alphanumeric Fields

If you've just placed an alphanumeric field on the report, the field template (or *mask*, as it is also called) will appear as a row of A's, which match the width of the field. The screen will display the prompt

**Now use → and ← to indicate how many characters to show...
press ◄┘ when finished.**

To make the field narrower, press the ← key as many times as necessary. To widen the field, use the → key. (Note, however, that you cannot widen the field beyond its width in the table.) Press Enter after selecting the appropriate width for the field.

Formatting Date Fields

If you are attempting to place a Date field on the report format, the screen will display a menu of date formats before placing the field.

These formats, along with sample dates, are listed below:

DATE FORMAT	EXAMPLE
1) mm/dd/yy	12/1/88
2) M o n t h dd, yy	December 1, 1988
3) mm/dd	12/01
4) mm/yy	12/88
5) dd-Mon-yy	1-Dec-88
6) Mon yy	Dec 88
7) dd-Mon-yyyy	1-Dec-1988
8) mm/dd/yyyy	12/01/1988
9) dd.mm.yy	12.01.88
10) dd/mm/yy	12/01/88
11) yy-mm-dd	88-12-01

Select a date format from the menu, and press Enter. The field mask will then appear on the report format.

Formatting Numeric Fields

If the field you've placed on the report is numeric or currency, the field mask will appear on the screen as a series of nines separated by commas (for example, 999,999,999,999). The screen will display the instructions

> Now use → and ← to adjust the number of whole digits to show...
> press ⏎ to set the number of digits.

Use the ← key to narrow the number display or → to widen it. Press Enter when done, and the screen will display the instructions

> Use the → and ← keys to adjust the number of decimal places...
> then press ⏎ to set the number of decimals.

Pressing → increases the number of digits displayed to the right of the decimal point, while pressing ← decreases the number of digits in the decimal portion. Press Enter after setting the number of decimal places you would like.

The maximum width of a numeric field is 12 whole digits, or 20 digits if decimal places are used. Once the field is placed and sized, you can use the Reformat option under the Field menu to reformat the number according to a variety of international standards.

PLACING REGULAR FIELDS

A *regular field* is any field that is stored in the table for which you are developing the report. When you select the Regular option from the Place menu, the screen displays a menu of field names on the current table. As usual, to select a field, just move the highlight to that field and press Enter. Once you've selected the field, place it on the report and format it using the general techniques discussed above.

Remember, you can place a regular field anywhere on the report. Referring back to Figure 14.1, the fields in the table band—Part No, Qty Sold, Sel Price, and so on—are all regular fields from the table named Sales. (These are the "suggested" fields that Paradox placed on the report automatically.)

PLACING CALCULATED FIELDS

A *calculated field* is one that is based on calculations of two or more other fields in the table. The calculations may involve any single data type, such as numeric (and currency) fields, date fields, and alphanumeric fields. Each type of calculation uses slightly different rules, as discussed below.

Calculated Numeric Fields

Numeric calculations are probably the most common ones used in reports. For example, the Sales table includes a field named Sel Price (the unit price), and a field named Qty Sold (the quantity sold). It does not include a field to store the *extended price*, which is the unit price times the quantity sold. However, you could still *display* the extended price by adding a calculated field to the report format.

To enter a calculated field, you must place the field names in square brackets ([]) and use any of the arithmetic operators below to create the appropriate calculation:

+   Addition

–   Subtraction

*   Multiplication

/   Division

()   Grouping

Numeric fields may also use the *summary operators* listed below in their expressions:

Sum	Sum of the field
Average	Average of the field
Count	Count of the field
High	Highest value in the field
Low	Lowest value in the field

These summary operators allow you to perform summary calculations within a report column. When using summary operators, you must place the expression within parentheses after the operator, using the general syntax

Sum(*field name or expression*)

For example, the expression

Sum([Sel Price] * [Qty Sold])

demonstrates the correct syntax for displaying the sum of the products of the Sel Price and Qty Sold fields.

Summary calculations are usually used in conjunction with *groups,* a topic we will discuss later in this chapter. A sample invoice-printing report format, shown towards the end of this chapter, demonstrates this use of summary operators.

You may also use constants in calculated fields. These are simply numbers that do not vary in value. For example, a calculation of 6 percent sales tax might be a constant, because the 6 percent is used for all calculations.

Let's look at some examples of calculated numeric fields. Suppose you wish to place a report column to show the extended price on a report for the Sales table. To do so, you would select the Calculated option from the menu, and enter the expression

[Sel Price] * [Qty Sold]

Note that the field names are placed within brackets, and the * symbol is used to signify multiplication.

If you wished to add 6 percent sales tax to the calculation, you could multiply the expression by the constant 1.06, as shown:

([Sel Price] * [Qty Sold]) * 1.06

Note that the constant is not enclosed in brackets. Furthermore, to ensure that the *Sel Price * Qty Sold* calculation is performed first, that part of the expression is enclosed in parentheses.

Parentheses are used in calculated fields the same way they are used in general math; they ensure that a particular operation takes place first, regardless of the normal order of precedence. For example, in general terms, the formula

10 + 5 * 2

equals 20, because the rules of operator precedence dictate that multiplication and division take place before addition and subtraction. However, the calculation

(10 + 5) * 2

equals 30 (15 times 2), because the parentheses force the addition to take place before the multiplication.

When using parentheses in expressions, make sure that the expression includes an equal number of open and closed parentheses, or the calculation will not work. For example, the sample expression

((([Qty]*[Price]) − ([Price]*[Discount])) * 1.06

is valid, because there are exactly three open and three closed parentheses. The expression below is incorrect, because there is one too many closing parentheses:

((([Qty]*[Price]) – ([Price]*[Discount])) * 1.06)

If you enter an expression with unbalanced parentheses (or some other syntax problem) Paradox will reject the entry and display the message

Syntax error in expression.

You can use the Backspace key or Field View (Alt-F5) to make corrections and try again.

The entire expression that you use in a calculated field can contain any number of fields, operators, and constants, so long as the overall length of the expression does not exceed 175 characters.

Figure 14.2 shows a sample printed report using data from the table named Sales. Note the various calculated fields used to display some of the columns.

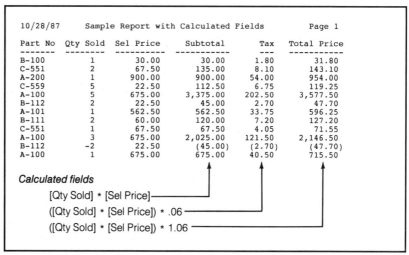

Figure 14.2: A sample report with calculated numeric fields

Calculated Date Fields

Date fields may also be calculated using the arithmetic operators + (plus) and – (minus). Date fields also support the use of the summary operators discussed in the previous section. A simple example of a calculated date field would be

[Date Sold] + 30

which would display the date 30 days after the date sold. The expression

[Date Sold] – 30

would display the date 30 days prior to the date sold.

Figure 14.3 shows a sample report, using a field named Date Shipped, which is a regular field in the table, and a calculated field displayed as Payment Due, which is not stored in the table. Instead, the Payment Due field is calculated using the expression *[Date Shipped] + 30*.

```
Customer                            Date
Number      Customer Name    Product Name    Shipped     Payment Due
----------  ---------------  ---------------  --------    ------------
1001        Joe Smith        Wool socks       10/28/88    11/27/88
1002        Wanda Miller     Wool muffler     10/30/88    11/29/88
1009        Jackson Ho       Oil lamp         10/30/88    11/29/88
1088        Basil Irwin      Wool socks       11/01/88    12/01/88
1088        Basil Irwin      Wool muffler     11/01/88    12/01/88


Calculated field
        [Date Shipped] + 30
```

Figure 14.3: A sample report with a calculated date field

Calculated Alphanumeric Fields

The only arithmetic operator allowed with alphanumeric fields is the + sign. Using this operator, alphanumeric fields can be joined to one another, to constants (enclosed in quotation marks), or to special printer codes.

In the sample calculated field below, the constants "Dear   " and ":" are both enclosed in quotation marks. Both constants are joined to the contents of the First Name field using the + operator:

"Dear   " + [First Name] + ":"

When printing a record with *Wanda* in the First Name field, this expression would display

Dear Wanda:

In the calculated field below, there is a single blank space between the two quotation marks. This blank space is used to join the First Name and Last Name fields, once again using the + operator:

[First Name] + "   " + [Last Name]

The expression above would display a record with *Wanda* in the First Name Field and *Smith* in the Last Name field as

Wanda Smith

If you know the codes your printer uses for special features such as boldface, underlining, expanded, and compressed print, you can use these codes in calculated alphanumeric fields to take advantage of these printer features. (All printers use different codes, so you'll need to look them up in your printer manual.)

Chapter 8 discussed general techniques for converting "written" codes to numeric codes for use in Paradox. For example, the Esc key is always code 27, which in Paradox is expressed as \027. (These codes are always preceded by a backslash.)

Suppose that your printer uses a particular set of special codes for the following printer attributes:

Begin expanded print	Esc-A
End expanded print	Esc-B
Begin compressed print	15
End compressed print	29

If you placed your report title on the report format using the calculated field

"\027A" + "Monthly Sales Summary" + "\027B"

the title would appear on the report in expanded print.

You may also place a calculated field with a printer code in it on the report with no other text. For example, using the sample codes above, if you were to place a calculated field containing *"\015"* (including the quotation marks) just above the report table, and the code *"\029"* (again including the quotation marks) just beneath the report table band, the body of the report (the column titles, underlines, and data) would be displayed in compressed print. Figure 14.4 shows the position of the title and the compressed print codes on a sample report format (these of course appear as AAA masks on the report specification screen).

Note in Figure 14.4 that the title is intentionally off center, to the left. This is because the title will be printed larger than appears on

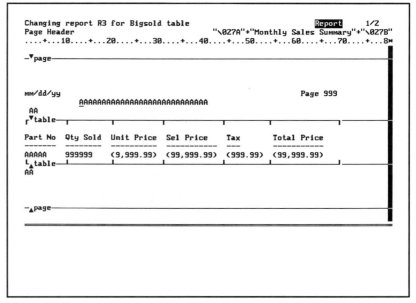

Figure 14.4: Special printer codes added to a report format

the screen, so some adjustment must be made to make the title appear centered on the printed report. You may have to use a little trial-and-error to get expanded print properly centered on your own printer.

You can see the AA field masks for the codes for starting and ending compressed print, just above and below the table band in the leftmost column.

Editing Calculated Fields

If you discover an error in a calculated field after placing it on the report format, you can edit it by calling up the report menu and selecting the Field and CalcEdit options. This method is particularly useful for correcting long expressions, because it saves you from having to retype the entire calculation.

When you select CalcEdit, Paradox presents the familiar instructions:

Press ↑ ↓ → ← to move to the field you want to edit...
then press ⏎ to correct it.

As instructed, move the cursor to the field you wish to edit and press Enter. The expression will be displayed at the top of the screen, with the cursor at the right end.

You can then enter the Field View mode (by typing Alt-F5) to help edit the expression. Once in Field View mode, you can use the Field View keys (shown in Appendix C) to make corrections. When done, press Enter to leave Field View, then press Enter again to place the edited expression back into the report.

Calculating Blanks as Zeros

By default, Paradox does not treat a blank value in a numeric field as a zero value. Instead, it ignores the record altogether, which might lead to misleading averages or lowest-value calculations in some reports. To have Paradox treat blanks as zeros, you need to reconfigure Paradox to use the Paradox Custom Configuration program, discussed in Chapter 16 of the *Paradox User's Guide*.

PLACING SUMMARY FIELDS

Summary fields are used to display totals and subtotals in reports. They can also be used to display an average, count, highest value, or lowest value. (We'll see some examples of summary fields in a later section of this chapter.) When you select Summary from the Place menu, you'll see the following options:

Regular   Calculated

If the field you want to summarize is a regular field from the table, select Regular. You'll see a list of field names from the current table. Select the field name you want to summarize.

If the field you wish to summarize is a calculated field, you will be asked to enter the calculation, rather than the name of the field to summarize. For example, if you wish to total (or summarize) the selling price times the quantity sold, you could enter the calculation

[Sel price] * [Qty Sold]

After you've selected the regular field, or defined the calculated field expression, you'll be given the options

Sum   Average   Count   High   Low

These options can be summarized as follows:

OPTION	FUNCTION
Sum	Displays the sum of the field
Average	Displays the average of the field
Count	Displays the number of fields
High	Displays the highest value in the field
Low	Displays the lowest value in the field

Select the type of calculation you want from the options listed. The next menu displayed is

PerGroup   Overall

The PerGroup option is used for subtotals. The Overall option is used for overall totals or running (cumulative) totals. Select the option you want, then place and format the field in the usual manner, as instructed on the screen. Figure 14.5 shows a sample report with summary fields used as subtotals and totals, and a highest date value.

PLACING THE DATE FIELD

The Date option under the Field and Place menus displays the current date on the report. (Note that Paradox automatically places the current date in the report heading as well.) When you select this option,

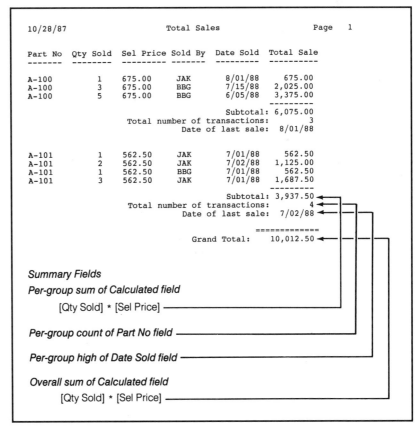

Figure 14.5: A sample report with summary fields

you'll be prompted to place and format the date in the usual manner.

The current date displayed is the one stored in your system. You can set that date directly from the DOS prompt, by entering the DATE command and pressing Enter. To change the system date from within Paradox, type Ctrl-O, enter the DATE command at the DOS prompt, and press Enter. Fill in the new date in the format shown on the screen. Then give the EXIT command and press Enter to return to Paradox.

PLACING THE TIME FIELD

The Time option under the Place menu lets you put the current time in the printed report. When you select this option, you'll be given two options for displaying the time:

```
Enter the time format to use:
1) hh:mm pm   2) hh:mm:ss (military)
```

The first option prints the time in the 12-hour clock format (with AM or PM). The second option displays the time in the 24-hour clock format used in the military.

Like the Date field mentioned above, the Time field uses the current system time. You can adjust the system time by entering the TIME command at the DOS prompt, and pressing Enter. (As with the Date field, you can escape to DOS temporarily using Ctrl-O to do this from within Paradox.) Be sure to enter the time in the format suggested on your screen.

PLACING THE PAGE FIELD

The Page field displays the page number on each page of the report. Paradox automatically places this field at the top of the report. However, if you prefer to place the page number elsewhere, you can use this option to place the page number wherever you wish (though you should place it in the Page band, and outside the other bands, to prevent the page number from being displayed in several places on the printed page).

PLACING THE #RECORD FIELD

The #Record field numbers records that are displayed in the report. When you select this option, Paradox displays the submenu

Overall   Per-Group

If you select Overall, records will be numbered consecutively from the top of the report to the bottom. If you select Per-Group, records will be numbered individually within groups (for example, subtotal groups). Once you select an option, you'll be prompted to place and format the #Record field in the usual manner.

If you place the #Record field in the report table band, each record will be assigned a number. If you place the #Record field in the page footer, it will count the number of records on each page. Placing the # Record field in the report footer displays the total count of all record numbers printed in the report.

Up to now, we've only briefly discussed *grouping* and the various tabular *report bands,* so some of this discussion about the #Record field may be a bit confusing at the moment. We'll deal with these important topics in a moment. But first, we need to discuss a couple of other options on the Field menu.

═══ *COLUMN ALIGNMENT* ═══

By default, Paradox automatically right-justifies Numeric and Currency values in report columns, and left-justifies Alphanumeric and Date fields. To change these default settings, call up the Report menu and select the Field and Justify options. You'll be given the standard instructions to

Use ↑ ↓ → ← to move into the field you want to justify...
then press ↵ to select it.

After moving the cursor to the report column of interest, and pressing Enter, you'll be given the options

Left   Center   Right   Default

These can be summarized as follows:

OPTION	FUNCTION
Left	Aligns values with the left edge of the column
Center	Centers values within the column
Right	Aligns values with the right edge of the column
Default	Returns to the alignment Paradox uses by default

Select the option you wish to use for the current field. You will see the effects of your selection when you print the report. Figure 14.6 shows examples of left-justified, centered, and right-justified columns.

```
Left                    Center                      Right    Default

Adams                   Adams                       Adams    Adams
Bartholomew             Bartholomew            Bartholomew    Bartholomew
Cat                     Cat                           Cat    Cat

9,876.54                9,876.54                 9,876.54            9,876.54
1.23                    1.23                         1.23                1.23
-11.00                  -11.00                     -11.00              -11.00

March 31, 1953          March 31, 1953       March 31, 1953    March 31, 1953
November 15, 1950       November 15, 1950    November 15, 1950    November 15, 1950
September 30, 1987      September 30, 1987   September 30, 1987    September 30, 1987
```

Figure 14.6: Examples of report-column justification

WORD-WRAP

Another feature of Paradox reports is word-wrapping, where long alphanumeric fields are broken into several lines, as necessary, on the printed report. For neatness, long text is broken between words, rather than between characters. Hence, this feature lets you display the full contents of a long alphanumeric field within in a narrow column, thereby allowing more room for other columns.

Figure 14.7 shows the "suggested" report format displayed by Paradox when developing a report for the Mastinv table. As you can see, the Pur Price field extends beyond the right margin. To make room for the Pur Price field within the margins, you could narrow, and word-wrap, the longer Part Name field.

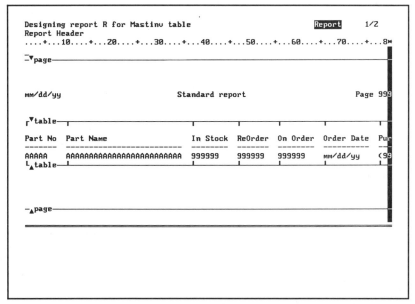

Figure 14.7: Paradox's suggested report format for the Mastinv table

To word-wrap the field, first reduce the size of the field to the width you desire. You can use the Field and Reformat menu options to do so. Then use the TableBand Resize options from the menu to narrow the entire column. Next, call up the menu and select Field and WordWrap. The screen asks that you move the cursor to the field to word-wrap, then press Enter to select that field (using the usual instructions at the top of the screen).

Next, the screen presents the prompt

> Number of lines: 1
> Enter the number of lines to wrap onto,
> or press ← to leave unchanged.

The maximum number of lines for displaying a single field is 255. Paradox will use only as many lines as necessary to display the entire contents of the field, up to the limit you set here. For this example, you can set a fairly small number, such as 3.

For the word-wrapped field, there will be an unpredictable number of lines printed on the row. (In this example, some Part Names may require only one line, some may require more lines.) If you wish to make sure that there is always a blank line between records displayed on the report, you can add the BLANKLINE keyword at the bottom of the table band. Figure 14.8 shows the narrowed Part Name field, with the BLANKLINE keyword added in the appropriate place.

Figure 14.9 shows a sample of the printed report. Notice that the part names are broken into two or more lines, where necessary, to fit

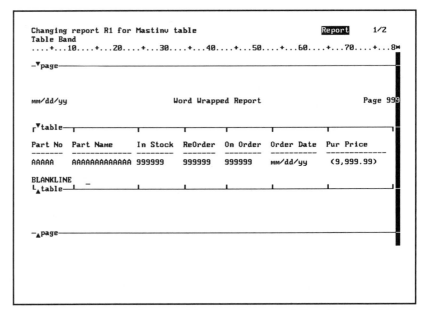

Figure 14.8: A report format with a word-wrapped Part Name field and BLANKLINE keyword

```
10/28/87               Sample Word Wrapped Report

Part No  Part Name       In Stock  ReOrder  Order Date  Pur Price
-------  --------------  --------  -------  ----------  -------------
A-100    Bicycle            10        5     1/31/88       450.00

B-112    Safety              0       10     1/31/88        15.00
         Helmet (Ozzy)

C-551    Hobie              50       75     4/15/88        45.00
         Skateboard

C-559    Flexie             25       75     4/15/88        15.00
         Skateboard
```

Figure 14.9: The sample report with a word-wrapped Part Name field

within the column. The names are broken between words (rather than between characters). Paradox will attempt to wrap every word in the field. However, if any single word is wider than the column, then Paradox will break the word between letters. Also, as you can see in the report, the BLANKLINE keyword has put a blank line between each printed record in the body of the report.

GROUPING

Grouping allows you to display subtotals and other calculations within like groups of data (for example, total sales for all part number A-100 sales, all part number B-200 sales, and so forth). But beyond subtotals, grouping also allows you to organize data for a display that is easier to read. For example, a customer list could be grouped by state or zip code and a financial report could be grouped by day, week, or month.

You can also nest groups within groups, to as many as 16 levels, to display subtotals and sub-subtotals (and sub-sub-subtotals, and so on). On a large customer list, you could group records by state and, within each state, group records by county. Within each county, you could group records by city. As you'll see in this section, there is almost no limit to the ways in which Paradox will allow you to define groups for your reports.

A NOTE ON REPORT BANDS

Before discussing grouping and *group bands* in detail, perhaps a brief discussion of tabular report bands, in general, will help reduce any confusion later in this section. When Paradox first displays its suggested report format on the screen, the report has two bands: the page band and the table band. A report can actually have up to four types of bands, as illustrated in Figure 14.10. The various types of bands can be summarized as follows:

- **Report band**: Everything in the report band is printed once each time the report is printed. Hence, the report band would be used to display a cover page for a lengthy report of several pages, or a grand total at the end of the report.

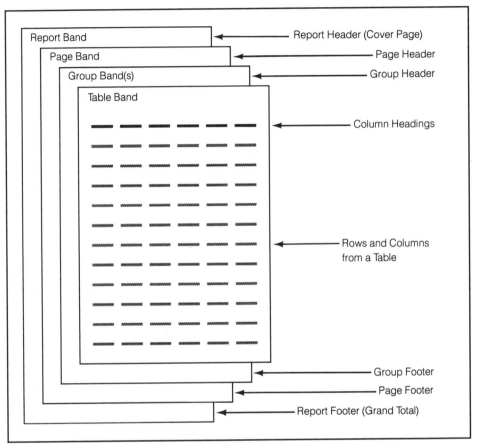

Figure 14.10: Bands in a report specification

- **Page band**: Information within the page band is printed once on each page of the report. Paradox automatically fills in the current date, report description, and page number in the page band, which you can use or delete.

- **Group band**: The optional group band is nested between the page band and the table band. This band determines how records from the table will be grouped on the printed page. A single report can contain up to 16 group bands, which means that you can have up to 16 levels of grouping. Any headers or footers placed within the group band will be displayed at the top and bottom of each group. If a report contains subtotals, you would typically place the subtotal as a footer in the group band, so that the subtotal is displayed at the bottom of each printed group.

- **Table band**: The table band is the innermost band and represents the main body of the report. The table band contains headings for fields from the table being displayed, as well as data from the table itself. The table band prints as many records from the table as will fit on the printed page.

PLACING GROUP BANDS IN THE REPORT

We'll discuss specific menu selections for defining group bands in a moment. But first, we need to discuss general techniques for inserting group bands. Remember that group bands must be inserted between the page and table bands, simply because a given page might contain several groups, and a given group might contain several records.

If your report contains several levels of groupings, the groups should be defined with the most important grouping level as the outermost band, and the least important group as the innermost band. In other words, the outermost group band specifies the broadest range of records, while the innermost group band specifies the narrowest range of records.

For example, if you were to group records in a report by State, County, and City, clearly State is the broadest range, and hence would be the outermost group band. County would be the next group band, because there are more counties than states, yet fewer counties than cities. City would be the innermost group band, because there are more cities than either states or counties.

Figure 14.11 shows a sample report specification with three levels of grouping for State, County, and City. Group bands appear with triangles, followed by the word *group,*, and the name of the field that the group is based on. Also, the group identification is indented to show its level within the group bands, as shown below (the table band is not shown so that you can see the group bands more clearly):

```
———— ▼group State ——————————————————
———————— ▼group County ——————————————
———————————— ▼group City ————————————
              Table band shown here
———————————— ▲group City ————————————
———————— ▲group County ——————————————
———— ▲group State ——————————————————
```

Figure 14.12 shows a page printed from the report specification shown in Figure 14.11. Even though this is only a single page from the report, you can see how the report is grouped by states, and by counties within the same state, and by cities within the same county. Additional pages would be in the same format.

Note also that Paradox has sorted each group: the states are in alphabetical order (California comes before Colorado); within the states, the counties are in alphabetical order (Los Angeles comes before San Diego); and within the counties, cities are alphabetized (Del Mar comes before Encinitas). Paradox automatically sorts the data within the groups, in either ascending or descending order.

The sample report in Figure 14.12 only shows a basic grouping. As we'll see, there are many ways to format the grouped report.

Whenever you insert a group into a report specification, Paradox will ask that you

USE ↑ ↓ → ← to show where you want the group inserted...
then press ← to place it.

If you are entering the first group band, move the cursor to any column position between the page band and the table band, and press Enter. If you are inserting an additional group band, be sure to move the cursor above, below, or between existing group bands, depending on the new band's logical position. (Using the example above, the County group band would be inserted between the existing State and City bands.) Press Enter when the cursor is properly positioned for the group.

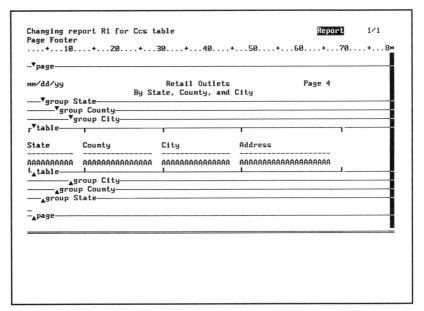

Figure 14.11: A Report specification with three grouping levels

```
10/29/88                   Retail Outlets                 Page 4
                      By State, County, and City

State        County            City              Address
----------   ----------------  ----------------  --------------------
California   Los Angeles       Culver City       123 A St.
California   Los Angeles       Culver City       2345 Beech St.
California   Los Angeles       Culver City       345 Callaway

California   Los Angeles       Duarte            2776 Adams Ave.
California   Los Angeles       Duarte            982 Vickers Way

California   Los Angeles       Whittier          1 Fashion Plaza
California   Los Angeles       Whittier          77 Alton Pkwy


California   San Diego         Del Mar           88 15th St.

California   San Diego         Encinitas         1086 Crest Dr.
California   San Diego         Encinitas         11 Santa Fe Dr.
California   San Diego         Encinitas         2001 Wotan St.

California   San Diego         La Jolla          191 Silverado
California   San Diego         La Jolla          21 Prospect Ave.
California   San Diego         La Jolla          71 Wall St.


Colorado     Acton             Boulder           11801 Rocky Hwy
Colorado     Acton             Boulder           27 Route 11
```

Figure 14.12: The printed report grouped by State, County, and City

THE GROUP MENU

When you select Group from the tabular Report menu, you'll see the following submenu:

Insert   Delete   Headings   SortDirection   Regroup

These options can be summarized as follows:

OPTION	FUNCTION
Insert	Adds a new grouping to the report
Delete	Deletes an existing group
Headings	Determines when group headings are printed
SortDirection	Specifies how data are sorted within groups
Regroup	Changes an existing grouping definition

INSERTING GROUPS

The Insert option under the Group menu lets you define a group for the report. When you select this option, you'll see the following submenu:

Field   Range   NumberRecords

These options are discussed individually in the sections below.

Grouping by Field

If you select the Field option from the Group Insert submenu, Paradox will display a list of all field names. Select the field you wish to group by in the usual manner (by highlighting and pressing Enter).

Paradox will then ask you to move the cursor to the place you want the group to be inserted. If this is the first grouping level, just move the cursor to anywhere between the page band and table band, then press Enter. If this is not the first defined group, be sure to place the cursor at the right grouping level, relative to other grouping levels, then press Enter.

Figures 14.11 and 14.12 display a report specification with three levels of grouping, each of these levels being a field from the table (State, County, and City). Figure 14.11 shows the proper nesting of the three fields, with State as the outermost, County in the middle, and City innermost.

Grouping By Range

The second option on the Group Insert submenu is Range. This option lets you define a range of values for a group that will depend on the data type of the group. Selecting this item first displays a menu of field names. Select the field to group by in the usual manner. Depending on the data type of that field, you'll be given one of three options, as outlined in the following sections.

Numeric Range   If the field you select under the Range option is Numeric or Currency, Paradox will display the prompt

Size of range:
Example: 10 produces 0-9, 10-19, etc.

The range you select determines how records are grouped. For example, if the field being grouped on was the price of a house, and you entered 25,000, the first displayed group would list houses costing in the range of 0 to $25,000.00. The second group would list houses costing in the range of $25,001 to $50,000. The third printed group would list houses costing in the range of $50,001 to $75,000, and so forth up to the most expensive house.

If, on the other hand, you had selected a field representing the number of bedrooms in a house, and specified 1 as the range, the report would group all houses with zero bedrooms (if any), then all houses with one bedroom, then all houses with two bedrooms, and so forth up to whatever the largest number of bedrooms available was.

After you select the range, you'll be prompted to place the cursor and insert the group. Again, move the cursor to anywhere between the page and table bands, or to the appropriate place in relation to other defined groups, and press Enter.

Date Range If the field you select under the Range option is the Date data type, you'll see the prompt

Day   Week   Month   Year

Selecting the Day option groups together records that have exactly the same date. For example, Jan. 1, 1988 would form one group, Jan. 2, 1988 would form the second group, and so forth for all the records in the table.

Selecting Week groups together records that fall within the same week (from Sunday to Saturday). Note that these records might cross two months, if the first of the month falls between a Sunday and the following Saturday. For example, records with dates in the range December 20, 1987 to December 26, 1987 would fall in one group, records with dates in the range December 27, 1987 to January 2, 1988 would form the next group, and so forth.

If you select the Month option, records that fall within the same month will be grouped together. For example, one group would contain all records with January dates, the next group would consist of records with all February dates, and so forth.

If you select Year, records that have dates with identical years will be grouped together. For example, all records with 1987 dates would be grouped together, followed by the 1988 records, and so forth.

After you have selected a date range, you'll be prompted to position the cursor at the group insertion point, and press Enter.

Alphanumeric Ranges If the field you select to group by under the Range option is the Alphanumeric data type, you'll see the prompt

Number of initial characters for range:
Use 1 to group by first letter, 2 to group by first two letters, etc.

If you enter a 1 in response to this prompt, all records that begin with the letter A will be grouped together, all records that begin with the letter B will be grouped together, all records that begin with the letter C will be grouped together, and so forth. If you selected 2, all records that begin with the letters AA would be grouped together, then all records beginning with the letters AB would be grouped together, followed by all records beginning with the letters AC, and so forth up to ZZ.

If the number you enter here equals the length of the field being grouped on, all records with identical values would be grouped together. For example, if you were to select Last Name, with a length of 15 characters, as the grouping field, and entered 15 as the number of initial characters, then all records with the last name Adams would be grouped together, followed by all records with the last name Bowser (or whatever last name was next in alphabetical order), and so forth.

After you specify the number of initial letters to group by, you'll be prompted to insert the group, as discussed previously.

Grouping by Number of Records

The NumberRecords option under the Range menu lets you define grouping sizes that are constant in size, and do not depend on values in any fields. When you select this option, you'll see the prompt

Number of records:
Enter number of records to group on:

If you were to enter a number such as 5, any group would have a maximum of five records in it. Blank lines (discussed in a moment) would separate each group of five records. (However, if the number of records in the report was not evenly divisible by five, the last group would have fewer records.)

Note that the NumberRecords option does not actually sort or organize records in any way. Instead, it merely creates "white space" on the report, which has the psychological effect of making the report more pleasing to the eye. For example, Figures 14.13 and 14.14 show two copies of the same report. The only difference between the two is that the report in Figure 14.14 displays records in groups of five, using the NumberRecords option.

In this example, there are 18 records in the table. As you can see, the last group on the report in Figure 14.14 has only three records, because there are no more records in the table to fill out the group.

Even though the reports displayed are not in any particular order, we could have used the Modify Sort options under the Main menu to presort these records into alphabetical order by name, prior to printing either report.

```
Mr/Mrs   Last Name         First Name        M.I.   Company
------   --------------    --------------    ----   ------------------------
Miss     Abzug             Ann               Z.
Mr.      Adams             Andy              A.
Ms.      Davis             Randi
Miss     Gladstone         Tara Rose                Waterside, Inc.
Ms.      Jackson           Janet             J.     Zeerox, Inc.
Mr.      Kenney            Clark             E.     Legal Aid
Mr.      Macallister       Mark              S.     BBC Publishing
Dr.      Rosiello          Richard           L.     Raydontic Labs
Mrs.     Simpson           Susita            M.     SMS Publishing
Dr.      Zastrow           Ruth                     Scripts Clinic
Mr.      Wilson            Jackson           J.     Rancho Enterprises
Mrs.     Salvatore         Annette           Q.
Ms.      Stark             Robin             D.     Starkland Systems
Dr.      Wallace           Doug                     Wallace Productions
Mr.      Newell            Jeff              J.     Irvine Construction
Mr.      Pickett           Scott             K.     Adept Software
Miss     Petricca          Mary Ann                 Biotech International
Mr.      Mendez            David                    Jet Plumbing, Inc.
```

Figure 14.13: A report with no groups

```
Mr/Mrs   Last Name         First Name        M.I.   Company
------   --------------    --------------    ----   ------------------------
Miss     Abzug             Ann               Z.
Mr.      Adams             Andy              A.
Ms.      Davis             Randi
Miss     Gladstone         Tara Rose                Waterside, Inc.
Ms.      Jackson           Janet             J.     Zeerox, Inc.

Mr.      Kenney            Clark             E.     Legal Aid
Mr.      Macallister       Mark              S.     BBC Publishing
Dr.      Rosiello          Richard           L.     Raydontic Labs
Mrs.     Simpson           Susita            M.     SMS Publishing
Dr.      Zastrow           Ruth                     Scripts Clinic

Mr.      Wilson            Jackson           J.     Rancho Enterprises
Mrs.     Salvatore         Annette           Q.
Ms.      Stark             Robin             D.     Starkland Systems
Dr.      Wallace           Doug                     Wallace Productions
Mr.      Newell            Jeff              J.     Irvine Construction

Mr.      Pickett           Scott             K.     Adept Software
Miss     Petricca          Mary Ann                 Biotech International
Mr.      Mendez            David                    Jet Plumbing, Inc.
```

Figure 14.14: A report with groups of five records

GROUP HEADERS, FOOTERS, AND BLANK LINES

You can place a header at the top and a footer at the bottom of each group on a printed report, to identify the group or display subtotals. The header or footer may consist of any number of lines you wish. A group header must appear inside its appropriate group band on the report specification, above the table band. The group footer must appear within the appropriate group band beneath the table band. Both the header and the footer can include fields from the table, which may be placed using the usual Field, Place, and Regular options from the Report menu.

Figure 14.15 shows a sample report with two levels of grouping and subtotals. Records are grouped and subtotaled by part number. Each part-number group has a header (for example, *Part number: A-100*) and a footer (for example, *Total sales for part number A-100:*).

```
                               Sales Summary
                       By Part Number and Sales Person
        10/29/87                                            Page 1

        Part No  Sold By  Date Sold  Qty  Unit Price   Total Price
        -------  -------  ---------  ---  -----------  -----------

        Part number: A-100

            Salesperson: BBG
        A-100     BBG       7/15/88    3       675.00     2,025.00
        A-100     BBG       6/05/88    5       675.00     3,375.00
        A-100     BBG       6/05/88    5       675.00     3,375.00
        A-100     BBG       8/01/88   10       675.00     6,750.00
                                                         -----------
                     Total sales for salesperson BBG:    15,525.00

            Salesperson: JAK
        A-100     JAK       6/01/88    1       675.00       675.00
        A-100     JAK       7/01/88    1       675.00       675.00
        A-100     JAK       8/01/88    1       675.00       675.00
        A-100     JAK       8/03/88    2       675.00     1,350.00
        A-100     JAK       8/02/88    3       675.00     2,025.00
                                                         -----------
                     Total sales for salesperson JAK:     5,400.00
                                                         ===========
                  Total sales for part number A-100:      2,025.00

        Part number: A-200

            Salesperson: BBG
        A-200     BBG       6/05/88    2       900.00     1,800.00
        A-200     BBG       6/21/88    2       900.00     1,800.00
        A-200     BBG       6/01/88    3       900.00     2,700.00
        A-200     BBG       6/15/88    5       900.00     4,500.00
                                                         -----------
                     Total sales for salesperson BBG:    10,800.00

            Salesperson: JAK
        A-200     JAK       7/01/88    1       900.00       900.00
        A-200     JAK       6/01/88    2       900.00     1,800.00
        A-200     JAK       7/01/88    2       900.00     1,800.00
        A-200     JAK       6/01/88   17       900.00    15,300.00
                                                         -----------
                     Total sales for salesperson JAK:    19,800.00
                                                         ===========
                  Total sales for part number A-200:     15,300.00

                           Grand Total of Sales:         51,525.00
```

Figure 14.15: A sample report with two levels of subtotals

Within each part-number group, records are grouped and subtotaled by salesperson. Each salesperson group also has a header (for example, *Salesperson: BBG*) and a footer (for example, *Total sales for salesperson BBG:*). Note also the use of blank lines to separate the various groups.

Figure 14.16 shows the report specification that was used to print the report shown in Figure 14.15. Let's take a look at it piece by piece, as it demonstrates many of the techniques we've discussed in this chapter.

Before looking at the group bands, take a look inside the table band. The Qty column contains the field Qty Sold, which appears as the mask *999*. The Unit Price column contains the Sel Price field, which is displayed as the mask *99,999.99*. The Total Price column is a calculated field, based on the expression *[Qty Sold] * [Sel Price]*. The fields are arranged and sized using the Field and TableBand options from the Report menu.

Now, locate the top of the group band for the Part No field. Within this group band, near the top, is a blank line and the group header

Part number: AAAAA

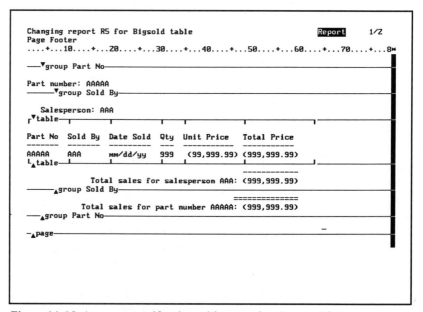

Figure 14.16: A report specification with group headers and footers

The blank line is inserted in the usual manner, by positioning the cursor, making sure the insert mode is on, and pressing Enter. (Remember, to remove lines, including blank lines, move the cursor to the leftmost column of the line to be deleted and type Ctrl-Y.) The text for the header is simply typed in. *AAAAA* is the mask for the Part No field, placed by positioning the cursor and selecting the Field, Place, and Regular options from the Report menu, and Part No from the menu of field names.

The footer for the Part No group appears between the Sold By and Part No group bands beneath the table band. The footer appears on the report specification as follows:

Total sales for part number AAAAA: (999,999.99)

The text is typed in, and *AAAAA* is once again the mask for the Part No field, placed using the Field, Place, and Regular options from the Report menu. The *(999,999.99)* mask shows the subtotal for the group on the printed report. It is placed by calling up the Report menu and selecting the Field, Place, Summary, and Calculated menu options. The expression for the field is once again *[Qty Sold] * [Sel Price]*, and the Sum and Per Group options have been selected to specify totals for the current group of records. Note also the equal-signs bar in the report footer, which is typed in from the keyboard.

Now locate the group band for the Sold By field. Above the table band, the group has a blank line and the header

Salesperson: AAA

Salesperson is typed in, and *AAA* is the mask for the Sold By field, placed using the usual Field, Place, and Regular options from the Report menu.

The footer for the Sold By group appears within the Sold By group band, beneath the table band. It appears as

Total sales for salesperson AAA: (999,999.99)

AAA is the mask for the Sold By field, again placed using the Field, Place, and Regular menu options. The *(999,999.99)* mask is placed using the Field, Place, Summary, Calculated, and Sum menu options and the expression *[Qty Sold]* * *[Sel Price]*. The Per-Group option is selected, rather than the Overall option, because this is a subtotal. This footer also includes a series of hyphens, which you can also see on the printed report in Figure 14.15.

Finally, notice the grand total at the bottom of the printed page in Figure 14.15. On the report specification, this appears beneath the page band, so that it is printed only once at the end of the report, rather than at the bottom of each page. (Though the screen does not show a marker for the report band, this grand total is actually in the report band.)

The *(999,999.99)* mask next to the *Grand Total of Sales:* title is another Summary field, placed using the usual Field, Place, Summary, and Calculated options. The expression for the calculation is once again *[Qty Sold]* * *[Sel Price]*. However, unlike the subtotal fields, this field is an Overall (rather than PerGroup) sum, because it displays the total of all records, not just individual groups of records.

REMOVING GROUPING VALUES FROM THE TABLE BAND

In some reports, you might prefer to display the grouping field in the group header only. For example, in the small group below, the part number A-100 appears only once at the top of the group. The part number does not appear within the records that fall into this group:

Part number: A-100				
BBG	7/15/88	3	675.00	2,025.00
BBG	6/05/88	5	675.00	3,375.00
BBG	6/05/88	5	675.00	3,375.00
BBG	8/01/88	10	675.00	6,750.00

To achieve this result, simply remove the grouping field from the Table band (using the TableBand Erase submenu). To leave an indentation beneath the group heading, as above, you can use the Field Erase options to remove the field without removing the entire column. Then use the Del (or Delete) key to remove the column heading and underline. Finally, use TableBand and Resize to adjust the blank column to the width you want for the indentation.

DELETING GROUPS

To delete a group band from a report specification, select the Delete option from the Group menu. Paradox will ask that you identify the group band by positioning the cursor. Before deleting the group, Paradox will ask for confirmation:

Cancel   Ok

Select Cancel to change your mind and keep the group band intact. Select Ok to delete the group band.

GROUP HEADINGS

Group headings are placed in the upper portion of a group band and, like footings, are printed once for each group. In addition, they are repeated on the next page if the group is split into two or more pages.

If you prefer that group headings not be repeated on a second page, select the Headings option from the Group menu. After you identify the group heading, Paradox will present these options:

Page   Group

The Group option prevents group headings from being displayed on a second page. The Page option retains the default setting (group headings at the top of each group, and on any "spillover" pages).

SORTING GROUPS

By default, Paradox will display groups sorted in ascending order. To display a group in descending order, select SortDirection from the Group submenu. Paradox will ask that you identify which group to sort by positioning the cursor. Then you'll be given these options:

Ascending   Descending

Ascending, the default setting, displays groups in the normal order (smallest to largest). Selecting Descending will display the group in descending (largest to smallest) order.

CHANGING GROUPS

You can always redefine groups in a report specification by selecting the Regroup option from the Group menu. When you choose Regroup, Paradox will ask that you identify the group to redefine by positioning the cursor. Then you'll be given the following options:

Field   Range   NumberRecords

From this point on, changing a group band definition is exactly the same as initially inserting a group.

TABULAR REPORT SETTINGS

You may recall that calling up the menu while designing a tabular report brings up these options:

Field   TableBand   Group   Output   Setting   Help   DO-IT!
Cancel

The Setting option allows you to define general report-format settings, as displayed on this submenu:

Format   GroupRepeats   PageLayout   Margin   Setup   Wait

These options can be summarized as follows:

OPTION	FUNCTION
Format	Defines how group and table headers should be displayed, whether as a table of groups or as a group of tables
GroupRepeats	Determines whether to repeat the constant field value within a group
PageLayout	Sets page dimensions (same as for a free-form report)
Margin	Specifies a left margin (same as for a free-form report)

Setup   Specifies a setup string (same as for a free-form report)

Wait   Pauses for paper change between pages (same as for a free-form report)

The Format option provides this submenu:

TablesOfGroups GroupsOfTables

Selecting the TablesOfGroups option (the default setting) produces a table that displays individual column headings only at the top of each page, as in Figure 14.17. The GroupsOfTables option produces a group of tables that repeats column headings each time the grouping changes, as in Figure 14.18.

```
10/11/88              Total Sales              Page 1

Part No  Sold By  Date Sold  Qty Sold  Unit Price        Total Sale
-------  -------  ---------  --------  ----------------  --------------


A-100    BBG      1/01/88       5          650.00           3,250.00
A-100    BBG      1/11/88       3          700.00           2,100.00
A-100    BBG      2/01/88       7          650.00           4,550.00
A-100    BBG      2/02/88       7          700.00           4,900.00
A-100    BBG      3/04/88       9          650.00           5,850.00
A-100    BBG      3/05/88       5          700.00           3,500.00
                                   Sales Person Subtotal:   24,150.00

A-100    JAK      1/01/88       1          700.00             700.00
A-100    JAK      1/11/88       3          700.00           2,100.00
A-100    JAK      1/31/88       5          700.00           3,500.00
A-100    JAK      2/06/88       1          450.00             450.00
A-100    JAK      3/03/88       3          450.00           1,350.00
                                   Sales Person Subtotal:    8,100.00
                                   Part Number Subtotal:    32,250.00


B-112    BBG      1/01/88      10           25.00             250.00
B-112    BBG      1/18/88       0           25.00               0.00
B-112    BBG      2/02/88       2           25.00              50.00
B-112    BBG      2/02/88       2           25.00              50.00
B-112    BBG      3/18/88       4           25.00             100.00
B-112    BBG      3/25/88       6           25.00             150.00
                                   Sales Person Subtotal:      600.00

B-112    JAK      1/21/88       2           70.00             140.00
B-112    JAK      2/02/88       3           55.00             165.00
B-112    JAK      2/02/88       5           55.00             275.00
B-112    JAK      3/01/88       4           70.00             280.00
B-112    JAK      3/15/88       6           70.00             420.00
B-112    JAK      3/25/88       1           55.00              55.00
                                   Sales Person Subtotal:    1,335.00
                                   Part Number Subtotal:     1,935.00
```

Figure 14.17: Tables of groups: column headings at top of page only

The GroupRepeats option lets you decide whether to repeat the constant value (for instance, the part number) used to define the group in each record. Your options are

Retain   Suppress

Retain is the default option, whereby the value is repeated in every record of the group, as follows:

PART NO	SOLD BY	DATE SOLD	QTY SOLD	SEL PRICE	TOTAL SALE
A-100	BBG	7/02/88	3	700.00	2,100.00
A-100	BBG	7/02/88	5	650.00	3,250.00
A-100	BBG	7/03/88	7	700.00	4,900.00
A-100	BBG	7/03/88	9	650.00	5,850.00

Selecting the Suppress option will suppress the grouping field after it is displayed in the first row of the group, as follows:

PART NO	SOLD BY	DATE SOLD	QTY SOLD	SEL PRICE	TOTAL SALE
A-100	BBG	7/02/88	3	700.00	2,100.00
	BBG	7/02/88	5	650.00	3,250.00
	BBG	7/03/88	7	700.00	4,900.00
	BBG	7/03/88	9	650.00	5,850.00

SUMMARY REPORTS

A commonly used report format in all kinds of business settings is the summary report. This type of report shows only totals rather than individual transactions. Figure 14.19 is an example of a summary report based on the Sales table, showing the total sales for each item.

To print such a report, you need to remove all fields from within the table band of the report specification, leaving only headings

```
10/11/88                  Total Sales              Page 1

Part No  Sold By  Date Sold  Qty Sold  Unit Price      Total Sale
-------  -------  ---------  --------  ---------------  --------------
A-100    BBG      1/01/88         5        650.00          3,250.00
A-100    BBG      1/11/88         3        700.00          2,100.00
A-100    BBG      2/01/88         7        650.00          4,550.00
A-100    BBG      2/02/88         7        700.00          4,900.00
A-100    BBG      3/04/88         9        650.00          5,850.00
A-100    BBG      3/05/88         5        700.00          3,500.00
                                      Sales Person Subtotal:   24,150.00

Part No  Sold By  Date Sold  Qty Sold  Unit Price      Total Sale
-------  -------  ---------  --------  ---------------  --------------
A-100    JAK      1/01/88         1        700.00            700.00
A-100    JAK      1/11/88         3        700.00          2,100.00
A-100    JAK      1/31/88         5        700.00          3,500.00
A-100    JAK      2/06/88         1        450.00            450.00
A-100    JAK      3/03/88         3        450.00          1,350.00
                                      Sales Person Subtotal:    8,100.00
                                      Part Number Subtotal:   32,250.00


Part No  Sold By  Date Sold  Qty Sold  Unit Price      Total Sale
-------  -------  ---------  --------  ---------------  --------------
B-112    BBG      1/01/88        10         25.00            250.00
B-112    BBG      1/18/88         0         25.00              0.00
B-112    BBG      2/02/88         2         25.00             50.00
B-112    BBG      2/02/88         2         25.00             50.00
B-112    BBG      3/18/88         4         25.00            100.00
B-112    BBG      3/25/88         6         25.00            150.00
                                      Sales Person Subtotal:      600.00

Part No  Sold By  Date Sold  Qty Sold  Unit Price      Total Sale
-------  -------  ---------  --------  ---------------  --------------
B-112    JAK      1/21/88         2         70.00            140.00
B-112    JAK      2/02/88         3         55.00            165.00
B-112    JAK      2/02/88         5         55.00            275.00
B-112    JAK      3/01/88         4         70.00            280.00
B-112    JAK      3/15/88         6         70.00            420.00
B-112    JAK      3/25/88         1         55.00             55.00
                                      Sales Person Subtotal:    1,335.00
                                      Part Number Subtotal:    1,935.00
```

Figure 14.18: Groups of tables: column headings repeated in each group

```
9/01/88    Summary Report    Page   1

                         Date of Most
Part No  Total Sales     Recent Sale
-------  -----------     ---------
A-100       6,050.00      8/01/88
A-101         450.00      7/01/88
A-200         800.00      6/01/88
B-100          55.00      6/01/88
B-111         100.00      7/01/88
B-112           0.00      8/01/88
C-551         195.00      7/01/88
C-559         155.00      6/05/88

Total:      7,805.00
```

Figure 14.19: A summary report based on the Sales Table

for the fields you want. Then you need to create a group band based on part number. Within the group band (but outside the table band), you can place Part No as a regular field. The Total is a per-group summary field with the formula *[Qty Sold]* * *[Sel Price]*. The Date of Most Recent Sale is a per-group summary field using the High option, rather than the Sum option, from the Summary submenu.

The grand total at the bottom of the report (outside the page band) is an overall summary field with the formula *[Qty Sold]* * *[Sel Price]*. Figure 14.20 shows the report specification for the Summary report. Note that the field masks for the report columns are outside of, and beneath, the table band.

━━ PRINTING
A REPORT FROM TWO TABLES ━━━

In Chapter 10 we saw how we could use the Tools, Copy, and Just-Family options to print a report from an Answer table after a query.

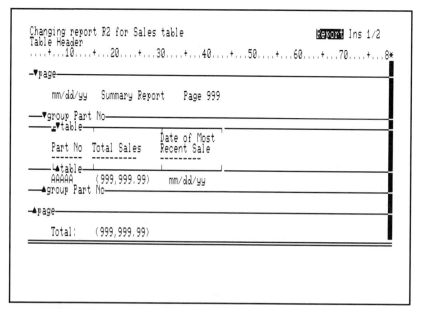

Figure 14.20: The report specification for the summary report

You can use a similar technique to print reports with data from two tables. For example, take a look at the sales report in Figure 14.21. Notice that most of the data are taken directly from the Sales table that we developed earlier, but the Part Name is borrowed from the Mastinv table. Let's take a look at how to design such a report using the Sales and Mastinv tables.

```
11/02/87                 Combined Tables              Page 1


Part No  Part Name                 Qty Sold  Unit Price   Total Sale
-------  ----------------------    --------  ----------   ----------
A-100    Gershwin Bicycle              1       675.00        675.00
A-100    Gershwin Bicycle              3       675.00      2,025.00
A-100    Gershwin Bicycle              5       675.00      3,375.00
A-101    Nikono Bicycle                1       562.50        562.50
A-200    Racing Bicycle                1       900.00        900.00
B-100    Safety Helmet (Nikono)        1        30.00         30.00
B-111    Safety Helmet (Carrera)       2        60.00        120.00
B-112    Safety Helmet (Ozzy)         -2        22.50        (45.00)
B-112    Safety Helmet (Ozzy)          2        22.50         45.00
C-551    Hobie Skateboard              1        67.50         67.50
C-551    Hobie Skateboard              2        67.50        135.00
C-559    Flexie Skateboard             5        22.50        112.50
```

Figure 14.21: A report with data from two tables

First, we'll use query forms to create an Answer table containing the fields we need for the report. Start by pressing Clear All (Alt-F8), then select Ask from the Main menu and specify Sales as the table. Call up the menu once again, select Ask, and specify the Mastinv table. Fill in the query forms as shown in Figure 14.22.

Notice that the query forms use the example *xxx* to link the Sales and Mastinv tables by part number. The Qty and Price examples are used to calculate a total sale price. The fields we want to use in the report—that is, Part No, Qty Sold, Sel Price, and Part Name—are checked.

To avoid repeating this process in the future, save this query by calling up the menu and selecting the Scripts and QuerySave options. Name the query script Smquery and press Enter. (We'll see how this will come in handy later.) Now press DO-IT! to perform the query. The Answer table will appear with the appropriate data.

Next, we want to build a report for the fields in the Answer table. However, we don't want to use the actual Answer table, because it is a temporary table that is deleted and recreated each time you do a query.

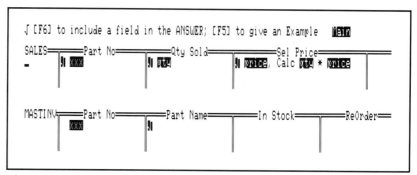

Figure 14.22: Two query forms filled out on the screen

Therefore, we'll rename this Answer table. To do so, call up the menu and select the Tools, Rename, and Table options. Enter Answer as the name of the table to rename, and Salmast as the new name, when requested. You'll notice that after the renaming is complete, the Answer table receives the new name Salmast right on the screen.

Now we can create a report format for this new Salmast table. From the menu, select the usual Report and Design options, and enter Salmast as the name of the associated table. Select 1 as the report number. Enter a description, such as Combined Tables, and press Enter. Finally, select the Tabular option.

When the report specification screen appears, you can design your report in any way you wish. In the example shown in Figure 14.23, I've rearranged the columns (using Ctrl-R), reformatted some numbers (using Field Reformat), changed some column widths (using TableBand Resize), and changed a few column titles. When you are done with the report specification, press DO-IT! to save it.

To print this combined report (now, as well as at any time in the future), we need to repeat the query process, copy the report format from the Salmast table to the current Answer table, and then print the report. Since there are several steps involved in doing so, we'll save all the necessary keystrokes as a script.

To begin recording the keystrokes, clear the screen by pressing Alt-F8, call up the menu, and select the Scripts and BeginRecord options. Name the script Salmast. (I've used the same name over again just to make it easier to remember. You can actually use any name you like.) Now, begin printing the report.

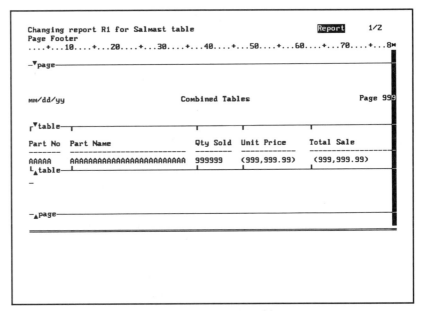

Figure 14.23: A report specification from two tables

First, call up the previously saved query by selecting Scripts and Play from the menus and specifying the Smquery script. Press DO-IT! after the query forms appear on the screen.

When the Answer table appears, call up the menu and select the Tools, Copy, and JustFamily options. Specify Salmast as the source table to copy from and Answer as the target table to copy to. Verify the copy by selecting the Replace option.

Now print the report by selecting the Report and Output options from the Main menu. Specify the Answer table and select report 1.

This is a good point to stop recording keystrokes, so that in the future you can decide whether you want the report to go to the screen, printer, or a file at this moment. We can't use the regular menu to stop recording just now, however, because there is already another menu on the screen. So use the PAL menu (press Alt-F10) and select the End-Record option. Now you can select either the Printer, Screen, or File options for your report.

At any time in the future, regardless of how many records you've added to your Sales table, you can get a current copy of this report by selecting Scripts and Play (or ShowPlay) from the menus and specifying the Salmast script. The entire process will be automated up to the point that you select either Printer, Screen, or File for your report output.

USING SUMMARY OPERATORS IN REPORTS

As mentioned earlier in this chapter, you can use *summary operators* in calculated fields, in place of Summary fields, to calculate totals, subtotals, and other group values. The summary operators are Sum(), Average(), Count(), High(), and Low(), each of which has the same function as the equivalent option from the Summary menu. In addition, the keyword *group* can be used inside a summary expression to specify calculations for a single group on the report (just as PerGroup is used with Summary fields).

In this section we'll demonstrate a report that prints invoices using summary calculations. The structure of the table that this report prints its data from is shown in Figure 14.24. (This table might actually be created from an Answer table that combines information from a customer list and a table of orders or charges.)

```
Viewing Struct table: Record 1 of 12                          Main

STRUCT        Field Name        Field Type
    1    Customer number        A5
    2    Last Name              A15
    3    First Name             A15
    4    Address                A30
    5    City                   A20
    6    State                  A2
    7    Zip Code               A10
    8    Part Number            A5
    9    Part Name              A20
   10    Qty                    S
   11    Unit Price             $
   12    Date Sold              D
```

Figure 14.24: The structure of a table used to print invoices

Samples of the invoices are shown in Figure 14.25. Though the figure shows two invoices on a single page, the report can easily print individual invoices on separate pages, as we'll demonstrate.

```
Customer number: 1001                  Invoice date:  2-Nov-87
   Andy Adams
   123 Grape St.
   Santa Monica, CA  91234

Date Sold  Part No.  Part Name            Qty  Unit Price    Item Total
---------  --------  --------------------  ---  -----------  -----------
  4/01/88  A-111     Avocado tree          5        75.00       375.00
  4/01/88  B-333     Rubber tree           1       120.00       120.00
  4/01/88  K-011     Wildflower seeds      1         5.00         5.00
  4/01/88  Z-901     Decorative ferns      5         7.50        37.50
                                                              -----------
                                           Order total:         537.50
                                           Sales Tax:            32.25
                                                              -----------
                                    Total amount due:           569.75
Thank you!


- - - - - - - - - - - - - - - - - - - - - - - - - - - - - - - - - -


Customer number: 8881                  Invoice date:  2-Nov-87
   Sandra Smith
   2071 Melba St.
   Venice, CA  92345

Date Sold  Part No.  Part Name            Qty  Unit Price    Item Total
---------  --------  --------------------  ---  -----------  -----------
  4/02/88  A-111     Avocado tree          1        75.00        75.00
  4/02/88  M-335     Fountain              1       250.00       250.00
  4/02/88  Z-901     Decorative ferns     10         7.50        75.00
                                                              -----------
                                           Order total:         400.00
                                           Sales Tax:            24.00
                                                              -----------
                                    Total amount due:           424.00
Thank you!


- - - - - - - - - - - - - - - - - - - - - - - - - - - - - - - - - -
```

Figure 14.25: Sample invoices

Figure 14.26 shows the report specification used to print the invoices. Notice that the customer information (name, address, and so forth) is displayed as a header in the Customer number group band, so that these are displayed only once on each invoice. The individual transactions are displayed in the table band. The order total, sales tax, and invoice total are displayed as the Customer number group band footer.

In the table band, the item total is a calculated field based on the expression

[Qty] * [Unit Price]

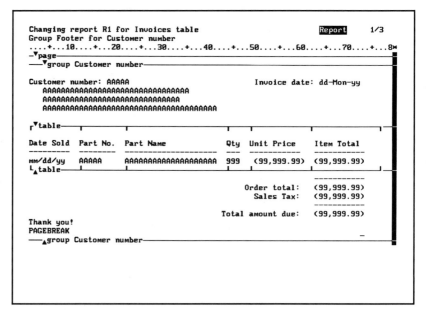

Figure 14.26: The report specification for printing invoices

In the group footer the order total is a calculated field based on the expression

Sum([Qty]*[Unit Price],group)

Note that the expression calculates the sum of the total sale (which is calculated as *Qty * Unit Price*). The *group* keyword, preceded by a comma, assures that the calculation is for the current group (invoice) only. (Note also that the *group* expression is placed inside the parentheses for the Sum operator, as required.)

The sales tax in the footer is also a calculated field, based on the expression

Sum([Qty]*[Unit Price],group)*.06

The invoice total is another calculated field, based on the expression

Sum([Qty]*[Unit Price],group)*1.06

For your general information (though this does not pertain to summary operators per se), the customer name is displayed in the group header as a calculated field using the expression

[First Name] + " " + [Last Name]

The city, state, and zip code are also a single calculated field, based on the expression

[City] + ", " + [State] + " " + [Zip Code]

The invoice date in the group header is placed using the usual Field, Place, and Date options from the Report menu.

To print each invoice on a separate page, the PAGEBREAK keyword appears at the bottom of the Customer number group band. Finally, to display column titles on each invoice, the GroupsOfTables option under the Setting Format menu options has been selected.

MULTIPLE-PAGE FORMS

On a table with many fields, it may not be possible to enter and edit data with a single custom form. In that case, you'll need to divide the form into several pages. Employment forms, tax forms, and others often require several pages of screens. A single Paradox form can consist of up to 15 "pages" of screens.

To add pages to a form, call up the menu (press F10) while editing the form, and select the Form option. You will be given these two new options:

Insert   Delete

To add a page, select the Insert option. Paradox will then display these options:

After   Before

To add a page following the form currently being edited, select the After option. To insert a page before the current form, select the Before option. A new screen for creating the new page will appear. Near the top of the screen, a symbol, such as 2/2, will tell you how many pages are on the form and which page you are viewing. For example, 1/2 indicates that you are viewing the first page of a two-page form.

While creating or editing a form with multiple pages, you can use the PgUp and PgDn keys to scroll up and down through the pages. You can also use PgUp and PgDn in conjunction with the Move command to move portions of a screen from one page to another.

When you use the multiple-page form to enter or edit data on a table, the PgUp and PgDn keys will move you from page to page, as well as through records. For example, if you are editing record number 1 (a two-page record), pressing PgDn will display the second page of record number 1. Pressing PgDn again will display the first page of record number 2.

To delete a page from a form, move to the page you want to delete and call up the menu. Select the Form option, then the Delete option. Be careful with this option. Once you delete a page, it cannot be retrieved. You would have to reinsert a new page, as well as reenter all the text and fields. (Of course, if you are editing an already existing form, you can Cancel all changes, in which case the deletion would not be saved and the page would remain intact.)

DISPLAY-ONLY FIELDS

When you use multiple-page forms, it's a good idea to carry over some identifying piece of information from one page to the next so you can always see, at a glance, which record you're working with.

Figure 14.27 shows the structure of a hypothetical table named Taxform. Suppose this table, which stores all the information to fill out a 1040 tax form, has 200 fields. You can easily set up a multiple-page form using the Page and Insert options, but let's look at a technique for carrying information over from one page to the next.

Figure 14.28 shows the first page of the custom form. All fields on this form were placed using the Put and Regular options. Therefore, you'll have complete access to all these data later when entering or editing information through the form.

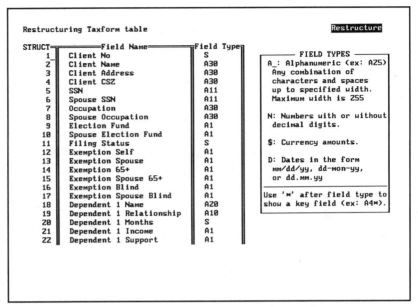

```
Restructuring Taxform table                              Restructure

STRUCT        Field Name            Field Type      ┌─── FIELD TYPES ───┐
    1    Client No                    S            A_: Alphanumeric (ex: A25)
    2    Client Name                  A30            Any combination of
    3    Client Address               A30            characters and spaces
    4    Client CSZ                   A30            up to specified width.
    5    SSN                          A11            Maximum width is 255
    6    Spouse SSN                   A11
    7    Occupation                   A30          N: Numbers with or without
    8    Spouse Occupation            A30            decimal digits.
    9    Election Fund                A1
   10    Spouse Election Fund         A1           $: Currency amounts.
   11    Filing Status                S
   12    Exemption Self               A1           D: Dates in the form
   13    Exemption Spouse             A1              mm/dd/yy, dd-mon-yy,
   14    Exemption 65+                A1              or dd.mm.yy
   15    Exemption Spouse 65+         A1
   16    Exemption Blind              A1           Use 'x' after field type to
   17    Exemption Spouse Blind       A1           show a key field (ex: A4x).
   18    Dependent 1 Name             A20
   19    Dependent 1 Relationship     A10
   20    Dependent 1 Months           S
   21    Dependent 1 Income           A1
   22    Dependent 1 Support          A1
```

Figure 14.27: The structure of a hypothetical Taxform table

```
Changing F1 form for TaxForm                          Form ◄    1/5


Client Number ------                    Social Security Number
Client Name   ----------------------    -----------
Address       ----------------------    Spouse's SSN
              ----------------------    -----------
                                        Occupation
                                        --------------------
                                        Spouse Occupation
                                        --------------------
        $1.00 to presidential election fund?   - (Y/N)
        If joint return, $1.00 from spouse?    - (Y/N)

FILING STATUS  ------      1. Single
                           2. Married filing joint return
                           3. Married filing separate return
                           4. Head of Household
                           5. Qualifying widow(er)
```

Figure 14.28: The first page of the custom form for tax table

Figure 14.29 shows the third page (of five, as indicated by *3/5* in the upper-right corner) of this form. The data inside the borders are carry-overs from the first page and cannot be changed. They are only to identify the individual for whom the tax form was entered. These were placed using the Field, Place, and DisplayOnly options from the menu. (The field on the left is Client No; the field on the right is Client Name.)

Figure 14.30 shows how this page of the form looks after entering some data into the completed form. The client name and number appear on the form for identification purposes but cannot be changed.

Since Paradox allows a regular field to be placed on a form only once, you cannot place the same regular field on different pages of a form. However, the DisplayOnly option allows you to place a field for display only on as many pages of the form as you wish. You can also use the Put and #Record options under the Forms menu to place a record number on any page of a form.

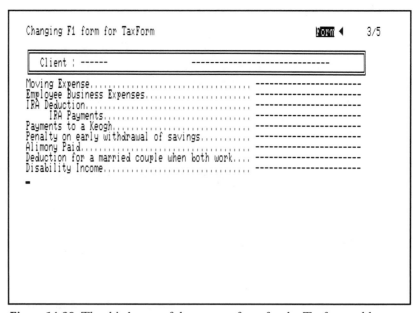

Figure 14.29: The third page of the custom form for the Taxform table

```
Editing Taxform table with form F1: Record 1 of 1            EDIT  ▲=▼

 ┌─────────────────────────────────────────────────────────────┐
 │   Client :   5001                   Albert McGinney          │
 └─────────────────────────────────────────────────────────────┘
 Moving Expense................................        500.00  ◄
 Employee Business Expenses.......................       0.00
 IRA Deduction..................................         0.00
          IRA Payments...............................     0.00
 Payments to a Keogh..............................       0.00
 Penalty on early withdrawal of savings...........      0.00
 Alimony Paid....................................        0.00
 Deduction for a married couple when both work....    400.00
 Disability Income................................      0.00
```

Figure 14.30: The third page of the Taxform data-entry form

CALCULATED FIELDS

We've seen how to perform calculations on data in tables using the Ask and Report options, but you can also perform immediate calculations on a custom form. For example, recall the structure of the Sales table, shown in Figure 14.31. Even though there is no field for storing the results of the calculation *[Qty Sold] * [Sel Price]*, we can display these results on a form using a calculated field.

Take a look at the form in Figure 14.32. All the fields except one were placed on this form using the usual Field, Place, and Regular options from the Forms menu. The field next to the *Total:* prompt was placed by selecting the Field, Place, and Calculated options from the menus. The expression entered into the field is *[Qty Sold] * [Sel Price]*.

When you use this form to enter or edit data, Paradox will not let you move the cursor to this calculated field. However, when you enter or change data in the Qty Sold and/or Sel Price fields, Paradox will immediately calculate and display the results of the calculation, as shown in Figure 14.33.

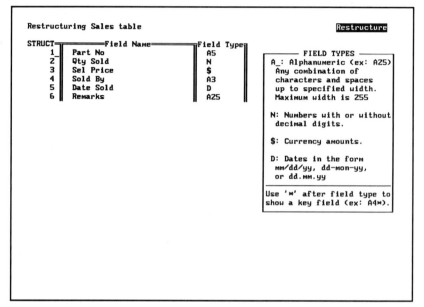

Figure 14.31: The structure of the Sales table

```
Changing F1 form for Sales                          FORM  ◄    1/1

 ┌──────────────────────────────────────────────────────────────┐
 │ Enter a Sales Transaction                                     │
 └──────────────────────────────────────────────────────────────┘

   Date: -----------              Sold By: ---


   Part Number : -----

   Quantity:        -----------------------

   Unit Price:      -----------------------

      Total:        -----------------------

 ╔══════════════════════════════════════════════════════════════╗
 ║                                                                ║
 ║   Remarks:      -----------------------                        ║
 ║                                                                ║
 ╚══════════════════════════════════════════════════════════════╝
                                        ▪
```

Figure 14.32: The form for the Sales table

```
Editing A:sales table with form F1: Record 1 of 12          Edit  ─▼

  ┌─────────────────────────────────────────────────────────────────┐
  │ Enter a Sales Transaction                                       │
  └─────────────────────────────────────────────────────────────────┘

  Date:  6/01/88                           Sold By: JAK


  Part Number : C-551

  Quantity:                          3

  Unit Price:                        67.50

     Total:                          202.5

  ┌─────────────────────────────────────────────────────────────────┐
  │                                                                   │
  │     Remarks:  _                          ◄                        │
  │                                                                   │
  └─────────────────────────────────────────────────────────────────┘
```

Figure 14.33: A calculated total on a data-entry form

UPDATING MULTIPLE TABLES

Paradox allows you to simultaneously enter or update data on two or more tables. With the use of keyed fields, you can even enter data in a one-to-many fashion quickly and efficiently using this technique. An example will demonstrate this best.

Suppose you decide to add a table of vendor names and addresses to the inventory system we developed earlier. For each record on the master inventory table, you wish to store a vendor code that will relate the product to a particular vendor. Your first task would be to add a vendor code field to the Mastinv table, following these steps:

1. Type Alt-F8 to clear the workspace.

2. Select Modify and Restructure from the Main menu, and specify Mastinv as the table to restructure.

3. Add a field named Vendor Code to the table, with A5 as the data type (as shown in Figure 14.34).

4. Press DO-IT! to save the new structure.

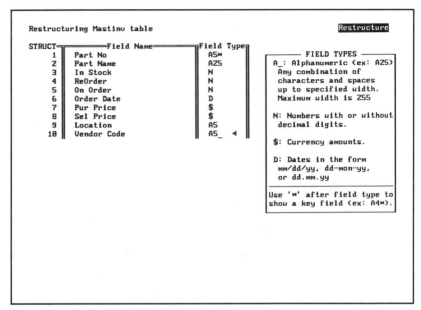

Figure 14.34: The Mastinv table with the Vendor Code field added

Next, you'll need a table to store vendor names and addresses in, with a vendor code to link the vendor to the product in the master inventory table. Here are the steps:

1. Type Alt-F8 to clear the workspace.

2. Select Create from the Main menu.

3. Enter Vendors as the name of the new table.

4. Structure the new table as in Figure 14.35.

5. Press DO-IT! to save the new structure.

Notice that Vendor Code is a key field in the Vendors table (marked with an asterisk). This ensures that each vendor in the Vendors table has a unique vendor code. Also, the data type and size (A5) is identical to the data type and size of the Vendor Code field in the Mastinv table, since this will be the common field used to link the two tables.

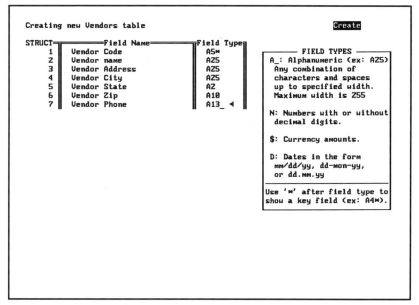

Figure 14.35: The structure of the Vendors table

SETTING UP MULTIENTRY TABLES

The next step is to set up a *source table* that contains fields from both the Mastinv and Vendors tables. You'll use this single table to enter data into both tables simultaneously. You'll also need a *map table,* which tells Paradox where to put the data from the source table. You use the Modify, MultiEntry, and SetUp options to create these tables. Here are the steps to follow:

1. Type Alt-F8 to clear the workspace.

2. Select Ask from the Main menu, and enter Vendors as the table to query.

3. Call up the menu once again, and select Ask.

4. Specify Mastinv as the table to query.

You'll then have two query forms on the workspace: one for the Vendors table and one for the Mastinv table. Now you put check marks into the fields that you want to appear in the source table. Also, you need to enter examples to link the two tables. In this instance, we'll put all the fields from both tables into the source table, and link the two tables by the common Vendor Code field. Here are the steps to do this:

1. Press Up Image (F3) to move to the Vendors query form.
2. Press F6 while in the leftmost column to place check marks in all the fields.
3. Press → to move to the Vendor Code field.
4. Press Example (F5).
5. Type **ABC** and press Enter.

Now the query form for the Vendors table has check marks in all fields and the example ABC in the Vendor Code field. Next let's set up the Mastinv query form:

1. Press Down Image (F4) to move to the Mastinv query form.
2. Press F6 to put check marks in all fields.
3. Use Ctrl-→ and → several times to move the cursor to the Vendor Code field in the Mastinv query form (the field farthest to the right).
4. Press F6 to erase the check mark.
5. Press Example (F5).
6. Type in **ABC**.

As usual, the example ABC is completely arbitrary. You can use any examples you like so long as they match on both query forms.

When creating a source table, only one of the example fields can have a check mark. Therefore, we had to delete the check mark in the Vendor Code field of the Mastinv table before entering the example. Your workspace should look something like Figure 14.36.

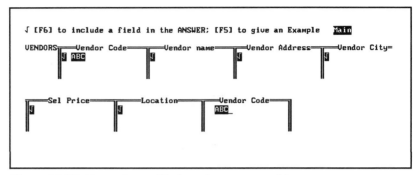

Figure 14.36: Query forms filled out for a source table

Next you need to create the map and source tables from these query forms. Call up the Main menu and select the Modify, MultiEntry, and SetUp options. Paradox asks for the name of the source table:

Source table:
Enter new name for the source table.

Enter a unique table name, such as Vendmast, and press Enter. Paradox now asks for the name of the map table:

Map table:
Enter new name for the map table.

Enter a unique name, such as Vmmap, and press Enter. A map describing the destinations for each field from the source table will appear in the middle of the screen. Beneath the map, you'll be able to see a portion of the source table, as shown in Figure 14.37.

You can use Up Image (F3) and Down Image (F4) to move the cursor to any of these tables and explore them further if you like. You'll notice that the Vmmap table consists of three fields:

- Source Field, which names the fields on the source table

- Target Field, which names the fields that will receive new data from the source table

```
Viewing Vendmast table: Table is empty                    Main  ▲═

VMMAP══════════Source Field════        ══════Target Field═══             ═════
      1   Vendor Code                  Vendor Code               Vendors
      2   Vendor name                  Vendor name               Vendors
      3   Vendor Address               Vendor Address            Vendors
      4   Vendor City                  Vendor City               Vendors
      5   Vendor State                 Vendor State              Vendors
      6   Vendor Zip                   Vendor Zip                Vendors
      7   Vendor Phone                 Vendor Phone              Vendors
      8   Part No                      Part No                   Mastinv
      9   Part Name                    Part Name                 Mastinv
     10   In Stock                     In Stock                  Mastinv
     11   ReOrder                      ReOrder                   Mastinv
     12   On Order                     On Order                  Mastinv
     13   Order Date                   Order Date                Mastinv
     14   Pur Price                    Pur Price                 Mastinv
     15   Sel Price                    Sel Price                 Mastinv
     16   Location                     Location                  Mastinv
     17   Vendor Code                  Vendor Code               Mastinv


VENDMAST═Vendor Code═      ═Vendor name═         ═Vendor Address═
      ─
```

Figure 14.37: The map and source tables on the screen

- Target Table, which specifies the table that will receive data from the source table

Notice that the Vendor Code field appears twice in the map. That's because the vendor code, though only entered once in the source table, will be stored on both the Mastinv and Vendors tables.

You can modify this table in any way you like, using the usual keys for editing a table. However, until you gain some practice with MultiEntry, it's best not to play around with the map.

So now you're done creating the source table and map. You can simply clear them from the workspace by typing Alt-F8. The new tables will be stored on disk in the usual manner.

ENTERING DATA WITH MULTIENTRY

To use the new source and map tables to enter data into the Mastinv and Vendors tables simultaneously, you select the Modify,

MultiEntry, and Entry options from the menu. In this example, follow these steps:

1. Select Modify, MultiEntry, and Entry from the menu.

2. Enter Vendmast as the name of the source table, and press Enter.

3. Enter Vmmap as the name of the map table, and press Enter.

The source table appears on the screen, and you can enter data as you would on any table. Of course, you can press Form Toggle (F7) to switch to Form View if you like. Figure 14.38 shows the source table in Form View with some sample data entered. If you are following along on-line, go ahead and type the sample data into the form.

Now, suppose you want to add another product, but from the same vendor. After entering data for the first record and pressing Enter, you can use the Ditto (^ D) key to fill in the vendor fields on

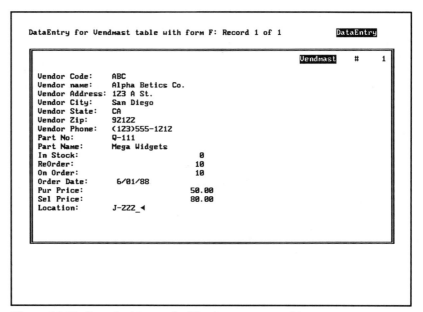

Figure 14.38: Sample data on the Vendmast source table

the form. (Just hold down the Ctrl key and type the letter D, followed by a press on the Enter key, seven times.) Then type in the product information shown in Figure 14.39.

Enter one more record on the form, as shown in Figure 14.40. Since this is a new vendor, you'll want to type in the vendor information rather than use the Ditto key.

Press the DO-IT! key to save the new records. (Of course, you could enter as many records as you wish, but for this example three records will suffice.)

So now, let's see what happened. Follow these steps to clear the workspace and view the Mastinv and Vendors tables:

1. Clear the workspace by pressing Alt-F8.

2. Select View from the menu, and enter Vendors as the table.

3. Call up the menu, select View, and specify Mastinv as the table.

You'll see both tables on the screen, as in Figure 14.41. (You can use the Rotate key to bring the Vendor Code field from the Mastinv table into view.) Let's discuss what has taken place here.

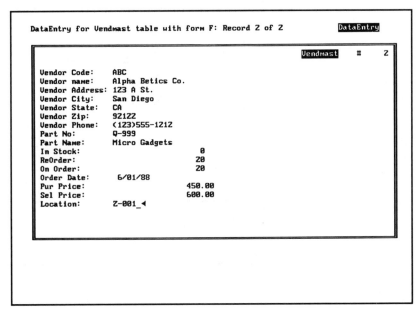

Figure 14.39: The second record entered on the Vendmast source table

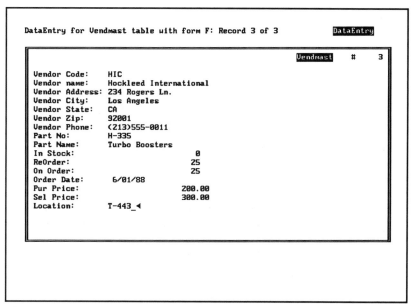

Figure 14.40: A third record added to the source table

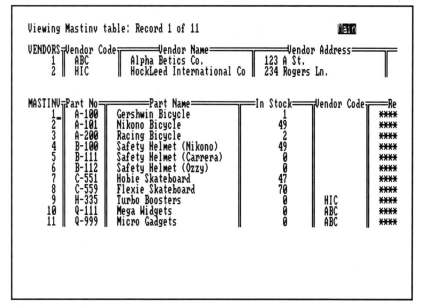

Figure 14.41: The Mastinv and Vendors tables on the screen

First, you'll notice that the vendor ABC has been entered into the Vendors table only once. This is good because, even though we may stock many products from this vendor, we only need to store his name and address in one place. However, all three new records have been added to the bottom of the Mastinv table. This is correct, since the two new products each deserve a record on the master inventory (another example of a one-to-many relationship).

How was Paradox so smart as to figure all this out? Well, we helped it along a little. Here's how. When using MultiEntry with a keyed table (like Vendors, which uses Vendor Code as a key field), Paradox will quickly analyze any records that have been entered with identical keys (Vendor Code in this example). If two records do have identical keys, then Paradox will do one of two things:

- If the two records fail to match exactly in every field, the new record will be sent to the Keyviol table.

- If the two records are identical in every way, the new record will be *absorbed* into the keyed table. It will not be added as a new record or considered an error.

By virtue of the fact that we used the Ditto key to enter the second record into the source table, we duplicated the previous entry exactly. Therefore, Paradox correctly absorbed the record into the Vendors table.

CUSTOM MULTIENTRY FORMS

You can build a custom form for a MultiEntry form just as you can for any single table. You need to build the form from the source table (not the map table). In this example, you would select Forms from the Paradox Main menu, and Design from the submenu. Then you'd specify VendMast as the table for the form. Select a form number, and enter a form description in the normal manner.

When you see the blank screen for designing the form, use the usual techniques to design the form. Press DO-IT! when done designing the form.

To use the custom form in the future, select Modify MultiEntry and Entry from the Main menu, as usual. When prompted, specify the name of the source table (VendMast in this example), and the name of the map table (Vmmap in this example).

The table image of the form will appear on the screen. To switch to your custom form, call up the menu (F10) and select the Image and PickForm options. Select the form number you want (1 in this example). Enter data as you normally would, then press DO-IT! when done.

An important note to keep in mind when designing forms for MultiEntry is that the cursor will move from field to field in the same order that the fields are listed in the MultiEntry table. If you wish to alter the order in which the cursor moves through the fields, view the MultiEntry table on the screen (VendMast in this example), switch toEdit mode (F9), and use the Rotate key or Image menu options to rearrange the field order. When the fields are in the order you want, save the new structure using the KeepSettings option from the Image menu, and press F2 to save your work.

ENTERING DATA WITH MULTIADD

Another technique for updating two or more tables simultaneously involves the MultiAdd option from the Tools menu. In this example, you would first use the usual Edit or DataEntry options from the Main menu to add records to the Vendmast table. Treating Vendmast as a single table will allow you to add records to the table without automatically adding the records to the associated Mastinv and Vendors tables. You can print a copy of the Vendmast table, make corrections, and then later add records from Vendmast to the two target tables.

You'll need to create both the source (Vendmast) and map (Vmmap) tables first (if you haven't already done so), as discussed above. Then select Modify and Edit, or Modify and DataEntry, to add new records to Vendmast. When you are ready to transfer data from Vendmast to Mastinv and Vendors, follow these steps:

1. Press Alt-F8 to clear the workspace.

2. Select Tools, More, and MultiAdd from the Main menu.

3. Specify Vendmast as the source table.

4. Specify Vmmap as the map table.

5. Select Update to perform the transfer.

Both the Mastinv and Vendors tables will be updated at that point. Records on the Vendmast table will remain in place as well.

The NewEntries option under Tools, More, and MultiAdd inserts new records into the target tables, rather than updating the existing records. Any duplicate key entries will show up in the Keyviol table.

KEY VIOLATIONS WITH MULTIENTRY

One problem with MultiEntry concerns the use of key fields. In the first example of data entry, the second entry with the identical vendor information (entered via the Ditto key) was absorbed into the Vendors table because every character of every field was identical to the previously entered vendor.

However, if you enter information into the MultiEntry screen with an existing vendor code (such as ABC), but do *not* type in the rest of the information *exactly* as it appears in all the existing fields, then the entire new entry is considered a key violation, and will appear in the Keyviol table when you attempt to save your work. This, in turn, means that information being sent to both the Mastinv table and the Vendors table will not be recorded.

The only way to salvage your work is to attempt to edit the Keyviol table so that existing vendor fields in the Keyviol table are *identical* to the entries in the Vendors table. This, however, is probably more work than it is worth, at least in this particular application. You may want to experiment with the MultiAdd option to determine if it is a useful data entry technique for your own particular Paradox applications.

The alternative, of course, is to enter data on the Vendors and Mastinv tables independently. When new items are to be added to the inventory, enter any new vendors in the Vendors table first. Then enter individual product descriptions into the Mastinv table. If you use a TableLookup ValCheck with HelpAndFill in the Vendor Code field on the Mastinv table form, it will reject invalid vendor codes immediately, and help you look up the correct vendor code. (Table look-ups are discussed in Chapter 12.)

SUMMARY

Complete mastery of the Paradox report generator will require some practice as well as a knowledge of the tools that are available to you. In this section, we've had a chance to develop a report with calculated fields, summary fields, subtotals, and totals. We've also been able to discuss many general options available from the Report menu. But the key to mastering the report generator is simply practice.

Creating reports is very much an iterative process. You design a little, make a quick printout (using Instant Report or the Output option from the Report menu), then design a little more and see the results. Keep doing so until your report looks exactly as you want it to, and save the report specification with the DO-IT! key.

Particular topics of importance that we've discussed in this chapter are summarized below:

- To insert, delete, copy, move, or modify fields in a tabular report, select the TableBand option from the Report menu.

- To place fields in a tabular report format, call up the Report menu and select Field.

- To display the results of calculations on fields in a record, enter a calculated field using the Field, Place, and Calculated options from the Report menu.

- To group records in a report, select the Group option from the Report menu.

- To display subtotals in a report, place a summary field at the bottom of a group band.

- To display grand totals in a report, place a summary field in the report band at the bottom of the report specification.

- To include multiple groups (or subtotals of subtotals), use nested group bands.

- To insert blank lines in a report specification, press Enter while Insert mode is on.

- To delete blank lines in a report specification, move the cursor to the leftmost column of the blank line and type Ctrl-Y.

- To specify sort orders for groups in a report, select the Sort-Direction option from the Group submenu.

- To print summary reports, remove all field templates from the table band and place them in the group band beneath.

- To print reports from two or more related tables, combine the tables into a single table using query forms, and develop the report format from a copy of the Answer table.

AUTOMATIC UPDATING

UPDATING IS A PROCESS WHEREBY THE CONTENTS OF one table are modified based on the contents of another. In this chapter, we'll show a technique for updating the Mastinv table based on the contents of the Sales and Purchase tables that we developed in Chapter 12. That is, the quantities of items sold will be subtracted from the in-stock quantities, and the purchases (items received) will be added to the in-stock quantities. Furthermore, items from the Purchase table will be subtracted from the on-order quantities (which assumes that these items were actually received), and the current purchase price in the Mastinv table will be changed to reflect the current purchase price in the Purchase table.

Before we begin, we need to discuss one problem that always accompanies an updating procedure. That is, how to differentiate between records that have already been updated (or *posted to* the Mastinv table) and those that have not. If we sell five racing bicycles and record this on the Sales table, then update the Mastinv table, the in-stock quantity of the racing bicycles will properly be decreased by five. However, we have to be sure not to update this same transaction again in the future, or the in-stock quantity on the Mastinv table will erroneously be decreased by five once again.

One way to handle this situation is to move all records that have already been updated from the Sales and Purchase tables onto separate *history tables*. This technique offers several advantages:

1. The current Sales and Purchase tables can be kept relatively small for quicker processing and easier access to current data.

2. On a floppy disk system, large history tables can periodically be transferred to other disks, thereby avoiding the problem of running out of disk space.

3. History tables encourage the use of *adjustment transactions* to make corrections, which leave a permanent audit trail of all events that have influenced the Mastinv table.

Let's set up some history tables for our inventory system.

HISTORY TABLES

A history table generally has the same structure as the associated transaction table. In this example, we'll create a history table named Salhist with the same structure as the Sales table. Select the Tools, Copy, and Table options from the Main and submenus. Specify Sales as the table to copy from and Salhist as the table to copy to.

Once the copy is complete, make sure the Salhist table is empty. To do so, select the Tools, More, and Empty options and specify Salhist as the table to empty. Select Ok when Paradox asks you to verify your request.

To create a history table for the Purchase table, named Purhist, select the Tools, Copy, and Table options, and specify Purchase as the table to copy from and Purhist as the table to copy to. Again, to ensure that you're starting with an empty table, select the Tools, More, and Empty options and specify Purhist as the table to empty. Select Ok when Paradox asks you to verify.

Now our entire inventory database consists of five tables, as shown in Figure 15.1. At the moment, the Sales and Purchase tables have some data on them, and both history tables are empty. After performing an update, the Sales and Purchase tables will be empty, and the Salhist and Purhist tables will contain the updated records.

As new sales and purchases occur, these will be added to the Sales and Purchase tables. However, as soon as an automated update takes place, the new records in Sales and Purchase will be added to the Salhist and Purhist tables. Hence, both history tables will tend to grow indefinitely, while Sales and Purchases grow only between updates.

AUTOMATING AN UPDATE PROCEDURE

Updating involves quite a few steps, so your best bet is to record all the required keystrokes in a script. If you're planning on following along

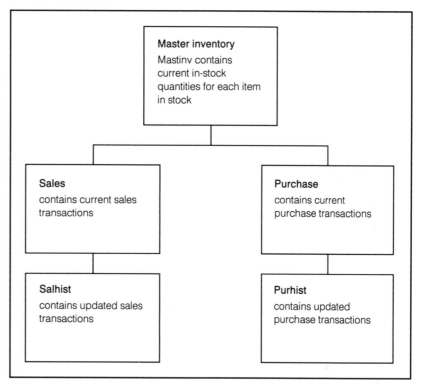

Figure 15.1: Five tables in the inventory system

on-line at this point, make sure you have a few minutes to complete all the necessary steps. Once you've saved all the keystrokes, you need only play the script to perform a complete update in the future.

RECORDING THE SCRIPT

To start recording the script, call up the Main menu and select the Scripts and BeginRecord options. Then enter the name Invupdat for the script. To be sure the script always starts with a clear screen, press Clear All (Alt-F8). Now we can begin the update.

SUMMARIZING THE SALES TRANSACTIONS

The first step in performing the update is to total and summarize all the sales transactions. To do so, select Ask from the Main menu and specify the Sales table. Place a check mark in the Part No column and the instruction

Calc sum

in the Qty Sold column, as shown in Figure 15.2. Press F2. The summarized table will appear on the screen as in the bottom of Figure 15.2.

SUBTRACTING SALES FROM MASTER QUANTITIES

The next step is to subtract the sums in this Sum of Qty Sold field from the Mastinv table. Follow these steps to do so:

1. Press Up Image (F3).

2. Press Clear Image (F8).

3. Call up a query form for the Answer table (call up the menu (F10), select Ask, and specify the Answer table).

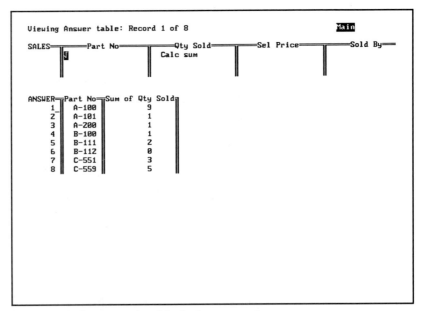

Figure 15.2: Summary (totals) of sales transactions

4. Enter an example in the Part No field (move the cursor to the Part No field, press F5, type **XXX**, and press Enter).

5. Enter an example in the Sum of Qty Sold field (press F5 and type Sqty).

The query form should now look like the top of Figure 15.3.

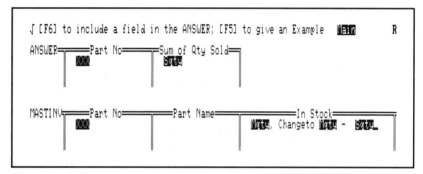

Figure 15.3: A query to update Mastinv from the Sales table

Next, fill in a query form for the Mastinv table that will subtract the sums of quantities sold from the in-stock quantities. Here are the steps:

1. Bring up a query form for Mastinv (call up the menu, select Ask, and specify the Mastinv table).

2. Enter an Example for the Part No field (move the cursor to the Part No field, press F5, type **XXX**, and press Enter).

3. Enter an example and formula in the In Stock field. (Move the cursor to the In Stock field, press F5, and type **Mqty**. Then type in a comma and a space, followed by the command

   Changeto Mqty − Sqty

   Remember to press the Example (F5) key before entering Mqty and Sqty.)

The query form for the Mastinv table should look like the lower one in Figure 15.3. Perform the query by pressing DO-IT!. You'll see the

Changed table, which displays copies of changed records with their original values. But before you check that actual changes have taken place on the Mastinv table, we have some more work to do.

MOVING RECORDS TO THE HISTORY TABLE

Next, we need to move the updated records from the Sales table to the Salhist table, then empty all records from the Sales table. Here are the steps:

1. Clear the screen (press Alt-F8).

2. Append records from the Sales table to the bottom of the Salhist table (select the Tools, More, and Add options, and specify Sales as the source table to copy from and Salhist as the target table to copy to).

3. Empty the Sales table (call up the menu, select Tools, More, and Empty, specify the Sales table, and select Ok).

That takes care of the Sales table. Now let's do the same for the Purchase table. This update is a little more complex, because we need to add quantities from Purchase to quantities in Mastinv, then subtract these same values from the Mastinv OnOrder field, updating the purchase price at the same time. The first task is to summarize the purchase transactions.

SUMMARIZING THE PURCHASE TRANSACTIONS

In order to summarize the purchase transactions, you must follow these steps:

1. Clear the screen (press Alt-F8).

2. Call up a query form (select Ask and specify Purchase).

3. Calculate the sum of the quantity ordered and the highest purchase price for each individual part number (place a check mark in the Part No field, the instruction Calc sum in the Qty Recd field, and the instruction Calc average in the Pur Price field, as shown in the top of Figure 15.4).

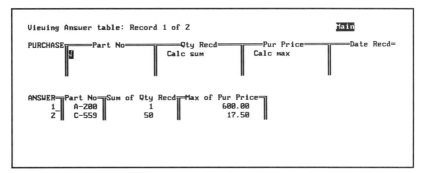

Figure 15.4: A query and answer summarizing purchase transactions

4. Press DO-IT! to perform the query.

Note that we've used Calc max to calculate the purchase price with which to update the Mastinv table purchase price. Ideally, we would want the most recent purchase price, but there is no command to calculate the most recent price. Calc max will calculate the most recent *date* when used in a Date field, but Pur Price is a Currency field. So, since we can't calculate the most recent purchase price, we've used the next best value—the highest purchase price. (Since prices seem to always go up, this is a reasonable alternative.)

ADDING PURCHASES TO MASTER QUANTITIES

After the Answer table has appeared, fill in query forms to update the Mastinv table from the Answer table. These are the steps:

1. Move up to the query form (press F3).

2. Delete the query form (press F8).

3. Call up a query form for the Answer table (call up the menu, select Ask, and specify Answer as the table to query).

4. Type in examples. (Put the cursor in the Part No field, press F5, and type **XXX**. Move the cursor to the Sum of Qty Recd field, press F5, and type **Pqty**. Move the cursor to the Average of Pur Price field, press F5, and type **Pprice**.)

Your query form should look like the top of Figure 15.5.

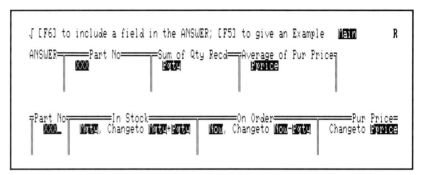

Figure 15.5: A query to update Mastinv from the Purchase table

Next, enter examples and formulas into a query form for the Mastinv table that will add purchases to the in-stock quantities, subtract them from the on-order quantities, and replace the value in the Pur Price field with the average of the latest purchase price. To do this, follow these steps:

1. Call up a query form for Mastinv (press Menu, select Ask, and specify Mastinv).

2. Place an example in the Part No field (move the cursor to the Part No field, press F5, and type **XXX**).

3. Place examples and a formula in the In Stock field. (Move the cursor to the In Stock field, press F5, and type **Mqty**. Then type a comma and the instruction **Changeto**, press F5 again, type **Mqty** and a + sign, press F5 again, and type **Pqty**.)

4. Place examples and a formula in the On Order field. (Move the cursor to the On Order field, press F5, type **Now**, a comma, and the **Changeto** instruction; press F5, type **Now**, then enter a minus sign (hyphen), press F5, and type **Pqty**.)

5. Place an example and formula in the Pur Price field. (Move the cursor to the Pur Price field, type in the command **Changeto**, press F5, and type **Pprice**.)

The examples and formulas in the Mastinv query should appear as they do in Figure 15.5. Note, however, that I've rearranged the columns to better fit them on the screen. Be sure to get the right formula in the right field. (Also note that the previous Answer table may still be showing on your screen.)

When both query forms are complete, perform the update by pressing F2.

MOVING PURCHASE TRANSACTIONS TO THE PURHIST TABLE

The last step in the update is to move all purchases from the Purchase table to the Purhist table, and then empty the Purchase table. This is done by following these steps:

1. Clear the screen (press Alt-F8).

2. Copy records to Purhist (select the Tools, More, and Add options, and specify Purchase as the source table with records to copy and Purhist as the target table to which the records will be copied).

3. Empty the Purchase table (call up the menu, select the Tools, More, and Empty options, specify Purchase as the table to empty, and select Ok).

4. Clear the screen (press Alt-F8).

COMPLETING THE SCRIPT

You can stop recording the Invupdat script now by selecting the Script and End-Record options from the menus.

VERIFYING THE UPDATE

To verify that the update worked properly, view the Mastinv table. As Figure 15.6 shows, some values in the In Stock, On Order, and Pur Price columns have changed. For example, part number C-559 now shows 70 units in stock, because five were sold and 50 were

```
Part No   Part Name                 In Stock  ReOrder  On Order  Order Date  Pur Price    Location
-------   ----------------------    --------  -------  --------  ----------  ------------ --------
A-100     Gershwin Bicycle             1         5         0      1/31/88       450.00    J-111
A-101     Nikono Bicycle              49        35         0      1/31/88       375.00    J-112
A-200     Racing Bicycle               2         3         0      2/01/88       600.00    M-991
B-100     Safety Helmet (Nikono)      49        10         0      2/15/88        20.00    L-111
B-111     Safety Helmet (Carrera)      0        10         0      2/15/88        40.00    J-333
B-112     Safety Helmet (Ozzy)         0        10        25      1/31/88        15.00    L-225
C-551     Hobie Skateboard            47        75         0      4/15/88        45.00    S-911
C-559     Flexie Skateboard           70        25         0      4/15/88        17.50    S-912
```

Figure 15.6: The Mastinv table after an automated update

received. There are no Flexie Skateboards on order because of the 50 that were received. The purchase price is now $17.50, as was indicated on the Purchase table.

Also, if you view either the Sales or Purchase tables, you'll see that both are empty. Viewing the Salhist and Purhist tables will show where the data went.

To test the whole procedure again, add a couple of records to both the Sales and Purchase tables. Now call up the menu, select Scripts and either Play or ShowPlay, and specify the Invupdat script. Then just sit back and relax for a couple of minutes while the script performs the new update and takes care of all the transactions.

DEVELOPING A SCHEDULE

Systems that use automated updating should be run on some kind of a schedule. In inventory systems, updates are often performed every day. (Bookkeeping systems, on the other hand, are often posted only once a month.) You should develop a routine for updating, such as the one below:

1. Add new transactions to the Sales and Purchase tables during business hours.

2. Print current Sales and Purchase reports at the end of each day.

3. Make any necessary corrections *before* the update is performed.

4. Perform the update after verifying sales and purchases.

5. Print the current master inventory data after the update.

Notice that the schedule specifies that current sales and purchases be printed before the update, since these records will be moved off the current Sales and Purchase tables during the update. Any corrections should be made before the update (though this is not essential). The master inventory table is then updated and contains only up-to-the-minute data.

CORRECTING UPDATED TRANSACTIONS

Occasionally, you may discover that a sales or purchase transaction which has already been updated was incorrect. This might be caused by a typographical error, or perhaps by an individual returning an item and receiving a refund.

One way to rectify this situation would be to edit the Salhist or Purhist table directly, then edit the Mastinv table directly. However, doing so leaves no audit trail to explain the change.

The preferred method for making such a correction would be to make an *adjustment transaction.* For example, you may have noticed that the Sales database (see Figure 12.9) contained a record with the following data:

Part_No	Qty_Sold	Sel_Price	Sold_By	Remarks
B-112	– 2	25.00	BBG	Return and Refund

Notice that the number sold is a negative number (– 2), and the Remarks field (which, as you see, can be a very useful field to have) explains the situation. During updating, this negative value will be subtracted from the In Stock quantity (thereby increasing the quantity). This method provides an accurate In Stock quantity as well as a record of the change in the Salhist table for future auditing.

A MASTER INVENTORY REPORT

You may want to develop some formatted reports for your master inventory table, though a simple Instant Report (Alt-F7) will tell you a lot. Perhaps the most important data you'll need, however, is a list of items that must be reordered. To get this information, simply view records with reorder points that are greater than the sum of the In Stock and On Order fields. Figure 15.7 shows a query that will pull these records out of the Mastinv table for you.

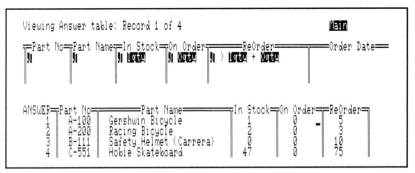

Figure 15.7: A query for items that must be ordered

Of course, you can develop formatted reports for your Mastinv table and use the JustFamily copying procedure we discussed earlier to print data based on queries from the table.

───── *SUMMARY* ─────

- Automatic updating allows you to change the values in one table based on the values in another.

- To avoid errors during updating procedures, you can copy updated records to separate history tables as soon as the update is complete.

- To perform an update, first summarize and total data in the transaction table, then set up query forms for the Answer and master tables with appropriate examples and formulas.

- To copy updated transactions to a history table, use the Tools, More, and Add options.

- To empty updated transactions from a transaction table, use the Tools, More, and Empty options.

- To correct transactions that have already been updated, enter *adjustment transactions* into the current transaction tables.

MANAGING FILES

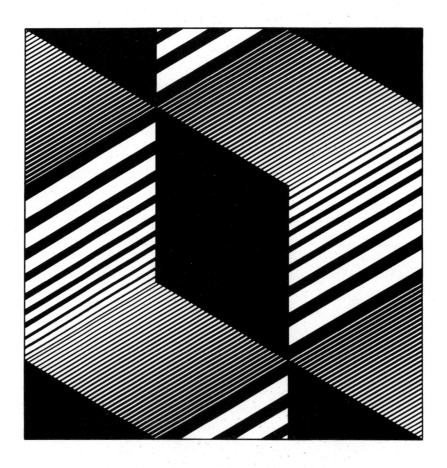

CHAPTER 16 _____

AS YOU DEVELOP MORE PARADOX *OBJECTS* (TABLES, forms, reports, and scripts), you'll need to learn techniques for managing them. The Tools option from the Main menu provides options for renaming, copying, deleting, and viewing objects. The Tools menu also provides options for importing and exporting data between Paradox and other database or spreadsheet programs, as well as for protecting data. We've used several options from the Tools menu already in previous chapters. In this chapter, we'll round out our knowledge of the Tools capability and discuss general techniques for managing objects.

When you select Tools from the Main menu, the submenu displays the following options:

Rename   QuerySpeedup   ExportImport   Copy   Delete
Info   Net   More

We'll discuss each of these options below (except for Net, which is discussed later under networking. If you are using Paradox on a network, be sure to read Chapter 22, as many of these options perform differently on a network).

_____ *RENAMING OBJECTS* _____

To rename a table or other object, select the Rename option from the Tools menu. The submenu will provide these options:

Table   Form   Report   Script

Once you select one of these options, Paradox will help you identify the object you want to rename, then ask for the new name. If the new name you enter is the same as an existing name, Paradox will ask for confirmation before deleting the original object and replacing it with the object being renamed.

The Rename option can be especially useful with the Answer table. If you perform a complex query whose results you wish to save for future use, simply rename the Answer table. The renamed Answer table will be as readily available as any other Paradox table.

COPYING OBJECTS

To make copies of objects, select Copy from the Tools menu. The submenu will display the following options:

Table   Form   Report   Script   JustFamily

Copying is useful for making backups of important data or for creating a new form or report that is similar to an existing form or report. When you decide to copy a table, Paradox will ask for the name of the table to copy and a name for the copy. The copy will include all the objects associated with the original table, including forms and reports.

The Form and Report options copy forms and reports within a table name. These are used primarily when you want to design a new form or report that is similar to an existing form or report.

The JustFamily option copies all the objects associated with a table (for instance, forms and reports) without copying the table itself. We've already seen how this can come in handy for using reports with query forms and printing reports from multiple tables.

COPYING ON A TWO-FLOPPY SYSTEM

If your computer does not have a hard disk, and you wish to copy a table from one floppy disk to another, you must follow the instructions below:

1. Press Clear All (Alt-F8).

2. Place the floppy disk containing the table you want to copy in drive B (if it is not already there).

3. Select the Tools and Copy options from the Main menu.

4. When prompted, enter the name of the table you wish to copy, and press Enter.

5. When prompted to enter the name of the copied file, be sure to enter A: in front of the file name. For example, if you want to copy to a table named MyData, type in the name of the table as A:MyData, but *do not* press Enter yet.

6. Remove the Paradox System Disk II (or System Disk I/II on a 3½-inch drive system) from drive A.

7. Place a formatted disk that is not write-protected in drive A.

8. Press the Enter key. Paradox will copy the table and associated forms, reports, and other objects to the disk in drive A.

9. As soon as the copy is complete, remove the disk in drive A, and put the Paradox System Disk II (or System Disk I/II) back into drive A.

DELETING OBJECTS

The Delete option from the Tools menu provides these options:

Table   Form   Report   Script   QuerySpeedup
KeepSettings   ValCheck

As you can see, the Delete option allows you to delete anything, including image settings and validity checks assigned to a table.

Do be careful, however, when deleting objects. Once deleted, they cannot be recovered. Before deleting an object, Paradox will double-check and allow you to change your mind, using the usual display:

Cancel   Ok

Select Ok to delete or Cancel to cancel your request.

COPYING RECORDS FROM ONE TABLE TO ANOTHER

In Chapter 15 we saw a technique for moving copies of records from one table to another using the Tools, More, and Add options.

These options can also be used to combine information from several tables into a single table. There are a few minor catches to watch out for when using the Tools, More, and Add options:

- The two tables must have compatible structures. This means that you cannot add records from a table containing Last Name, First Name, and Address fields to a table containing Amount, Qty, and Date fields. If you wish to combine tables with incompatible structures, you should use multiple-query forms, then rename the Answer table, thereby creating a new table with a new structure.

- If two compatible tables are combined but the receiving table has a key field, records that violate the rule of uniqueness in the key field will be displayed in the Keyviol table. As discussed earlier, you can edit or delete records in the Keyviol table, then use Tools, More, and Add once again to add records from the Keyviol table to the receiving table. You must do so immediately though, because the Keyviol table is erased when you exit Paradox. (Optionally, just copy the Keyviol table using Tools Copy, and edit the copied Answer table when it's convenient to do so.)

▬▬ *REMOVING RECORDS FROM A TABLE* ▬▬

You can remove individual records from a table by simply pressing the Del key while in the Edit mode, or by using the Delete option in a query form. But you can also remove records from a table that match records in another table by using the Tools, More, and Subtract options. Let's look at an example.

Suppose you have an accounts-receivable system in which you bill clients at the end of the month for purchases made during the previous month. You store these charges on a table named Charges, as shown in Figure 16.1.

At the end of November, you want to isolate charges for the month of October. You could set up a query like the one in Figure 16.2 to pull out all records with purchase dates in October.

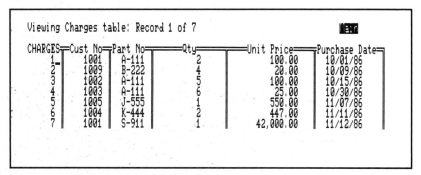

Figure 16.1: Charges on the Charges table

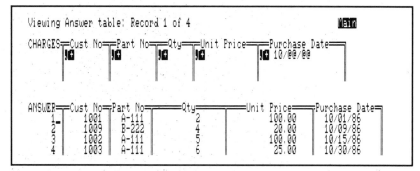

Figure 16.2: A query for charges in the month of October

Next, using the Tools, Rename, and Table options, you rename the Answer table as Billed. Now the Billed table contains only transactions for the month of October, as shown in Figure 16.3. Now you could use Tools, Copy, and JustFamily to copy a report specification for printing invoices from any other table to the Billed table in order to print invoices.

Once the October transactions have been billed, they should be removed from the Charges table using the Tools, More, and Subtract options. Paradox will prompt you for the table names. Specify Billed as the table containing the transactions to be subtracted and Charges as the table from which to subtract these records. When done, the Charges table will no longer contain charges for the month of October, as shown in Figure 16.4.

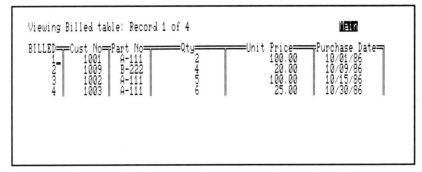

Figure 16.3: Charges for the month of October on the Billed table

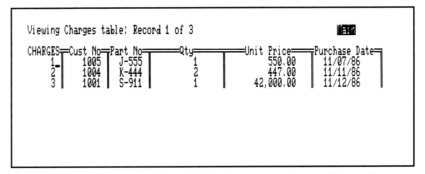

Figure 16.4: The Charges table with October transactions subtracted

_____ *EMPTYING A TABLE* _____

In the last chapter, we saw how the Tools, More, and Empty options allow you to empty all transactions from a table. This is particularly useful in systems with automated updating, where updated transactions are copied to a history file (using Tools, More, and Add), then deleted from the current transactions table.

Selecting the Tools, More, and Empty options always asks for the name of the table to empty records from. Before actually erasing all the records, Paradox presents these options:

Cancel   Ok

To proceed, select Ok. If you change your mind, select Cancel. Use caution when making this decision. Once records are erased from a table, they cannot be retrieved.

PROTECTING DATA

There are two ways to protect a table or other object in Paradox. The *password* technique ensures that unauthorized users, who don't know the password you assign, can neither read nor change information in a table. The *write-protect* technique allows anybody to read data in a table, but prevents accidental changes to the data in a table.

Both protection schemes are available from the Tools, More, and Protect options. When selected, Paradox displays the following options:

    Password   ClearPasswords   Write-protect

PASSWORD PROTECTION

If you select the Password option from the Protect submenu, Paradox will first display this menu:

    Table   Script

(As discussed in Chapter 19, scripts can be encrypted so that they cannot be read or changed by users.) Once you select an option, Paradox will ask for the name of the table or script to protect. Then you'll see these instructions:

    Password:
    Enter new owner password, or press ◄─┘ to remove all passwords.

Before you type in your password, note these important points:

- Case counts. That is, the password *Hello* is *not* the same as *hello*. Therefore, pay attention to case as you enter your password.

- The password does not appear on the screen as you type it. This is a safety precaution to prevent others from watching what you enter on the screen. If you type away madly waiting for something to appear on the screen, you will actually be entering your password as you do so.

- Once you enter your password, there is no way to view the table or script, or to remove the password if you do not know the password. Therefore, you should write down your password and store it in a safe place where you can find it easily.

- For obvious reasons, if your data is sensitive enough to deserve password protection, you should avoid obvious passwords like you first name, initials, or nickname. (Pet names are also common, and obvious, passwords.)

- If you decide to bail out now after reading the above, you can just press the Esc key to do so.

Once you decide on a password, type it in and press Enter. The screen will verify that you've typed it correctly by displaying the prompt

Password:
Enter password a second time to confirm.

Type in the same password again. (If you don't get it right, the screen will inform you of this. You can try again, or press Esc until the Main menu reappears to start all over.)

If you correctly enter your password a second time, you'll see a large form for entering *auxiliary passwords*. Unless you are working on a network, auxiliary passwords will probably not be necessary. To bypass the auxiliary passwords, press F2. You'll see the message

Encrypting...

at the bottom right corner of the screen, and then be returned to the Main menu.

In the future, when you attempt to view or work with the password-protected table, you'll see the message below before Paradox gives you any access to the table:

Password:
Enter password for this table to view it.

If you attempt to edit a protected script, using the Scripts Editor and Edit options from the menu, you'll be given the instructions

Password:
Enter script password before you can edit it.

You must type in the correct password to proceed. Again, the password will *not* appear on the screen as you type it, so type carefully. Press Enter after typing in the password.

If you do not enter the correct password, Paradox will display the error message

Invalid password

and allow you to try again. If you cannot enter the correct password, your only alternative is to press Esc and return to the higher-level menu.

REACTIVATING PASSWORDS

Once you access a password-protected table or script by entering the appropriate password, Paradox allows you to access that table or script as often as you wish during the current session (that is, until you exit Paradox) without reentering the password.

This is convenient, as it can become tedious to reenter the password each time you need a table or script. But there is a drawback: If you walk away from your computer during the current session, anybody who sits down at your computer can also access all your password-protected tables and scripts without reentering the passwords. (This is even more of a problem on a network.)

To work around this problem, you can select the Tools, More, Protect, and ClearPasswords options from the menus. Doing so clears all the passwords that you've entered in the current session, so that the passwords will need to be reentered to access the tables or scripts again. (This option also clears the screen, as Alt-F8 does.)

When you select ClearPasswords, you'll be given the options

Cancel   Ok

Selecting Ok will clear the previous password entries. Selecting Cancel cancels the commands, and retains free access to the scripts and tables during the current session.

WRITE PROTECTION

The Write-protect option on the Protect submenu acts as a temporary stopgap measure to prevent accidental changes to a table. A write-protected table can be viewed at any time, but cannot be changed in any way until the write-protection is removed. Unlike password-protection, write-protection can easily be removed by anyone without the use of a password.

If you attempt to change a write-protected table, Paradox will display a message such as

This table is write-protected and cannot be modified

You cannot modify the table until the write-protection is removed.

When you select Write-protect from the Protect submenu, Paradox will ask for the name of the table to protect. Enter the table name in the usual manner. The screen will then display the options:

Set   Clear

Select Set to enforce write-protection on the table. Select Clear to disable the previous write-protection.

SETTING A DIRECTORY

If you are a hard disk user who stores files on many different directories, you may occasionally wish to change the default directory for accessing files (objects). Normally, Paradox assumes that all objects are stored on the current directory (C:\PARADOX2 on most hard disk systems). You can change this by selecting the Tools, More, and Directory options. Paradox will then ask for the new working directory, as below:

Directory: C:\PARADOX2
Enter new working directory specification (e.g. a:\data or b:)

Type in the drive specification (for instance, C:) and the directory name.

When you change directories, Paradox will delete all current temporary tables (for example, Answer and Keyviol). This avoids splitting a single application (such as accounts-receivable tables) onto separate directories.

Before changing directories, Paradox will ask for verification using the usual options:

Cancel   Ok

GENERAL FILE INFORMATION

The Info option from the Tools menu provides a powerful and convenient way for viewing and printing your Paradox objects. When you select the Info option, the following submenu is displayed:

Structure   Inventory   Family   Who   Lock

VIEWING TABLE STRUCTURES

If you select the Structure option from the Info submenu, Paradox will ask for the name of the table for which you wish to view the structure. As usual, you can type in a table name or press Enter to see a menu of existing tables, and then select a table by highlighting and pressing Enter. Paradox will then display the table structure as in Figure 16.5.

Although you can edit this structure using the usual arrow, Ins, and Del keys, you should not do so unless you plan on renaming the table after making your modifications. Info is really designed only to allow you to view a structure. Use the Modify and Restructure options to modify the structure of a table.

VIEWING THE FILE INVENTORY

Selecting the Inventory option from the Info submenu presents the following options:

Tables   Scripts   Files

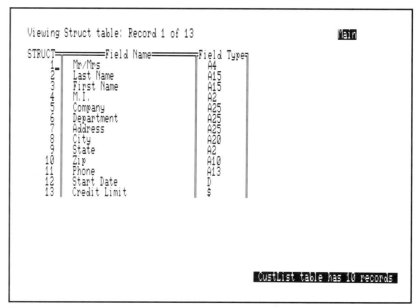

Figure 16.5: A sample display from the Tools Info Structure option series

These options present directories of existing objects. As the option names imply, selecting Tables displays the names of existing tables, Scripts displays the names of scripts, and Files displays the names of any files. Each option shows the name and the date of the last modification displayed in a special table named List, as shown in Figure 16.6.

When you first select either the Tables or Scripts option, Paradox will display this prompt:

Directory:
Enter directory for list of tables, or press ◀── for working directory

Just pressing the Enter key will display tables or scripts on the currently logged drive (usually drive B on a floppy disk system, or C:\PARA-DOX2 on a hard disk). You can enter another drive or directory name instead, using the usual syntax (for instance, A: or C:\accounts).

Selecting the Files option from the Inventory submenu lets you view any group of files. When selected, Paradox will show this prompt:

Pattern:
Enter DOS directory pattern (e.g. *.TXT, or ◀── for working directory)

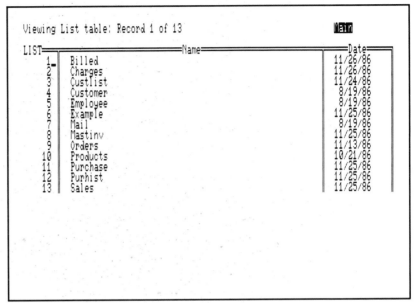

```
Viewing List table: Record 1 of 13                          Main

 LIST                           ═══Name═══                        ═══Date═══
    1    Billed                                                  11/26/86
    2    Charges                                                 11/26/86
    3    Custlist                                                11/24/86
    4    Customer                                                 8/19/86
    5    Employee                                                 8/19/86
    6    Example                                                 11/25/86
    7    Mail                                                     8/19/86
    8    Mastinv                                                 11/25/86
    9    Orders                                                  11/13/86
   10    Products                                                10/21/86
   11    Purchase                                                11/25/86
   12    Purhist                                                 11/25/86
   13    Sales                                                   11/25/86
```

Figure 16.6: Table names displayed with the Tools Info Inventory option series

You can use a question mark as a "wild-card" for a single character, or an asterisk for a group of characters. For example, *.* displays all files, while *.WRK displays only those files with the extension .WRK (Symphony worksheets, for example). The pattern *.DB? displays files with any first name and the letters DB as the first two characters of a three-character extension (that is, .DB, .DBF, .DBA, and so on).

You can specify a drive and directory as well. For example, the pattern C:\dbase*.DBF will display the names of all dBASE database files on a directory named dbase on drive C.

To print a copy of the screen, press Instant Report (Alt-F7). To clear the display, press Clear Image (F8).

VIEWING FAMILIES

The Family option from the Info submenu displays a table name and its associated objects (or *family*). When you select this option, Paradox will ask that you enter the table name, and then it will display the family as shown in Figure 16.7. Notice that the Custlist table includes validity checks in a VAL file (that is, a file named Custlist.VAL), two forms (named Custlist.F and Custlist.F1), and four reports (Custlist.R, .R1, .R2, .R3). (Your screen might show other family members.)

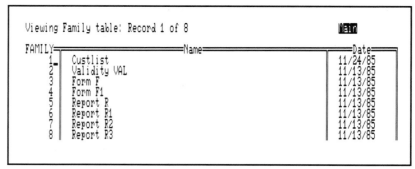

```
 Viewing Family table: Record 1 of 8                         Main

 FAMILY┌──────────────────────Name──────────────────────┬═══Date═══┐
      1─│  Custlist                                      ║ 11/24/85
      2 │  Validity VAL                                  ║ 11/13/85
      3 │  Form F                                        ║ 11/13/85
      4 │  Form F1                                       ║ 11/13/85
      5 │  Report R                                      ║ 11/13/85
      6 │  Report R1                                     ║ 11/13/85
      7 │  Report R2                                     ║ 11/13/85
      8 │  Report R3                                     ║ 11/13/85
```

Figure 16.7: The family of objects for the Custlist table

SPEEDING UP QUERIES

The QuerySpeedup option from the Tools menu allows you to enhance the speed of often-used queries. For example, if you regularly perform an automated update, you can use QuerySpeedup to reduce the time required to perform the update.

To use this feature, fill out query forms as you normally would. (You can use the Scripts and QuerySave options to save the query.) While the query form is displayed, select the Tools and Query-Speedup options from the menu. In most cases, future queries using the same fields will run more quickly.

There are situations where QuerySpeedup will not speed up or will even slow down a query. For example, if a query is based on a key field, Paradox will display this message:

No speedup possible

That's because the key field is already used to maximize the speed of the query.

The QuerySpeedup option works by creating secondary index files (or key fields) that are updated whenever a query is performed. These secondary index files have two costs associated with them:

- They consume disk space.
- They require some time to update.

The significance of the first cost depends on how much disk space you have on your computer. If you're using a hard disk, this cost will be negligible for a single speed-up. However, each speed-up will require more index files, and the disk space will mount up if you attempt to use this option with every query form.

The second cost, time, is a different matter. If a table is very small, it may very well take more time to update the index and perform the query than it did to perform the query in the first place. Hence, QuerySpeedup could actually slow things down. However, for an average-to-large-size table, QuerySpeedup will probably enhance the speed noticeably.

INTERFACING WITH OTHER SOFTWARE SYSTEMS

The ExportImport option under the Tools menu allows you to transfer data to and from other software systems. When you select this option, your choices are

Export   Import

Selecting either option displays the following submenu:

1-2-3   Symphony   dBase   Pfs   Visicalc   Ascii

Let's first discuss each of these options in general terms, then look at some creative ways to import and export data. One important point to keep in mind is that Paradox always converts data through copies of files. In all cases, your original data are left unchanged, and converted data are copied to a new file with a name you provide. (Paradox will prompt you for the name before converting.)

1-2-3 AND SYMPHONY

If you select 1-2-3 from the Export or Import submenu, you'll be given the options

1) 1-2-3 Release 1A   2) 1-2-3 Release 2

Select the appropriate option for your version of 1-2-3. (The version number appears on the copyright screen when you first run 1-2-3.)

If you select the Symphony option from the Export or Import submenu, you'll see the options

1) Symphony Release 1.0   2) Symphony Release 1.1

Select the appropriate option for your version of Symphony. (Again, the version number is displayed on the copyright screen when you first run Symphony.)

When importing or exporting on a hard disk with several directories, be sure to include the directory name as required. For example, to import a 1-2-3 spreadsheet named Sales from the directory named Lotus on drive C, enter the name of the file to import as *C:\Lotus\Sales*.

When you export data to Symphony or 1-2-3, the table fields and records will be stored in individual columns and rows. The file will have the name you assigned, plus the appropriate extension for your version of 1-2-3 or Symphony; .WKS for Release 1A of 1-2-3, .WK1 for Release 2 of 1-2-3, .WRK for Symphony Release 1.0, and .WR1 for Symphony Release 1.1. Once you export the Paradox file, you can use the usual File Retrieve options in Symphony or 1-2-3 to read the exported file into the spreadsheet. (Examples later in the chapter demonstrate techniques for exporting and graphing Paradox data using Lotus products.)

When importing 1-2-3 or Symphony data, Paradox will look for files on the specified directory, with the appropriate extension. For example, if you opt to import a 1-2-3 spreadsheet from Release 2 of 1-2-3, and specify C:\Lotus\Sales as the file to import, Paradox will search the Lotus directory in drive C for a file named Sales.WK1.

Paradox cannot reliably import the data that are randomly placed about a spreadsheet. Instead, it needs to import even columns and rows, where the top row contains the field names for the database table. If your spreadsheet contains labels or formulas outside of an even row-and-column orientation, you should first use the File Xtract option in 1-2-3 or Symphony to extract only the field names and values beneath them. (On a Symphony spreadsheet, this would be the database [_DB] range.) Then from Paradox, import the extracted file only.

Paradox will assign data types to the imported data based on the following table:

LOTUS COLUMN	*PARADOX FIELD*
Label	Alphanumeric (A)
Number	Numeric (N)
Number formatted as Currency, or with fixed two decimals	Currency ($)
Date (formatted as Date)	Date (D)

Any column storing the results of calculations will be imported as values. Paradox will not import the formulas themselves.

DBASE II, III, AND III PLUS

Transferring data to and from dBASE II, III, or III PLUS is a simple, straightforward process, since both systems store data in records and fields. To export data to dBASE, select the dBase option from the menu, then either dBASE II or dBASE III from the submenu. Paradox will copy data to the file name you provide, adding the usual dBASE .DBF extension (for instance, Partodb3.DBF).

Importing dBASE II or III data is just as easy as exporting. When importing data, however, dBASE logical fields will be converted to alphanumeric fields with a length of one character, and memo fields will be trimmed to a maximum of 255 characters and stored as alphanumeric data.

FRAMEWORK

Though there is no command to interface with Framework, you can bypass this simply by using the dBase or Ascii option. Just export a Paradox table as a dBASE III database, then use the Framework @dbasefilter function to read the converted file.

When you're working with Framework and you want to send data to Paradox, bring the data you want to transfer to the desktop and select the Write DOS Text File option from the Disk menu. Framework will create a delimited file with the extension .TXT (such as Fwtopar.TXT).

In Paradox, create an empty table that resembles the Framework file structure and use the Ascii and Delimited options to import the file.

PFS

The Pfs option stores data in Pfs (or IBM Filing Assistant) format with the file name extension .PFS.

When importing data from Pfs or IBM Filing Assistant, first make sure that the file you are importing has the file name extension .PFS. (If it does not, use the DOS Rename command to change the file name.)

Since Pfs does not use data types, Paradox will make reasonable assumptions about data types during the conversion. Attachment pages will be trimmed to a maximum length of 255 characters and stored as alphanumeric data.

VISICALC

The Visicalc option lets you import and export data stored in Data Interchange Format (DIF). The exported file will be assigned the file name extension .DIF.

VisiCalc and many other spreadsheet programs allow you to store data in DIF format. Any file that you convert to DIF format can be imported into Paradox by selecting the Import and Visicalc options from the ExportImport submenus. Keep in mind that Paradox stores data in fields and records, and therefore the data being imported should have a consistent row-and-column format. Paradox cannot import a spreadsheet that contains data stored randomly throughout the rows and columns. Also, extraneous characters like boxes and asterisks, used to enhance the appearance of the spreadsheet on the screen, will not be converted easily. Remove these before exporting to Paradox.

ASCII

When you select the Export and Ascii options from the ExportImport menu, you'll be given the options below:

Delimited   Text

If you select Import, and then Ascii, you'll be given the choice

Delimited   AppendDelimited   Text

A delimited file is one in which fields are separated by commas and each record is terminated by a carriage return/linefeed combination. Typically, character data are enclosed in quotation marks. When you use the DOS TYPE command to view a delimited file, it will typically look something like the example in Figure 16.8. The carriage return/linefeed at the end of each record causes each new record to begin on a new line in the screen, as in the figure.

When you export a delimited file, Paradox creates a file with the name you provide and the extension .TXT (unless you provide a different file name extension). The ASCII file shown in Figure 16.8 is

```
C:\paradox > type transfer.dat
"Miss","Abzug","Ann","Z.","","","","301 Crest Dr.","Encinitas","CA","92024","(123)5
55-1111","3/01/1986",7500.00
"Mr.","Adams","Andy","A.","","","","234 Ocean View Dr.","San Diego","CA","92038","(
213)555-9999","1/15/1986",2500.00
"Ms.","Davis","Randi","","","","","371 Oceanic Way","Manhattan Beach","CA","90001",
"(555)555-1111","3/01/1986",7500.00
"Miss","Gladstone","Tara Rose","","Waterside, Inc.","Acquisitions","P.O. Box 121
","New York","NY","12345","(415)555-1111","2/28/1986",15000.00
"Ms.","Jackson","Janet","J.","Zeerox, Inc.","Accounts Payable","1234 Corporate H
wy.","Los Angeles","CA","91234","(616)555-0011","1/01/1986",10000.00
"Mr.","Kenney","Clark","E.","Legal Aid","","371 Ave. of the Americas","New York"
,"NY","12345","(333)222-1111","1/31/1986",5000.00
"Mr.","Macallister","Mark","S.","BBC Publishing","Foreign Sales","121 Revelation
Dr.","Bangor","ME","00001","(333)888-0109","3/15/1986",7500.00
"Dr.","Rosiello","Richard","L.","Raydontic Labs","Accounts Payable","P.O. Box 77
112","Newark","NJ","00123","(222)555-9898","3/15/1986",7500.00
"Mrs.","Simpson","Susan","M.","SMS Publishing","Software Division","P.O. Box 280
2","Philadelphia","PA","23456","(333)555-0101","1/01/1986",15000.00
"Dr.","Zastrow","Ruth","","Scripts Clinic","Internal Medicine","4331 La Jolla Sc
enic Dr.","La Jolla","CA","92037","(818)555-3258","1/01/1986",10000.00

C:\paradox > _
```

Figure 16.8: The Custlist table exported to ASCII delimited format

a Paradox table exported in delimited format. This is a common format that many software systems can import. Hence, you can export data from Paradox to just about any software system by exporting to a delimited ASCII file, then using the other software package to import the delimited file. (Examples using word processors are presented in the next section.)

Paradox can also import delimited ASCII files (also called *text files* and *sequential data files* in some software systems). When importing delimited ASCII files, Paradox assumes that individual fields are separated by commas. (You can, however, use the Paradox Custom Configuration program to specify a different delimiter.) The imported data will be stored on a new table with the field names Field 1, Field 2, Field 3, and so forth. Data types in the imported table are determined on a "best guess" basis. (Of course, you can use the Modify and Restructure options from the Paradox Main menu to change the field names and data types in the imported table if you wish.)

AppendDelimit lets you import ASCII data into an existing Paradox table. If the table you are importing records into is keyed, you'll be given the options below:

NewEntries   UpDate

If you select NewEntries, Paradox attempts to append the imported records to the bottom of an existing table. If you select Update, Paradox attempts to replace records in an existing table with imported records that have identical key fields.

Because the ASCII file has no field names, Paradox simply attempts to append records based upon the order of the fields. That is, the first field in the ASCII file is imported into the first field in the Paradox table, the second field in the ASCII file is imported into the second field of the Paradox table, and so on.

Any data that cannot be imported, because of non-matching fields or conflicting data types are stored in a table named Problems. This table shows the record number of the record that could not be imported, the first 80 characters of that record, and the reason that the importation failed. You can use this information, if necessary, to modify the ASCII file (using any text editor with a "nondocument" mode), and try again later.

The Text option lets you import and export text files consisting of single lines of information. When importing Text files, the new table will have a single field named Text, containing a single line from the imported file. When exporting Text files, the Paradox table may contain only a single alphanumeric field. Each record in the Paradox table becomes a line in the exported text file.

INTERFACING WITH WORD PROCESSORS

The Ascii option from the ExportImport menu is particularly useful for interfacing with word processors. In the following exercises, we'll use WordStar as the example word processor, although most word processors have similar capabilities.

EXPORTING A REPORT

You can export Paradox reports to word processors either for further editing or for inclusion in other documents. To send a copy of a report to a word processor, first make an ASCII text file copy of the report. Call up the Paradox Report menu and select the Output option. Enter a table name when requested (such as Custlist), and specify a report (for example, 1 for the directory). From the submenu, select the File option and enter a file name (such as Transfer). When complete, there will be a copy of your report on disk with the file name you assigned plus the extension .RPT (in this example, Transfer.RPT).

Exit Paradox and call up your word processor. Then, simply edit the Transfer.RPT file as you would any other.

If you wish to embed the transferred report in an existing document, first begin editing the existing document. Move the cursor to the place where you want to embed the Paradox report and simply read in the file. For example, in WordStar, type ^ KR and the name of the file to read in (that is, Transfer.RPT), then press Enter.

MAILMERGE FILES FOR FORM LETTERS

Word processors with mailmerge capabilities for writing form letters mostly use the ASCII delimited format for storing data. In this section, we'll see how to export Paradox data to a WordStar MailMerge file. First, from the Paradox Main menu, choose the Tools option, then select the ExportImport, Export, Ascii, and Delimited options. Enter the name of the table to export (such as Custlist), and a name for the exported file (such as Transfer.DAT). When the export is complete, exit Paradox.

From the DOS A> or C> prompt, you can use the TYPE command to verify that the export took place. On a hard disk system, enter the command

TYPE Transfer.DAT

On a floppy disk system, enter the command

TYPE B:Transfer.DAT

(assuming, of course, that you named the exported file Transfer- .DAT). You'll see the data from the table stored on a delimited file, with commas as the delimiters. (Incidentally, this is also the format used to store BASIC sequential data files.) Figure 16.8 shows the Custlist table exported to ASCII delimited format.

Next, call up your word processor and enter the appropriate commands to set up a form letter. Figure 16.9 shows a sample form letter set up in WordStar. The .OP command eliminates page numbers, the .DF (Data File) command specifies the name of the file with names and addresses (Transfer.DAT in this example). The .RV (Read Variable) command defines the structure of the file. Notice that the .RV command lists all fields, even though we do not use all of the fields in the letter. Keep in mind that the .RV command assigns names to *all* fields in the data file, not just the ones you want to use. The number of fields in the .RV command must match exactly the number of fields in the data file. The .PA command at the bottom of the letter starts each letter on a new page.

Within the form letter, variable names defined in the .RV command are placed by surrounding the name with ampersands (for instance, &LName&). The /o used in some variable names means "omit if no data." This keeps blank fields from appearing as blank lines or spaces.

```
            C:FORMLET.TXT  PAGE 1 LINE 14 COL 52        INSERT ON
L----!----!----!----!----!----!----!----!----!----!----!--------R
.OP                                                              <
.DF Transfer.DAT                                                 M
.RV Title, Lname, FName, MI, Co, Dept, Add, City, State, Zip, Date, Amount  M
                                                                <
&Title/o& &Fname& &MI/o& &LName&                                <
&Co/o&                                                          <
&Dept/o&                                                        <
&Add&                                                           <
&City&, &State&  &Zip&                                          <
                                                                <
Dear &Fname&:                                                   <
                                                                <
     How  do you like getting these form letters from me?  I'll
bet  you  thought I hand typed this  letter,  but  not  so.  By
combining  Paradox and Wordstar,  I was able to use Paradox with
Wordstar's  nifty  formatting capabilities,  like  justified  right
margin, ^Sunderline^S, ^Bboldface^B, ^Xstrikeout^X,  and so on._  <
                                                                <
Best Regards                                                    <
                                                                <
Albert Winney                                                   <
.PA
```

Figure 16.9: A WordStar form letter

WORDPERFECT FORM-LETTER FILES

WordPerfect uses a very unusual format for storing data to be merged into form letters. Each field is terminated with a ^R (Ctrl-R) and a carriage return, and each record is terminated with a ^E (Ctrl-E) and a carriage return. You can't export Paradox files to this exact format, but you can use WordPerfect's search-and-replace capabilities to convert the ASCII file field delimiters to ^R characters and insert the ^E at the end of each record. Below, we'll work through the steps to convert an exported Paradox ASCII file to a WordPerfect data file for printing form letters.

First of all, you should probably use some character other than a comma as the delimiter (field separator) in the converted ASCII file, because this character might actually exist inside one of the fields, as in the company name *ABC Records, Inc*. We wouldn't want WordPerfect to convert this comma to a ^R character, because it is not a field delimiter. To avoid any confusion about the field delimiters, we'll have Paradox use an unusual character (@ in this example) as a field separator in the exported text file.

To change the field delimiter, run Paradox in the usual fashion, and select the menu options Scripts and Play. Enter Custom as the script to play. If Paradox cannot find that script, you'll need to copy the file Custom.SC from your Paradox Installation Disk to the Paradox2 directory on your hard disk, or place the Installation disk in drive B on a two-floppy system. If you are using two floppies, use the the name B:Custom when Paradox asks for the name of the script to play.

When the Configuration menu appears at the top of the screen, select the options More, AsciiConvert, and Separator. Press Backspace to erase the default delimiter (a comma) and type in the @ character. Press Return, then select the options Return, Return, and DO-IT!. Select either TwoFloppy, HardDisk, or Network from the next menu, depending on the type of computer you have. You've just reconfigured Paradox to place an @ sign, instead of a comma, between fields in exported ASCII text files. (After completing this exercise, you might want to repeat the process and put a comma back in as the separator.)

Now, run Paradox in the usual manner. Select Tools, ExportImport, Export, Ascii, and Delimited from the menus. Specify the name of the table to export (we'll use the CustList table in this example). Enter a drive, directory, and name for the copied file. On a hard disk, this might be C:\WP\Data.TXT, assuming WordPerfect is stored on a directory named WP on drive C. On a two-floppy system, place a disk in drive B, and name the file B:Data.TXT.

Next, exit Paradox using the usual Exit and Yes menu options. To verify the exportation, use the TYPE command to view the contents of the Data.TXT file. On a hard disk, log onto the WordPerfect disk (enter the command CD\WP and press Enter). Then enter the command TYPE DATA.TXT and press Enter. On a floppy disk system, enter the command TYPE B:DATA.TXT. The file should look something like the example in Figure 16.8.

Now, run WordPerfect in the usual manner, specifying Data.-TXT as the file to edit. (That is, at the DOS prompt, type in the command WP DATA.TXT and press Enter.) You should see the delimited ASCII file on your screen.

Now, you need to place a ^ E and carriage return at the end of each record. To do so, follow these steps:

1. Type Alt-F2.

2. Enter N in response to the *Confirm?* prompt.

3. Press Enter in response to the *Srch:* prompt (this appears as [HRt]).

4. Press F2.

5. Type Ctrl-E and press Enter in response to the *Replace with:* prompt (it appears on the screen as ^ E[HRt]).

6. Press F2.

WordPerfect will put a ^ E at the end of each record; you'll be able to see the effect on your screen.

Next, you need to replace all the @ delimiters with a Ctrl-R and carriage return. To do so, follow these steps:

1. Press Home-Home-↑ to move to the top of the file.

2. Type Alt-F2.

3. Enter N in response to the *Confirm?* prompt.

4. Type @ in response to the *Srch:* prompt.

5. Press F2.

6. Type Ctrl-R and press Enter in response to the *Replace with:* prompt (it appears on the screen as ^ R[HRt]).

7. Press F2.

Finally, you need to get rid of the quotation marks. Here are the steps to do so:

1. Press Home-Home-↑ to move to the top of the file.

2. Type Alt-F2.

3. Enter N in response to the *Confirm?* prompt.

4. Type " in response to the *Srch:* prompt.

5. Press F2.

6. Type F2 in response to the *Replace with:* prompt.

All of the quotation marks are removed from the file. If you now type Home-Home-↑ to move the cursor to the top of the screen, the first Paradox record should look something like the following (of course, the actual data might be different):

```
Miss ^ R
Abzug ^ R
Ann ^ R
Z. ^ R
 ^ R
301 Crest Dr. ^ R
Encinitas ^ R
CA ^ R
92024 ^ R
(555)555-1212 ^ R
3/01/1987 ^ R
7500.00 ^ E
```

Notice that each field starts on a new line (The Company and Department fields are blank in this record). Each field ends with a Ctrl-R, and each record ends with a ^ E, just as WordPerfect requires. Save the data file by pressing F7, selecting Yes, pressing Enter, and selecting Yes again.

Next you can use WordPerfect to create your form letter. We can't go into detail on how to do that here, but basically you need to use the Alt-F9 menu to place fields in the document. The field numbers on the CustList table are listed below:

FIELD	CODE
Mr/Mrs	F1
LName	F2
FName	F3
M.I.	F4

Company	F5
Department	F6
Address	F7
City	F8
State	F9
Zip code	F10
Phone	F11
Start Date	F12
Credit Limit	F13

You'll want to use the Alt-F9 and F options to lay out the recipient's address at the top of the form letter (but below the letter date) so that it looks something like this:

```
^F1^ ^F3^ ^F4^ ^F2^
^F5?^
^F6?^
^F7^
^F8^, ^F9^ ^F10^
```

Note the use of a single space between each field position. The question marks prevent any empty Company or Department fields from being printed as blank lines, like Paradox's LineSqueeze option. The comma in the last line is the comma placed between the City and State fields.

Type in the body of the letter. (You can also use Alt-F9, F to place fields in the body of the letter.) Save the completed form letter in the usual manner (the F7 key), using a file name such as FormLet.TXT.

To merge the form letter with the data file, run WordPerfect, type Ctrl-F9, and select 1 (Merge). Specify FormLet.TXT (in this example) as the Primary file, and Data.TXT (in this example) as the Secondary file. The letters will be created on the screen, and you can scroll through them and make any necessary changes using the usual WordPerfect techniques. You might want to save the completed form letters under a new file name, or perhaps print them immediately (using Shift-F7 1).

SYMPHONY DATABASES

Since Paradox data are exported as simple spreadsheets with rows and columns, there are a few additional steps you need to take to transfer Symphony databases to and from Paradox. Let's look at a couple of examples.

EXPORTING TO A SYMPHONY DATABASE

To export a Paradox table to a Symphony database, first keep in mind that Symphony can hold only a limited number of records, and that number varies with the amount of RAM your computer has. Realistically, Symphony can probably store about 2000 records. If your Paradox table is larger than this, you might want to use the Paradox Ask function to pull out only a portion of the records, as we'll discuss next.

Let's assume you want to pull the records of all California residents from your Paradox Custlist table and transfer them to a Symphony database. In Paradox, call up the Ask menu and specify Custlist as the table to query. Fill in a formula to specify only California residents and press DO-IT!. The query and some of the results are shown in Figure 16.10.

Make a note of all the field names in the Answer table and jot them down if you are not certain that you can remember their order. Next, export the Answer table to a Symphony file by calling up the Main menu and selecting the Tools, ExportImport, Export, and Symphony options. Specify Answer as the table to copy and assign it a file name (such as Partosym). When the export is complete, exit Paradox.

Run Symphony in the usual fashion. When a blank spreadsheet appears on the screen, type in the database field names across row 1, each field name in a separate cell. In Symphony, use single words for field names (for example, Date rather than Start Date). You need not use the same field names as the Paradox database, but the order must be the same. Make sure there are no blank columns between field names. Then press HOME to put the cell pointer in cell A1. Figure 16.11 shows a Symphony screen with field names typed in (though some are beyond the right edge of the screen).

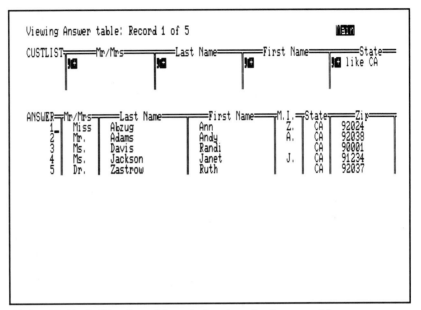

Figure 16.10: California residents isolated on the Answer table

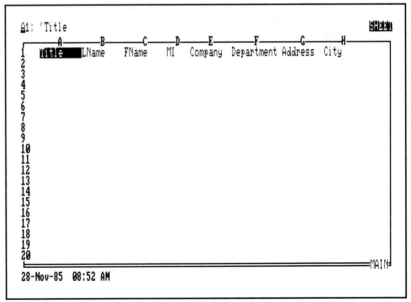

Figure 16.11: Symphony screen with field names typed in

Next, you need to create a Symphony Form window, as described in the following steps:

1. Press Services (F9).

2. Select Window Create.

3. Enter a name for the window (for instance, Pardat).

4. Press Enter.

5. Select Form from the next menu.

6. Press Enter to highlight the entire screen.

7. Quit the menu (select Q).

You'll see this message at the top of the screen:

(No Definition range defined)

Create the definition range by following these steps:

1. Press Menu (F10).

2. Select Generate.

3. Select Label.

4. Type in the length of the longest field from the Paradox database (30 in this example). (*Note*: If the longest field in your Paradox database is wider than 60 characters, enter 60 instead.)

5. Enter a name for the database (for example, Pardat).

6. Press Enter.

7. Highlight the field names when requested (press the Period, End, and → keys).

8. Press Enter.

A database data-entry form will appear on the screen, as shown in Figure 16.12.

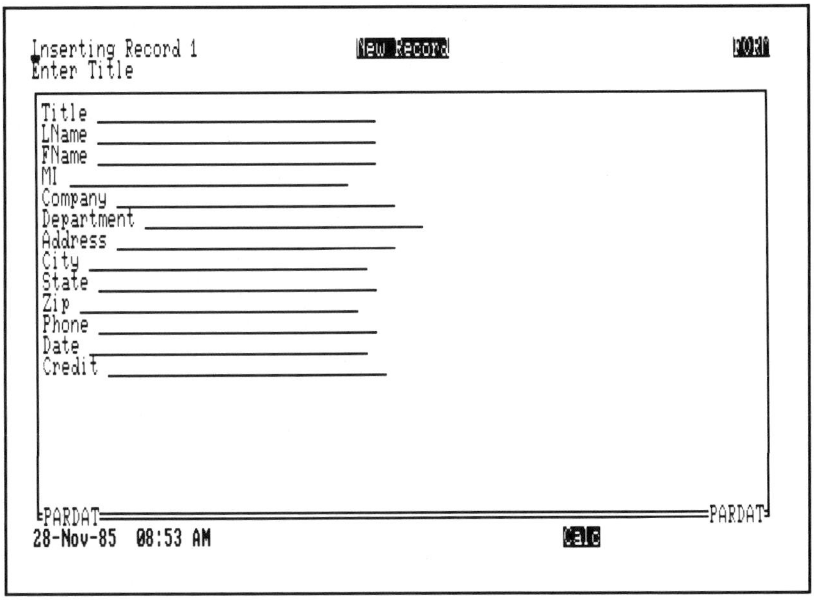

Figure 16.12: A Symphony database FORM window

Next, you need to move the highlight to the Symphony Database range. Use the following steps to do so:

1. Press Window (F6).

2. Press Goto (F5).

3. Enter the database range database name (for example, Pardat_DB).

4. Press Enter.

The database field names will appear at or near the top of the screen. Press the ↓ key once to move the highlight to the first blank row beneath the field names. Then use the File and Combine options to read in the Paradox data using the following steps:

1. Press Services (F9).

2. Select the File option.

3. Select the Combine option.

4. Select the Copy, EntireFile, Read, and Values options.

5. Enter the name of the file to read in (in this example, Partosym).

All the records from the Paradox database will be read into the Symphony database. Delete the imported field names (second row of field names) using the Menu, Delete, and Row options in Symphony. Your screen should look like Figure 16.13. (Even though the narrow columns hide some of the data, all the information is in the Symphony database.)

Next, you'll need to inform Symphony that the new records are in the database. Follow these steps:

1. Press Window (F6).

2. Press Menu (F10).

3. Select the Settings option.

4. Select the Basic option.

5. Select the Database option.

Highlight the entire database by pressing the End and ↓ keys, and then press Enter. Select the Quit option from the next two menus.

The first record from the transferred database will appear in the Symphony database window, as shown in Figure 16.14. You can use the PgUp and PgDn keys to browse through the new records in the Symphony database. Use the Services File Save command to save the new Symphony database.

IMPORTING FROM SYMPHONY TO PARADOX

To import a Symphony database to Paradox, run Symphony and use the Services File Retrieve command to retrieve the database that you want to transfer. Then follow these steps to create a separate file for the transfer:

1. Press the Window (F6) key until the database SHEET window appears.

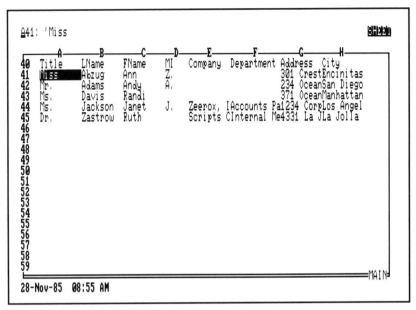

Figure 16.13: Paradox data read into a Symphony database

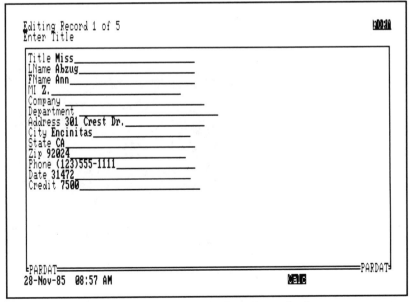

Figure 16.14: A transferred record in the Symphony database

2. Go to the _DB range by pressing GOTO (F5) and typing in the database name followed by _DB (for example, Mail_DB).

Next, you'll need to make a disk file of the records from the Symphony database. Simply follow these steps:

1. Press Services (F9).

2. Select the File, Xtract, and Values options.

3. Specify a file name (for example, Symtopar).

4. Highlight the field names, rows, and columns, as shown in Figure 16.15. Press Enter after highlighting.

Next, exit Symphony and run Paradox. Select the Tools, Export-Import, and Symphony options, and enter the file name (in this case, Symtopar). Enter a name for the new table (for example, Newpar). The Symphony database data will appear in the table, as shown in Figure 16.16.

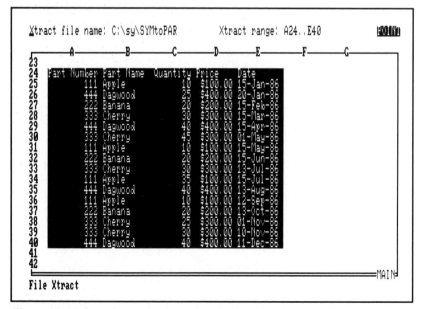

Figure 16.15: Symphony database data highlighted for exporting

```
Viewing Newpar table: Record 1 of 16                          Main

NEWPAR══Part number══╤═Part name══╤═Quantity══╤═══Price══╤═══════Date════
     1─         111         Apple          10        100.00       1/15/86
     2          444         Dagwood        25        400.00       1/20/86
     3          222         Banana         20        200.00       2/15/86
     4          333         Cherry         30        300.00       3/15/86
     5          444         Dagwood        40        400.00       4/15/86
     6          333         Cherry         45        300.00       5/01/86
     7          111         Apple          10        100.00       5/15/86
     8          222         Banana         20        200.00       6/15/86
     9          333         Cherry         30        300.00       7/13/86
    10          111         Apple          35        100.00       7/15/86
    11          444         Dagwood        40        400.00       8/13/86
    12          111         Apple          10        100.00       9/12/86
    13          222         Banana         20        200.00      10/13/86
    14          333         Cherry         25        300.00      11/01/86
    15          333         Cherry         30        300.00      11/10/86
    16          444         Dagwood        40        400.00      12/11/86
```

Figure 16.16: Symphony data transferred to a Paradox database

If you use Lotus 1-2-3 rather than Symphony, you'll need to use the same basic technique of extracting rows and fields of data from the 1-2-3 database, and saving only these data on a file. Then run Paradox and import the data using the Tools, ExportImport, Import, and 1-2-3 options.

GRAPHING MONTHLY TOTALS

One of the beauties of being able to interface with 1-2-3 and Symphony is the ability to plot Paradox data on graphs. Typically, you'll want to plot monthly totals on these graphs, so we should discuss techniques for obtaining monthly totals in Paradox first.

Let's assume you want to plot monthly totals from a table like the Totsales table shown in Figure 16.17. The first thing you'll need to do is add a field for storing the month (rather than the date). To do so, use Modify and Restructure to add the new Month field, as shown in Figure 16.18. (Note that this is an instance where the short field type is useful.)

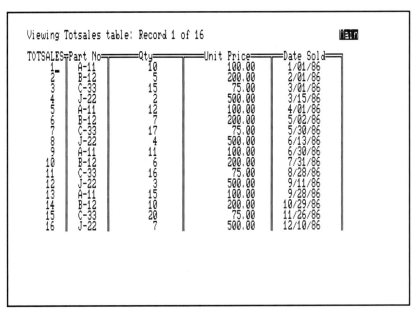

Figure 16.17: The Totsales example table

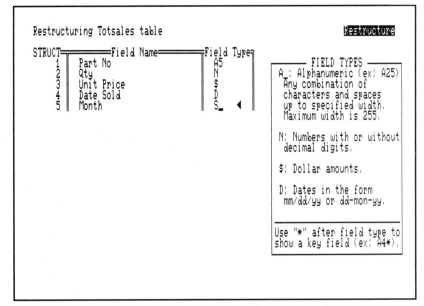

Figure 16.18: The new Month field added to the Totsales table

Save the new structure, and then select Ask from the menu. Specify the Totsales table, and fill in the query form as in Figure 16.19. Notice that a series of Changeto queries changes the entry in the Month field from a date to the number of the month. For example, the number 1 will be entered if the date starts with 1/, 2 if the month starts with 2/, and so on. If you plan on performing this query often, use Scripts and QuerySave to record a copy of the query.

After you perform this query, you'll see the Changed table as usual. If you view the Totsales table instead, you'll see the month number in the Month field.

Next, we need to calculate the product of the Qty by the Unit Price in each field. To do so, clear the screen (Alt-F8) and select the Ask option, specify the Totsales table, and fill in the query form as in Figure 16.20. Note that the Price and Qty entries are examples, and must be entered using the Example (F5) key. When you perform this query with F2, the Answer table will contain a field representing the results of the calculations, as shown in Figure 16.20.

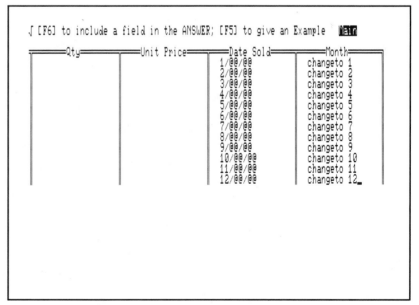

Figure 16.19: Query to fill in month numbers on the Totsales table

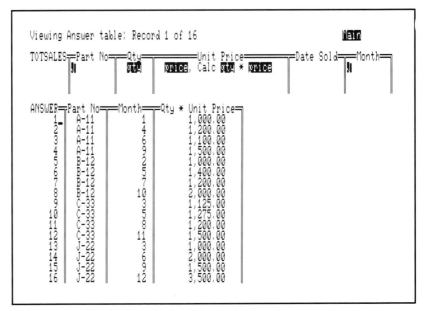

Figure 16.20: Total sales calculated for each record

Next, we need to summarize these data with monthly totals. Clear the screen, select Ask, specify Answer as the table to query, and fill in the query form as shown in Figure 16.21. When you press F2, the new Answer table shows the summarized totals (though the query form will disappear from your screen).

Next, call up the menu and select the Tools, ExportImport, and Export options; then choose either 1-2-3 or Symphony, and select the appropriate version. Specify Answer as the table to export and enter a name for the transfer file (for instance, Pargraf).

Now you can exit Paradox and run either Lotus or Symphony. Use the File and Retrieve options to call up the transfer file (in this case, Pargraf, or C:\Pargraf if you've changed directories. If Paradox is not on the PARADOX2 directory on your computer, substitute the appropriate directory name). You'll see it on the screen as a small spreadsheet, as shown in Figure 16.22. (In this example, I've inserted a new column and typed in month names for use on the graph.)

Use the usual 1-2-3 or Symphony Graph options to design your graph. In this example, the month names are defined as the X range

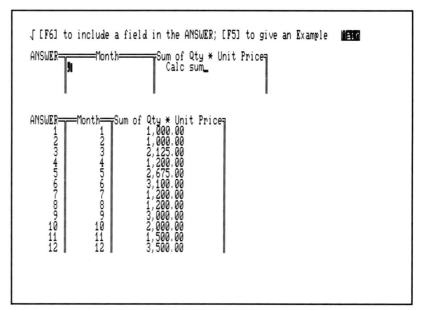

Figure 16.21: A summary of total sales by month

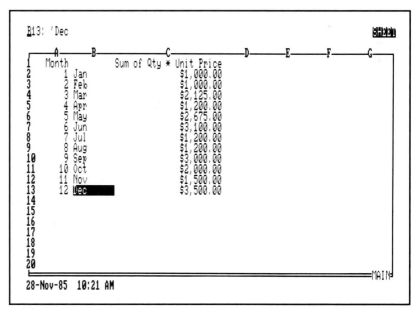

Figure 16.22: Summarized Paradox data on the Symphony worksheet

and the totals are defined as the A range. I've added a few titles to the graph as well. Figure 16.23 shows a Symphony graph of the Paradox data.

GRAPHING QUARTERLY TOTALS

If you prefer to plot quarterly rather than monthly totals, you can use a technique similar to the one outlined above. Again using the Totsales table as the example, add a new field to the table named Quarter using the usual Paradox Modify and Restructure options. Figure 16.24 shows the new structure for the table.

Save the new structure, then select Ask from the menu and specify Totsales as the table to query. Fill in the query form as in Figure 16.25. Notice that the Quarter field is changed to 1 for dates less than or equal to March 31. Dates in the range of April 1 to June 30 are assigned the quarter 2, and so on. (Once again, if you plan on performing this query often, save it using Scripts and QuerySave.) When you perform the query, the Changed table will appear. To view the results of the query, clear the screen and view the Totsales table.

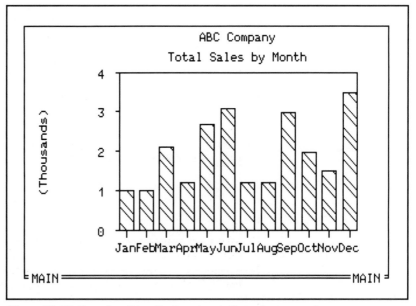

Figure 16.23: Paradox data displayed on a Symphony graph

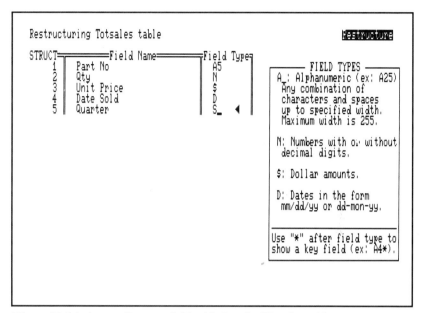

Figure 16.24: A new Quarter field added to the Totsales table

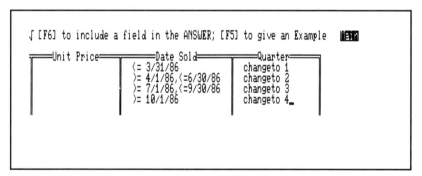

Figure 16.25: A query to assign quarters to records

Next, calculate the total sales for each transaction by selecting Ask and specifying Totsales as the table to query. Fill in the query form as in Figure 16.26. Note that once again the Price and Qty entries are examples, and must be entered using the F5 key. Notice also that the Part No and Quarter columns are checked. When you press F2, the results of the query will display the total sales, as shown in the lower part of the figure.

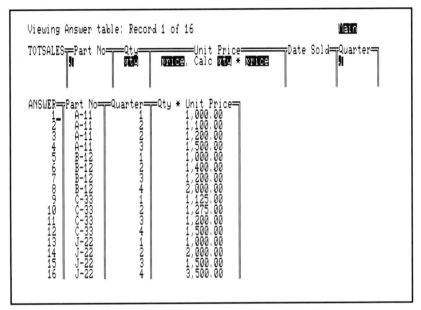

Figure 16.26: Total sales for each record in the Totsales table

Next, clear the screen and summarize the total sales by selecting Ask from the menu and specifying the Answer table. Fill in the query form as in Figure 16.27, then perform the query. The results will appear as shown in Figure 16.27.

To plot these data on a graph, call up the menu and select Tools, ExportImport, Export, and either 1-2-3 or Symphony and the

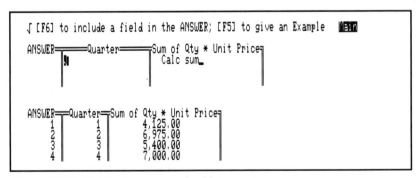

Figure 16.27: Total sales summarized by quarter

appropriate version number. Specify Answer as the table to export, and assign a file name to the exported file (for example, Pargraf2). Then exit Paradox.

Next, run 1-2-3 or Symphony, and use the File and Retrieve options to read in the Pargraf2 file from the Paradox2 directory. The data will appear as a spreadsheet, as shown in Figure 16.28.

Of course, once the data are in the spreadsheet, you can use the usual Symphony or 1-2-3 menu options to plot a graph. Figure 16.29 shows quarterly data on a bar graph, with graph and column titles.

——— *RUNNING EXTERNAL PROGRAMS* ———

You can temporarily suspend Paradox and exit back to the DOS A> or C> prompt without having to save or clear any open tables. This is very useful for using DOS commands such as FORMAT or COPY during a session in Paradox. You can even change floppy

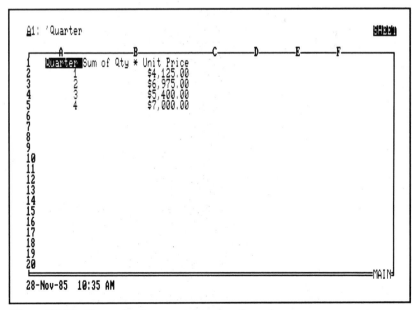

Figure 16.28: Quarterly data transferred to Symphony

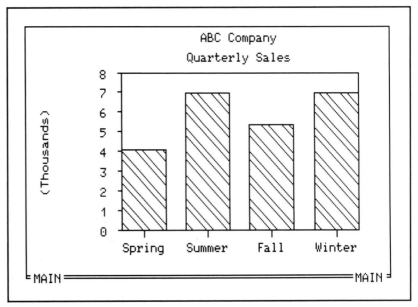

Figure 16.29: Quarterly data on a Symphony graph

disks while the DOS prompt is showing, as long as you put the original disks back in their drives before returning to Paradox.

To suspend the current Paradox session, first try to work your way back to the Main menu. For example, if you happen to be editing a table, form, or report specification, save these. While it is not absolutely necessary, it is safer to do so. (Should anything go wrong while Paradox is suspended, any data being edited might be lost.) You need not clear any tables from the screen, however.

Next, select the Tools, More, and ToDOS options from the menu, or type Ctrl-O. On a hard disk system, Paradox will display a warning message and the DOS C> prompt. On a floppy disk system, DOS may first ask that you insert a disk with COMMAND.COM on it. In most cases, you can just remove the Paradox System Disk from drive A, then insert your DOS boot (or DOS System) disk in drive A. Press any key, and the DOS A> prompt will appear. While

Paradox is suspended, and the DOS prompt is showing, you'll need to keep in mind a few rules to protect the suspended Paradox:

- Don't load any RAM resident programs, such as desktop tools, keyboard enhancers, or memory-resident spelling checkers. Similarly, don't use the DOS PRINT or MODE commands.

- Do not ERASE, RENAME, or modify any Paradox objects that were in use when you suspended the current Paradox session.

- If you use the DOS CHDIR or CD command to change directories, be sure to go back to the original directory before returning to Paradox.

- If you change floppy disks, be sure to put the original disks back in their drives before returning to Paradox. On a floppy disk system, be especially sure to put the Paradox System Disk #2 into drive A.

- Always return to Paradox and exit properly before turning off the computer.

To return to your Paradox session from the DOS A> or C> prompt, just type the command EXIT at the DOS prompt, then press Enter. Your Paradox session will reappear on the screen as though you'd never left (assuming you've followed the rules above). If at anytime you forget whether or not Paradox is suspended, enter the EXIT command at the DOS prompt (after replacing the appropriate disks if necessary). If Paradox is not in suspension, the DOS prompt will simply reappear.

Note that while Paradox is suspended, you may not be able to run all of your programs, because the suspended Paradox still occupies 420K of memory. If you need more memory, you can exit to DOS using the DOS Big key (Alt-O). DOS Big leaves only 100K of Paradox in memory while Paradox is suspended, leaving more room for other programs. The only disadvantage to using DOS Big is that it takes longer to get back into Paradox from the DOS prompt when you enter the EXIT command. Note also that DOS Big works only on hard disk systems, and not on computers with floppy disk drives only.

SUMMARY

- To rename a Paradox object, use the Tools and Rename options.

- To copy Paradox objects, use the Tools and Copy options.

- To delete Paradox objects, use the Tools and Delete options.

- To copy records from one table to another, use the Tools, More, and Add options.

- To remove records from one table that match records in another table, use the Tools, More, and Subtract options.

- To empty a table of all records (thereby closing the table), use the Tools, More, and Empty options.

- To protect data with passwords or write-protection, use the Tools, More, and Protect options.

- To define a new working directory, use the Tools, More, and Directory options.

- To view general information about files, use the Tools and Info options.

- To speed up often used queries, use the Tools and Query-Speedup options.

- To import and export data, use the Tools and ExportImport options.

- You can read a delimited ASCII text file into an existing table using the AppendDelimited option.

- You can temporarily suspend Paradox and return to the DOS prompt using the Tools, More, and ToDOS menu options, the Ctrl-O key, or the DOS Big (Alt-O) key.

P A R T   III

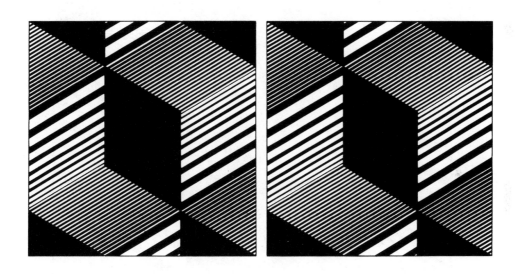

THE PARADOX APPLICATION
LANGUAGE

INTRODUCTION TO PAL PROGRAMMING

CHAPTER 17

MOST DATABASE-MANAGEMENT SYSTEMS REQUIRE A considerable amount of programming to gain full control in accessing data. Paradox, on the other hand, provides substantial power in managing data without any programming whatsoever. Nonetheless, there will always be "power users" who want to extend the built-in capabilities of Paradox to create custom systems for special applications.

For the power users Paradox offers PAL, the Paradox Application Language. We've already seen how to record a series of keystrokes and store them in a script using the Script and BeginRecord options. With PAL, you can extend the power of scripts beyond recorded keystrokes to entire programs.

In this chapter, we'll cover the basics of designing and developing PAL programs, and discuss in detail some of the more commonly used commands. In the next chapter, we'll look at some PAL programs designed to manage a mailing system. We'll use the more common commands in examples so you can see how they work. For more technical information on all the PAL commands and functions, refer to the *PAL User's Guide,* which comes with Paradox.

CREATING A PAL PROGRAM

To create a PAL program, you can use the PAL editor or any word processor that has a nondocument mode. (If you use an external word processor, be sure to use the extension .SC in your file name.) To access the PAL editor, call up the Paradox Main menu and select the Scripts, Editor, and Write options. Paradox will ask for a file name. Enter a name (eight letters maximum with no spaces or punctuation) and press Enter. In this example, enter the name Test1.

The PAL editor provides a blank screen to work with. The keys for creating and editing command files are the same as those used for creating forms and reports, as listed in Table 17.1.

We can test a simple program here. Type the lines below, *exactly* as shown:

```
? "Test Test Test"
SLEEP 10000
```

Use the various editing keys to make corrections if necessary.

KEY	FUNCTION
←	Moves left one character
Ctrl-←	Moves left one screen
→	Moves right one character
Ctrl-→	Moves right one screen
↑	Moves up a line
↓	Moves down a line
Home	Moves to first line
Ctrl-Home	Moves to first character on line
End	Moves to last line
Ctrl-End	Moves to last character of line
Ins	Toggles Insert mode on/off
Del	Erases character at cursor
Ctrl-Y	Deletes all to right of cursor, or entire line if cursor is in leftmost column
Enter	Moves down a line, or creates a new blank line if Insert mode is on
Ctrl-V	Turns vertical ruler on or off

Table 17.1: Keys used for creating and editing command files

SAVING A PAL PROGRAM

When you've entered your program, call up the Editor menu by pressing Menu (F10). You'll be given these options:

Read   Go   Help   DO-IT!   Cancel

The Go option will save your program as well as play it right away. The DO-IT! option will save the program and return to the Paradox menu. The Cancel option allows you to abandon the current program (and the current changes), and Help provides a help screen.

The Read option allows you to combine scripts, which is very useful to more advanced programmers. For example, you might find that you can write a large portion of a program by recording keystrokes or saving a query form. With the Read option, you can incorporate a recorded script or query form directly into the current PAL program.

For now, select the DO-IT! option to save your program and return to the Paradox menu. Paradox automatically adds the extension .SC to the file name you provide. Hence, if you name your program Test1, it will be stored on disk as Test1.SC.

RUNNING A PAL PROGRAM

A PAL program is no different than any other script. To run the program, call up the Main menu and select the Scripts and Play options. When requested, enter the name of the script, or press Enter to view a menu of existing scripts and select one by highlighting it. In this example, enter or highlight the name Test1. You'll see the screen clear, then the message

Test Test Test

appear on the screen for about 10 seconds. Then the Paradox Main menu reappears. Let's discuss why.

The ? command means "display." Therefore, the command

? "Test Test Test"

displays the words in quotes on the screen. The SLEEP command causes Paradox to pause. The 10000 tells Paradox to pause for 10,000 milliseconds, or 10 seconds. Therefore, the "Test Test Test" message stays on the screen for about 10 seconds before the program ends and returns to the Paradox Main menu.

Notice that the menu disappeared while the program was running, then reappeared when the program was done. This has to do with the *PAL canvas,* which we'll discuss next.

THE PAL CANVAS

When you become involved with programming in PAL, you have to become familiar with the concept of the PAL canvas. Basically, whenever a PAL program is running, it takes over the screen and "hides" any events that might be occurring on the Paradox workspace (for example, menus, tables, and so on). This keeps Paradox invisible and in the background. As we'll see later, the WAIT and ECHO commands allow you to bring Paradox out of the background into the foreground temporarily, even while a program is running.

CANCELING A PAL SCRIPT

Once you begin running a PAL script, it keeps running until it is fully played out, or until Paradox encounters an error. When you develop more complex scripts, particularly those that use *looping,* you may make a mistake that makes the script behave unpredictably and go into a performance of some routine without ever stopping. To get out of such a dilemma, press the Break key (the Ctrl-ScrollLock combination on IBM PC keyboards, and Ctrl-Pause on the IBM AT keyboard) to cancel the script. You'll be given the option to Cancel or Debug. Select Cancel to terminate the script and return to the Paradox workspace. Select Debug to use the PAL debugger, discussed in Chapter 19.

DEBUGGING

When you write your own programs in PAL, you're likely to make errors quite often. Programming errors are called "bugs" in computer jargon (because an error was once caused by a moth flying into the earliest computer). Getting rid of errors is therefore called *debugging*.

When Paradox encounters a bug in a program, it will stop running the program and present you with these options:

    Cancel   Debug

Selecting Cancel simply stops the program and returns you to the Paradox Main menu. Selecting the Debug option displays the line where the error occurred, and a brief description of the problem. (In some cases, the line below the offending line will appear, but the error message will help you figure out the problem.) The instructions

    Type Ctrl-Q to Quit

will also appear. After viewing and understanding the error, you can type Ctrl-Q to quit and return to the Paradox menu. Then use the editor to correct the line and try again. (*Note:* For more advanced debugging techniques with complex programs, see Chapter 19 in this book, and Chapter 11 of the *PAL User's Guide.*)

EDITING A PAL PROGRAM

To fix or change a PAL program, select the Scripts, Editor, and Edit options, and enter the name of the program to edit. The script will appear on the screen. At this point, all editing keys work as they usually do. After editing the program, call up the menu and select Go to run the program, or DO-IT! to save the program and run it later using the Scripts and Play options.

With the basics of creating, running, debugging, and editing PAL programs under our belts, let's take a look at the basic commands used in creating and running PAL programs.

═══ *INTERACTING WITH THE USER* ═══

Most programs use commands for presenting information to and getting information from the user. PAL includes many commands for such interactions, a few of which are listed below:

COMMAND	FUNCTION
CLEAR	Erases the PAL canvas
ACCEPT	Gets information from the user
?	Prints information on a new line
??	Prints information on the same line
@	Positions the cursor
STYLE	Defines colors, blinking, and other effects on the PAL canvas
GETCHAR( )	Gets a character of information from the user

Let's try out some of these commands to see how they work. From the Paradox menu, select the Scripts, Editor, and Write options, and enter the file name Testuser. Then enter the program shown in Figure 17.1. After typing in each line, press the Enter key to move to the beginning of the next line. To put blank lines into the script, press the Enter key while the cursor is still on a blank line. Notice that some lines start with a semicolon (;). Be sure you don't leave these semicolons out, or the program won't run correctly. (We'll discuss the function of these semicolons and the text that follows them later in the chapter.)

Let's discuss what each *routine* in this sample program does. The first routine simply states the name of the program (Testuser.SC) and its function:

```
;------------------------------------------------------------- Testuser.SC
;------------------------------------------- Test user-interface commands.
CLEAR                       ;Clear the screen
STYLE ATTRIBUTE 30          ;Yellow letters on blue
@ 1,10                      ;Cursor to row 1, column 10
?? "This is yellow on blue"
```

```
;---------------------------------------- Testuser.SC
;---------------------- Test user-interface commands.
CLEAR                            ;Clear the screen
STYLE ATTRIBUTE 30               ;Yellow letters on blue
@ 1,10                           ;Cursor to row 1, column 10
?? "This is yellow on blue"

STYLE REVERSE                    ;Reverse video
@ 3,10
?? "This is reverse video"

STYLE REVERSE, BLINK             ;Reverse and blinking
@ 5,10
?? "This is blinking"

STYLE ATTRIBUTE 40               ;Get user name
@ 7,10
?? "Enter your name, then press <-' : "
ACCEPT "A25" TO MyName

@ 9,10
?? "Enter a number from 1 to 5 then press <-' : "
ACCEPT "N" PICTURE "#" MIN 1 MAX 5 TO X

STYLE ATTRIBUTE 95
@ 20,10
?? "Your Name is ",MyName," and you entered ",X

STYLE ATTRIBUTE 175
@ 24,10
?? "Press any key to return to Paradox menu..."
Y = GETCHAR()
```

Figure 17.1: The Testuser.SC PAL program

The CLEAR command makes sure that the PAL canvas is clear before running the rest of the program. The STYLE ATTRIBUTE 30 command sets the display style for a color monitor to yellow letters on a blue background. (I'll show you all the color combinations a little later in this chapter.) The command @ 1,10 places the cursor at the first row of the tenth column on the screen. The command *?? "This is yellow on blue"* displays the sentence enclosed in quotation marks on the screen, beginning at the cursor position.

The next routine displays the sentence "This is reverse video" in reverse video on the third row, tenth column of the screen:

```
STYLE REVERSE    ;Reverse video
@ 3,10
?? "This is reverse video"
```

Notice that the word ATTRIBUTE is not used when selecting a display enhancement rather than a color combination. Display enhancements include REVERSE, BLINK, and INTENSE.

The next routine displays the sentence "This is blinking" on the fifth row, tenth column, of the screen:

```
STYLE REVERSE, BLINK     ;Reverse and blinking
@ 5,10
?? "This is blinking"
```

Two STYLE parameters are defined: REVERSE and BLINK. The two enhancements are separated by a comma, and once again the ATTRIBUTE command is not used.

Now the routine gets a little trickier, as shown below:

```
STYLE ATTRIBUTE 40     ;Get user name
@ 7,10
?? "Enter your name, then press <-' : "
ACCEPT "A25" TO MyName
```

The colors are changed using STYLE ATTRIBUTE, and on the seventh row, tenth column, the sentence "Enter your name, then press <-' :" is displayed. (The Enter key is represented by a less-than sign followed by a hyphen and apostrophe.) The ACCEPT command then waits for alphanumeric data with a maximum length of 25 characters ("A25") to be typed in. Whatever the user types is stored in a *variable* named MyName.

The variable name MyName is completely arbitrary. I could have used the variable name X, HaHaHa, or Bowser. Any variable name would do. The important point about variables is that they can store data which can be used later in the program, as we'll see in a moment. However, unlike data stored in tables, variables are transient and cease to exist when the program stops running. For now, keep in mind that whatever the user (or yourself) types in response to the "Enter your name" request is stored in the variable named MyName.

The next routine positions the cursor on the screen at row 9, column 10:

```
@ 9,10
?? "Enter a number from 1 to 5 then press <-' : "
ACCEPT "N" PICTURE "#" MIN 1 MAX 5 TO X
```

The ?? command then displays the request to enter a number between 1 and 5, followed by a press on the Enter key. The ACCEPT command waits for a number ("N") that is one digit long (PIC-TURE "#") and has a minimum value of 1 and a maximum value of 5. Whatever the user types is stored in a variable named X. (If a number out of the range is typed in, Paradox will reject it and ask for a new number. The program will continue running only after a number within the defined range has been entered.)

Next the program uses the data stored in the variables to display a simple message at row 20, column 10, using yet another color combination. This routine is shown below:

```
STYLE ATTRIBUTE 95
@ 20,10
?? "Your Name is ",MyName," and you entered ",X
```

Notice how the variable data is combined with *literal* data. That is, Paradox displays "Your Name is", followed by the contents of the MyName variable, followed by the words " and you entered ", and the contents of variable X. Hence, had you entered "Albert" as your name, and "2" as the number, this line would display

Your Name is Albert and you entered 2

Notice that the literal data is enclosed in quotation marks, while variable names are not. Commas are used to separate the literals from the variables. This syntax is very common and often used in PAL programs.

The last routine in the program displays the message "Press any key to return to Paradox menu..." at the bottom of the screen (row 24):

```
STYLE ATTRIBUTE 175
@ 24,10
?? "Press any key to return to Paradox menu..."
Y = GETCHAR( )
```

The GETCHAR( ) function, rather than the ACCEPT command, is used in this example. That's because ACCEPT allows data of any length to be entered, followed by a press on the Enter key. The GET-CHAR( ) function "expects" only a single keystroke and stores the results of that keystroke in a variable. (Actually, GETCHAR( ) stores the ASCII code of the keystroke in the variable, but we need not concern ourselves with such details yet.)

Figure 17.2 shows the results of running the Testuser program, though your screen may look slightly different depending on the type of monitor you have. Pressing any key will end the program and return you to the Paradox Main menu.

⎯⎯ *LOOPING* ⎯⎯

One of the most common techniques used in programming is *looping*. Looping allows a program to perform a task repeatedly without repeating many lines. For example, we briefly discussed the STYLE ATTRIBUTE command, which allows you set up color combinations on the screen. Suppose you wish to know what all the possible color combinations are? Well, since there are 255 of them, you could spend a great deal of time and effort trying each one out individually. A better way would be to write a program with a loop that repeats itself 255 times, incrementing the attribute number, and displaying each one on the screen.

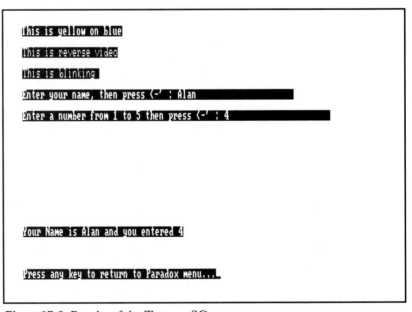

Figure 17.2: Results of the Testuser.SC program

Loops are set up in PAL programs using the WHILE and ENDWHILE commands. There *must* be an ENDWHILE command associated with each WHILE command in a program. This is the general syntax for the WHILE and ENDWHILE loop:

```
WHILE <some condition exists>
    <do this command>
    <and this command>
    <and whatever other commands you want to do>
ENDWHILE
```

Often, a variable is used with a loop to terminate the loop after a certain number of repetitions. If you have a color monitor, try entering and running the program named Colors in Figure 17.3 to test this out. As in the last example, select Scripts, Editor, and Write to enter the PAL editor. Type in the script name **Colors** when prompted, and press Enter. Then type in the script *exactly* as it is shown in Figure 17.3. After typing in the script, call up the PAL menu (press F10), and select Go to save and play the script.

```
;--------------------------------------- Colors.SC.
;-- Shows colors used with STYLE ATTRIBUTE command.
;--------------------------- Loop from 0 to 255.
Counter = 0
WHILE Counter <= 255
       STYLE ATTRIBUTE Counter
       ?? FORMAT("W5",Counter)
       Counter = Counter + 1
ENDWHILE
@ 24,1
?? "Press any key when done viewing colors..."
X = GETCHAR()
```

Figure 17.3: The Colors.SC program

As you'll see, the script displays all the possible color combinations in each of the attribute numbers. In the future, you can use these numbers with the STYLE ATTRIBUTE command to set up a color combination. For example, to display yellow letters on a blue background, use the following command in your program:

STYLE ATTRIBUTE 30

Now let's discuss how the Colors program produces its display. The first three lines in the program are simply programmer comments (they don't affect the program in any way):

```
; ------------------------------------------------------------------- Colors.SC.
; ------------ Shows colors used with STYLE ATTRIBUTE command.
; -------------------------------------------------------- Loop from 0 to 255.
```

The next line creates a variable named Counter and assigns the number zero to it:

```
Counter = 0
```

Next, a loop is set up that will repeat itself as long as the number stored in the Counter variable is less than or equal to 255:

```
WHILE Counter < = 255
```

Within the loop, the program sets the STYLE ATTRIBUTE to whatever number is currently stored in the Counter variable:

```
STYLE ATTRIBUTE Counter
```

The next line displays the number currently stored in the Counter variable on the screen. To standardize the format of the displayed number, the PAL FORMAT command is used. It specifies that the Counter variable must be displayed with a width of five characters ("W5"):

```
?? FORMAT("W5",Counter)
```

Since we don't want the next pass through the loop to repeat the same STYLE ATTRIBUTE, the next line in the program increments the number stored in the Counter variable by 1. This is accomplished by indicating that the variable equals itself plus 1, as shown below:

```
Counter = Counter + 1
```

The ENDWHILE command marks the bottom of the loop. All commands between the WHILE and ENDWHILE loop will be repeated until the stated condition, Counter < = 255, is no longer true.

To keep the color display from suddenly disappearing from the screen when the looping is done, the GETCHAR( ) function waits for the user to press any key, as shown below:

```
@ 24,1
?? "Press any key when done viewing colors..."
X = GETCHAR( )
```

When the user presses any key after viewing colors, the PAL canvas with all the colors displayed disappears from the screen, and the Paradox Main menu reappears.

AVOIDING THE INFAMOUS INFINITE LOOP

The command *Counter = Counter + 1* in the Colors.SC script is a very important one, not only because it makes sure that the next STYLE ATTRIBUTE is displayed, but also because it guarantees that the loop will end at some point. WHILE...ENDWHILE loops must *always* include some command to assure that the loop does not attempt to run forever (called an *infinite loop*).

For example, if you look at the small routine below, you'll see that the WHILE condition says, "Repeat this loop as long as the value of counter is less than 10001":

```
Counter = 1
WHILE Counter < 1001
  ? "Hello"
ENDWHILE
```

However, the value of the Counter variable never changes; it is *always* equal to 1. Hence, this script would attempt to print the word *Hello* on the screen forever. The only way to terminate this loop would be to press the Break key on the keyboard when you grew tired of seeing Hellos written on the screen.

To avoid an infinite loop, be sure there is some way for the WHILE condition to end eventually. In the above example, you would merely need to increment the Counter variable with each pass through the loop so that Counter eventually reaches a number greater than 1000, as shown here:

```
Counter = 1
WHILE Counter < 1001
   ? "Hello"
   Counter = Counter + 1
ENDWHILE
```

There are other ways to ensure that loops will not run forever, as future examples in this book will demonstrate.

MAKING DECISIONS

There are basically two techniques used in PAL to make decisions while a program is running. One is the fairly simple IF...THEN...ELSE...ENDIF command clause, used for making decisions when there are only one or two possible outcomes. The other is the SWITCH...CASE...OTHERWISE...ENDSWITCH clause, used for making a decision when several mutually exclusive alternatives exist. We'll discuss and test each type independently.

IF...THEN...ELSE...ENDIF

The PAL IF...THEN...ELSE...ENDIF commands mean pretty much the same thing they do in English. The basic syntax for this structure is as follows:

```
IF <this condition exists> THEN
   <do this command>
   <and this command>
   <and whatever other commands are listed here>
ELSE
   <do this command instead>
   <and this one too>
   <and any others listed here>
ENDIF
```

The ELSE command is entirely optional. That is, an IF decision might also have this syntax:

```
IF <this condition exists> THEN
    <do this command>
    <and any others listed here>
ENDIF
```

In this case, the ELSE situation is assumed to be, "Don't do anything." The required ENDIF command marks the end of the decision clause; commands beneath ENDIF are not dependent on anything that happened within the IF...ENDIF clause. Let's look at an example by typing in the command file shown in Figure 17.4.

```
;------------------------------ Iftest.SC
;---- Test IF...THEN...ELSE...ENDIF commands.
CLEAR
@ 10,1
;---------------------- Get a number from the user.
?? "Enter a whole number "
ACCEPT "N" TO X
;----------------- Display one message or the other.
IF MOD(X,5) = 0 THEN
    @ 15,1
    ?? X, " is evenly divisible by 5"
ELSE
    @ 15,1
    ?? X, " is NOT evenly divisible by 5"
ENDIF
SLEEP 5000
```

Figure 17.4: A program to test the IF...ENDIF clause

The program is a relatively simple one. First it asks the user to enter a whole number. The user's answer is stored in a variable named X:

```
;------------------------------------------------------------- Iftest.SC
; ---------------------------- Test IF...THEN...ELSE...ENDIF commands.
CLEAR
@ 10,1
;------------------------------------------------- Get a number from the user.
?? "Enter a whole number "
ACCEPT "N" TO X
```

Next, an IF command tests to see if the number entered is evenly divisible by 5. It does so by testing the *modulus* of the number when divided by 5. The PAL MOD function divides the two numbers and tests the result. If the modulus (remainder) is zero, the number is evenly divisible by 5. Otherwise, the number is not evenly divisible by 5. Hence, if the number is indeed evenly divisible by 5, the program displays the number (X) followed by the message "is evenly divisible by 5", as shown below:

```
;-------------------------------------------- Display one message or the other.
IF MOD(X,5) = 0 THEN
    @ 15,1
    ?? X, " is evenly divisible by 5"
```

However, if the number is not evenly divisible by 5 (ELSE), the program displays the number and the message "is NOT evenly divisible by 5", as shown below:

```
ELSE
    @ 15,1
    ?? X, " is NOT evenly divisible by 5"
ENDIF
```

The ENDIF command marks the end of the IF clause, so the last command pauses the program for about five seconds before returning control to the Paradox Main menu, regardless of what occurred within the IF...ENDIF commands:

```
SLEEP 5000
```

SWITCH...CASE...OTHERWISE...ENDSWITCH

In some situations, decisions may involve more alternatives than a simple IF...ELSE...ENDIF clause can handle. In such situations, a SWITCH...CASE...OTHERWISE...ENDSWITCH clause can be called into play. This is the basic syntax for this clause:

```
SWITCH
    CASE <this occurs> :
        <do these commands>
```

```
CASE <this occurs> :
   <do these commands>
CASE <this occurs> :
   <do these commands>
OTHERWISE <if none of the above> :
   <do these commands>
ENDSWITCH
```

There can be any number of CASE commands within the SWITCH-...ENDSWITCH commands. The OTHERWISE command is entirely optional. Hence, the following syntax is acceptable:

```
SWITCH
   CASE <this occurs> :
      <do these commands>
   CASE <this occurs> :
      <do these commands>
   CASE <this occurs> :
      <do these commands>
ENDSWITCH
```

The difference is that in the first syntax, if none of the CASE options occurs, the OTHERWISE option performs its commands. In the latter syntax, if none of the CASE options occurs, nothing at all happens. (That is, nothing between the SWITCH and ENDSWITCH commands happens.)

It is important to keep in mind that options within a SWITCH-...ENDSWITCH clause are mutually exclusive. That is, as soon as a CASE option performs its commands, all other CASEs and the OTHERWISE are ignored. Figure 17.5 shows a sample program named Testcase that demonstrates the SWITCH...ENDSWITCH clause.

This program begins by clearing the screen, setting a color combination, and asking the user to enter a number between 1 and 4. The user's answer is stored in a variable named X, as shown below:

```
;------------------------------------------------------------------------- Testcase.SC
;------------- Test SWITCH, CASE, OTHERWISE, and ENDSWITCH.
CLEAR
STYLE ATTRIBUTE 40
@ 12,10
```

```
;------------------------------- Testcase.SC
;--- Test SWITCH, CASE, OTHERWISE, and ENDSWITCH.
CLEAR
STYLE ATTRIBUTE 40
@ 12,10
?? "Enter a number from 1 to 4, then press <-' : "
ACCEPT "N" PICTURE "#" TO X

;------------------- Respond to entry.
@ 15,10
STYLE REVERSE, BLINK
SWITCH
     CASE X = 1 :
          ?? "You entered a one"
     CASE X = 2 :
          ?? "You entered a two"
     CASE X = 3 :
          ?? "You entered a three"
     CASE X = 4 :
          ?? "You entered a four"
     OTHERWISE  :
          BEEP BEEP BEEP
          ?? "I said from 1 to 4!"
ENDSWITCH
SLEEP 4000
STYLE
```

Figure 17.5: The Testcase.sc program

```
?? "Enter a number from 1 to 4, then press <-' : "
ACCEPT "N" PICTURE "#" TO X
```

Next, the program positions the cursor at row 15, column 10 on the screen, and sets the style to reverse video and blinking:

```
; ------------------------------------------------------------- Respond to entry.
@ 15,10
STYLE REVERSE, BLINK
```

Next, a SWITCH...ENDSWITCH clause decides what to do based on the user's entry. If the user entered a 1, the program displays the message "You entered a one". If the user entered a 2, the program displays "You entered a two", and so on. If the user did not enter a number between 1 and 4, the OTHERWISE option takes over, sounds three beeps (via the PAL BEEP command), and displays the message "I said from 1 to 4!"

```
SWITCH
   CASE X = 1 :
      ?? "You entered a one"
```

```
          CASE X = 2 :
            ?? "You entered a two"
          CASE X = 3 :
            ?? "You entered a three"
          CASE X = 4 :
            ?? "You entered a four"
          OTHERWISE :
            BEEP BEEP BEEP
            ?? "I said from 1 to 4!"
ENDSWITCH
```

The SLEEP command then pauses for about four seconds, the STYLE command (with no attributes) sets the STYLE back to the default settings, and control is returned to the Paradox Main menu.

```
SLEEP 4000
STYLE
```

Note that each CASE statement, as well as the optional OTHERWISE statement, is followed by a colon. Also, even though there is only a single command associated with each CASE statement in this example, a CASE statement may have any number of commands associated with it. The same holds true for the OTHERWISE command.

The SWITCH...ENDSWITCH clause is often used with custom menus in PAL. We'll see how next.

CUSTOM MENUS

You can create your own menus, which are similar to the menus Paradox shows at the top of the screen, using the SHOWMENU...TO <variable> commands. Your menus can include help messages, which appear below the menu as each option is highlighted. This is the basic syntax for the SHOWMENU command:

```
SHOWMENU
    <option 1> : <help message 1>,
    <option 2> : <help message 2>,
    <option n> : <help message n>
TO <choice>
```

where options are displayed at the top of the screen, help messages (descriptions of the menu items) are displayed beneath highlighted menu options, and <choice> is any variable name to store the selected option. Note that commas separate the options. To try this out, enter and play the PAL program named Testmenu, shown in Figure 17.6.

This sample program demonstrates both the SHOWMENU command and a technique for responding to a menu selection with a SWITCH...ENDSWITCH clause. When you play this program, you'll see this menu at the top of the screen:

```
Beep   Flash   Colors   Nothing
Make a few beeps
```

If you move the highlight to other menu options, their help messages will be displayed beneath the menu. You can select a menu option by typing the first letter of the option or by moving the highlight to the option and pressing Enter (as with any other Paradox menu).

The menu appears on the screen because of the SHOW-MENU...TO <variable> clause in the Testmenu program, shown below:

```
; ---------------------------------- Display a menu, store selection in Choice.
SHOWMENU
    "Beep"      : "Make a few beeps",
    "Flash"     : "Display a flashing message",
    "Colors"    : "Play the Colors script",
    "Nothing"   : "Don't do anything"
TO Choice
```

Whichever option is selected from the menu when the program is run is stored in the variable Choice. Once again, this variable name is entirely arbitrary. I've used the name Choice only because it is descriptive.

Note the syntax of the SHOWMENU...TO <variable> clause. Within the clause, menu options to be displayed are enclosed in quotation marks. (To ensure that the "first-letter" method of choosing menu items works properly, you should make each option start with a unique letter.)

```
;---------------------------------- TestMenu.SC
;-------------- Test commands for displaying menus.
CLEAR
SHOWMENU
    "Beep"    : "Make a few beeps",
    "Flash"   : "Display a flashing message",
    "Colors"  : "Play the Colors script",
    "Nothing" : "Don't do anything"
TO Choice

;-------------- Respond to menu choice.
SWITCH
      CASE Choice = "Beep" :
           BEEP BEEP BEEP BEEP
      CASE Choice = "Flash" :
           @ 12,20
           STYLE BLINK
           ?? "Here is your flashing message..."
           SLEEP 5000
      CASE Choice = "Colors" :
           CLEAR
           PLAY "Colors"
ENDSWITCH
```

Figure 17.6: The Testmenu program

Next to each menu option, after a colon, is the help message to be associated with the option. This, too, is enclosed in quotation marks. Each menu option and help message, except the last, is followed by a comma.

Beneath the SHOWMENU...TO clause is a SWITCH-...ENDSWITCH clause that responds to the selected menu item. Within the SWITCH...ENDSWITCH clause, the first CASE sounds four beeps if the user selects Beep from the menu:

```
; ------------------------------------------------------- Respond to menu choice.
SWITCH
   CASE Choice = "Beep" :
      BEEP BEEP BEEP BEEP
```

The second CASE displays a flashing message if the Flash option is selected:

```
CASE Choice = "Flash" :
   @ 12,20
   STYLE BLINK
   ?? "Here is your flashing message..."
   SLEEP 5000
```

The third CASE runs the Colors.SC program if the Colors option is selected:

```
CASE Choice = "Colors" :
   CLEAR
   PLAY "Colors"
ENDSWITCH
```

(This choice works only if the Colors program, discussed earlier in this chapter, has already been created and is stored on the same disk as the Testmenu program.) Notice the syntax of the command. The PLAY command in a PAL program is identical to selecting the Scripts and Play options from the Paradox Main menu. The script or program name is enclosed in quotation marks.

If the Nothing option is selected, nothing happens, because there is no CASE or OTHERWISE option to cover this alternative. In any case, control is returned to the Paradox Main menu after a selection is made and the appropriate commands, if any, are performed.

SCRIPT CONVENTIONS

In previous examples in this chapter and in Chapter 11 we've seen many different types of scripts, in several different forms. Chapter 6 discussed *instant scripts*, which are recorded as you select commands and then stored in a script named Instant.SC. This chapter includes more complex scripts, which you create with the PAL editor. In the next chapter, we'll see yet another type of script called the *keyboard macro*.

All of these different types of scripts have certain elements in common, and any type of script may use any of these elements. The conventions that all scripts use are discussed in this section.

MENU SELECTIONS

If a script is designed to select items from one of the Paradox menus, the appropriate menu selection must be enclosed in curly braces and spelled exactly as it is spelled on the menu. For example, if the script is to select the Modify and Sort options from the Paradox

Main menu, then the instructions to do so would be written into the script as

> {Modify} {Sort}

A script can select any menu item, as long as the item is available on the current menu. For example, the selection {Sort} alone will generate an error if the {Modify} menu has not already been called up. If you are not sure of the series of menu selections you need, try selecting the items from the keyboard without any scripts involved, and jot down notes as you select menu items. Optionally, record the menu selections as you make them, and then copy the recorded keystrokes from the Instant.SC script to a new script name.

LITERAL KEYSTROKES

Literal keystrokes refer to any keystrokes that would otherwise be typed in at the keyboard. Literal keystrokes must be enclosed in double quotation marks within the script. When Paradox sees text enclosed in quotation marks within a script, it types those exact letters, just as though they were being typed in from the keyboard by a person. For example, if you want your script to type the name *Palm Springs*, then that section of the script must be written as

> "Palm Springs"

Suppose you want your script to select the Modify and Restructure options from the menu, then type in the name CustList as the table to restructure. The series of elements would need to be

> {Modify} {Restructure} "CustList"

Here, the menu selections are enclosed in curly braces, and the literal name CustList is enclosed in quotation marks.

SPECIAL KEYS

In addition to the basic letters and numbers that appear on your keyboard, a script can also press the special keys such as Enter, ↑, ↓, and so forth. These special key names are *not* enclosed in quotation marks, but are instead typed in by name. The names for these keys are listed in Table 17.2.

Suppose you want your script to call up the Paradox Main menu, select the the Tools, More, Inventory, and Files options, type in *.TXT as the pattern of file names to view, and then press Enter. The script would look like this:

Menu {Tools} {Info} {Inventory} {Files} "*.TXT" Enter

KEY NAME	PAL NAME
(space)	Space
”	"\""
↓	Down
←	Left
→	Right
↑	Up
Alt-F10	PalMenu
Alt-F3	InstantRecord
Alt-F4	InstantPlay
Alt-F5	FieldView
Alt-F6	CheckPlus
Alt-F7	InstantReport
Alt-F8	ClearAll
Alt-F9	CoeditKey
Backspace	Backspace
Ctrl-←	CtrlLeft
Ctrl-→	CtrlRight
Ctrl-Backspace	CtrlBackspace
Ctrl-Break	CtrlBreak

Table 17.2: Key names used in scripts

KEY NAME	PAL NAME
Ctrl-D	Ditto
Ctrl-End	CtrlEnd
Ctrl-F	FieldView
Ctrl-Home	CtrlHome
Ctrl-PgDn	CtrlPgDn
Ctrl-R	Rotate
Ctrl-V	VertRuler
Ctrl-Y	DeleteLine
Del (or Delete)	Del
End	End
Enter	Enter
Esc	Esc
F1	Help
F10	Menu
F2	DO_IT!
F3	UpImage
F4	DownImage
F5	Example
F6	Check
F7	FormKey
F8	ClearImage
Home	Home
Ins (or Insert)	Ins
PgDn	PgDn
PgUp	PgUp
Shift-Tab	ReverseTab
Tab	Tab

Table 17.2: Key names used in scripts (continued)

where *Menu* presses the Menu (F10) key, {*Tools*} {*Info*} {*Inventory*} {*Files*} select items from the menu, "*.*TXT*" is typed in literally when Paradox displays the prompt for entering a file name pattern, and *Enter* presses the Enter key.

COMMANDS AND FUNCTIONS

Any PAL script may also contain any one of the many PAL commands and functions. We've seen some examples of commands, such as STYLE, CLEAR, and WHILE...ENDWHILE in this chapter, and some functions as well, such as UPPER( ), GETCHAR( ), and MOD( ). There are many more PAL commands and functions, and these are discussed in the *PAL User's Guide.*

Commands and functions have very specific rules of syntax and other requirements that must be adhered to strictly. Those many requirements are far too numerous to list here, and your best source for the specifics about a PAL command or function is the *PAL User's Guide* that comes with your Paradox package.

Commands and functions are usually entered in all uppercase, (though this is more for stylistic, rather than technical, reasons). All of the sample scripts in this chapter demonstrate the use of PAL commands in scripts.

FIELD NAMES

Field Names from the currently open table can be used in scripts by placing square brackets around the name of the field. Note, however, that the field name must refer to a field that is on the currently active table. In the sample routine below, the first line uses the VIEW command to make the CustList table active. The second command displays the data in the Last Name field, for the current record, on the screen:

```
VIEW "CustList" Enter
? [Last Name]
```

VARIABLES

In this chapter we've seen the use of *variables* in PAL scripts as well. As discussed, a variable is a temporary "holding place" for information used in a script. Unlike information stored in tables, information stored in variables is temporary—it ceases to exist when the script stops running.

There are a few basic rules about variables that you need to adhere to for successful use in macros, as listed below:

- Variable names may be up to 132 characters in length.

- The first character must be a letter, A-Z or a-z.

- Subsequent characters in the variable name may be letters, numbers, or the punctuation marks ., $, !, or _.

- Blank spaces are *not* allowed in variable names.

- Variable names cannot be the same as a Paradox keyword—a PAL command, a PAL function, a menu selection, or a key name.

Examples of valid and invalid variable names are listed in Table 17.3.

The trickiest variable names to avoid are those that duplicate commands, function names, and key names. Again, Appendix F lists all the commands and functions, and Table 17.2 lists all the key names. If you do inadvertently use a reserved word as a variable name, PAL will display an error message such as

Syntax error: Expecting a variable name

You'll need to edit the script and use a different variable name.

For your own convenience, you might also want to avoid using table names as variable names. For example, if your script operates on a table named Mastinv, you can avoid potential confusion by not using Mastinv as a variable name in that script.

Variables are assigned values in several ways within scripts. One is to use the equal sign (=), as you would in general mathematics. For

Variable Name	Type	Explanation
YourName	Valid	
My_Name	Valid	
X15	Valid	
Any_Day_Now	Valid	
Fig13.33	Valid	
Income$	Valid	
Hardy Har	Invalid	Contains a blank space
1stEntry	Invalid	Does not begin with a letter
$Income	Invalid	Does not begin with a letter
"Hello"	Invalid	Does not begin with a letter
Style	Invalid	Same as a command
MenuChoice	Invalid	Same as a function name
Ditto	Invalid	Same as a key name

Table 17.3: Examples of valid and invalid variable names

example, the command below creates a variable named LoopCounter, and stores the number 1 in it:

    LoopCounter = 1

The command below stores the name Albert in a variable named PersonName:

    PersonName = "Albert"

The value in a variable may be changed using the equal sign operator as well. For example, the command below adds 1 to the current value of the LoopCounter variable:

```
LoopCounter = LoopCounter + 1
```

The command below adds the word *Dear* and a blank space to the front of whatever is stored in the variable named PersonName:

```
Salute = "Dear " + PersonName
```

In the above example, if the variable named PersonName contains Albert, then this command stores *Dear Albert* in a variable named Salute.

Many commands, such as SHOWMENU and ACCEPT, also automatically assign values to variables, as earlier examples demonstrated. For example, the command below:

```
ACCEPT A25 TO PersonName
```

waits for the user to type in an alphanumeric value with a maximum length of 25 characters, and stores that entry in a variable named PersonName.

Other commands and functions operate on data already stored in variables. For example, the small script below displays the prompt *Enter you name:* on the screen, then waits for the user to type in his name and press Enter. The ? command displays the user's name on the screen in all uppercase letters (because of the UPPER function):

```
? "Enter your name: "
ACCEPT "A20" TO PersonName
? UPPER(PersonName)
```

In the next chapter, we'll see all of these elements used within a practical application of PAL scripts.

STRUCTURED PROGRAMMING

Now, before we try to do anything too practical with our new knowledge of basic PAL programming techniques, we should discuss why the sample programs in this chapter look the way they do. You'll notice that most programs include comments (sentences in plain English preceded by a semicolon) and indentations. Such techniques are part of the *structured* approach to programming, and are designed to help you write programs that are easy to debug and modify.

There are two basic and fairly simple rules for structured programming that you can use to make your PAL programming a bit easier:

1. Use comments to identify the program and major routines in plain English.

2. Indent commands that fall within "clauses."

Figure 17.7 shows a program, identical to the Testmenu program that we just developed, which does not follow these two basic rules of structured programming.

```
CLEAR
SHOWMENU "Beep":"Make a few beeps","Flash":
"Display a flashing message","Colors":
"Play the Colors script","Nothing":
"Don't do anything" TO
Choice
SWITCH
CASE Choice = "Beep":BEEP BEEP BEEP BEEP
CASE Choice = "Flash":@ 12,20
STYLE BLINK
?? "Here is your flashing message..."
SLEEP 5000
CASE Choice = "Colors":CLEAR
PLAY "Colors"
ENDSWITCH
```

Figure 17.7: An unstructured PAL program

The unstructured program will run as well as the structured one, but it is difficult to decipher the purpose of the program and the function of each major section of the program. Figure 17.6 shows the same program with comments and indentations.

Notice that the comments stand out very clearly and, therefore, make the program easy to decipher. Even though Paradox requires only that a comment be preceded by a semicolon, the use of hyphens brings the comments to the foreground, making it easy to scan through the comments quickly to review the purpose of the major routines in the program.

Indentations are used in all commands that form clauses to make the clauses stand out more clearly. In the unstructured program, all the commands look like a single string of indecipherable code. In the structured program, it is clear that there are two major clauses in the program: one for displaying the menu (SHOWMENU...TO <variable>) and another for making decisions (SWITCH...ENDSWITCH).

In the sample programs in the next chapter, we'll adhere to the basic rules of structured programming to try to make the programs as readable as possible. First, take a moment to review the various programming techniques we discussed in this chapter.

━━━━ *SUMMARY* ━━━━━━━━━━━━━━━━━━━━━━━━━

- To create or edit a PAL program, use the Scripts and Editor options from the Paradox Main menu.

- To run a PAL program, use the Scripts and Play options from the Paradox Main menu, or the Go option from the Editor menu.

- To display information on the screen from within a program, use the STYLE, ?, ??, and @ commands.

- To get information from the user while a program is running, use the ACCEPT command or GETCHAR( ) function.

- To set up a loop in a program, use the WHILE- ...ENDWHILE commands.

- To make simple if...then decisions in a program, use the IF...THEN...ELSE...ENDIF commands.

- To make decisions where several mutually exclusive alternatives exist, use the SWITCH...CASE...OTHER- WISE...ENDSWITCH commands.

- To generate menus from within a program, use the SHOW- MENU...TO <variable> commands.

- A script is composed of any combination of the basic script elements: menu selections, literal keystrokes, special key names, PAL commands and functions, field names, and variables.

A SAMPLE PAL APPLICATION

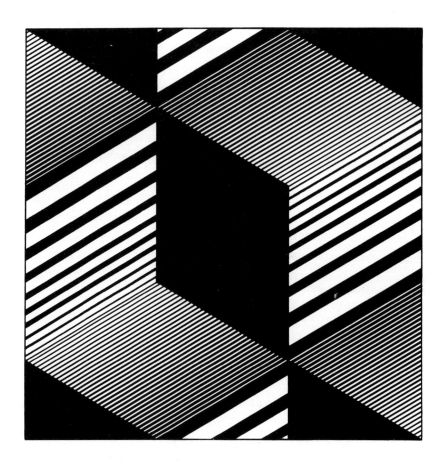

ONE OF THE MAIN REASONS THAT PEOPLE DEVELOP custom applications with a programming language is to simplify the use of the end product. As an example of this, in this chapter we'll develop some PAL programs that automate a mailing-list management system, using the Custlist table. When the user plays the script named Mail, the screen displays a menu containing these options:

Add   Sort   Print   Change   Exit

The user can select items from this custom menu to perform a variety of tasks. He need not know anything about Paradox itself, because all options are fully automated.

Each of the menu options has a PAL script associated with it. Each of the scripts is accessed from the Mail script, which presents the menu. We can envision the relationship among the various scripts (programs) as shown in Figure 18.1.

We'll discuss each program in the sample application independently. If you are planning to follow along on-line, be sure to store these programs on the same disk as your Custlist table, which we created in the first few chapters of this book.

THE MAIN MENU

The main menu program for the sample application is named Mail.SC. You can create it with the PAL editor. Type it in as shown in Figure 18.2.

Let's discuss how the Mail.SC program works. The program begins with some opening comments and the CLEARALL command, as shown below. CLEARALL clears any existing tables from

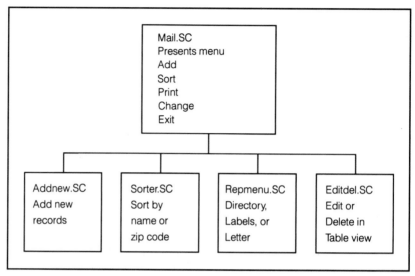

Figure 18.1: Relationships of programs in the mailing system

the Paradox workspace, so the program begins with a "clean slate":

```
;------------------------------------------------------------------------------ Mail.SC
; ---------------------------------------- Script to integrate mailing system.
CLEARALL
```

The next routine in the program sets a style attribute and prints the title "Mailing List Management System" and some opening instructions. Any information between the TEXT...ENDTEXT commands in a program is displayed on the screen exactly as typed into the program:

```
; -------------------------------------------------------- Display opening screen.
STYLE ATTRIBUTE 30
CLEAR
@ 8,25
?? "Mailing List Management System"
STYLE
@ 10,1
TEXT
    Select options from the menu above, either by highlighting and
    pressing Enter, or by typing in the first letter of the option.
```

```
;-------------------------------------- Mail.SC
;---------- Script to integrate mailing system.
CLEARALL
;---------------- Display opening screen.
STYLE ATTRIBUTE 30
CLEAR
@ 8,25
?? "Mailing List Management System"
STYLE
@ 10,1
TEXT

        Select options from the menu above, either by highlighting
        and pressing Enter, or by typing in the first letter of
        the option.  Moving the highlight with the cursor arrow
        keys displays a brief description of each option.

ENDTEXT
;------------- Set up loop to repeat menu.
Choice = " "
WHILE Choice <> "Exit"
        ;---------------- Show Paradox-style menu.
        SHOWMENU
           "Add"  : "Add new records",
           "Sort" : "Sort data into alphabetical or zip code order",
           "Print" : "Print directory, labels, or letters",
           "Change" : "Change or delete data",
           "Exit" : "Return to Paradox"
        TO Choice
        ;---------- Branch to new script based on choice.
        SWITCH
           CASE Choice = "Add" :
                PLAY "Addnew"
           CASE Choice = "Sort" :
                PLAY "Sorter"
           CASE Choice = "Print" :
                PLAY "Repmenu"
           CASE Choice = "Change" :
                PLAY "Editdel"
        ENDSWITCH
ENDWHILE
;------------- Exit selected.
CLEAR
STYLE REVERSE
@ 12,24
?? "Returning to Paradox Main menu..."
SLEEP 1000
```

Figure 18.2: The Mail.SC program

> Moving the highlight with the cursor arrow keys displays a brief
> description of each option.
> **ENDTEXT**

Next, a WHILE...ENDWHILE loop is set up that will repeatedly redisplay the menu on the screen, as long as the user does not opt to exit from the mailing system. Note that the variable Choice is used to control the loop, which repeats as long as this variable does not contain the word *Exit:*

```
;------------------------------------------------- Set up loop to repeat menu.
Choice = " "
WHILE Choice <> "Exit"
```

Within the WHILE loop, the SHOWMENU command displays the menu and help messages. The user's selection is stored in the variable named Choice:

```
; ---------------------------------------------------- Show Paradox-style menu.
SHOWMENU
    "Add" : "Add new records",
    "Sort" : "Sort data into alphabetical or zip code order",
    "Print" : "Print directory, labels, or letters",
    "Change" : "Change or delete data",
    "Exit" : "Return to Paradox"
TO Choice
```

Next, a SWITCH...ENDSWITCH clause passes control to another program, based on the user's menu selection. (This part of the program will work properly only after you've created the other programs discussed in this chapter.)

```
;--------------------------------- Branch to new script based on choice.
SWITCH
    CASE Choice = "Add" :
        PLAY "AddNew"
    CASE Choice = "Sort" :
        PLAY "Sorter"
    CASE Choice = "Print" :
        PLAY "RepMenu"
    CASE Choice = "Change" :
        PLAY "EditDel"
ENDSWITCH
ENDWHILE
```

When an outside script is accessed by this program, it will perform its tasks and then return control to the Mail.SC program. At this point, all other CASE options are ignored, and control falls to the ENDWHILE command. If the user did not select Exit, the loop will repeat and the menu will reappear at the top of the screen.

When the user does select Exit, none of the CASE statements will be selected, and the WHILE...ENDWHILE loop will end. At this point, control will fall to the last routine in the program, which displays a closing message, pauses briefly, and then returns to the Paradox Main menu:

```
; ------------------------------------------------------------------ Exit selected.
CLEAR
STYLE REVERSE
@ 12,24
?? "Returning to Paradox main menu..."
SLEEP 1000
```

When first played, the Mail.SC program displays the opening messages and menu shown in Figure 18.3. After a menu option is selected and a task is performed, the menu will reappear on the screen and the user can either make another selection or choose Exit to leave the mailing system and return to the Paradox Main menu.

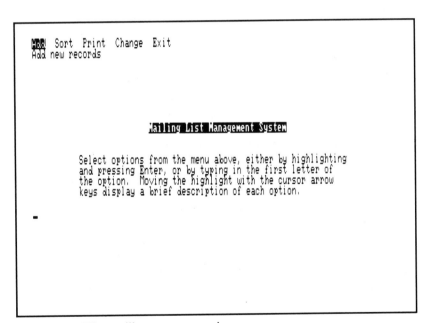

Figure 18.3: The mailing system opening screen

——— *ADDING NEW RECORDS* ———

When the user selects Add from the main menu, Paradox displays the custom form (which we developed earlier), ready to accept new data, as shown in Figure 18.4. The Addnew.SC program, shown in Figure 18.5, allows the user to enter new data through this custom form.

This program begins with the usual opening comments, the CLEARALL command to clear the workspace, and then keystrokes similar to those in a recorded script, as shown below:

```
CLEARALL {Modify} {DataEntry} {Custlist}
MENU {Image} {PickForm} {1}
```

The keystrokes *{Modify} {DataEntry} {Custlist}* select the Modify and DataEntry options from the menu and specify Custlist as the table to add records to. Notice that the keystrokes are placed inside curly braces, as discussed in Chapter 17.

The second set of keystrokes, *MENU {Image} {PickForm} {1}*, calls up the menu and selects the Image and PickForm options and form number 1. MENU is a command that calls up the menu, so it is not enclosed in braces.

The next routine keeps the custom form for entering records on the screen until the user presses DO-IT! (F2). The WAIT command is used in situations where a Paradox table or form is displayed on the screen, and you want to hold that table or form until a certain key is pressed. This keeps the PAL canvas in the background and the Paradox workspace in the foreground until some event occurs. Notice the syntax of the command, shown below:

```
; – Allow new records until F2 is pressed.
WAIT TABLE
    MESSAGE "Press F2 when done"
UNTIL "F2"
```

The WAIT TABLE portion tells Paradox to wait before returning to the PAL canvas, and allows changes to the entire table. The MESSAGE portion displays the message "Press F2 when done" in the lower-right corner of the screen, so the user knows how to get back to

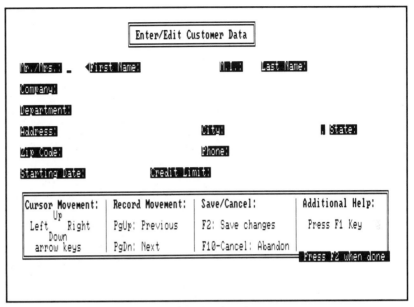

Figure 18.4: The custom screen for entering data

```
;-------------------------------- Addnew.SC.
;--- Script to add new records to Custlist table.

;--- Make menu selections.
CLEARALL {Modify} {DataEntry} {Custlist}
MENU {Image} {PickForm} {1}
;--- Allow new records until F2 is pressed.
WAIT TABLE
     MESSAGE "Press F2 when done"
UNTIL "F2"
;--- Save new records, then clear everything.
DO_IT!
CLEARALL
CLEAR
```

Figure 18.5: The Addnew.SC program

the PAL program. The UNTIL portion defines which key terminates the WAIT.

Other options for the WAIT command are WAIT RECORD, which allows a single record to be modified or added, and WAIT FIELD, which allows changes to only a single field.

Once the user is done entering records and presses F2, the last lines in the program are played:

```
; – Save new records, then clear everything.
DO_IT!
CLEARALL
CLEAR
```

The DO_IT! command (which uses an underline rather than a hyphen when used as a PAL command) saves the newly added records. (When the user presses DO-IT! (F2) in the performance of this program, the only action that takes place is that the WAIT pause ends. The program itself then performs a DO_IT! to actually save the new records.) The CLEARALL command clears the form from the workspace, and the CLEAR command clears the PAL canvas. At this point, the program is done and returns control to the calling program, Mail.SC, which in turn redisplays the mailing-system menu.

SORTING DATA

When the user selects Sort from the menu, the screen displays this submenu:

Alphabetical   ZipCode   None

The user can select a sorting option, and PAL will automatically perform the sort. If the user selects None, control is simply returned to the mailing-system menu. This portion of the mailing system is handled by the Sorter.SC program, shown in Figure 18.6.

The Sorter program begins with the usual opening programmer comments, followed by a routine that displays a menu of sort options, as shown below:

```
;------------------------------------------------------------------ Sorter.SC.
;---------------------------------------------- Script to display options and sort.
CLEARALL
CLEAR
SHOWMENU
   "Alphabetical" : "Alphabetical order by name",
   "ZipCode" : "Zip code order for bulk mailing",
```

```
;----------------------------------------- Sorter.SC.
;----------------- Script to display options and sort.
CLEARALL
CLEAR
SHOWMENU
   "Alphabetical" : "Alphabetical order by name",
   "ZipCode" : "Zip code order for bulk mailing",
   "None" : "Don't sort, return to menu"
TO SChoice

;--- Create message about waiting.
IF SChoice <> "None" THEN
   Msg = "Sorting the data, please wait"
   STYLE REVERSE, BLINK
   @ 12,25
   ?? Msg
ENDIF

;---------- Sort accordingly.
SWITCH
   CASE SChoice = "Alphabetical" :
        SORT "Custlist" ON "Last Name", "First Name"
   CASE SChoice = "Zip Code" :
        SORT "Custlist" ON "Zip", "Last Name"
ENDSWITCH
CLEAR
```

Figure 18.6: The Sorter.SC program

```
    "None" : "Don't sort, return to menu"
    TO SChoice
```

The user's selection is stored in a variable named SChoice. If the user does not select the None option, the program displays a blinking message: "Sorting the data, please wait". The IF clause shown below displays the message (assuming the user did not select None):

```
; ---------------------------------------------- Create message about waiting.
IF SChoice < > "None" THEN
    Msg = "Sorting the data, please wait"
    STYLE REVERSE, BLINK
    @ 12,25
    ?? Msg
ENDIF
```

The final routine sorts the database according to the user's request. Note the use and syntax of the PAL SORT command, which bypasses the need to fill out the sort form:

```
; ----------------------------------------------------------------- Sort accordingly.
SWITCH
    CASE SChoice = "Alphabetical" :
        SORT "Custlist" ON "Last Name", "First Name"
```

```
        CASE SChoice = "Zip Code" :
            SORT "Custlist" ON "Zip", "Last Name"
        ENDSWITCH
        CLEAR
```

The general syntax for the SORT command is as follows:

```
SORT "<table name>" ON "<field 1>",
"<field 2>",... "<field n>"
```

This form of the command will sort the table to itself (just as selecting the Same option from the Sort submenu). An optional TO clause can be used to store sorted data on a separate table, using this syntax:

```
SORT "<table name>" ON "<field 1>",..."<field n>" TO
"<table name>"
```

In this example, sorted records will be stored on the second table name in the command. You can also specify descending orders with the SORT command by placing the letter D after the field name but before the comma. For example, the command

```
SORT "Custlist" ON "Zip" D, "Last Name", TO "Zipdesc"
```

sorts the Custlist table in descending zip code order, with last names in alphabetical order within common zip codes. The sorted records are placed in a table named Zipdesc.

PRINTING REPORTS

If the user selects Print from the mailing-system main menu, the following submenu appears:

    Directory   Labels   FormLetter   None

The user can pick any option and the program will automatically print the report. After selecting the type of report to print, the following submenu appears, offering the user a simplified querying capability:

AllRecords   City   State   ZipCode

Selecting AllRecords displays data for every record in the table. Selecting City presents the prompt

Limit print run to what city?

The user can type in the name of any city, and press Enter. The printed report will then contain only those records that contain the requested city.

The State option displays the prompt

Limit print run to what State?

In response to this prompt, the user may type in the two-letter abbreviation of any state, and the report will include records for only that state.

Selecting ZipCode allows the user to specify a range of zip codes to print the directory, mailing labels, or form letter from. This option first presents the prompt

Enter lowest zip code to include:

The user can type in any zip code value and press Enter. The screen then displays the prompt

Enter highest zip code to include:

The user types in the highest zip code value, and presses Enter. For example, if the user types in 90000 as the lowest zip code, and 99999 as the highest zip code, the report will include only records with zip codes in the range 90000 to 99999.

Of course, the user might request a query value for which there are no records. For example, if the user asks to print records for Kalamazoo residents, but there are no Kalamazoo records, the script displays the message

No records matched the requested query!

and passes control back to the main menu.

However, assuming the user enters a search value for which there are matching records, the program proceeds normally, beginning with the next prompt:

Are records already sorted into desired order? (Y/N)

If the records have not already been sorted, then the user can enter N, for No. In this case, the screen displays the message

Sorting records...

and sorts the records. (For a directory report, the records are sorted into alphabetical order by name. For mailing labels for a form letter, records are sorted into zip code order.)

If for some reason the printer is not ready to display the report when the sorting is complete, the screen displays the prompt

Prepare printer then press any key!

The user can turn on the printer (or set it on-line), and press any key to proceed. The requested report is printed, in the appropriate sorted order, and limited to the city, state, or zip code range requested (unless, of course, the AllRecords option was selected to print all the records). The PAL script to perform all of these tasks and present the menus and prompts, RepMenu.SC, is shown in Figure 18.7. We'll examine the various routines that the program uses in the following discussion.

The program begins with the usual identifying comments and then displays the menu of report options using the usual SHOW-MENU command. The user's selection is stored in a variable named RChoice, as shown below:

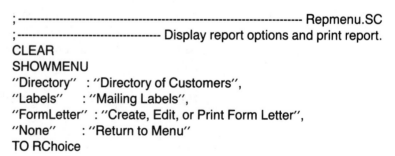

```
; ---------------------------------------------------------------------- Repmenu.SC
; ------------------------------------ Display report options and print report.
CLEAR
SHOWMENU
"Directory"  : "Directory of Customers",
"Labels"     : "Mailing Labels",
"FormLetter" : "Create, Edit, or Print Form Letter",
"None"       : "Return to Menu"
TO RChoice
```

```
;---------------------------------------- RepMenu.SC
;------------ Display report options and print report.
CLEAR
SHOWMENU
    "Directory" : "Directory of Customers",
    "Labels" : "Mailing Labels",
    "Form Letter" : "Create, Edit, or Print Form Letter",
    "None" : "Return to Menu"
TO RChoice

;---------------- If no report selected, return to menu.
IF RChoice = "None" THEN
    CLEAR
    RETURN
ENDIF

;--------- Display simple menu of query options.
CLEAR
SHOWMENU
    "AllRecords" : "Print data for all records",
    "City"       : "Limit mailing to a particular city",
    "State"      : "Limit mailing to a particular state",
    "ZipCode"    : "Limit mailing to a particular zip code range"
TO QChoice

;--- Bring up the query form, and
;--- fill in all fields with CheckPlus.
MENU {Ask}{CustList}CHECKPLUS

;--- Ask for query information,
;--- and fill in query form.
STYLE ATTRIBUTE 30
SWITCH
    CASE QChoice = "City":
        @ 12,5
        ?? "Limit print run to what city? "
        ACCEPT "A25" TO LookUp
        [City] = LookUp
    CASE QChoice = "State":
        @ 12,5
        ?? "Limit print run to what State? "
        ACCEPT "A5" TO LookUp
        [State] = LookUp
    CASE QChoice = "ZipCode":
        @ 12,5
        ?? "Enter lowest zip code to include: "
        ACCEPT "A10" TO LookUp1
        @ 14,5
        ?? "Enter highest zip code to include: "
        ACCEPT "A10" TO LookUp2
        [Zip] = ">="+LookUp1+",<="+LookUp2
ENDSWITCH

@ 24,1 CLEAR EOL
?? "Querying..."
;----- Perform the query, and copy report
;----- formats to the Answer table.
DO_IT!

;--- If Answer table ends up empty,
;--- cancel the operation.
IF (NRECORDS("Answer")=0) THEN
    BEEP BEEP
    @ 24,1 CLEAR EOL
    ?? "No records matched the requested query!"
    SLEEP 5000
    CLEARALL
    CLEAR
    RETURN
ENDIF

;--- If Answer table OK, copy report formats to it.
{Tools}{Copy}{JustFamily}{CustList}{Answer}
{Replace}
```

Figure 18.7: The RepMenu.SC program

```
;-------- Check on sort order, allow only Y or N answer.
Answer = " "
WHILE Answer <> "Y" AND Answer <> "N"
    @ 12,1 CLEAR EOS
    @ 12,10
    STYLE ATTRIBUTE 30
    ?? "Are records already sorted into desired order? (Y/N) "
    Answer = UPPER(CHR(GETCHAR()))
    ?? Answer
ENDWHILE

;-------- Sort if No selected.
IF Answer = "N" THEN
    STYLE REVERSE, BLINK
    @ 24,1 CLEAR EOL
    STYLE BLINK
    ?? "Sorting records..."
    IF RChoice = "Directory" THEN
        SORT "Answer" ON "Last Name", "First Name"
    ELSE
        SORT "Answer" ON "Zip", "Last Name"
    ENDIF ;(rchoice)
    CLEAR
ENDIF ;(answer)

;------------------------- Make sure printer is ready.
WHILE PRINTERSTATUS() = False
    BEEP
    @ 12,1 CLEAR EOS
    @ 12,10
    STYLE REVERSE,BLINK
    ?? "Prepare printer then press any key!"
    Nothing = GETCHAR()
ENDWHILE

;------------------------- Print requested report.
STYLE
CLEAR
? "Printing requested report..."
SWITCH
    CASE RChoice = "Directory" :
        REPORT "Answer" "1"

    CASE RChoice = "Labels" :
        REPORT "Answer" "2"

    CASE RChoice = "Form Letter" :
        REPORT "Answer" "3"

ENDSWITCH
;--- Eject one more page (optional).
PRINT "\F"

CLEARALL
CLEAR
```

Figure 18.7: The RepMenu.SC program (continued)

If the user decides not to print any reports (by selecting None), the program simply clears the screen and returns control to the calling program (Mail.SC). Note the use of the RETURN command to exit the program and return to the calling program:

```
;------------------------------------- If no report selected, return to menu.
```

```
IF RChoice = "None" THEN
   CLEAR
   RETURN
ENDIF
```

Next, the program displays its simplified "mini-query" menu to the user. Once again, it uses the SHOWMENU command, as shown below. Note that the user's menu selection is stored in a variable named QChoice:

```
;----------------------------------- Display simple menu of query options.
CLEAR
SHOWMENU
   "AllRecords" : "Print data for all records",
   "City"       : "Limit mailing to a particular city",
   "State"      : "Limit mailing to a particular state",
   "ZipCode"    : "Limit mailing to a particular zip code range"
TO QChoice
```

After the user makes his selection, the program calls up the query form for the CustList table, and places checkmarks in all the fields. (Since the PAL canvas is still in control of the screen, the user does not see this take place.) Because the cursor is automatically in the leftmost column of the query form when it is brought to the screen, the single CHECKPLUS keystroke places check-plus marks in every field:

```
;---------------------------------------------- Bring up the query form, and
;---------------------------------------------- fill in all fields with CheckPlus.
MENU {Ask} {CustList} CHECKPLUS
```

Now the program asks the user for the value to search for. If the user opts to limit records to a particular city, the routine below asks for the name of the city, stores the user's entry in a variable named LookUp, and then places that value into the City field on the query form. Once again, the field name [City] is enclosed in brackets, while the variable name LookUp is not:

```
;--- Ask for query information,
;--- and fill in query form.
STYLE ATTRIBUTE 30
SWITCH
```

```
CASE QChoice = "City":
  @ 12,5
  ?? "Limit print run to what city? "
  ACCEPT "A25" TO LookUp
  [City] = LookUp
```

If the user opts to limit the report to a particular state, a routine similar to the one above asks for the name of the state, and places that name in the State field on the query form:

```
CASE QChoice = "State":
  @ 12,5
  ?? "Limit print run to what State? "
  ACCEPT "A5" TO LookUp
  [State] = LookUp
```

If the user opts to limit records to a range of zip codes, the program asks for the highest and lowest zip code values:

```
CASE QChoice = "ZipCode":
  @ 12,5
  ?? "Enter lowest zip code to include: "
  ACCEPT "A10" TO LookUp1
  @ 14,5
  ?? "Enter highest zip code to include: "
  ACCEPT "A10" TO LookUp2
  [Zip] = ">=" + LookUp1 + ",<=" + LookUp2
ENDSWITCH
```

The low value is stored in a variable named LookUp1, and the high value is stored in a variable named LookUp2. The appropriate expression is then placed into the Zip field of the query form. Note that this is done with the line

```
[Zip] = ">=" + LookUp1 + ",<=" + LookUp2
```

where *[Zip]* is the field name on the currently active query form, "$>=$" and ",$<=$" are literal text, and *LookUp1* and *LookUp2* are variables. Hence, if the user entered 10000 as the low value, and 19999 as the high value, the Zip field on the query form would receive the proper expression $>= 10000, <= 19999$.

Notice that there is no CASE clause for the AllRecords menu

option. If the user selects this option, we want the query form to contain only the check-plus marks, because we want the query to display all the records in the table.

Next, the program clears the bottom line of the screen, presents the message "Querying...", and performs the query by pressing the DO-IT! key, as shown below:

```
@ 24,1 CLEAR EOL
?? "Querying..."
;---------------------------------------- Perform the query, and copy report
;---------------------------------------------------- formats to the Answer table.
DO_IT!
```

As a safety precaution, the program checks to make sure that some records made it to the Answer table. It uses the NRECORDS function to count how many records are in the Answer table. If this value is zero, the routine below beeps twice, displays an error message for about 5 seconds, clears the PAL canvas and the Answer table, and passes control back to the main menu, Mail.SC, using the RETURN command:

```
;------------------------------------------------- If Answer table ends up empty,
; ----------------------------------------------------------- cancel the operation.
IF (NRECORDS("Answer") = 0) THEN
    BEEP BEEP
    @ 24,1 CLEAR EOL
    ?? "No records matched the requested query!"
    SLEEP 5000
    CLEARALL
    CLEAR
    RETURN
ENDIF
```

Assuming that the Answer table does not end up empty, the PAL keystrokes below copy all the report formats from the CustList table to the Answer table, using the usual Tools, Copy, and JustFamily menu options:

```
; ---------------------------- If Answer table OK, copy report formats to it.
{Tools} {Copy} {JustFamily} {CustList} {Answer}
{Replace}
```

It is necessary to copy the report formats into the Answer table so that they can be used to print only those records that are in the Answer table.

Now the program asks about the sort order. It uses a technique that forces the user to enter either Y or N as a response. It uses a variable named Answer (which has nothing to do with the Answer table) to store the user's answer.

The WHILE loop repeats as long as the variable named Answer does not equal Y and does not equal N. Within the loop, the @ 12,1 CLEAR EOS command clears the screen from row 12 down (EOS stands for End Of Screen). The GETCHAR( ) function reads the next keystroke, storing it as an ASCII number. The CHR function converts this number to the appropriate letter (the one that was actually typed), and the UPPER function converts that letter to upper-case (so that a *y* or *n* entry is converted to *Y* or *N*). The ?? Answer command displays this converted answer on the screen:

```
; ------------------------- Check on sort order, allow only Y or N answer.
Answer = " "
WHILE Answer < > "Y" AND Answer < > "N"
    @ 12,1 CLEAR EOS
    @ 12,10
    STYLE ATTRIBUTE 30
    ?? "Are records already sorted into desired order? (Y/N) "
    Answer = UPPER(CHR(GETCHAR( )))
    ?? Answer
ENDWHILE
```

If the user recently sorted the table using the Sort option from the Mail.SC main menu, he can answer Y to the "Are records already sorted into the desired order?" prompt, and bypass the wait required to sort the records at this point. If the user answers N in response to the prompt, the routine below presents a blinking message, "Sorting records...", on the screen. Then it sorts the Answer table into the appropriate order for the report being printed: into alphabetical order by last and first name for directory reports, or into zip code order for the other report options:

```
; ------------------------------------------------------------ Sort if No selected.
IF Answer = "N" THEN
    STYLE REVERSE, BLINK
    @ 24,1 CLEAR EOL
```

```
      STYLE BLINK
      ?? "Sorting records..."
      IF RChoice = "Directory" THEN
         SORT "Answer" ON "Last Name", "First Name"
      ELSE
         SORT "Answer" ON "Zip", "Last Name"
      ENDIF ;(rchoice)
      CLEAR
   ENDIF ;(answer)
```

Note the use of nested IF clauses in the routine above. The first IF clause bypasses all the commands within the routine if the user's answer was not N. However, if the user's answer was N, all of the commands within that routine are executed. As required, each IF clause has its own ENDIF associated with it. To keep track of which ENDIF goes with which IF, the comments *;(rchoice)* and *;(answer)* are placed next to the ENDIFs. Since these are only comments (because of the leading semicolon), they do not have any effect on the routine. Paradox automatically assumes that an ENDIF relates to the IF at its same level of nesting. The comments next to the ENDIFs are simply for our own clarification.

Next, the program contains a routine to ensure that the printer is ready to accept the report. The PAL PRINTERSTATUS( ) function evaluates to false if the printer is not ready, or true if the printer is ready. A WHILE loop holds the program in suspension until the printer is ready (that is, it repeats itself as long as the printer is not ready). Within this WHILE loop, the program beeps and displays a blinking message. The CLEAR EOL command clears the screen from the cursor position to the end of the line. The GETCHAR( ) function waits for any key to be pressed. The results of the keypress are stored in a variable named Nothing (since this variable only exists to make the GETCHAR( ) funtion work properly):

```
; ------------------------------------------------------ Make sure printer is ready.
WHILE PRINTERSTATUS( ) = False
   BEEP
   STYLE REVERSE, BLINK
   @ 12,10 CLEAR EOL
   ?? "Prepare printer then press any key!"
   Nothing = GETCHAR( )
ENDWHILE
CLEAR
```

Finally, the program is ready to print the reports. In the routine below, the CLEAR and ? commands clear the screen and display a message on the screen. Then a SWITCH...ENDSWITCH clause prints the appropriate report, based on the user's earlier request (stored in the RChoice variable).

The routine uses the PAL REPORT command, which follows the general syntax

REPORT "<table name>","<report identifier>"

where <*table name*> is the name of the table containing the data to print, and <*report identifier*> is the number of the report assigned when the report was initially designed. As you may recall from Chapter 8, we assigned the number 1 to the directory report, the number 2 to the mailing labels, and 3 to the form letter. Furthermore, this program already used the Tools, Copy, and JustFamily options to copy these report formats to the Answer table. Therefore, the command below prints mailing labels for the Answer table:

REPORT "Answer","2"

The routine to print the appropriate report is shown below:

```
;---------------------------------------------------------- Print requested report.
STYLE
CLEAR
? "Printing requested report..."
SWITCH
  CASE RChoice = "Directory" :
    REPORT "Answer" "1"
  CASE RChoice = "Labels" :
    REPORT "Answer" "2"
  CASE RChoice = "Form Letter" :
    REPORT "Answer" "3"
ENDSWITCH
```

The small routine below causes the printer to eject an extra page after the report is printed. Many printers will not need this extra page, though some laser printers might require it. If your printer automatically ejects an extra page at the end of the printed reports, you can just leave this entire routine out:

```
; ----------------------------------------------- This small routine is optional.
PRINT "\F"
```

On some printers, you may need to eject only the last page when printing mailing labels. (That's because mailing labels use a "continuous" page length, and leave the printer waiting for an "eject" after the last "page" is printed.) If that is the case, leave out the small routine above, and place the PRINT "\F" statement in the CASE clause for printing labels, as shown below:

```
CASE RChoice = "Labels" :
    REPORT "Answer" "2"
    PRINT "\F"
```

The last two commands in the RepMenu.SC simply clear the workspace and the PAL canvas:

```
CLEARALL
CLEAR
```

Then, the program ends and passes control back to the calling program: Mail.SC in this example.

——— *EDITING THE MAILING LIST* ———

When the user selects the Change option from the mailing-system main menu, the program first presorts the table into alphabetical order, making it easier to find a particular person by name, and then displays this prompt:

```
Enter last name to look up
Or just press Enter to exit: _
```

The user can enter a last name, and the Custlist table will appear on the screen, ready for editing, with the cursor at the first record with the requested last name. Since the table is sorted, any other individuals with the same last name will be beneath the cursor, as shown in Figure 18.8.

If there is no name that matches the requested name, the program displays this message:

There is nobody named <Smith>

The user can edit and delete as many records as he wishes using this program. Pressing Enter rather than entering a name to look up returns control to the mailing-system menu. This portion of the mailing system is handled by the EditDel.SC program, shown in Figure 18.9.

Let's look at how the EditDel program works. The program begins with opening comments and then sorts that table into alphabetical order, as shown below:

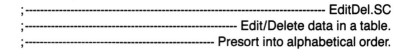

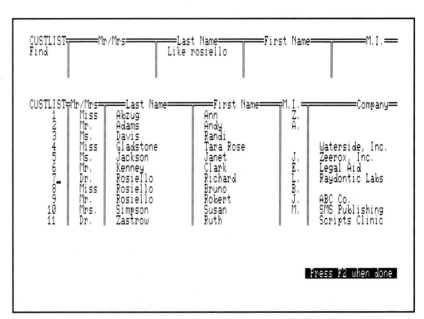

Figure 18.8: The screen after requesting to edit Rosiello's data

```
; ---------------------------------------- EditDel.SC
; ---------------------- Edit/Delete data in a table.
;-------------------- Presort into alphabetical order.
STYLE REVERSE,BLINK
CLEAR
@ 12,10
?? "Presorting to simplify editing..."
SORT "Custlist" ON "Last Name" "First Name" "M.I."
BEEP
;-------------------- Set up loop for editing.
CLEAR
StillAtIt = TRUE
WHILE StillAtIt
        CLEARALL
        CLEAR
        STYLE ATTRIBUTE 30
        @ 12,10
        ?? "Enter last name to look up "
        @ 14,10
        ?? "Or just press Enter to exit: "
        ACCEPT "A20" TO LookUp

        ;---------- If no entry, exit.
        IF ISBLANK(LookUp) THEN
            @ 24,1 CLEAR EOL
            ?? "Returning to menu..."
            QUITLOOP
        ENDIF

        @ 24,1
        ?? "Setting pointer to " + Lookup
        ;----- Perform a "find" query.
        MENU {Ask} {Custlist}
        [Last Name] = "Like " + LookUp
        [#] = "Find"
        DO_IT!

        ;----- If no match, warn user.
        IF (NRECORDS("Answer") = 0) THEN
            BEEP
            @ 24,1 CLEAR EOL
            ?? "There is nobody named "+LookUp
            SLEEP 5000
            LOOP
        ENDIF

        ;-- Allow full editing from cursor position.
        EDITKEY
        WAIT TABLE
            MESSAGE "Press F2 when done"
            UNTIL "F2"
        ;-- Save changes.
        DO_IT!
ENDWHILE
CLEAR
```

Figure 18.9: The EditDel.SC program

```
STYLE REVERSE,BLINK
CLEAR
@ 12,10
?? "Presorting to simplify editing..."
SORT "CustList" ON "Last Name" "First Name" "M.I."
BEEP
```

Next, a loop is set up so the user can repeatedly enter names to look up and edit. This loop is controlled by a variable named StillAtIt. Within the loop, the program asks the user to enter a name to look up (or press Enter), and stores the user's entry in a variable named LookUp, as shown below:

```
;------------------------------------------------------------- Set up loop for editing.
CLEAR
StillAtIt = TRUE
WHILE StillAtIt
   CLEARALL
   CLEAR
   STYLE ATTRIBUTE 30
   @ 12,10
   ?? "Enter last name to look up "
   @ 14,10
   ?? "Or just press Enter to exit: "
   ACCEPT "A20" TO LookUp
```

If the user simply presses Enter, rather than entering a name, the program drops out of the loop immediately. Note the use of the PAL ISBLANK function to test whether the LookUp variable is a blank. The PAL QUITLOOP command terminates the WHILE loop in this case, passing control to the first command beneath the ENDWHILE command:

```
;----------------------------------------------------------------------- If no entry, exit.
IF ISBLANK(LookUp) THEN
   @ 24,1 CLEAR EOL
   ?? "Returning to menu..."
   QUITLOOP
ENDIF
```

If the user enters a name, the program displays a message indicating that it is looking up the requested individual, as shown below:

```
@ 24,1
?? "Looking for " + LookUp
```

Next, the program calls up the Paradox menu, selects Ask, and specifies CustList as the table to query, as shown below:

```
;------------------------------------------------------------ Perform a "find" query.
MENU {Ask} {CustList}
```

Next, the word "Like" and the requested last name are placed into the Last Name field on the query form, and the command "Find" is placed into the leftmost column. Note the use of square brackets to indicate fields on the query form. The [#] symbol stands for the leftmost column, where commands like Find and Delete are entered. The DO_IT! command then performs the "Find" query (which displays actual table data ready for editing, rather than an Answer table):

```
[Last Name] = "Like " + LookUp
[#] = "Find"
DO_IT!
```

Now it gets a little tricky. Although a find query displays the original table rather than the Answer table, it does create an Answer table that is simply not shown on the screen. Therefore, we can determine whether the program found an individual with the requested last name by counting the number of records in the (invisible) Answer table. If there are no records in the Answer table (NRECORDS = 0)—that is, no record matches the requested last name—the program informs the user of this fact in the routine below:

```
;------------------------------------------------------------ If no match, warn user.
IF (NRECORDS("Answer") = 0) THEN
    BEEP
    @ 24,1 CLEAR EOL
    ?? "There is nobody named " + LookUp
    SLEEP 5000
    LOOP
ENDIF
```

(The LOOP command skips all remaining commands between the current position and the ENDWHILE command, but does not in itself terminate the loop.)

If there is a match (or several matches) for the requested last name, the program switches the user to Edit mode (by issuing the EDITKEY command), then waits for the user to finish editing. When the user has finished editing (signified by pressing F2), the program saves his changes and repeats the loop asking for the next person to edit:

```
; – Allow full editing from cursor position.
EDITKEY
WAIT TABLE
   MESSAGE "Press F2 when done"
   UNTIL "F2"
; – Save changes.
   DO_IT!
ENDWHILE
CLEAR
```

This marks the end of the program and the end of the mailing-list system.

After you have typed in all of the programs (scripts) shown in this chapter using the PAL editor (or an outside word processor), you can use the mailing system. (Of course, you'll also need the CustList table we created in Chapter 2, and the report formats we created in Chapter 8.)

To use the mailing system anytime, select the Scripts and Play options from the Paradox Main menu. Specify Mail as the name of the script to play. The Mail menu will replace the Paradox Main menu until you select Exit. At that point, you'll be returned to the Paradox Main menu, and all your work with the Mail system will be safely stored on disk.

═══ *SPEEDING UP MAIL* ═══

For all its user-friendliness, and constant resorting, the Mail system has one drawback: it can get to be rather slow when there are many records in the CustList table. To speed things up, you can create *secondary indexes* of fields that are commonly used for searching. (They are called secondary indexes because Paradox automatically creates a primary index for the key field in the table, if it has one.) In this application, the Last Name field is searched quite regularly to locate a record to edit. Also, the Zip field might be searched often if you often specify ranges of zip codes for mailings.

The QuerySpeedup menu option we discussed earlier creates secondary indexes, but does not necessarily create the best possible indexes for a given application. For example, if you use Query-Speedup to create an index for a query on the State field, but don't really search the State field often, the secondary index is somewhat wasteful, because there is some extra time involved in keeping all secondary indexes up to date. Instead of using the QuerySpeedup option, you can use the PAL INDEX command to create indexes for specific, and often used, fields.

The basic syntax of the INDEX command is

INDEX [MAINTAINED] "<table name>" ON "<field name>"

where the optional *[MAINTAINED]* portion is used only with tables that already have a primary index (based on a key field). *<table name>* is the name of the table the index file is for, and *<field name>* is the name of the field that is indexed.

To create indexes of the Last Name and Zip fields for the CustList table, enter the PAL script editor using the usual Scripts, Edit, and Write menu options. Enter a name, such as MIndex, for the script when prompted, and type in the two commands below:

INDEX "CustList" ON "Last Name"
INDEX "CustList" ON "Zip"

Press F2 when done, then select Scripts, Play, and MIndex from the Main menu to run the script.

Though you won't see any immediate effects, Paradox will create four files, named CustList.X02, CustList.Y02, CustList.X0A, and CustList.Y0A. Paradox will automatically maintain and use these files as necessary in the future. You need not do anything else after running the MIndex script once. (However, if a blackout or some other small disaster causes Paradox to terminate abruptly, the indexes may become corrupted, and your searches may then behave strangely. If that occurs, just play the MIndex script again to rebuild the index files.)

I hope this sample system has given you a basic idea of how PAL programs work, and has presented enough general techniques to get you started on your own programs, if you are so inclined. Again, let me state that it is not necessary to program Paradox; most work can be handled easily working through the normal Paradox menus. But if you enjoy programming or have a strong desire to develop a customized application, PAL will allow you to do so.

There is also another way to create customized applications in Paradox, and that is to use the Paradox Personal Programmer, which comes with your Paradox package. The Personal Programmer lets you build custom applications through menu selections, much like the menu selections on the Paradox Main menu. You tell the Personal Programmer what you want your custom application to do, and it writes the PAL scripts for you. We'll discuss the Paradox Personal Programmer in Chapter 20.

SUMMARY

In this chapter, we've discussed some general programming techniques that you can use to create custom applications using PAL. Some of the commands that are especially useful to programmers are summarized below:

- The TEXT...ENDTEXT commands allow a program to display many lines of text without repeated ? or ?? commands.

- The WAIT command halts a PAL program while the user interacts with a form or table display.

- The SORT command sorts a table without going through the usual menu procedures.

- The REPORT command prints a report without going through the usual menu selection process.

HANDY TIPS AND SCRIPTS

THIS CHAPTER DISCUSSES GENERAL TECHNIQUES
for managing scripts, and also presents some handy scripts that you
can use in your own custom applications. One particularly useful
script converts numbers (such as *123.45*) to words (such as *one hundred
twenty three and 45/100*) for applications that write checks. Another
handy script prints multicolumn mailing labels in any format you
desire. Both of these scripts also involve some advanced PAL programming concepts and techniques.

TIPS ON SCRIPTS

We shall begin our discussion by looking at several handy techniques you can use with your scripts.

RUNNING SCRIPTS FROM DOS

To run an existing script without first going through the Paradox
opening screen, simply enter the name of the script next to the Para-
dox2 command from the DOS prompt. For example, on a hard disk,
the command

    C> PARADOX2 Mail

runs Paradox and the Mail.SC script immediately.

AUTOMATIC SCRIPTS

Another way to make a script run immediately is to assign it the
name Init.SC. When Paradox first runs, it looks for a script named

Init.SC and processes all commands in the script immediately, before providing access to the Main menu. If a script contains the EXIT command, it will return to the DOS prompt when done.

PROTECTING SCRIPTS

Using the Tools, More, Protect, Password, and Script options, you can assign passwords to scripts. Once the password is assigned, the script cannot be viewed or edited by anyone who does not know the password. Furthermore, the script will be encrypted, so that neither the DOS TYPE command nor an external word processor can view its contents. Passwords are discussed in greater detail in Chapter 16.

PRINTING SCRIPTS

To print a PAL script, press Menu (F10) while the script is displayed in the PAL editor. Then simply select Print from the menu to print your script.

USING EXTERNAL WORD PROCESSORS TO EDIT SCRIPTS

An unprotected script is a simple ASCII file that can be created and edited with any text editor or word processor. When you use an external word processor to create or edit a script, be sure to follow these guidelines:

- Store the script on a directory or disk that is available to Paradox.

- Always specify the extension .SC with the script file name. The PAL editor does this automatically, but an external word processor will not.

- Create or save the script as an ASCII file (also called a DOS text file).

The last point is an important one, because most word processors add formatting codes, which Paradox cannot read, if you do not explicitly store the file as an ASCII file. In WordStar, you create ASCII files by specifying N (Nondocument), rather than D (Document) mode before you enter the name of the file to edit or create. With WordPerfect, you need to press Ctrl-F5 and select 1 (DOS Text File Format Save) when saving the completed script. Other word processors will use other techniques for storing ASCII files (or DOS text files).

You can configure Paradox to invoke the word processor of your choosing automatically when you select Script Editor from the Main menu. For instructions on how to do so, see the discussion of the PAL editor configuration in Chapter 16 of the *Paradox User's Guide*.

RUNNING EXTERNAL PROGRAMS FROM SCRIPTS

To run an external DOS program from within a PAL script, use the PAL RUN command. Doing so has the same effect as selecting Tools, More, and ToDos from the menus, or typing Ctrl-O. (You can also mimic the DOS Big key, Alt-O, by using the command RUN BIG instead.)

With RUN or RUN BIG, you can run any DOS command (such as DIR, COPY, MKDIR), any DOS batch file (with the extension .BAT), or any program that is normally run from the DOS prompt (such as Lotus 1-2-3, dBASE, or a word processor). Within the script, put the name of the command or program in quotation marks. For example, the following command runs the DOS COPY program, and copies all scripts (.SC files) from the current drive to drive A:

```
RUN "COPY *.SC A:"
```

The command below runs Lotus 1-2-3, assuming that 1-2-3 is accessible from the current disk and directory (either because it is stored on the same directory as Paradox or because of the DOS PATH setting). Note the use of RUN BIG in this case, to make more memory available to 1-2-3:

```
RUN BIG "123"
```

Do not use the RUN or RUN BIG commands to run programs that stay resident in memory (like the DOS MODE and PRINT commands). These programs will likely prevent you from returning to the suspended Paradox program.

If you want your script to exit to the DOS prompt without running a program, you can use the commands below in the script instead of the RUN command:

{Tools} {More} {ToDos}

With this option, you'll need to enter the EXIT command at the DOS prompt to get back into Paradox. The script will resume playing where it left off.

You can use the SLEEP command with RUN to set up a delay before Paradox is reinstated. This is useful if you want the user to read something on the screen before Paradox erases it. The maximum delay is 30 seconds (entered in the SLEEP command as 30,000 milliseconds). As an example, the command below exits to DOS from within a script, displays a directory of Paradox database (.DB) files, then pauses for 20 seconds before returning to Paradox:

RUN SLEEP 20000 "DIR *.DB"

See the discussion of running external programs in Chapter 16 for more important information on suspending Paradox.

KEYBOARD MACROS

A *keyboard* macro is a sort of miniature script that is assigned to a particular key or pair of keys (such as Alt-1). You assign a script to a particular keystroke using the PAL SETKEY command, using the general syntax

SETKEY <key code> <commands>

The *<key code>* is a special code that represents the key to be pressed. You can assign a macro to any key you want—even the letter A, for instance. However, you really wouldn't want to do that, because you need the letter A for general typing. Instead, you'll probably want to assign macros to keys that are not already used in Paradox, such as Alt-F or Ctrl-F10. The codes for these unassigned keys are listed in Table 19.1. (*Note*: Though listed, the Alt-Z key is actually used as Zoom Next in Paradox, and Alt-R and Alt-L are used in networked environments for locking records and refreshing the screen. If you use these options in Paradox, you'll want to avoid assigning custom macros to these keys.)

The <*commands*> portion of the keyboard macro is the text, keystrokes, or commands that you want the key to perform. Some examples will best demonstrate the use of SETKEY.

A KEYBOARD MACRO TO TYPE A NAME

Suppose you have a table containing names and addresses, and most of the addresses have Los Angeles as the city name. You can create a keyboard macro that automatically types Los Angeles for you when you type a particular key. Suppose you decide to use Alt-C as the key for the macro (the letter C reminds you that this macro is for typing in the City). The PAL command to set up the macro would be

SETKEY – 46 "Los Angeles"

In this case, the command portion (Los Angeles) is enclosed in quotation marks because the macro types literal text (as opposed to performing PAL commands). The – 46 is the code for the Alt-C keystrokes, derived from Table 19.1.

A MACRO TO EJECT A PAGE

If you have a laser printer, chances are you know how it often leaves a printed page inside the machine until you eject the page. You can set up a keyboard macro that will eject a page from the printer right from the keyboard. In the example below, the appropriate command, PRINT ''\F'', is assigned to the Alt-E (for eject) keystroke:

SETKEY – 18 PRINT "\F"

In this example, – 18 is the code for the Alt-E keystroke, and PRINT ''\F'' is the command to eject a page from the printer. PRINT is not enclosed in quotation marks, because it is a PAL command.

Keys	Code	Keys	Code	Keys	Code
Alt-A	−30	Alt-1	−120	Shift-F1	F11
Alt-B	−48	Alt-2	−121	Shift-F2	F12
Alt-C	−46	Alt-3	−122	Shift-F3	F13
Alt-D	−32	Alt-4	−123	Shift-F4	F14
Alt-E	−18	Alt-5	−124	Shift-F5	F15
Alt-F	−33	Alt-6	−125	Shift-F6	F16
Alt-G	−34	Alt-7	−126	Shift-F7	F17
Alt-H	−35	Alt-8	−127	Shift-F8	F18
Alt-I	−23	Alt-9	−128	Shift-F9	F19
Alt-J	−36	Alt-0	−129	Shift-F10	F20
Alt-K	−37				
Alt-L	−38	Alt-F1	F31	Ctrl-F1	F21
Alt-M	−50	Alt-F2	F32	Ctrl-F2	F22
Alt-N	−49	Alt-F10	F30	Ctrl-F3	F23
Alt-O	−24			Ctrl-F4	F24
Alt-P	−25			Ctrl-F5	F25
Alt-Q	−16			Ctrl-F6	F26
Alt-R	−19			Ctrl-F7	F27
Alt-S	−31			Ctrl-F8	F28
Alt-T	−20			Ctrl-F9	F29
Alt-U	−22			Ctrl-F10	F30
Alt-V	−47				
Alt-W	−17				
Alt-X	−45				
Alt-Y	−21				
Alt-Z	−44				

Table 19.1: Common key codes for keyboard macros

A MACRO TO DISPLAY SCRIPT INVENTORY

This sample macro demonstrates how to select Paradox menu items from within a keyboard macro. To display all script names on the screen, you select the menu items Tools, Info, Inventory, and Scripts. To store these in a script assigned to the Alt-S (for scripts) keystrokes, you would use the command

SETKEY – 31 MENU{Tools}{Info}{Inventory}{Scripts}Enter

Note that in this example, menu selections are enclosed in curly braces. Pressing the Enter key is signified by the key name Enter, which is not enclosed in curly braces because it is the name of a key rather than a menu item.

ACTIVATING THE SETKEY COMMANDS

To activate the keyboard macros, you need to place the SETKEY commands in a PAL script and play that script using the usual Scripts and Play menu options. For example, to place the three sample keyboard macros in a script named KeyMacs.SC, you would select Scripts, Editor, and Write from the Paradox Main menu, and type in the SETKEY commands as shown in Figure 19.1. Note that several comments are included to clarify what each SETKEY command does. After you've created the script shown in the figure, save it using the usual DO-IT! key.

```
;-- Assign keyboard macros.
;--- Alt-C types Los Angeles.
SETKEY -46 "Los Angeles"
;--- Alt-E ejects a page.
SETKEY -18 PRINT "\F"
;--- Alt-S displays script inventory.
SETKEY -31 MENU{Tools}{Info}{Inventory}{Scripts}Enter
```

Figure 19.1: Keyboard macros assigned in a script

Before the keyboard macros will actually work, you need to play the script. In this example, just select Scripts and Play from the Paradox Main menu, and specify KeyMacs as the script to play. Nothing will appear on your screen, as this script does not display anything. However, the keyboard macros will be available to you for the rest of the current Paradox session.

Once assigned, typing Alt-E will eject a page from the printer, while typing Alt-S will display a list of all scripts on the current disk and directory. If you call up a table in the Edit mode, and place the cursor in a new blank record, then type Alt-C, the name *Los Angeles* will be typed automatically into the field.

Of course, you can store all of your SETKEY commands in a script named Init.SC. As discussed above, Paradox *always* runs the script named Init.SC at startup. Therefore, your keyboard macros will be available as soon as Paradox is up and running on your computer.

KEYBOARD MACRO LIMITATIONS

A SETKEY command cannot be longer than a single line. Using the PAL editor, that means your limit is about 130 characters. If a script is longer than that, you'll need to treat it as a script played with the usual Scripts and Play menu options, rather than as a keyboard macro.

Of course, there is a way around this problem. Suppose you have a macro named BigGuy.SC that is many lines long, but you would like to invoke it by pressing Alt-B. Simply have your Alt-B command activate the BigGuy.SC script using the PAL PLAY command as shown:

```
SETKEY – 48 PLAY "BigGuy"
```

Note that the PLAY command is not enclosed in quotation marks, but the script name (BigGuy in this example) is.

CANCELING KEYBOARD MACROS

If at any time you want to cancel a macro assignment to a keystroke, run a script containing the SETKEY command with the appropriate keystroke code but no command. For example, the script below cancels the effects of the Alt-C, Alt-E, and Alt-S keys whenever the script is run:

```
;---- Cancel previous keyboard macro assignments.
SETKEY – 46
SETKEY – 18
SETKEY – 31
```

DEBUGGING PAL SCRIPTS

Whenever Paradox encounters something in a PAL script that it cannot "digest," it stops executing the script and displays the options

Cancel   Debug

If you select Cancel, you'll simply be returned to the Paradox workspace. Optionally, you can select Debug to enter the PAL Debugger and get some help in correcting the problem.

When you select Debug, the screen displays the *current command* (the one that caused the error), a brief description of the error (called an *error message*), the name of the script with the error in it, the line number of the current command, and the option

Type Control-Q to Quit

to exit the debugger.

There are two other ways to enter the PAL debugger. One is to interrupt the script as it is playing by pressing the Break key. Doing so will display the Cancel and Debug options. Select Debug at that point. A second way to start the debugger is to place the command DEBUG right in your script at exactly the point where you want debugging to begin. Then save and play the script.

While the debugger is active, you can press PALMenu (Alt-F10) to call up the Debugger menu. This menu displays the options

Value Step Next Go MiniScript Where? Quit Pop Editor

Each of these options is discussed below.

THE VALUE OPTION

The Value option on the Debugger menu let's you enter an expression to test its current value. This option is particularly useful when an expression caused the error. For example, suppose you receive the error message while a script is attempting to execute the line

? SQRT(X)

(which means, "Print the square root of the value stored in the variable named X"). If you call up the debugger, select Value, and enter X as the value to check, the bottom right corner of the screen will display the value stored in the variable named X. If, for example, this number is then displayed as -123, you will know the problem: you cannot take the square root of a negative number, and X contains a negative number.

You may also enter a complete expression, or even a PAL function, as the value to check. For example, if the error occurred in a long expression such as

(Cost − (Discount * Cost)) * 1.06

you could enter just the expression *Discount * Cost* to see what this portion of the faulty expression evaluates to.

The PAL functions listed in Table 19.2 can also provide useful information about the current environment in which the error occurred. (See the *PAL User's Guide* that comes with your Paradox package, for more information on these functions.)

FUNCTION	DISPLAY
ARRAYSIZE(*arrayname*)	Dimensions of named array
ATFIRST( )	*Is current record the first record?*
ATLAST( )	*Is current record the last record?*
CHECKMARKSTATUS( )	*Is field in query form checked?*
DIRECTORY( )	Name of current directory

Table 19.2: Functions that can help in debugging

FUNCTION	DISPLAY
DIREXISTS(*directory name*)	*Does named directory exist?*
DRIVESPACE( )	Amount of space available on disk
FIELD( )	Name of current field
FIELDSTR( )	Contents of current field
FIELDTYPE( )	Type of current field
IMAGETYPE( )	Type of current image
ISASSIGNED(*variable*)	*Has variable been assigned a value?*
ISENCRYPTED(*table name*)	*Is table password-protected?*
ISEMPTY(*table name*)	*Is the named table empty?*
ISFIELDVIEW( )	*Is the current field in Field View?*
ISFILE(*file name*)	*Does the named file exist?*
ISFORMVIEW( )	*Is the current table in form view?*
ISINSERTMODE( )	*Is the insert mode on?*
ISTABLE(*table name*)	*Does the table exist?*
ISVALID( )	*Are the field contents valid?*
MEMLEFT( )	*How much RAM memory is left?*
NIMAGES( )	Number of images on the workspace
NKEYFIELDS(*table name*)	Number of key fields in the table
NRECORDS(*table name*)	Number of records in the table
PRINTERSTATUS( )	*Is printer ready to accept data?*
RECNO( )	Current table record number
SYSMODE( )	Current operating mode
TABLE( )	Table currently in use
VERSION( )	Version of Paradox in use

Table 19.2: Functions that can help in debugging (continued)

As an example of using PAL functions as values, suppose a script fails because it cannot find a value in a table named Charges. To see if the Charges table exists, select Value and enter the expression

ISTABLE("Charges")

If the table exists, the lower right corner of the screen will display *True*. Otherwise, it will display *False*.

Perhaps the table exists (the screen displays *True*), but the script is still not working properly. Perhaps the table is empty. Entering the value

ISEMPTY("Charges")

will display *True* if the table is empty, *False* if it is not.

Suppose in the above example, the screen displays *False* in response to the ISTABLE( ) function. In that case, perhaps the script is currently logged onto the wrong directory. You could test this by typing in the function

DIRECTORY( )

as the value to check; the screen will display the current directory.

Note that if the expression you enter as the value to test causes an error in itself, then you'll be placed in the debug mode to debug *that* error. To "pop" back up to the original error, call up the PAL menu (Alt-F10), and select Pop.

THE STEP OPTION

If you entered the Debugger through the Break key or the DEBUG command in a script, you can select Step from the Debugger menu, or just type Ctrl-S, to play the script one step at a time. Stepping through a script a single line at a time lets you follow the logic of the script in a slower one-command-at-a-time manner. When the stepping process comes to an erroneous line, it will display the error as it normally would. At that point, you may have enough information from the previous steps to figure out what caused the error.

THE NEXT OPTION

This option is used in conjunction with Step to skip over the line that caused the error in the script and proceed with the next line. This lets you check the script for other errors, if possible, before dealing with the current error. You can activate Next either from the Debugger menu or by typing Ctrl-N.

THE GO OPTION

Selecting Go from the Debugger menu, or typing Ctrl-G, resumes executing the script from the current command. This is particularly handy if you've corrected the error with the Editor option from the Debugger menu and want to proceed with the script without starting it from the first line.

THE MINISCRIPT OPTION

The MiniScript option lets you create and execute a small script on the spot, which may help you to proceed with your debugging. For example, if the error in your script was caused by a nonexistent variable (such as the calculation $X = Y + Z$, where the Z variable is not defined), you can enter a miniscript such as $Z = 0$ to assign a value to the variable Z temporarily. Then select Go from the debugger menu to proceed with the script. (Later, you'll have to come back and edit the script so that Z does actually have a value.)

Like Value on the debugger menu, it is possible to enter a miniscript that contains an error of its own. When that occurs, the debugger will again detect *that* new error and allow you to fix it. As discussed before, you need to select Pop from the Debugger menu to pop back up to the level that caused the original problem in the script.

THE WHERE? OPTION

Selecting Where? from the debugger, or typing Ctrl-W, displays the nesting level at which the error occurred. For example, suppose the script named Mail.SC plays a script named RepMenu.SC, and

RepMenu.SC in turn plays a script named Labels.SC. If an error occurs in Labels.SC, you want to know what series of scripts led to the error. Where? will show you, as in Figure 19.2. As you can see, Mail.SC called RepMenu.SC, which in turn called Labels.SC, which is where the error occurred.

THE POP OPTION

As discussed under Value and MiniScript above, the Pop option (which can also be activated by typing Ctrl-P) leaves the current level of debugging and pops back up to the next highest level (and thus to the previous error).

THE EDITOR OPTION

Selecting the Editor option, or typing Ctrl-E, brings you straight from the debugger into the PAL editor, with the cursor at the line that caused the error. You can correct the error at that point using the

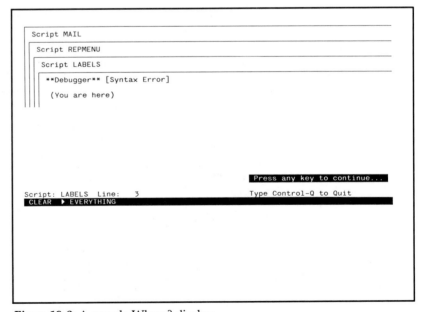

```
Script MAIL
  Script REPMENU
    Script LABELS
      **Debugger** [Syntax Error]
      (You are here)




                                      Press any key to continue...
  Script: LABELS  Line:   3           Type Control-Q to Quit
  CLEAR  ▶ EVERYTHING
```

Figure 19.2: A sample Where? display

usual PAL Editor editing keys. When done, call up the menu (F10) and select Go to save and replay the corrected script.

THE QUIT OPTION

Selecting Quit from the Debugger menu, or typing Ctrl-Q, ends the debugger and cancels the entire script play. You'll be returned to the Paradox workspace with no scripts running.

USING RECORD NUMBERS IN TABLES

You may have noticed by now that the record numbers in Paradox tables are not constant. For example, when you sort a table to itself (by using the Same rather than the New option), each record in the table receives a new number. Similarly, when you query a table, the Answer table assigns new record numbers to records, which will not match the record numbers in the original table.

You can add your own constant record number to a table simply by adding a field to store record numbers in. To simplify the maintenance of this field, I'll show you a script that will automatically assign a record number to each new record in a table.

Let's use the Custlist table to demonstrate a technique for managing constant record numbers. Figure 19.3 shows the original Custlist table with a new field, named RecNo, added via the Modify and Restructure options. Notice that I've used the short number (S) data type. (If your table is likely to have more than 32,000 records in it, be sure to use the N data type instead.)

Figure 19.4 shows the Custlist table after adding the new field and saving the structure. Notice that the RecNo field is still blank in every record.

Figure 19.5 shows a PAL script named Fillrec.SC that will automatically scan the Custlist table for records that have a blank in the RecNo field and enter the record number into the RecNo field.

To use a similar script for a different table, just change the table name *Custlist* in the following command to whatever table name you wish to use:

```
EDIT "Custlist"
```

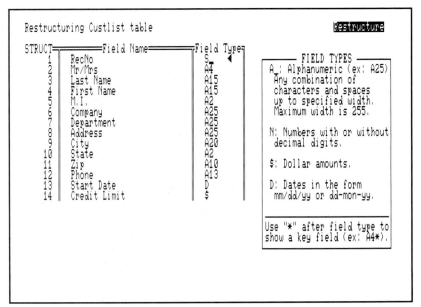

Figure 19.3: The Custlist table with a new field added

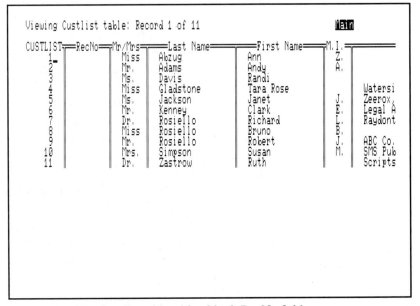

Figure 19.4: The Custlist table with a blank RecNo field

```
;----------------------------------------- Fillrec.SC
;--- Automatically fills in RecNo field on Names table.
CLEARALL
EDIT "Custlist"                      ; edit custlist table
MOVETO [RecNo]                       ; move to RecNo field
SCAN FOR ISBLANK([RecNo])            ; find blank record
    TYPEIN RECNO()                   ; enter record number
    MESSAGE RECNO()                  ; show progress
ENDSCAN                              ; repeat for next blank
? "All Done!"
BEEP
DO_IT!                               ; save changes
```

Figure 19.5: The Fillrec script

If you use a field name other than RecNo, change the name *RecNo* in the following commands to the appropriate field name:

```
MOVETO [RecNo]
SCAN FOR ISBLANK([RecNo])
```

The TYPEIN command types the record number (RecNo) into the field, and MESSAGE displays the record number on the screen so you can see the script's progress.

After you play the Fillrec script (using the Scripts and Play options), the Custlist table will have record numbers in the RecNo field, as shown in Figure 19.6.

After you sort the table to itself, the RecNo field will still contain the original record numbers, as shown in Figure 19.7. To get the records back in their original order, simply sort the table again, based on the RecNo field.

If you query the table, the Answer table will still show the original record numbers, as shown in Figure 19.8. After the query, you can use the Image, GoTo, and Record options to jump to the appropriate record in the original table and make changes if you wish.

TRANSLATING NUMBERS INTO WORDS

If you were to write a script to manage accounts payable using Paradox and you wanted to print checks from a table, you'd need the ability

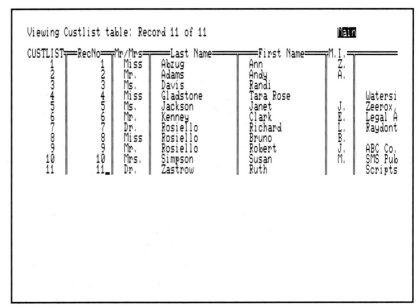

Figure 19.6: Record numbers in the RecNo field

```
Viewing Custlist table: Record 1 of 11                    Main
CUSTLIST==RecNo==Mr/Mrs======Last Name======First Name======Zip=====
     1        7    Dr.    Rosiello       Richard        00123
     2        9    Mr.    Rosiello       Robert         11111
     3        4    Miss   Gladstone      Tara Rose      12345
     4        6    Mr.    Kenney         Clark          12345
     5       10    Mrs.   Simpson        Susan          23456
     6        3    Ms.    Davis          Randi          90001
     7        5    Ms.    Jackson        Janet          91234
     8        1    Miss   Abzug          Ann            92024
     9       11    Dr.    Zastrow        Ruth           92037
    10        2    Mr.    Adams          Andy           92038
    11        8    Miss   Rosiello       Bruno          99999
```

Figure 19.7: The Custlist table sorted by zip code

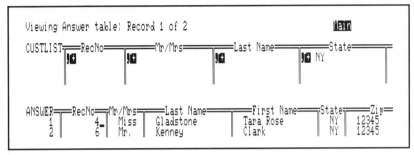

Figure 19.8: The Answer table with original record numbers

to translate dollar amounts, expressed as figures, into words. This is one of the few capabilities that Paradox does not already have. However, you can write a PAL script to perform the translation for you.

The first thing you'll need is an *array* that contains all the unique English words for numbers. You can create this by entering and playing the Numwords.SC script shown in Figure 19.9.

The Numwords script creates an array of 90 subscripted variables named Word. (Subscripted variables all have the same name, but different subscripts.) The subscript, in this example, matches the

```
;---------------------------------- Numwords.SC
;-- Create an array of unique words for numbers.
ARRAY Word[90]
Word[1]  = "ONE"
Word[2]  = "TWO"
Word[3]  = "THREE"
Word[4]  = "FOUR"
Word[5]  = "FIVE"
Word[6]  = "SIX"
Word[7]  = "SEVEN"
Word[8]  = "EIGHT"
Word[9]  = "NINE"
Word[10] = "TEN"
Word[11] = "ELEVEN"
Word[12] = "TWELVE"
Word[13] = "THIRTEEN"
Word[14] = "FOURTEEN"
Word[15] = "FIFTEEN"
Word[16] = "SIXTEEN"
Word[17] = "SEVENTEEN"
Word[18] = "EIGHTEEN"
Word[19] = "NINETEEN"
Word[20] = "TWENTY"
Word[30] = "THIRTY"
Word[40] = "FORTY"
Word[50] = "FIFTY"
Word[60] = "SIXTY"
Word[70] = "SEVENTY"
Word[80] = "EIGHTY"
Word[90] = "NINETY"
```

Figure 19.9: The Numwords.SC script

word stored in the variable. Hence, Word[17] is "SEVENTEEN", and Word[90] is "NINETY".

Once you play the Numwords script, other PAL procedures will have full access to these subscripted variables. Next, you'll need a *procedure* to translate a number to words. Figure 19.10 shows such a procedure, named Translat.SC. You can type it in using the usual Scripts editor.

What makes a procedure different from a regular script is that when you play a procedure, it is loaded into RAM memory but not immediately executed. To access the procedure after loading it into memory, treat the procedure name as any PAL function. For example, after creating the Numwords and Translat scripts, you can create a third script, as below, to test the procedure:

```
; ------------------------------------------------------------------------ Trantest.SC
; ------------------------------------------------------ Test the translation procedure.
PLAY "NumWords";---------------------------------- Load English words.
PLAY "Translat"; ---------------------------- Load translation procedure.
AnyNumber = 1
WHILE AnyNumber > 0
    @ 9,2
    ?? "Enter a number from 1 to 999999.99"
    @ 11,2
    ?? "(or 0 to exit) : "
    ACCEPT "$" TO AnyNumber
    @ 15,1 CLEAR EOS
    ? TRANSLAT(AnyNumber)
    SLEEP 3000
ENDWHILE
CLEAR
```

In the Trantest script, the command

```
PLAY "Numwords"
```

loads the array of words into memory, and

```
PLAY "Translat"
```

loads the translation procedure. The command

```
ACCEPT "$" TO AnyNumber
```

```
;----------------------------------- Translat.SC
;------- PAL procedure to convert a $ number to words.

PROC TransLat(Amount)

;------------------------- Set up initial variables.
Counter = 1
Start = 1
Hold = STRVAL(Amount)
String = SPACES(9-LEN(Hold))+Hold
English = " "

;--------------- Loop through thousands and hundreds.
WHILE Counter <= 2

    ;------ Split out hundreds, tens, and ones.
    Chunk = SUBSTR(String,Start,3)
    Hun = NUMVAL(SUBSTR(Chunk,1,1))
    Ten = NUMVAL(SUBSTR(Chunk,2,2))
    One = NUMVAL(SUBSTR(Chunk,3,1))

    ;------------- Fix possible error in Ten variable.
    IF Ten = "Error" THEN
        Ten = One
    ENDIF

    ;------------------------- Handle hundreds portion.
    IF NUMVAL(Chunk) > 99 THEN
        English = English + Word[Hun] + " HUNDRED "
    ENDIF

    ;------------------------ Handle second 2 digits.
    IF Ten > 0 THEN
        SWITCH

            ;------------- Translate even tens and teens.
            CASE MOD(Ten,10)=0 OR (Ten>9 AND Ten<20) :
                English = English + Word[Ten]

            ;-- Translate numbers evenly divisible by 10.
            CASE Ten > 9  AND MOD(Ten,10) <> 0 :
                Ten=NUMVAL(SUBSTR(STRVAL(Ten),1,1))*10
                English=English+Word[Ten]+" "+Word[One]

            ; -------------Translate number less than 10.
            CASE Ten < 10 :
                English = English + Word[One]

        ENDSWITCH

    ENDIF ;(Ten > 0)

    ;-------------------- Add "Thousand" if necessary.
    IF Amount > 999.99 AND Counter = 1 THEN
        English = English +" THOUSAND "
    ENDIF

    ;--------------- Prepare for pass through hundreds.
    Start = 4
    Counter = Counter + 1

ENDWHILE ;(counter <= 2)

;----------------------------- Tack on the pennies.
IF INT(Amount) > 0 THEN
    English = English + " AND "
ENDIF

English = English + SUBSTR(String,8,2)+"/100"

;---------- End procedure, return English translation.
RETURN English
ENDPROC
```

Figure 19.10: The Translat.SC procedure

allows the user to enter any number. (The Translat procedure works only with the $ data type, with numbers in the range of 0.01 to 999,999.99.) To translate a number to words, the Trantest script simply uses the command

? TRANSLAT(AnyNumber)

Notice how the syntax is identical to any other PAL function. Once a script is defined and loaded as a procedure, it can be treated as though it were a built-in Paradox capability.

Let's take a look at the Translat procedure now. Notice that the first command (beneath the comments) is PROC. It is this command, in conjunction with ENDPROC, that causes this script to be treated as a procedure. The procedure name is defined (Translat), and a single parameter named Amount is passed, as shown below:

```
; ------------------------------------------------------------------------- Translat.SC
; ------------------------ PAL procedure to convert a $ number to words.

PROC Translat(Amount)
```

Within the main body of the procedure, numerous commands manipulate the passed number and build an English translation using variables from the Words array. At the bottom of the procedure are these commands:

```
; --------------------------------- End procedure, return English translation.
RETURN English
ENDPROC
```

The *RETURN English* command returns control to the calling program, along with the translated number stored in the variable named English. The *ENDPROC* command marks the end of the procedure.

A practical application of the translation procedure would be, of course, to print checks from data stored in a table. Figure 19.11 shows a sample table named Checks, which stores data to write checks from. Notice that the field named Written is blank in all records.

Figure 19.12 shows a sample script named Checkprn.SC that can print a check for each record in the Checks table. The routine also

```
CheckNo  Check Date  To Whom                   Amount  Written
-------  ----------  ----------------------  --------  -------
   1001  12/02/88    American Financial         20.00
   1002  12/02/88    Federated Partners         13.11
   1003  12/15/88    Sandy Eggo Utilities        6.01
   1004  12/15/88    Frankly Unctuous          100.00
   1005  12/16/88    Borscht Microprocessors   123.45
   1006  12/16/88    MicroPotatoChips        1,234.56
   1007  12/20/88    Salisbury Finance      12,345.67
   1008  12/21/88    Woosk Matilda         123,456.78
   1009  12/02/88    HereWeGo Enterprises      888.08
   1010  12/02/88    StillAtIt Co.             808.08
   1011  12/02/88    UpForGrabs, Ltd.        8,080.80
```

Figure 19.11: A table with data for writing checks

```
; --------------------------------------- Checkprn.SC
; -------------------- Sample program to print checks.
CLEARALL
CLEAR
; -------------------- Create index of English words.
PLAY "Numwords"
; ----------------------- Load translation procedure.
PLAY "Translat"

; --------------- Call in "Checks" table in Edit mode.
EDIT "Checks"

;---------------- Send ? and ?? outputs to printer.
PRINTER ON

; --- Loop through records with blank "printed" field.
SCAN FOR ISBLANK([Written])
     Dollars = FORMAT("W12.2,E$C*",[Amount])
     ? [Checkno],SPACES(40),[Check Date]
     ?
     ? [To Whom], SPACES(10), Dollars
     ?
     ? TRANSLAT([Amount])
     ?
     ;---------------- Mark check as written.
     MOVETO [Written]
     TYPEIN "Y"
ENDSCAN ;--------------- (for checks not printed yet)

;------------------------- End of Checkprn.SC script.
DO_IT!            ;---- Save edits to the Checks table.
CLEARALL
CLEAR
```

Figure 19.12: The Checkprn.SC script

marks each check as having been written by placing the letter Y in the Written field. Hence, this script never prints the same check twice, because the SCAN command accesses only records that have a blank Written field.

Within the SCAN . . . ENDSCAN loop, the script prints the check number, followed by 40 blank spaces, followed by the check date.

Then the script prints a blank line and the name of the recipient, followed by 10 blank spaces and the dollar amount. The script then prints another blank line and the translated dollar amount. Undoubtedly, the lines that control spacing within the SCAN . . . ENDSCAN loop will have to be modified for different check formats.

MULTICOLUMN MAILING LABELS

With the help of the PAL script named Labels.SC, shown in Figure 19.13, you can print multicolumn labels from a Paradox table. The script will work with any Paradox table that has (at least) the fields listed below:

Mr/Mrs
First Name
M.I.
Last Name
Company
Address
City
State
Zip

```
; --------------------------------------------- Labels.SC
; -------- Script to print multi-column mailing labels.
CLEARALL
CLEAR

; --------------------- Get label format information.
@ 5,5
? "How many labels across (1-5): "
    ACCEPT "N" PICTURE "#" TO Across

@ 7,5
? "How wide each label (X.X inches) ? "
    ACCEPT "N" PICTURE "#.#" TO Width
;-- Convert width in inches to characters.
Width = Width * 10

@ 9,5
? "How tall each label (X.X inches) ? "
    ACCEPT "N" PICTURE "#.#" TO Height
;-- Convert height in inches to lines.
Height = Height * 6
```

Figure 19.13: The Labels.SC script

```
; ------------------------- Sort the Answer table.
@ 22,1
? "Presorting into zip code order..."
VIEW "Answer"
SORT "Answer" ON "Zip"
ToTRecs = NRECORDS(TABLE())
@ 0,0
CLEAR

; ---------------------- Send labels to the printer.
PRINTER ON

; --------------------------- Loop through records.
OutLoop = 1
WHILE OutLoop <= TotRecs
    ; --------------- Make four blank lines of labels.
    L1=" "
    L2=" "
    L3=" "
    L4=" "
    ; -------------------------------- Make labels.
    InLoop = 1
    WHILE InLoop <= Across AND OutLoop <= ToTRecs
        L1 = L1+SUBSTR([Mr/Mrs]+" "+[First Name]+
                " "+[M.I.]+" "+[Last Name]+
                SPACES(Width),1,Width)

        ; -------------- Make label with Company field.
        IF ISBLANK([Company]) THEN
            L2 = L2+SUBSTR([Address]+
                    SPACES(Width),1,Width)
            L3 = L3+SUBSTR([City]+", "+[State]+
                    " "+[Zip]+SPACES(Width),1,Width)
            L4 = L4+SPACES(Width)

        ; ----------- Make label without Company field.
        ELSE
            L2 = L2+SUBSTR([Company]+
                    SPACES(Width),1,Width)
            L3 = L3+SUBSTR([Address]+
                    SPACES(Width),1,Width)
            L4 = L4+SUBSTR([City]+", "+[State]+
                    " "+[Zip]+SPACES(Width),1,Width)
        ENDIF ;(isblank)

        ; -------------------- Increment loop counters.
        InLoop = InLoop + 1
        OutLoop = OutLoop + 1
        Down                 ;--------Move down 1 record.
    ENDWHILE ;(inLoop)
    ;------------------------- Print a row of labels.
    ? L1
    ? L2
    ? L3
    ? L4
    ;-- Print blank lines to fill in label (height).
    Printed = 4
    WHILE Printed < Height
        ?
        Printed = Printed + 1
    ENDWHILE ;(printed)

ENDWHILE ;(outLoop)

;------------------------- End of Labels.SC script.
PRINTER OFF
@ 23,0
? "Press any key to finish..."
X = GetChar()
CLEARALL
CLEAR
PRINT "\F"
```

Figure 19.13: The Labels.SC script (continued)

You can use the PAL editor to key in and save the Labels.SC script.

To use the Labels.SC script, first place blank mailing labels in your printer and make sure the printer is online and ready. Then call up the Paradox Main menu and select Ask. Specify the name of the table that contains the data to print labels from. Place check marks in all the fields of the query form (press F6 while the cursor is in the left-most column), then fill in a query (such as State = CA). Of course, if you place the check marks but do not specify a search criterion, the script will print mailing labels for all the records in the table.

When the Answer table appears on the screen, call up the Main menu (F10) and select the Scripts and Play options. Specify Labels as the script to play. The screen will display this prompt:

How many labels across (1–5):

Enter a number between one and five, indicating the number of labels across. Next the screen will ask for the width of each label:

How wide is each label (X.X inches) ?

Enter the width of the label in inches. (Most mailing labels are 3.5 inches wide.)

Next the screen displays the prompt

How tall is each label (X.X inches) ?

Enter the label height in inches. (If the label package uses a fraction, such as 15/16 of an inch, this is just to account for the space between labels. You can just round up this value. For example, a label height of 15/16 of an inch is in fact one inch, so you would enter 1.0 as the label height.)

After you've defined the label measurements, the script will display the message:

Presorting into zip code order . . .

and print the labels.

Let's take a moment to discuss how the Labels.SC script works.

The opening lines simply display a title, description, and then clear the screen, as shown below:

```
;-------------------------------------------------------------------------- Labels.SC
;-------------------------------- Script to print multicolumn mailing labels.
CLEARALL
CLEAR
```

Next the script uses a series of @, ?, and ACCEPT commands to position the cursor and display prompts, and to ask for the label measurements. The number of labels across is stored in a variable named Across. The label width and height are stored in variables named Width and Height, respectively. The width is converted from inches to character widths, assuming the printer is set to the usual ten characters per inch, while the height is converted from inches to lines, assuming the usual setting of six lines per inch:

```
; ------------------------------------------------- Get label format information.
@ 5,5
? "How many labels across (1-5): "
    ACCEPT "N" PICTURE "#" TO Across

@ 7,5
? "How wide each label (X.X inches) ? "
    ACCEPT "N" PICTURE "#.#" TO Width
;-- Convert width in inches to characters.
Width = Width * 10

@ 9,5
? "How tall each label (X.X inches) ? "
    ACCEPT "N" PICTURE "#.#" TO Height
;-- Convert height in inches to lines.
Height = Height * 6
```

The next routine displays the message

Presorting into zip code order...

on the screen, then sorts the Answer table into zip code order:

```
; ------------------------------------------------------------- Sort the Answer table.
@ 22,1
? "Presorting into zip code order..."
VIEW "Answer"
SORT "Answer" ON "Zip"
```

Next the script counts how many records are in the Answer table, clears the screen, and turns on the printer:

```
ToTRecs = NRECORDS(TABLE())
@ 0,0
CLEAR


; ------------------------------------------------------ Send labels to the printer.
PRINTER ON
```

Next a WHILE loop is set up to read each record in the table. Within this loop, the variables L1 through L4 (which represent four lines on each label) are created as blanks:

```
; ----------------------------------------------------------- Loop through records.
OutLoop = 1
WHILE OutLoop < = TotRecs
; ---------------------------------------------- Make four blank lines of labels.
L1 = " "
L2 = " "
L3 = " "
L4 = " "
```

Next, an inner loop repeats for as many loops as there are columns of labels. Each time through the loop it creates another label. First, it strings together the Title, First, Middle, and Last Names, making sure that they are exactly the width of the label by using a combination of the PAL SUBSTR and SPACES functions:

```
;------------------------------------------------------------------------- Make labels.
InLoop = 1
WHILE InLoop < = Across AND OutLoop < = ToTRecs
```

```
L1 = L1 + SUBSTR([Mr/Mrs] + " " + [First Name] +
   " " + [M.I.] + " " + [Last Name] +
   SPACES(Width),1,Width)
```

The SPACES function adds spaces to ensure that the line is at least the width of the label. Then the SUBSTR function cuts off all characters beyond the width of the label, making sure the line is the exact width required.

Next, the script creates the company (if any), address, and city-state-zip rows of the labels, again using the PAL SUBSTR and SPACES function to ensure an exact width. An IF clause ensures that labels with no data in the Company field do not end up with a blank line between the name and address:

```
;---------------------------------------------- Make label with Company field.
IF ISBLANK([Company]) THEN
   L2 = L2 + SUBSTR([Address] +
      SPACES(Width),1,Width)
   L3 = L3 + SUBSTR([City] + ", " + [State] +
      " " + [Zip] + SPACES(Width),1,Width)
   L4 = L4 + SPACES(Width)

;------------------------------------------- Make label without Company field.
ELSE
   L2 = L2 + SUBSTR([Company] +
      SPACES(Width),1,Width)
   L3 = L3 + SUBSTR([Address] +
      SPACES(Width),1,Width)
   L4 = L4 + SUBSTR([City] + ", " + [State] +
      " " + [Zip] + SPACES(Width),1,Width)
ENDIF ;(isblank)
```

The inner loop is incremented to keep track of the number of columns of labels created and the number of records processed:

```
;------------------------------------------------ Increment loop counters.
InLoop = InLoop + 1
OutLoop = OutLoop + 1
Down    ;---------------------------------------------- Move down 1 record.
ENDWHILE ;(inLoop)
```

When the inner loop is done, one row of labels is ready for printing. The ? commands below print the label information, then the WHILE...ENDWHILE loop prints enough blank lines to fill in the full height of the label. The bottom ENDWHILE repeats the outermost loop to process the next record in the table:

```
; ---------------------------------------------------------- Print a row of labels.
? L1
? L2
? L3
? L4
; --------------------------------- Print blank lines to fill in label (height).
Printed = 4
WHILE Printed < Height
    ?
    Printed = Printed + 1
ENDWHILE ;(Printed)

ENDWHILE ;(outLoop)
```

When all labels are printed, the script disconnects from the printer before clearing the workspace and returning to the Paradox Main menu:

```
; ----------------------------------------------------------- End of Labels.SC script.
PRINTER OFF
@ 23,0
? "Press any key to finish . . . "
X = GetChar( )
CLEARALL
CLEAR
```

If you would like to use the Labels.SC script in the custom Mail application we developed in Chapter 18, a couple of simple modifications will allow you to do so. First, in the RepMenu.SC script, change the routine which reads

```
CASE RChoice = "Labels" :
        REPORT "Answer" "2"
```

to

```
CASE RChoice = "Labels" :
      PLAY "Labels"
```

Also, since the RepMenu.SC script already takes care of sorting, you can delete this feature from the label-printing script. To do so, remove the following lines from the Labels.SC script:

```
; ---------------------------------------------------------- Sort the Answer table.
@ 22,1
? "Presorting into zip code order..."
```

and

```
SORT "Answer" ON "Zip"
```

PREPARSED PROCEDURE LIBRARIES

For the more advanced database programmer, Paradox offers *preparsed procedure libraries*. Like the Translat procedure we created earlier in this chapter, a preparsed procedure is loaded into memory, and can be played at any time from within a script. There are, however, certain advantages to preparsed procedures. They are already translated from PAL into a language more readily understood by the computer (preparsed), and therefore are executed much more quickly than regular procedures. Also, you can store up to 50 different procedures in a single library, which helps organize many procedures into a single file.

The commands used for preparsed procedure libraries are CREATELIB, WRITELIB, READLIB, and INFOLIB. Let's try one out to get a feel for them.

PROCEDURE TO CREATE A LIBRARY

We'll begin by developing a couple of procedures to translate dates from the Paradox MM/DD/YY or Mon-DD-YY format to the

English format of Month Date, Year (for example, January 1, 1988). Two procedures will be required, one to assign all the month names to variables in an array, and another to perform the translation. Since we want to store both procedures in a single library, we'll put them in a single file named Makelib.SC. So, use the Scripts, Editor, and Write options to first create the script shown in Figure 19.14.

Let's discuss the Makelib.SC script. The CREATELIB command beneath the opening comments tells Paradox that it is to create a pre-parsed procedure library named Dateproc.LIB (Paradox automatically assigns the extension .LIB to the file name you specify):

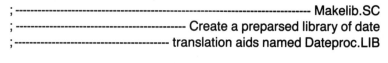

```
; ------------------------------------------------------------------------- Makelib.SC
; ----------------------------------------- Create a preparsed library of date
; ------------------------------------- translation aids named Dateproc.LIB


CREATELIB "Dateproc"
```

```
;-------------------------------- Makelib.SC
;--- Create a preparsed library of date
;--- translation aids named Dateproc.LIB

CREATELIB "Dateproc"

;------------ Make an Array of month names.
PROC Dateword()
    ARRAY CMonth[12]
    CMonth[1] = "January"
    CMonth[2] = "February"
    CMonth[3] = "March"
    CMonth[4] = "April"
    CMonth[5] = "May"
    CMonth[6] = "June"
    CMonth[7] = "July"
    CMonth[8] = "August"
    CMonth[9] = "September"
    CMonth[10] = "October"
    CMonth[11] = "November"
    CMonth[12] = "December"
    RETURN
ENDPROC

;----- Engdate procedure to convert
;----- MMDDYY dates to English.
PROC Engdate(mmddyy)
    Engdate = CMonth[MONTH(mmddyy)] + " "+
            STRVAL(DAY(mmddyy))+", "+
            STRVAL(YEAR(mmddyy))
RETURN Engdate
ENDPROC

WRITELIB "Dateproc" Dateword
WRITELIB "Dateproc" Engdate
```

Figure 19.14: The Makelib.SC script

Next, a procedure named Dateword is listed. Like all procedures, it begins with the PROC command and ends with the ENDPROC command. Since no parameters are passed to this procedure, empty parentheses follow the procedure name. Within the procedure, an array named CMonth consisting of 12 variables is defined. Each array element is assigned the name of a month, (in proper order, of course). Hence, after the Dateword procedure is executed, the variable CMonth(6) will equal "June", CMonth(10) will equal "October", and so on:

```
;---------------------------------------------- Make an Array of month names.
PROC Dateword( )
    ARRAY CMonth[12]
    CMonth[1] = "January"
    CMonth[2] = "February"
    CMonth[3] = "March"
    CMonth[4] = "April"
    CMonth[5] = "May"
    CMonth[6] = "June"
    CMonth[7] = "July"
    CMonth[8] = "August"
    CMonth[9] = "September"
    CMonth[10] = "October"
    CMonth[11] = "November"
    CMonth[12] = "December"
    RETURN
ENDPROC
```

The next procedure, named Engdate, actually translates the Paradox Date data into an English date. Since one parameter is passed to this procedure (a date in MM/DD/YY format), a single parameter is specified after the procedure name, Engdate.

Within the Engdate procedure, a variable named Engdate is assigned the English month name corresponding to the date number, followed by a blank space, followed by the day converted to a character string, followed by a comma and a space, followed by the year converted to a character string. The procedure uses the PAL MONTH, DAY, and YEAR functions to isolate these portions of the date. Since CMonth is a character string, all the pieces of the Engdate variable need to be character strings. Therefore, the

PAL STRVAL function, which converts numeric values to character strings, is used in the procedure. The procedure ends by returning the variable Engdate:

```
;---------------------------------------------- Engdate procedure to convert
;---------------------------------------------- MMDDYY dates to English.
PROC Engdate(mmddyy)
   Engdate = CMonth[MONTH(mmddyy)] + " " +
      STRVAL(DAY(mmddyy)) + ", " +
      STRVAL(YEAR(mmddyy))
RETURN Engdate
ENDPROC
```

The last two lines of the Makelib.SC script store the Dateword and Engdate procedures in the Dateproc.LIB procedure file:

```
WRITELIB "Dateproc" Dateword
WRITELIB "Dateproc" Engdate
```

After creating and saving the Makelib.SC script, you can play it using the usual Scripts and Play options from the menu. Nothing will happen on the screen, however the new Dateproc.LIB procedure file will be created and stored on disk.

USING THE PROCEDURE LIBRARY

To use the procedure library, you need to create a script that uses the READLIB command to load the procedures into memory. Figure 19.15 shows an example. You can create this script using the usual Scripts, Editor, and Write options from the menu, assigning the name Testlib.

The Testlib.SC script works in the following fashion. First, the READLIB command loads the Dateword and Engdate procedures from the Dateproc.LIB library into memory. The Dateword( ) command accesses the Dateword procedure, which in turn creates the array of words for dates:

```
;---------------------------------------------------- Open procedure library.
READLIB "Dateproc" Dateword, Engdate
```

```
;-------------------------------- Testlib.SC
;------ Script to test the Dateproc procedures.

;--------------- Open procedure library.
READLIB "Dateproc" Dateword, Engdate

;--------------- Execute the Dateword procedure
;--------------- to load array.
Dateword()

;--------------- Ask for a MM/DD/YY date.
@ 12,5
?? "Enter a valid date in MM/DD/YY format : "
ACCEPT "D" TO Anydate

;---------------'Print results.
@ 15,5
?? Engdate(AnyDate)

SLEEP 3000
```

Figure 19.15: The Testlib.SC script

```
; ---------------------------------------- Execute the Dateword procedure
; ------------------------------------------------------------------ to load array.
Dateword( )
```

Next, the script asks that you enter a date in MM/DD/YY format. It stores your entry in a variable named AnyDate:

```
;---------------------------------------------- Ask for a MM/DD/YY date.
@ 12,5
?? "Enter a valid date in MM/DD/YY format : "
ACCEPT "D" TO AnyDate
```

Next the script displays the English translation of the date you entered at row 15, column 5 on the screen:

```
;------------------------------------------------------------------ Print results.
@ 15,5
?? Engdate(AnyDate)
```

Finally, the script pauses for a few seconds before returning to the Paradox Main menu:

```
SLEEP 3000
```

To test the Testlib.SC script, use the usual Scripts and Play options after creating and saving the script. Fill in a date when requested, such as 12/10/88. The script will display the English translation, December 10, 1988.

MODIFYING PROCEDURE LIBRARIES

Since procedure libraries are stored in a special preprocessed format, you cannot edit them directly. Instead, you need to edit the script used to create the library (Makelib.SC in this example), then play that script again to recreate the .LIB procedure library. You can add, delete, or change procedures in the Makelib.SC script as often as you wish. Just be sure to play that procedure after any changes so that the .LIB script is updated accordingly.

CHECK-PRINTING REVISITED

Let's take a look at a way to combine some existing scripts and procedures into a single procedure library to speed up the process of printing checks. We'll use a few fancy techniques with the PAL editor to create the procedure library. We'll name the procedure library Proclib1.LIB (for procedure library 1), and create it with a script named Proclib1.SC.

First, use Scripts, Edit, and Write from the menu to create a script named Proclib1. When the script editor appears, press Menu and select Read. Enter the name Makelib to read the Makelib script onto the screen. Change the line that reads

```
CREATELIB "Dateproc"
```

to

```
CREATELIB "Proclib1"
```

so that the script will create a library named Proclib1.SC. You may also want to change the opening comments, as I've done in Figure 19.16.

Next, press the End key to move the cursor to the bottom of the script. Move the cursor so that it is above the two WRITELIB commands, press Insert, and then press Return a few times to add a few

```
;----------------------------- ProcLib1.SC
;--- Create a pre-parsed library of check
;--- writing procedures named DateProc.LIB

CREATELIB "ProcLib1"

;----------- Make an Array of month names.
PROC DateWord()
      ARRAY CMonth[12]
      CMonth[1] = "January"
      CMonth[2] = "February"
      CMonth[3] = "March"
      CMonth[4] = "April"
      CMonth[5] = "May"
      CMonth[6] = "June"
      CMonth[7] = "July"
      CMonth[8] = "August"
      CMonth[9] = "September"
      CMonth[10] = "October"
      CMonth[11] = "November"
      CMonth[12] = "December"
      RETURN
ENDPROC

;----- EngDate procedure to convert
;----- MMDDYY dates to English.
PROC EngDate(mmddyy)
      EngDate = CMonth[MONTH(mmddyy)] + " "+
                STRVAL(DAY(mmddyy))+", "+
                STRVAL(YEAR(mmddyy))
RETURN EngDate
ENDPROC

PROC NumWords()
      ;-- Create an array of unique words for numbers.
      ARRAY Word[90]
      Word[1] = "ONE"
      Word[2] = "TWO"
      Word[3] = "THREE"
      Word[4] = "FOUR"
      Word[5] = "FIVE"
      Word[6] = "SIX"
      Word[7] = "SEVEN"
      Word[8] = "EIGHT"
      Word[9] = "NINE"
      Word[10] = "TEN"
      Word[11] = "ELEVEN"
      Word[12] = "TWELVE"
      Word[13] = "THIRTEEN"
      Word[14] = "FOURTEEN"
      Word[15] = "FIFTEEN"
      Word[16] = "SIXTEEN"
      Word[17] = "SEVENTEEN"
      Word[18] = "EIGHTEEN"
      Word[19] = "NINETEEN"
      Word[20] = "TWENTY"
      Word[30] = "THIRTY"
      Word[40] = "FORTY"
      Word[50] = "FIFTY"
      Word[60] = "SIXTY"
      Word[70] = "SEVENTY"
      Word[80] = "EIGHTY"
      Word[90] = "NINETY"
      RETURN
ENDPROC

PROC TransLat(Amount)
;-- Procedure to convert a $ number to words.
;------------------------- Set up initial variables.
Counter = 1
Start = 1
Hold = STRVAL(Amount)
String = SPACES(9-LEN(Hold))+Hold
English = " "
```

Figure 19.16: The Proclib1.SC script

```
;--------------- Loop through thousands and hundreds.
WHILE Counter <= 2

    ;------ Split out hundreds, tens, and ones.
    Chunk = SUBSTR(String,Start,3)
    Hun = NUMVAL(SUBSTR(Chunk,1,1))
    Ten = NUMVAL(SUBSTR(Chunk,2,2))
    One = NUMVAL(SUBSTR(Chunk,3,1))

    ;------------ Fix potential error in Ten variable.
    IF Ten = "Error" THEN
        Ten = One
    ENDIF

    ;------------------------ Handle hundreds portion.
    IF NUMVAL(Chunk) > 99 THEN
        English = English + Word[Hun] + " HUNDRED "
    ENDIF

    ;------------------------- Handle second 2 digits.
    IF Ten > 0 THEN
        SWITCH

            ;------------ Translate even tens and teens.
            CASE MOD(Ten,10)=0 OR (Ten>9 AND Ten<20) :
                English = English + Word[Ten]

                ;-- Translate numbers evenly divisible by 10.
                CASE Ten > 9  AND MOD(Ten,10) <> 0 :
                    Ten=NUMVAL(SUBSTR(STRVAL(Ten),1,1))*10
                    English=English+Word[Ten]+" "+Word[One]

                ; ------------Translate number less than 10.
                CASE Ten < 10 :
                    English = English + Word[One]

        ENDSWITCH

    ENDIF ;(Ten > 0)

    ;-------------------- Add "Thousand" if necessary.
    IF Amount > 999.99 AND Counter = 1 THEN
        English = English +" THOUSAND "
    ENDIF

    ;--------------- Prepare for pass through hundreds.
    Start = 4
    Counter = Counter + 1

ENDWHILE ;(counter <= 2)

;----------------------------- Tack on the pennies.
IF INT(Amount) > 0 THEN
    English = English + " AND "
ENDIF

English = English + SUBSTR(String,8,2)+"/100"

;---------- End procedure, return English translation.
RETURN English
ENDPROC

WRITELIB "ProcLib1" DateWord
WRITELIB "ProcLib1" EngDate
WRITELIB "ProcLib1" NumWords
WRITELIB "ProcLib1" Translat
```

Figure 19.16: The Proclib1.SC script (continued)

blank lines. Then, press Menu and select Read. Enter Numwords as the name of the procedure to read in, and press Enter. You'll see the Numwords.SC script appear on the screen. To change this into a procedure, place the command

```
PROC NumWords( )
```

above the ARRAY command, and the commands

```
RETURN
ENDPROC
```

at the bottom of Numwords, as shown in Figure 19.16. You may also want to add indentations just to pretty things up, as I've done in Figure 19.16. (Move the cursor to the beginning of each line, make sure Insert mode is on, and press the Space bar 5 times. Tedious, I know!)

Next, read the Translat.SC procedure into this procedure file. To do so, first make sure the cursor is below the Numwords procedure, but above the two WRITELIB commands. Then, call up the menu, select Read, and enter Translat as the name of the file to read. The Translat procedure was originally created with the PROC and ENDPROC commands, so you don't need to add anything to it.

Finally, move the cursor to the bottom of the procedure file. Replace the two lines that read

```
WRITELIB "Dateproc" Dateword
WRITELIB "Dateproc" Engdate
```

with the four lines below:

```
WRITELIB "Proclib1" Dateword
WRITELIB "Proclib1" Engdate
WRITELIB "Proclib1" Numwords
WRITELIB "Proclib1" Translat
```

This will make sure that all four procedures are stored in the new Proclib1 procedure library. Press DO-IT! to save the new script. Figure 19.16 shows the Proclib1.SC script in its entirety.

To create the new Proclib1.LIB procedure library, select the Scripts and Play options as usual, and play Proclib1. Not much will happen on the screen, but when the Main menu returns, the Proclib1.LIB library will have been created.

Now, we need a script that can access these procedures to print checks. Our original Checkprn.SC script (Figure 19.12) is close, but not quite adequate. So, we'll use Checkprn.SC to create a new script named Chekprn2.SC.

To do so, select Scripts, Editor, and Write from the menu. Enter **Chekprn2** as the name of the new script. Then, press Menu, select Read, and specify Checkprn as the file to read in.

Next, you'll need to remove the two PLAY commands shown below (using Ctry-Y):

```
; ----------------------------------------------- Create index of English words.
PLAY "Numwords"
; ----------------------------------------------- Load translation procedure.
PLAY "Translat"
```

and put in these lines instead:

```
; ----------------------------------------------------- Load procedure library.
READLIB "Proclib1" Dateword, Engdate, Numwords, Translat
; ----------------------------------------------- Load date and number arrays.
Dateword( )
Numwords( )
```

The READLIB command will read in the preparsed procedures, and the Dateword( ) and Numwords( ) commands will set up the number and month arrays we've discussed earlier in the chapter.

To use the new date-translation procedure on printed checks, change the line that reads

```
? [Checkno],SPACES(40),[Check Date]
```

to

```
? [Checkno],SPACES(40),Engdate([Check Date])
```

which uses the Engdate procedure to translate the [Check Date] field from the Checks table. Figure 19.17 shows the entire Chekprn2.SC script.

```
; ----------------------------------- Chekprn2.SC
; ------------------ Sample program to print checks.
CLEARALL
CLEAR

;--------------- Load procedure library.
READLIB "Proclibl" Dateword, Engdate, Numwords, Translat

;--------------- Load date and number arrays.
Dateword()
Numwords()

; -------------- Call in "Checks" table in Edit mode.
EDIT "Checks"

; -------------- Send ? and ?? output to printer.
PRINTER ON

; --- Loop through records with blank "printed" field.
SCAN FOR ISBLANK([Written])
     Dollars = FORMAT("W12.2,E$C*",[Amount])
     ? [Checkno],SPACES(40),EngDate([Check Date])
     ?
     ? [To Whom], SPACES(10), Dollars
     ? "    "
     ? TRANSLAT([Amount])
     ? "    "
     ;----------------- Mark check as written.
     MOVETO [Written]
     TYPEIN "Y"
ENDSCAN ;--------------- (for checks not printed yet)

;------------------------- End of Checkprn.SC script.
DO_IT!            ;---- Save edits to the Checks table.
CLEARALL
CLEAR
```

Figure 19.17: The Chekprn2.SC script

Before you can test it all, you'll need to call up the Checks table (described earlier in this chapter) using the Modify and Edit options from the menu. Then, use → to scroll over to the field named Written and remove the *Y* from any records that might have it. (Recall that the check printing procedure puts a Y in the Written field, so that it does not accidentally print the same check twice. Of course, if you have real check data in the Checks table, you'd do better to wait until you've added some more checks before printing.)

To test the new script and procedures, save the Checks table with DO-IT!, call up the menu, select Scripts and Play, and specify Chekprn2 as the script to play. Unless you have a particularly slow printer, you should notice increased speed over the previous script used to print checks.

———— *LOOKING INTO PROCEDURES* ————

You can look at the names and sizes of procedures in a procedure library using the INFOLIB command. To see a list of procedures in the Proclib1.LIB procedure file, select Scripts, Editor, and Write from the menu, enter a name for the script, such as PeekLib, and enter this single line:

    INFOLIB "Proclib1"

Call up the menu and select Go. You'll see a temporary table named List containing the names and sizes of the procedures in the Proclib1.LIB file, as shown in Figure 19.18.

———— *SUMMARY* ————

In this chapter, we've discussed more basic techniques for managing scripts, and looked at some sample scripts using advanced PAL

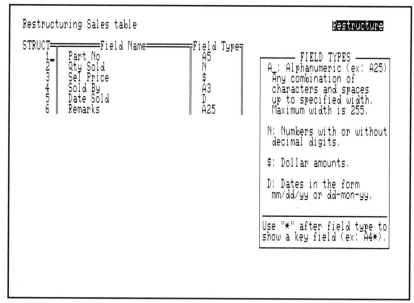

Figure 19.18: The contents of the Proclib1.LIB procedure file

techniques. Space here does not permit us to go into as much detail as the 500-plus page *PAL User's Guide* that comes with your Paradox package, but hopefully the information presented here has given you a good overview of the potential of PAL scripts and enough basic techniques to get you started on developing scripts of your own.

Some specific points to keep in mind that were discussed in this chapter are listed below:

- You can include a script name next to the PARADOX2 command at the DOS prompt to have Paradox run the script immediately at startup.

- You can have a script run automatically every time Paradox is first run by assigning the name Init.SC to the script.

- The Tools, More, Protect, Password, and Script options let you assign passwords to scripts to prevent others from viewing or changing the script's contents.

- To print a copy of a script, call up the menu while editing the script and select Print.

- You can use any text editor or word processor to create or modify a script, as long as you remember to include the extension .SC in the file name, and save the script as an ASCII (DOS Text) file.

- The RUN and RUN BIG commands let you run external programs from within a PAL script.

- Keyboard macros are miniature scripts that are assigned to a particular keystroke through the SETKEY command.

- The PAL debugger provides menu options that can help you locate and correct errors in a script.

THE PARADOX PERSONAL PROGRAMMER

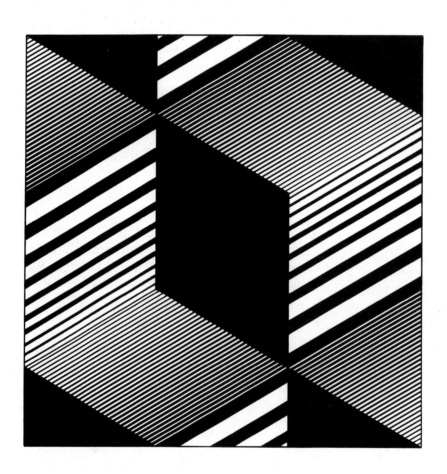

CHAPTER 20

AS DISCUSSED PREVIOUSLY, AN *APPLICATION* IS A SET of Paradox tables, report formats, forms, PAL programs, and perhaps other objects that work together to perform a particular job, such as managing an inventory, an account, or a payroll. The application typically has a menu system of its own that temporarily replaces the more general Paradox menus with menus that are specific to the job at hand.

The real beauty of an application is that it allows you to develop complete systems that others can use easily; even people with no Paradox experience whatsoever. In fact, others who may be interested in using your application don't even need to have Paradox at all! Instead, they can use a smaller *Paradox Runtime* package, which costs less than Paradox, and requires less disk space. This is particularly beneficial if you decide to market your application on a large scale.

One way to develop applications, as we saw in Chapter 18, is to write a lot of PAL scripts. This technique can be quite tedious, and also requires a good deal of knowledge about PAL and general programming techniques. A second way to develop applications is with the Paradox Personal Programmer, which came with your Paradox package.

The Personal Programmer lets you develop applications by presenting menus and asking you to *describe* the application you wish to develop. You define what tables, reports, and forms are required, and design a system of menus that link the various pieces of the application into an integrated system. After you've described your application through your menu selections, the Personal Programmer automatically writes all the necessary PAL scripts to convert your description into a real working application.

REQUIREMENTS AND LIMITATIONS

The Personal Programmer is a very large program; to use it you will need quite a bit of computer hardware and a little Paradox experience.

HARDWARE REQUIREMENTS

As a minimum, your computer system must have the following features:

- At least 640K RAM
- A hard disk with at least 2 megabytes (2,000K) of available space
- All other basic requirements for running Paradox, and the Paradox program already installed on the computer

Though you can't use the Personal Programmer on a computer without a hard disk, your users may be able to use the application you develop with the Personal Programmer on a computer with only two floppy disk drives. Whether or not other users can use the developed application on smaller computers will, of course, be determined by how much disk space the final application requires.

EXPERIENCE REQUIREMENTS

As an application developer, you need to know the basics of using Paradox. You don't need to know anything about PAL, the Paradox Application Language (discussed in Chapters 17 through 19 of this book), but it certainly doesn't hurt to have some familiarity with PAL. In some cases, very complex or sophisticated applications may require some PAL programming.

In this chapter, we'll see how ability to record a PAL script (discussed in Chapter 11) can help overcome some of the limitations of the Personal Programmer.

If you already are an experienced PAL programmer, you'll find the Personal Programmer a great productivity tool in helping you build applications. The PAL programs that the Personal Programmer develops adhere to the basic principals of *structured programming*, making it easy to modify the applications that the Personal Programmer develops, if you are so inclined.

There are a few limitations that the Personal Programmer imposes, although these are by no means strict. Briefly, Paradox sets the following limits for a single application:

- A maximum of 15 tables

- A maximum of 15 selections per custom menu

- A maximum of 10 levels of menus

The applications that you develop with the Personal Programmer will even run on a network. However, the application will use only the most fundamental networking techniques, which network programmers may wish to enhance by modifying the scripts that the Personal Programmer generates.

INSTALLING THE PERSONAL PROGRAMMER

Using the Personal Programmer requires some basic knowledge of DOS directories. While the examples in this chapter will help you manage your directories, you should take some time to familiarize yourself with the following basic DOS commands if you plan on developing many applications of your own with the Personal Programmer:

- MKDIR or MD
- CHDIR or CD
- PROMPT
- COPY

Information on these basic DOS commands is available in the DOS manual that (probably) came with your computer.

Note that the instructions for installing the Personal Programmer presented here are for a single-user system. On a network, the network administrator (the person assigned to managing the network) should install the personal programmer using the appropriate instructions from the *Network Administrator's Guide* that came with your Paradox package.

To install the Personal Programmer, start your computer in the usual manner so that the DOS prompt (usually C>) appears. To help you keep track of what directory you are on, enter the command

PROMPT PG

at the DOS prompt. (Note: You may want to include this handy command in your DOS AUTOEXEC.BAT file so it is always activated when you boot up your computer.)

From the DOS prompt, follow these steps to install the Personal Programmer:

1. Enter the command

   CD\PARADOX2

   to log onto the Paradox directory. (If you've installed Paradox on a different directory, log onto that directory instead.)

2. Insert the Personal Programmer Disk I into drive A of your computer.

3. Enter the command

   A:PINSTALL

   and press Enter to start the installation program. The installation program will create a subdirectory named \PARADOX2\PPROG and copy the files from the current disk onto it. It will then prompt you to remove Disk I and insert Disk II. Follow the instructions as they appear on the screen, removing and inserting the appropriate disk as instructed. When the installation process is complete, the DOS prompt will reappear.

4. Update the PATH or SET PATH command in your DOS AUTOEXEC.BAT file to include the directories

   C:\PARADOX2;C:\PARADOX2\PPROG

You can use any word processor (in nondocument mode) or text editor to do so. The AUTOEXEC.BAT file must be stored on the root directory of your hard disk (the one that is automatically logged when you first boot up—usually C:\).

Before editing an existing AUTOEXEC.BAT file, check to see if there is already a PATH set, with either the SET PATH or PATH command. If there is already a PATH or SET PATH command, add the directive

   ;C:\PARADOX2;C:\PARADOX2\PPROG

to the right end of the command. For example, if your PATH command is

   PATH C:\;C:\WS4

change it to

   PATH C:\;C:\WS4;C:\PARADOX2;C:\PARADOX2\PPROG

If there is not already a PATH or SET PATH command in your AUTOEXEC.BAT file, create one by typing in

   PATH C:\PARADOX2;C:\PARADOX2\PPROG

(For more information on the AUTOEXEC.BAT file, see your DOS manual.)

While the AUTOEXEC.BAT file is still on your screen, you may also want to add the command

   PROMPT PG

if there is not already a PROMPT command in the file. Be sure to place this command on a separate line, and press Enter after typing in the command. The PROMPT PG command will ensure that the name of the directory you are logged onto appears next to the DOS prompt on your screen.

Save the AUTOEXEC.BAT file after making your changes, using the usual commands to do so for your word processor (remembering that the AUTOEXEC.BAT file must be stored as an ASCII or DOS text file).

When the DOS prompt reappears, reboot your computer to activate the new PATH setting. (To reboot, hold down the Ctrl and Alt keys simultaneously, then press the Del key.) Now that the basic installation is complete, you need not repeat any of these steps in the future.

PLANNING AN APPLICATION

In this section, we'll discuss general techniques for planning an application, using an inventory-management system as an example. Rather than plan an application that the Personal Programmer is able to create easily, we'll purposely design an application that goes a bit beyond the capabilities of the Personal Programmer. After all, in any "real-world" situation, you'll probably want to design your own applications without limitations. When the Personal Programmer falls short of meeting the needs of our example application, I'll show you how to bypass the Personal Programmer's limitations to develop the application you want.

AN INVENTORY MANAGEMENT SYSTEM

When you want to build your own application, it's a good idea to start with a large goal, such as the development of an inventory-management system, and break it down into smaller, easier goals. To do this, you must create a diagram of the various tables used in the application and a *menu tree* of the tasks required to manage those data.

THE INVENTORY SYSTEM TABLES

The database structure we'll use for the inventory example will be identical to the structure discussed in Chapter 15, and shown in Figure 15.1. To recap, the master inventory table will hold a single record for each item that the business keeps in stock. Each of these items must be assigned a unique part number (or product number). This table will also store information about the current status of each item, including the quantity in stock, the reorder point, the quantity on order, the date the last order was placed, and so forth.

The Sales table will store current sales transactions. The SalHist table stores sales transactions that have already been posted (their quantities have already been subtracted from the in-stock quantities in the Mastinv table). The Purchase table will store items received from the manufacturers (or distributors). The Purhist table will store posted transactions (items that have been received and their quantities already added to the Mastinv table in-stock quantities).

Figure 20.1 shows the the five tables used in the inventory system we'll develop in this chapter. There are a couple of one-to-many relationships in this database structure. For each item in the Mastinv table, there will likely be many sales transactions and many purchase transactions.

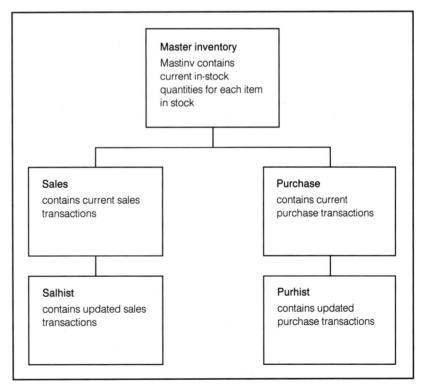

Figure 20.1: The five tables used in the inventory application

THE APPLICATION MENU TREE

After deciding how to store the data for the application, you'll want to develop a *menu structure* that simplifies the task of managing the data. A general rule of thumb when developing applications with multiple tables is to provide an individual menu for managing each table. That is, each table should have a menu selection that allows the user to add new data, edit and delete data, look up information, and print reports. Any general tasks, such as updating, can also be assigned a menu selection. All of the various tasks and submenus can then be linked together through a higher level main menu.

Planning the menu structure (or *menu tree* as it is often called) before using the Personal Programmer will greatly simplify the development of your application. A preplanned menu structure breaks the larger task of developing the application into smaller, more manageable chunks. It also provides a road map to guide you through the Personal Programmer, and makes it easier to take a break from time to time and resume your work at a later point.

The menu structure for the sample inventory-management system we'll develop in this chapter is shown in Figure 20.2. Notice that several of the main menu options branch to submenus for managing information on the Mastinv, Sales, and Purchase tables. The master inventory submenu branches down even further to a second submenu, to allow the user of the application to select a particular report to print.

As we develop the sample application, you might want to refer back to this figure from time to time to keep track of where we are in the development process.

Now, be forewarned that in this chapter, I will intentionally take you into some "dead-ends" where the Personal Programmer falls short. If you are just trying to follow instructions to get the job done, you might be irritated by these intentional dead-ends. But be patient. Learning how to react to, and overcome, the limitations of the Personal Programmer is an important part of mastering this valuable tool. Hopefully, the intentional dead-ends that I overcome in this chapter will help you to do the same when developing custom applications of your own.

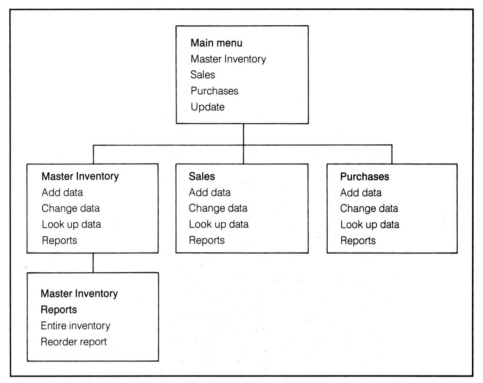

Figure 20.2: The menu structure for the inventory application

CREATING A DIRECTORY FOR THE APPLICATION

Each application that you develop should be stored on its own directory on your hard disk, to avoid conflicting file names and general confusion. To create a new directory for your application, start from your root directory (the one that is logged when you first start your computer), and use the DOS MKDIR or MD command to enter the name of the new directory. The directory name can be up to eight characters long, with no spaces or punctuation.

We'll store the sample application in this chapter on a directory named InvMgr. To create the directory, enter the series of commands below at the DOS prompt (pressing Enter after each command):

```
CD\
MD\INVMGR
CD\INVMGR
```

These commands ensure that you start from the root directory (*CD*), create a new directory named INVMGR (*MD\INVMGR*), and log onto that new directory (*CD\INVMGR*).

When developing or modifying your application, you'll want to be sure to always log onto the appropriate directory first.

COPYING OBJECTS

If you plan to use existing tables, report formats, forms, or scripts for your application, you may want to copy these onto the new directory before starting the Personal Programmer. To do so, be sure you are logged onto the new directory, and use the DOS COPY command with the appropriate file name and extension. The file-name extensions that Paradox uses for various objects are listed in Table 20.1.

As an example, a table named CustList would be stored on disk as Custlist.DB. Its validity checks, if any, would be stored in the file Custlist.VAL. Its image settings, if any, would be stored in Custlist.SET.

OBJECT	EXTENSION
Table	.DB
Form	.F <number>
Report format	.R <number>
Script	.SC
Validity check	.VAL
Image setting	.SET

Table 20.1: Paradox file-name extensions

Report and form file-name extensions use the number you selected when designing the report. For example, report number 1 for the Custlist table is Custlist.R1. Form number 3 for the Custlist table is Custlist.F3.

To use the DOS COPY command to copy objects to the application directory, enter the COPY command, followed by the name of the directory that the object is stored on, and the name of the object to copy. For example, to copy the Custlist table to the current directory, you would enter the command

COPY C:\PARADOX2\Custlist.DB

at the DOS prompt.

For the current example application, you need not copy any Paradox objects. We'll begin with a blank directory.

STARTING THE PERSONAL PROGRAMMER

When logged onto the appropriate directory for your application, you can begin the Personal Programmer by typing in the command

PPROG

at the DOS prompt and pressing Enter.

You'll see an introductory graphic screen similar to the one you see when first starting Paradox, and then the Personal Programmer Main menu and initial instructions, as shown in Figure 20.3.

The options on the Main menu are summarized below:

OPTION	EFFECT
Create	Creates a new application
Modify	Changes an existing application
Summarize	Prints a summary of the application
Review	Views the menu structure of the application
Play	Runs the application or a PAL script

```
Create Modify Summarize Review Play Tools Exit_
Create a new application.




                      ══ The Paradox Personal Programmer ══
  ┌─────────────────────────────────────────────────────────────────────────┐
  │  ▶ Select an action from the menu.                                        │
  ├───────────────────────────────────────────────────────────────────────────┤
  │  The information in these boxes will help you to create applications.  The │
  │  top box shows the current status of the application on which you are      │
  │  working.  This bottom box contains additional information and help.       │
  │                                                                            │
  │  The Personal Programmer menu works just like the Paradox menu --          │
  │  Use the ← and → keys to move the highlight to the selection you want...   │
  │  then press ◄┘ to choose the highlighted selection.  Press [Esc] to return │
  │  to the previous menu.                                                      │
  └────────────────────────────────────────────────────────────────────────────┘
```

Figure 20.3: The opening screen for the Personal Programmer

Tools	Copies, deletes, or renames the application, changes settings or the current directory
Exit	Leaves the Personal Programmer and returns to DOS

You select items from the Personal Programmer menu in exactly the same way you select them from the Paradox menus. To leave a submenu and return to a higher-level menu, press the Esc key; select DO-IT! or Cancel if the options are presented. We'll see examples of these various options as we develop the sample inventory manager.

CREATING THE APPLICATION

It will take quite a bit of time to develop the entire inventory application, so we'll break it down into pieces so that you can take a break from time to time, and resume where you left off.

To create an application, select Create from the Personal Programmer Main menu. The screen displays the prompt

> Application name:
> Enter a name for the new application:

The application name can be from one to five characters long, with no spaces or punctuation. For this example, type in the application name **Inv** and press Enter.

SELECTING TABLES FOR THE APPLICATION

The next step in creating an application is to create the tables or specify which existing tables to use for the application. The menu at the top of the screen displays the options

> ExistingTable NewTable RemoveTable DO-IT! Cancel

These options can be summarized as follows:

ExistingTable	Selects an existing table for use in the application
NewTable	Creates a new table for use in the application
RemoveTable	Removes a table from the application
DO-IT!	Finishes selection of tables for the application
Cancel	Cancels table selections and returns to the Main menu

For the inventory example, we'll assume that the tables do not already exist. Therefore, select the NewTable option, type in the table name **Mastinv** when prompted, and press Enter. Figure 20.4 shows the structure of the Mastinv table. You can type it in exactly as shown in the figure. (Optionally, if you already created the Mastinv table back in Chapter 12, call up the Menu (F10), select Borrow, and type **\PARADOX2\Mastinv** as the structure to borrow.) When you have the structure entered correctly, as in Figure 20.4, press the DO-IT key (F2) to save it.

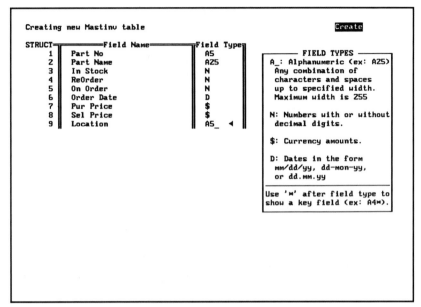

Figure 20.4: The structure of the Mastinv table

Next, create the structure of the Sales table. Select NewTable, and enter **Sales** as the table name. Type in the structure exactly as shown in Figure 20.5. (If you previously created the Sales table back in Chapter 12, you can borrow its structure by pressing Menu (F10) and selecting Borrow. Specify **\PARADOX2\Sales** as the structure to borrow. Note that you must also change the name of the Sel Price field to Unit Price, so the structure matches that in Figure 20.5.) Press F2 to save the completed Sales table structure.

Next, create the structure for the Purchase table. Select NewTable from the menu, and enter the table name **Purchase**. Structure the table exactly as shown in Figure 20.6. (Once again, if you already created this table back in Chapter 12, press F10, select Borrow, and specify **\PARADOX2\Purchase** as the structure to borrow.) Press F2 when the table structure matches that shown in Figure 20.6.

Next, create the history files. Select NewTable, and enter the table name **Salhist**. Since its structure is identical to the Sales table structure, press Menu (F10), select Borrow, and enter **Sales** as the name of the structure to borrow. Press F2 when the structure of the Salhist table matches the structure of the Sales table shown in Figure 20.5.

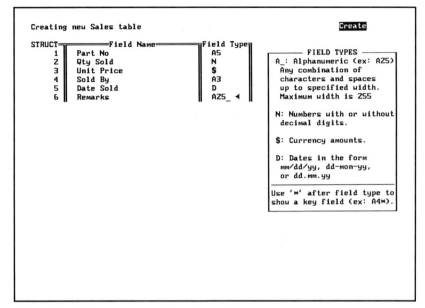

Figure 20.5: The structure of the Sales table

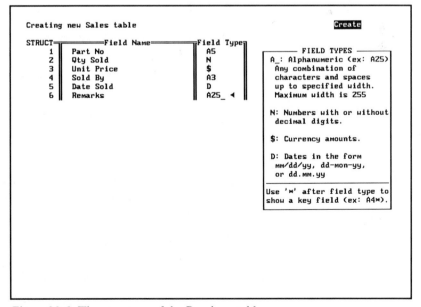

Figure 20.6: The structure of the Purchase table

To create the Purhist table, select NewTable, and enter the table name **Purhist**. Since its structure is identical to the Purchase table structure, press Menu (F10), select Borrow, and enter **Purchase** as the name of the structure to borrow. Press F2 when the structure of the Purhist table matches the structure of the Purchase table shown in Figure 20.6.

The screen displays the names of the tables selected for the application, as shown below:

Selected tables:
Mastinv Sales Purchase Salhist Purhist

These are the five tables we'll use in this application, so select DO-IT! from the top menu to finish selecting tables. The Personal Programmer will now ask you to type in a description of each table.

Type in **Master inventory file** as the description of the Mastinv table, and press Enter. Type in **Current sales transactions** as the description of the Sales table, and press Enter. Enter **Current purchases (items received)** as the description of the Purchase table. Enter **Posted sales transactions** as the description of the Salhist table, and **Posted purchases (items received)** as the description of the Purhist table. After entering all the table descriptions, you'll see the message

Preparing to create the main menu

at the bottom of the screen.

DEFINING THE MAIN MENU

Your next task is to define the main menu for the application. You define each menu item, up to a maximum of 20 characters, as it is to appear on the screen, and a descriptive message, up to 60 characters, for each item. You'll notice on the screen that the word *Main* appears in the upper-right corner of the box, and the reminder

Designing MAIN menu

appears within the help box on the screen, as shown in Figure 20.7 (yours won't show the inventory system main menu yet). Later, when

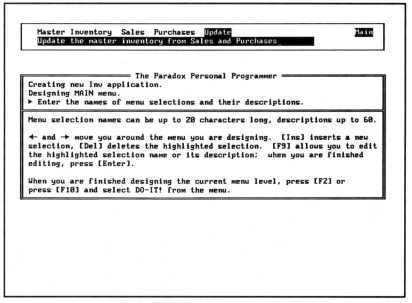

```
  Master Inventory Sales Purchases [Update]                          [Main]
  Update the master inventory from Sales and Purchases

  ═══════════════ The Paradox Personal Programmer ═══════════════
  Creating new Inv application.
  Designing MAIN menu.
  ▶ Enter the names of menu selections and their descriptions.
  ───────────────────────────────────────────────────────────────
  Menu selection names can be up to 20 characters long, descriptions up to 60.

  ← and → move you around the menu you are designing. [Ins] inserts a new
  selection, [Del] deletes the highlighted selection.  [F9] allows you to edit
  the highlighted selection name or its description;  when you are finished
  editing, press [Enter].

  When you are finished designing the current menu level, press [F2] or
  press [F10] and select DO-IT! from the menu.
```

Figure 20.7: The main menu for the inventory system defined

you develop submenus, these same messages will help you keep track of which submenu you are working on.

When entering menu items, remember that these menus will work just like the Paradox menus. The user of your application can select options either by highlighting and pressing Return, or by typing in the first letter of the option. Therefore, you might want to ensure that each option begins with a unique letter.

As you enter menu items and descriptions, you can use the following keys to make changes and corrections if necessary:

KEY	EFFECT
→, ←	Moves the highlight between menu items
Ins	Inserts a new item to the left of the current one
Del	Deletes the highlighted menu item
F9	Edits the highlighted selection below

The F9 key makes use of the following keys to edit the highlighted item:

KEY	*EFFECT*
Backspace	Moves cursor back and erases
Ctrl-Backspace	Erases entire entry
Enter	Finishes item edit and moves to description
Esc	Cancels the edit
DO-IT!	Finishes editing session

For the inventory application, enter the menu selections shown in the main menu of Figure 20.2. That is, for the first item, type in the item **Master Inventory,** press Enter, and then type the description **Manage the master inventory file.** For the second main menu item, type in **Sales**, press Enter, and type in the description **Manage current sales transactions**. For the third menu item, type in **Purchases** and the description **Manage current purchases (items received)**. As the fourth selection, type in the name **Update**, and enter the description **Update the master inventory from Sales and Purchases**.

When you've finished creating the main menu, your screen will look like Figure 20.7. To save the main menu, press F2. The Personal Programmer will add the menu option Leave to your menu, then display a menu of options for assigning actions to menu selections, as shown below:

SpecifyAction   DO-IT!   Cancel

TAKING A BREAK

To take a break now, you can select DO-IT! from this menu, and NoSplashScreen from the next menu. Then select DO-IT! from the next menu. The Personal Programmer will create as much of the application as you've defined. When the Main menu appears select the Exit and Yes options to return to DOS. Your work so far is saved, and you can continue with the application development in the next section when convenient.

At any time during the application development process, you can follow these same steps to take a break. Just work your way "backwards" through the menu selections (by pressing the Esc key, and selecting DO-IT! when available), until the Personal Programmer Main menu appears. From that Main menu, select Exit and Yes to return to the DOS prompt.

To resume your work later, follow these steps:

1. Log onto the application's directory with the DOS CHDIR or CD command (**CD\INVMGR** in this example).

2. Start the Personal Programmer by entering the command **PPROG** at the DOS prompt.

3. Select Modify from the Main menu, and enter the name of the application to change (**Inv** in this example).

4. Select NotDefined from the next menu to go directly to the first menu item that has not been assigned an action yet (which is where you left off).

5. As instructed on the screen, press Menu (F10) to call up the menu, and select Action to begin assigning actions to menu items.

In this particular example, you want to select Define next to start defining menu actions. (If you are modifying an existing application, rather than resuming your work after taking a break, you can select Revise rather than Define to change a menu item or the action it performs.)

ASSIGNING ACTIONS TO MENU ITEMS

The next phase in the application development process is to begin assigning actions to menu items. In other words, now is the time to tell the Personal Programmer what to do when the user selects the currently highlighted menu item. The menu below appears on the screen (if you took a break in the last section, you've already bypassed this option—you'll instead be at the next menu):

SpecifyAction   DO-IT!   Cancel

These options can be summarized as follows:

OPTION	EFFECT
SpecifyAction	Assigns actions to menu items
DO-IT!	Saves work so far and returns to Main menu
Cancel	Abandons work so far and returns to Main menu

As discussed previously, you can select DO-IT! at any time if you just want to take a break (you also select this option when you are done). For now, select the SpecifyAction option to assign actions to the Master menu item (which is blinking on the screen).

After you select SpecifyAction, the Action menu appears on the screen, as shown below:

Menu   View   Report   DataEntry   Edit   Script   Help
NotDefined   Cancel

These options can be summarized as follows:

OPTION	EFFECT
Menu	Displays a submenu to the user
View	Lets the user view data
Report	Lets the user print a report
DataEntry	Lets the user enter new data
Edit	Lets the user change or delete data
Script	Plays a script for the user
Help	Shows a help screen to the user
NotDefined	Skips the current item
Cancel	Sends the user back to the previous menu

The Action menu is where you'll do most of your work in the Personal Programmer. You need to assign an action to every menu item in your system. If for some reason you are not ready to assign an action to an item, you can select NotDefined and come back to that item later. You can also press Esc to work backwards and exit the Personal Programmer, as discussed earlier.

THE MASTER INVENTORY SUBMENU

In the current inventory application, the Master Inventory menu selection branches to a submenu of choices for managing the master inventory file. To assign this action to the item, select Menu from the Action menu.

As you begin to design the submenu of the master-inventory table, the upper-right corner of the screen reminds you that you are now designing a submenu for the Master Inventory selection from the inventory-system main menu. You create a submenu using the same technique as for a main menu: type in the menu items and a brief description of each item. Referring back to Figure 20.2, recall that we want this menu to display the options Add data, Change data, Look up data, and Reports.

Type in **Add data** as the first menu item, and **Add new products to the master inventory** as the description. As the second submenu item, enter **Change data** as the menu item, and **Edit/delete master inventory items** as the description. For the third submenu item, enter **Look up data** as the item, and **Look up information in the master inventory** as the description. Finally, enter **Reports** as the fourth menu item, and **Print master inventory reports** as the description. Your screen should look like Figure 20.8 when done.

Press F2 when you've finished defining the submenu. Your next step is to assign an action to each item on this submenu.

Master Inventory Data Entry

When users select *Add data* from the submenu, we want them to be able to add new records to the master inventory file. So, select SpecifyAction from the top menu, then DataEntry from the Action menu. The screen will ask which table or tables you want the user to add data to, using the following menu:

SelectTable   AllTables   DO-IT!   Cancel

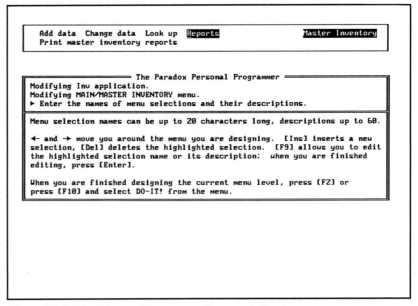

Figure 20.8: The Master Inventory submenu defined

The SelectTable option lets you select a table (or several tables) to add data to. The AllTables option selects all tables for entering data. Obviously, we only want to add data to a single table here, so select SelectTable. When prompted, specify Mastinv as the name of the table to use, and then select DO-IT! to indicate that you are finished selecting tables for this menu item.

The next options to appear are

FormView   TableView   FormToggle

If you want the application to display data on a custom form, select FormView. If you want the application to display data in Table view during data entry, select TableView. If you want the user to be able to switch back and forth between Table and Form views, select the FormToggle option.

In this example, we'll develop a custom form for data entry, so select FormView. The next menu options are

Design   Borrow   StandardForm

The Design option lets you design a new form. The Borrow option lets you borrow another form in the table. The StandardForm option displays the Paradox standard form. Select Design in this case to design a new form.

Select option 1 from the forms menu to assign the number 1 to the new form we'll be designing. For the form description, enter **Enter/ edit master inventory data**. The screen for designing forms (discussed in Chapter 9) appears on the screen.

Using the usual techniques, design the form to your liking. Figure 20.9 shows an example you might want to follow. All of the field masks are placed on the form using the Field, Place, and Regular options from the menu (accessed by pressing F10).

Press F2 after you've created form. Your next menu options are

       Settings   DO-IT!   Cancel

We'll explore the Settings option later. For now, select DO-IT! to save the current form. You'll be returned to the Action menu, to define an Action for the next Master Inventory submenu option.

```
Changing F1 form for mastinv                              Form ◄ Ins 1/1
<18, 4>
  ┌──────────────────────────────────────────────────────────────────┐
  │                      Master Inventory File                        │
  └──────────────────────────────────────────────────────────────────┘

    Part number: -----

    Part name:   -------------------------

       In            Reorder         On            Date
      Stock           Point         Order         Ordered
   ----------      ----------    ----------     -----------

    Purchase price: ----------------------

    Selling price:  ----------------------

    Location: -----
    _
```

Figure 20.9: A custom form for the Mastinv table

Master Inventory Editing

The second item in the Master Inventory submenu is *Change data*. The action you'll want to assign to this item is Edit, so select the Edit option from the Action menu.

Once again, you'll be asked to define tables to use. Select Select-Table, and specify Mastinv as the table to use. Then select DO-IT! to stop selecting tables.

The next menu lets you decide how the edit takes place. Your options are

SelectRecords   AllRecords

The AllRecords option displays all the records in the table during the edit. The SelectRecords option lets your application help the user to locate a particular record to edit. For this example, select SelectRecords.

A query form for performing the search appears on the screen. However, we don't want to specify a particular record to search for right now; rather, we want the user to be able to specify a record to edit while he is using the application. So, to tell the Personal Programmer that this is the case, you enter a *tilde variable* into the field you want the user to search. A tilde variable is a tilde (~) followed by a variable name (which must begin with a letter, and may not contain spaces or punctuation).

In this example, move the cursor to the Part No field, and type in ~ **partnum**. The screen should look like Figure 20.10. Press F2 after entering the tilde variable.

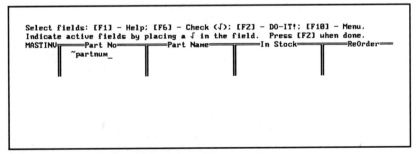

Figure 20.10: A tilde variable in the edit query form

The Personal Programmer then displays the message

Prompt:
Enter the prompt for "partnum".

Type in the question that you want your application to present to users to prompt them for the desired part number. In this example, type in the prompt **Enter part number to edit:**, then press Enter. The screen displays the data type, as below:

Data type: A5
Enter the correct data type for variable "partnum"

The default data type shown is correct, so press Enter.
    Once again the screen displays the options

FormView   TableView   FormToggle

and once again, you select FormView to allow editing through a custom form. From the next submenu, select Borrow to borrow an existing form for editing. Select 1 to select the previously defined form for the Mastinv table. After a brief pause, you'll be given the options

Modify   DO-IT!
Change the form so the key fields are display-only

If you select Modify, the user will not be able to edit the part number (the only key field in this table). Since there is only one table, and one key field on this screen, you can select DO-IT! to save the form as is.
    The next menu presents the options

Settings   InsertDelete   DO-IT!   Cancel

The Settings option lets you change settings, such as validity checks and image settings, on the custom form, which we don't need to do right now. The InsertDelete option lets you decide whether or not the user can insert and/or delete records in this edit mode. There is no need for the user to be able to insert records, as we have a data-entry menu item for that. However, the user must be able to delete a record in this mode. So select InsertDelete, Insert, and No, and then select InsertDelete, Delete, and Yes.

At this point, you are done defining the Change data option on the Master Inventory submenu. Select DO-IT!

Master Inventory Lookup

For the *Look up data* selection, we'll allow the user to look up an item in the master inventory by either part number or name (in case he or she does not know the part number). To define the action for this menu selection, select View from the Action menu. As usual, you'll be prompted to define a table to use. Select the SelectTable option, the Mastinv table, and then select DO-IT!

Next you'll be given the options

SelectFields   AllFields

The SelectFields option lets you select specific fields to include in the view. The AllFields selection automatically displays all fields in the view. Select AllFields for this example.

The next menu displays the options

SelectRecords   AllRecords

As with editing, we want to allow the user to specify a particular record to view. So select the SelectRecords option, and you'll see query form for the Mastinv table.

In this case, we want the user to be able to search by either part number or part name. Once again, we need tilde variables that accept an entry while the user is running the application. In addition, we need to specify an OR search; since we don't know if the user will enter a part name or part number, the query must be able to search for either a part name or a part number. Furthermore, since the part name that the user enters to search for may not exactly match the part name in the table, we need to use the *like* command on the query form.

Figure 20.11 shows how to set up the query form on the screen. Note that both entries use tilde variables. Also notice that each entry is placed on a separate row to specify an OR search. Press F2 after filling in the query form as shown in Figure 20.11.

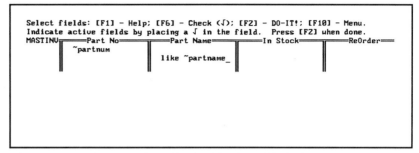

Figure 20.11: The query form for the Mastinv table look-up

Now the screen asks for prompts for the tilde variables. For the partnum variable, type in the prompt

    Enter part number to locate, or press Enter:

Press Enter to accept the suggested data type, A5. For the partname variable, enter the prompt

    Optionally, enter the part name to locate:

Press Enter to accept the suggested data type, A25.

From the next menu, select FormView to display the data on a form. Select Borrow to use an existing form, select 1 to use form number one. That completes the action for the Master Inventory Look up data menu item. Next, you'll want to define an action for the *Reports* menu item.

Master Inventory Reports

When the user selects *Reports* from the Master Inventory submenu, we want to display yet another menu of report options, as shown in Figure 20.2. Therefore, select Menu as the action for the Reports option. Define the first submenu (or, actually sub-submenu) item as **Entire inventory**, and enter the description **Display entire master inventory**. Enter **Reorder report** as the second menu option, and **List items below reorder point** as the description. Press F2 after entering the menu descriptions.

The *Entire inventory* option blinks to tell you that you are ready to work with this menu item. Select SpecifyAction from the top menu to begin. Select Report as the action, select SelectTable, Mastinv, and DO-IT!, and then select AllRecords so the report displays all the records. Select Design to design a report format, and select 1 as the report number.

Enter **Master inventory display** as the description of the form; you can then design the report format to your liking (as discussed in Chapter 8). For this example, I designed a free-form report as shown in Figure 20.12, (though you, of course, can develop a report format to your own liking).

Press F2 after designing your report format. Your next options will be:

Printer   Screen   File

Select Printer so the report will be displayed on the printer.

Next you'll define an action for the *Reorder report* menu option. Again, select Report, SelectTable, Mastinv, and DO-IT!. Because

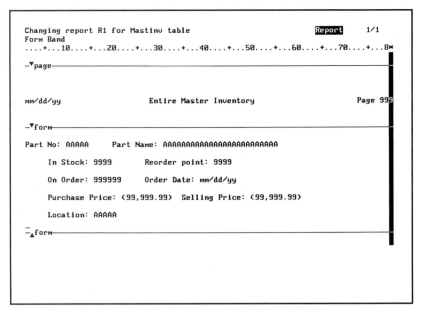

Figure 20.12: A suggested format for the Entire inventory report

this report is to display only certain records (those with in-stock and on-order quantities below the reorder point), select the SelectRecords option to specify records to display.

When the first query appears, you'll want to define the search condition, which is records whose reorder point is greater than the sum of the in-stock and on-order quantities. You'll need to use some F5 examples to set up the query. This is where we hit our first dead end. This query form does not allow the use of examples. How should we deal with this?

Well, we know that *Paradox* is capable of printing such a report; only the Personal Programmer is having trouble here. The solution will be to create a script (later) that goes through all the necessary steps to print the report we want, and attach that script to this menu item.

For now, we need to back out of our current position. You can always do so using a combination of the Esc key and the Cancel options from the menus until you're back at the Action menu. In this example, press F10 to call up the menu, then select Cancel and Yes. To move up another menu level, press Esc. Select Cancel and Yes again to move back to the Action menu. Select NotDefined to leave this menu option undefined for the time being.

INVENTORY SALES SUBMENU

Now we need to develop the submenu and its actions for the sales system submenu. In this section we'll look at a more advanced feature of the Personal Programmer, called *MultiTable views*. Like the MultiEntry form we discussed in Chapter 19, MultiTable views let you view data from two or more tables at once. This can be very handy in the Sales system, because when the user enters the part number for a sales transaction, we can display the part name and other information about the part to provide some feedback to the person at the keyboard.

We'll also see how to use MultiTable views to print reports. Once again, we can display the part name and other information to provide additional information that is available only from the Mastinv table.

The only restriction on MultiTable views within the Personal Programmer is that you cannot use them to edit information, unless all the tables used in the MultiTable edit are keyed. Usually, only one table is keyed, because the two tables are in a one-to-many relationship, and only the table on the "one" side of the relationship has a true key field. Nonetheless, these views are very useful tools when developing applications with multiple tables.

THE SALES SUBMENU

To begin developing the submenu for the sales system, move the highlight to the Sales option and press F10 to call up the menu. While the Sales option is blinking, select Action to define an action for this main menu item. From the next menu, select Define to view the Action menu.

The Sales option on the main menu needs to branch to a submenu of choices for managing the Sales table. Therefore, select Menu from the Action menu and begin. You'll be prompted to type in menu items and descriptions using the same techniques we've used with previous menus. For this example, type in the following menu items and descriptions:

ITEM	DESCRIPTION
Add data	Add new sales transactions
Change data	Edit/delete current sales transactions
Look up	Look up a current sales transaction
Report	Print current sales transactions

Press F2 when done entering the menu items and descriptions.

Sales Table Data Entry

After you enter the menu options and descriptions, you are ready to define actions for the *Add data* menu option. *Add data* blinks on the screen. Select SpecifyAction to define an action for the item. We'll develop a custom form for entering data into the Sales table that also displays data from the Mastinv table.

From the Action menu, select DataEntry. To define the tables to use during data entry, select SelectTable, the Sales table, SelectTable again, and then the Mastinv table. Notice that both the Sales and

Mastinv tables are listed as selected tables. Select DO-IT! to stop selecting tables for this menu action.

Next, the screen needs to know which fields are involved in the MultiTable view of the inventory data and presents two options to you:

Create   Borrow

As implied, the Create option lets you create a new MultiTable view, while Borrow lets you use a previously defined MultiTable view. As we have not created a MultiTable view, you need to select Create.

Two query forms will appear on the screen: one for each table in the MultiTable view. Using these query forms, you need to place checkmarks in fields that you want to use in the MultiTable view, and enter an example that links the two tables via a common field.

For this example, press F6 with the cursor in the leftmost column of the Sales query forms, so that all the fields have check marks. Move the cursor into the Part No field, and enter the example ABC (by pressing F5 and then typing **ABC**).

Press F4 to move down to the Mastinv query form. Type in the example that links Mastinv to Sales. (In this case, move the cursor to the Part No field, press F5, and type in **ABC**.) Next, place check marks in any fields that you want to display from this table. For this example, place a check mark (using the usual F6 key) in the Part Name and Sel Price fields. Figure 20.13 shows the two query forms on the screen (I've manipulated the image a bit so that you can see all the fields). Press F2 after completing the query forms.

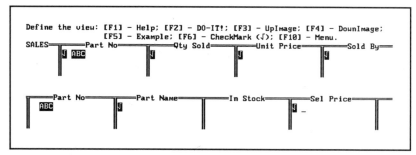

Figure 20.13: Query forms completed for the MultiTable view

Next you'll see the following familiar menu:

FormView   TableView   FormToggle

Once again, select FormView to allow the user to enter data through a custom screen. Select Design and 1 to design form number 1 for the Sales table data entry. Enter **Current sales transactions** as the form description.

The standard screen for developing a custom form will appear. You can use the usual Field and Place options to place fields on the screen, but there is one very important point to keep in mind. When placing fields from the Mastinv table onto the form, use the Field, Place, and DisplayOnly menu options, rather than the Field, Place, and Regular options. This is an important point, because we do not want the user to change information on the Mastinv table while entering Sales transactions. Instead, we want to display this information on the form only to provide feedback.

When developing your own applications, you'll want to do the same. That is, use Field, Place, and Regular to place fields that will be changed, and Field, Place, and DisplayOnly to place fields from the related table.

Figure 20.14 shows a suggested format for the custom Sales form. The fields were placed on the screen as listed below (note that Regular refers to the Field, Place, and Regular menu options; DisplayOnly refers to the Field, Place, and DisplayOnly menu options; and Calculated refers to the Field, Place, and Calculated menu options):

OPTION	*LOCATION*	*FIELD NAME*
Regular	< 5,15>	Part No
Regular	<12, 2>	Qty Sold
Regular	<12,13>	Unit Price
Regular	<12,30>	Date Sold
Regular	<12,49>	Sold By
Regular	<16,11>	Remarks
DisplayOnly	< 5,46>	Part Name
DisplayOnly	< 6,46>	Sel Price
Calculated	<12,59>	[Qty Sold] * [Unit Price]

The boxes are drawn using the usual Border and Place options from the menu, and all the rest of the form is simply typed in. When you've finished designing your form, call up the menu and select DO-IT!.

This selection brings up the options

Settings   DO-IT!   Cancel

You can add validity checks and HelpAndFill to this form by selecting Settings. Note that the cursor is in the Part No field. You can move the cursor to any field and then call up the menu to define a validity check. In this case, leave the cursor in the Part No field, and press F10 to call up the menu. Select ValCheck and Define to define a validity check.

The standard options for validity checks appear on the next menu. Select TableLookup, enter Mastinv as the table to check entries against, then select AllCorrespondingFields and HelpAndFill. This validity check is sufficient for entering Sales data. Press F2 to save the validity check, and you'll see the menu

Settings   DO-IT!   Cancel

```
Changing F1 form for Invs1                          Form ◄     1/1
<22, 2>
╔═══════════════════════════════════════════════════════════════╗
║                   Current Sales Transactions                  ║
╚═══════════════════════════════════════════════════════════════╝

  Part Number: -----          ┌─────────────────────────────────┐
                              │ Part name: ──────────────────── │
                              │ List price: ─────────────────── │
                              └─────────────────────────────────┘

     Qty       Unit Price     Date Sold     Salesperson's        Total
                                              Initials
  ----------  -------------  -----------        ---         ---------------


  Remarks: ────────────────────────
 ╔═══════════════════════════════════════════════════════════════╗
 ║ When cursor is in Part Number field, press F1 to view part numbers. ║
 ║ When part number table is displayed, press F2 to select current part. ║
 ╚═══════════════════════════════════════════════════════════════╝

  _
```

Figure 20.14: The suggested format for the custom Sales form

again. Select DO-IT! to save the form.

At this point, you've finished defining the action and the custom form for Sales data entry. You'll be prompted to define an action for the *Change data* submenu item.

Sales Table Editing

The *Change data* menu option should now be blinking on the screen. You cannot use MultiTable view during editing, because the Personal Programmer requires that both tables be keyed for editing (as discussed earlier). Therefore, we'll use a simple TableView to allow edits to the Sales table.

From the Action menu, select Edit, then select SelectTable, Sales, and DO-IT! to define the table to use. Select TableView as the format for editing, and Settings to set up a validity check for editing. Move the cursor to the Part No field, press F10, select ValCheck, Define, TableLookup, and enter Mastinv as the lookup table. Select JustCurrentField and HelpAndFill. These selections will make sure the user enters valid part numbers, and will also help him to look up part numbers and part names. Press F2.

Next you can define whether or not the user can insert and delete records during editing. To limit this menu option to editing and deleting, select InsertDelete, Delete, and Yes. (The default setting for Insert is No, so you need not respecify that option.) Select DO-IT! to save the setting.

This completes the action for the Change data option on the Sales menu. Now the *Look up data* option blinks, and you can define its action.

Sales Table Lookup

For the *Look up data* option on the Sales submenu, we'll display data using the MultiTable view we developed for the data-entry portion of the menu. Rather than recreating the MultiTable view, we'll borrow that existing view and its custom form.

From the Action menu, select View. Then select SelectTable, Sales, SelectTable, Mastinv, and DO-IT! to specify the Sales and

Mastinv tables for the Look up data menu option. Once again, your options are

Create   Borrow

To borrow the previously created MultiTable view, select the Borrow option. This brings up the options

Menu   Name

The Name option lets you specify the MultiTable view by name, and is generally used only with MultiTable views you create outside of the Personal Programmer. The Menu option let's you borrow the view from another previously defined menu item. In this example, you want to select Menu.

Recall that the MultiTable view we created earlier was defined under the Add data option from the Sales submenu. You now need to select items that lead to that existing menu choice. In this example, select Sales. When the Add data option is displayed, press F10 to call up the menu. Select BorrowView from the next menu to appear, to indicate that you want to borrow the MultiTable view from the Sales Add data menu action.

After a brief pause while the Personal Programmer copies and validates information, you'll be given the standard menu:

SelectRecords   AllRecords

Again, we want the user to be able to specify a particular record to view, so select the SelectRecords options. A query form will appear on the screen. To help the user locate a particular transaction, we'll have the application prompt him or her for a part number and salesperson's initials. Place the tilde variable

~ partno

in the Part No field, and

~ person

in the Sold By field, as shown in Figure 20.15.

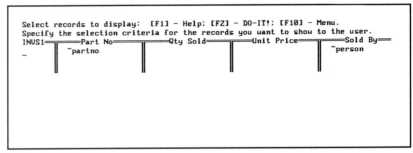

```
Select records to display:  [F1] - Help; [F2] - DO-IT!; [F10] - Menu.
Specify the selection criteria for the records you want to show to the user.
INUS1═══════Part No═══════╤═══════Qty Sold═══════╤═══════Unit Price═══════╤═══════Sold By═══
    _                    │   ~partno            │                       │          ~person
```

Figure 20.15: Tilde variables in the Sales query form

Press F2 after entering the tilde variables. You'll be asked to provide prompts for the tilde variables. For the *partno* variable, enter the prompt

> Enter part number to locate:

Press Enter to accept the suggested data type. For the *person* tilde variable, enter the prompt

> Enter sales person's initials:

Press Enter to accept the suggested data type, A3.

Now you'll be given the options to display data in FormView, TableView, or FormToggle. Select FormView to use a custom form, select Borrow to use the existing form from the Add data option, and then select 1 to indicate the specific custom form.

This completes the action for the Look up data option from the Sales menu. Now you are ready to define the action for the Sales table Reports option.

Sales Table Reports

Once again, we'll use a MultiTable view to display data from the Sales and Mastinv tables simultaneously, this time using a report format to print the data. While the Report menu item is blinking, select Report from the Action menu. To select tables, select the options SelectTable, Sales, SelectTable, Mastinv, and press DO-IT!

Because you've selected multiple tables, the screen will once again present the options

    Create   Borrow

to help you create or borrow a MultiTable view. We can again use the MultiTable view created for the data entry option on the Sales submenu, so select Borrow, Menu, and Sales. With the Add data option highlighted on the submenu, press F10 to call up the menu, and select BorrowView.

The screen asks if the report should print some records (SelectRecords) or all records (AllRecords). For this example, select AllRecords. Now you can define a format for the Sales table report.

Select Design from the report menu, 1 as the report format, and enter the report description as **Current Sales Transactions**. You can next select whether you want your report to be tabular or free-form. For this example, I selected Tabular and designed the format as shown in Figure 20.16. Of course, you may design the report to your own liking.

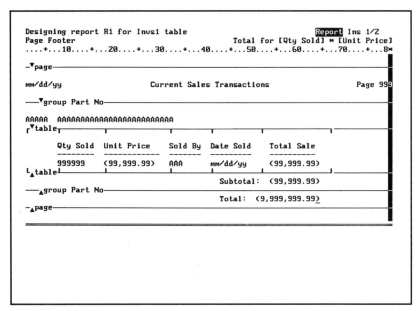

Figure 20.16: The suggested format for the Sales report

In Figure 20.16, the TableBand and Erase options are also used to delete the Part No, Part Name, Remarks, and Sel Price columns from the suggested report format.

I've used the Group, Insert, and Field options to define a group band based on the Part No field. Within the group band, but outside of the table band, I've placed the Part No and Part Name fields, using the usual Field, Place, and Regular menu options. (These appear as AAA masks in the Part No group heading area.)

The TableBand and Insert options are used to insert the blank column at the left of the table band. This column is then narrowed using TableBand and Resize. This blank column appears as an indentation on the final printed report.

To reduce the size of the Unit Price field, use Field and Erase to erase the current field contents, and then Field, Place, and Regular to put the Unit Price field back. When you place the field back into its column, you'll be given the option to specify the size of the field. (The Field, Reformat, and Comma options do not allow you to resize the field; you need to use this delete-and-replace technique instead.)

The TableBand and Insert options are used to create the Total Sale column at the right of the table band. The heading and underline are typed in as shown, and the Field, Place, and Calculated options are used to place the expression *[Qty Sold] * [Unit Price]* within the report column.

The subtotal calculation is placed using the Field, Place, Summary, and Calculated menu options; these place the expression *[Qty Sold] * [Unit Price]* beneath the table band (but within the group band). The Sum and PerGroup options are selected to ensure proper subtotaling. The grand total, outside the group band, is placed using the Field, Place, Summary, and Calculated menu options, again using *[Qty Sold] * [Unit Price]* as the expression. Then, the Sum and Overall options are selected to ensure a grand total.

After designing the report specification to your liking, press F2, and select Printer as the destination for the report. That concludes the action definition for the Sales menu Reports option, and for the entire Sales submenu as well.

THE PURCHASES SUBMENU

The Purchases section in the inventory system also requires a submenu of options for managing the Purchase table. This submenu uses basically the same techniques that the Sales submenu does to present information from multiple tables, and does not present any new Personal Programmer techniques. Therefore, to help you develop this module quickly, we'll just run through the required entries and menu selections involved in an abbreviated format.

Move the highlight to the Purchases item on the main menu, and press F10 to call up the menu. Select Action, Define, and Menu to begin defining the submenu. Enter the menu items and descriptions as listed below:

ITEM	*DESCRIPTION*
Add data	Add new purchases (items received)
Change data	Edit/delete current purchases
Look up data	Look up a current purchase (item received)
Reports	Print current purchases (items received)

Press F2 when done entering the menu items and descriptions.

Purchase Table Data Entry

When the *Add data* option is blinking, select SpecifyAction, DataEntry, SelectTable, Purchase, SelectTable, Mastinv, and DO-IT! to define the tables. Select Create to create a MultiTable view, and fill in the query forms as shown in Figure 20.17. Note that all the fields in the Purchase query form are checked, and the XXX examples are entered using the F5 key to define an example. Press F2 after filling in the query forms.

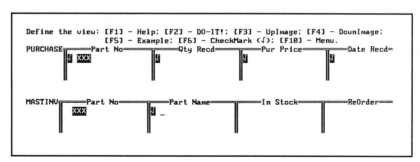

Figure 20.17: Query forms for the Purchases MultiTable view

Select FormView, Design, and 1, and enter **Current Purchases (items received)** as the form description. You'll be given the standard screen for designing a new form. Once again, when placing the Part Name field from the Mastinv table, be sure to use the Field, Place, and DisplayOnly options (rather than Field, Place, and Regular options) so that the field cannot be changed during data entry. Figure 20.18 shows a sample form. Press F2 after designing the form to your liking.

Select Setting and, with the cursor in the Part No field, press F10. Select ValCheck, Define, and TableLookup, then enter Mastinv as the table name. Select AllCorrespondingFields and HelpAndFill. Press F2 and select DO-IT!.

Purchase Table Editing

When the Change data submenu option blinks, select Edit, SelectTable, Purchase, DO-IT!, TableView, and Settings, and make sure the cursor is in the Part No field. Press F10, and select ValCheck, Define, TableLookup, and Mastinv as the look-up table.

```
Changing F1 form for Invs2                              Form ◄ Ins 1/1
<21, 1>
┌────────────────────────────────────────────────────────────────────┐
│                   Current Purchases (Items Received)                │
└────────────────────────────────────────────────────────────────────┘


   Part Number: -----        ┌── Part name: ───────────────────────┐
                             └─────────────────────────────────────┘


       Date                        Purchase
     Received          Qty           Price
   ------------      ----------    ---------------


   Remarks : ------------------------------


   ┌────────────────────────────────────────────────────────────────┐
   │ When cursor is in the Part Number field, press F1 for part number list. │
   │ When part number list is displayed, press F2 to select part number.    │
   └────────────────────────────────────────────────────────────────┘

   _
```

Figure 20.18: The Purchases data-entry form

Select JustCurrentField and HelpAndFill. Press F2. Select InsertDelete, Delete, Yes, and DO-IT!.

Purchase Table Lookup

When the *Look up data* option blinks, select View, SelectTable, Purchase, SelectTable, Mastinv, and DO-IT!. Select Borrow, Menu, Purchases, and with the highlight on the Add data option, press F10 and select BorrowView.

From the next menu, select SelectRecords, enter ˜**partno** in the Part No field, and press F2 to save the tilde variable. Enter the prompt **Enter part number to locate**, and press Enter to accept the default data type, A5.

Select FormView, Borrow, and 1 to use the current Purchases form, defined earlier.

Purchase Table Reports

When *Reports* is blinking on the Purchases submenu, select Report from the Action menu. Select SelectTable, Purchase, SelectTable, Mastinv, and DO-IT! to specify the Purchase and Mastinv tables for this menu action.

To borrow the existing MultiTable view, select Borrow, Menu, and Purchases, press F10 while *Add data* is highlighted, and select BorrowView.

Select AllRecords to have the report print all records. Select Design and 1, and enter the report description as **Current Purchases**. You can select Tabular to design a tabular report format, and use a format similar to that presented in Figure 20.19. Note that in this format, the TableBand and Erase options are used to remove the Remarks column and the Part Name field is moved using the TableBand and Move options. To ensure sorting by part number, select Group, Insert, Field, and Part No to insert a group band, and use Ctrl-Y with the cursor in the leftmost column to delete any unwanted blank lines between the group and table bands.

Press F2 after designing your report format, and select Printer to channel the printed report to the printer.

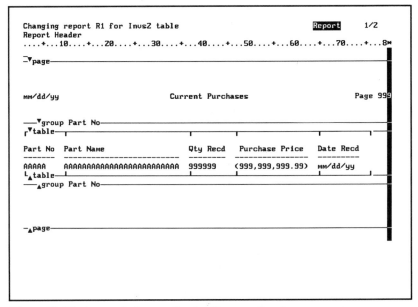

Figure 20.19: A sample format for the Current Purchases report

That concludes the submenu for the Purchase table. Now we have two more items to create. First, we still need a script to print the reorder report, and another script to perform updates. (This script will be identical to the recorded script discussed in Chapter 15.) We'll need to put some sample data in the various tables to create these scripts, so now would be a good time to leave the Personal Programmer, and try out some aspects of the application developed so far.

For now, move the highlight to the *Update* option, press F10 to call up the menu, and select DO-IT! to leave the Update option undefined. Select DO-IT! from the next menu to save your work so far. You'll see the scripts that the Personal Programmer creates whiz by on the screen as it does its work. The Personal Programmer menu will reappear. You can either select Exit and Yes to leave the Personal Programmer now, or continue with the next section.

TESTING OUR PROGRESS

Let's take a look at our work so far by adding some records to the Mastinv, Sales, and Purchase tables, using the application system developed by the Personal Programmer. To do so, select Play from the Personal Programmer Main menu, and enter **Inv** as the name of the application. Press Enter rather than entering a password. (You could also run the application directly from Paradox, as we'll discuss later.)

You'll see the inventory system main menu appear on the screen, displaying the menu options and option descriptions that you defined within the Personal Programmer, as below:

Master Inventory   Sales   Purchases   Update   Leave
Manage the master inventory file.

If you use the arrow keys to scroll around the menu options, you'll see the other report descriptions you defined in the Personal Programmer.

First, let's add a couple of records to the Master Inventory (Mastinv) table. Select Master Inventory and Add data from the custom menus, and you'll see the custom form for entering master-inventory records. For the first record, enter the sample data below (of course, you can add some real data from your own inventory if you prefer):

Part number:	**1001**
Part name:	**Artichokes**
In stock:	**1**
Reorder point:	**10**
On order:	**5**
Date order:	**11/10/88**
Purchase price:	**100.00**
Selling Price:	**150.00**
Location:	**LZ1**

As a second sample record, enter the data below:

Part number:	**1002**
Part name:	**Bananas**
In stock:	**50**
Reorder point:	**10**
On order:	**0**
Date order:	**11/10/88**
Purchase price:	**20.00**
Selling Price:	**30.00**
Location:	**BZ1**

Press F2 after entering the second record.

Now let's add a couple of transactions to the Sales table. Select Sales from the main menu, and Add data from the submenu. Enter the information below. (You'll notice that the appropriate information from the Mastinv appears on the screen after you enter the part number):

Part number:	**1001**
Qty sold:	**2**
Unit price:	**150.00**
Sold by:	**SAM**
Date sold:	**10/11/88**

Before entering the second record, you might want to try the HelpAndFill feature we added. Press F1 to see a list of part numbers and names. Move the cursor to part number 1002. (You can also use Zoom [Ctrl-Z] to locate information in any field on the look-up table.) Press F2 to copy the selected part number to the current form. Fill in the form with the following sample data:

Part number:	**1002**
Qty sold:	**5**
Unit price:	**30.00**
Sold by:	**SAM**
Date sold:	**10/11/88**

Press F2 after entering the second record.

Now we'll add a single record to the Purchase table. Select Purchases from the main menu, and Add data from the submenu. Again, you can use the F1 and F2 keys to select a part number from the Mastinv table, or just type in the sample record below:

Part no:	**1001**
Qty received:	**100**
Purchase price:	**110.00**
Date received:	**12/1/88**

Press F2 after entering the sample record.

You might want to take some time now to try out other options from the custom menu (though remember, the reorder report and update options have not been assigned actions yet). When you are done experimenting with the inventory system menus, select Leave.

CUSTOM SCRIPTS FOR THE INVENTORY SYSTEM

We'll need to create a couple of scripts now: one to print the reorder report and one to perform updates. To do so, exit the Personal Programmer (if necessary) by selecting Exit and Yes from its Main menu. The DOS prompt should appear on your screen when you've successfully exited.

The custom scripts that you tie into an application can be either hand-written or recorded. For these examples, we'll use recorded scripts. We'll also need to create a new report format for the reorder report.

First, you'll want to run Paradox in the usual manner, but from the current directory so that it uses the tables on the same directory as the application and stores any files on this same directory. While still logged onto the INVMGR directory, enter the command

PARADOX2

and press Enter to run Paradox.

THE REORDER REPORT

To create the reorder report format, select Report and Design, and enter Mastinv as the table to use. Select report number 2, and enter the description **Reorder report**. Select Tabular, and design the report to your liking. Figure 20.20 shows a sample format.

In the example, I have shortened the Part Name field slightly by backspacing over some of the hyphens and using the Field and Resize options from the menu to narrow the field. The Location, Sel Price, and Order Date fields are deleted using TableBand and Erase. To reduce the size of the Purchase Price field, I have deleted it and reinserted it using TableBand Erase, TableBand Insert, and Field, Place, and Regular. Press F2 after designing the report format to your liking, and return to the Paradox Main menu.

To begin recording the script, type Alt-F3. Select Ask from the menu, and specify Mastinv as the table to ask about. Press F6 so that all the fields receive a check mark. Move the cursor to the In Stock field, press F5, and type in the example **In**. Move the cursor to the

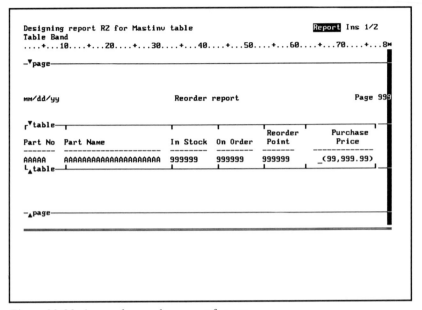

Figure 20.20: A sample reorder report format

On Order field, press F5, and enter the example **Coming**. Move back to the Reorder field, and enter the expression

> > In + Coming

where *In* and *Coming* are both examples (each preceded by a press on the F5 key before being typed in). This query limits records displayed to those which have Reorder values greater than the sums of the In Stock and On Order quantities. Figure 20.21 shows the completed query form on the screen. Press F2 to perform the completed query.

Next, copy the report formats from the Mastinv table to the Answer table. To do so, press Menu (F10), and select Tools, Copy, and JustFamily. Enter Mastinv as the source table to copy from, and Answer as the target table to copy to.

Next, call up the menu, select Report and Output, and specify Answer as the table to print from. Select Printer, and you should see the only item that needs reordering appear on the report.

Clear the screen by typing Clear All (Alt-F8), and then stop recording the script by typing Alt-F3 again. The completed script is

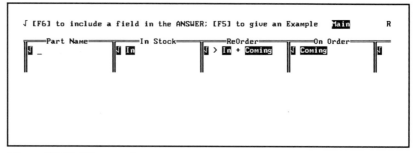

Figure 20.21: The reorder report query

stored as Instant.SC, but you'll want to change its name. To do so, call up the menu, select Tools, Rename, and Scripts, and change the name of the Instant script to Reorder.

To verify that the Reorder script exists, select Scripts, Editor, and Edit, and enter Reorder as the name of the script. It should appear on your screen looking something like Figure 20.22. Then call up the menu, and select Cancel and Yes to return to the Paradox Main menu.

```
Changing script C:\invmgr\reorder                           Script
....+...10....+...20....+...30....+...40....+...50....+...60....+...70....+...80
{Ask} {MastInv} Check Right Right Right Example  "In" Right
">" Example  "In + " Example  "Coming" Right Example  "Com"
"ing" Do_It! Menu {Tools} {Copy} {JustFamily} {MastInv} {Answer}
{Replace} Menu {Report} {Output} {Answer} {2} {Printer} ClearAll
```

Figure 20.22: The Reorder script

INVENTORY SYSTEM UPDATE SCRIPTS

You can use the InvUpdat script developed back in Chapter 15 for the current inventory application. If you have not already created that script, find the section entitled ''Automating an Update Procedure,'' and follow all the steps presented to create the InvUpdat script. (Note that the sample data in the figures won't match the sample data you see when working with these versions of the Mastinv, Sales, and Purchase tables, but the query forms in the figures will be the same.)

You might also want to provide the option to "back out" from the update procedure in the custom application. To do so, use the Scripts, Edit, and Write options to create a script named Updater. Type in the script exactly as shown in Figure 20.23. Note that this script plays the InvUpdat script only if the user selects Proceed from the submenu. (You could have also used the Personal Programmer to create this same simple Proceed and Cancel menu, but this example will demonstrate how to attach a hand-written script to the inventory application.) Press F10 and select DO-IT! after creating the Updater script.

```
;-------- Double-check on automatic update.
CLEAR
SHOWMENU
    "Proceed" : "Proceed with the update",
    "Cancel"  : "Cancel this selection"
TO UChoice
IF UChoice = "Proceed" THEN
    CLEAR
    STYLE BLINK
    @ 5,10
    ? "Performing the update... Please wait."
    ;---- Play the updating script.
    PLAY "InvUpdat"
ENDIF
RETURN
```

Figure 20.23: The Updater script

After defining the additional scripts for the inventory application, you can go back to the Personal Programmer and prepare to attach them to their menu items; we'll look at this process next.

ATTACHING THE CUSTOM SCRIPTS

To attach custom scripts to the inventory application, run the Personal Programmer from the inventory directory, and select Modify. In this example, first make sure that you are still logged onto the

InvMgr directory, and enter the command PPROG to run the Personal Programmer. Select Modify from the Main Menu, and enter the application name **Inv**.

From the Main menu, select NotDefined to move directly to the first undefined menu option, which in this case will be Update. As instructed on the screen, press F10 to call up the menu. Select Action and Define from the next menus to define an action for the item. We want this menu option to play the Updater script developed in the last section, so select Scripts, and enter **Updater** as the name of the script that this menu option should play.

Next, you'll be instructed to move to the next menu selection you want to modify. In this case, we want to define an action for the Reorder report menu option on the Master Inventory Reports submenu. So, move the highlighter to the *Master Inventory* option, and press Enter to move down to its submenu. On the submenu, move the highlighter to the Reports option, and press Enter to move down another menu level.

Next, move the highlighter to the Reorder report option, and press F10. Select Action and Define from the next menus to define an action for the item. We want this menu option to play the Reorder script developed in the last section, so select Scripts, and enter **Reorder** as the name of the script that this menu option should play.

Now the new custom scripts are attached to the appropriate application menu items. Save all your work by calling up the menu (F10) and selecting DO-IT! from the remaining menus. Select Exit and Yes from the Personal Programmer Main menu to return to the DOS prompt.

RUNNING THE INVENTORY APPLICATION

Whenever you want to use the completed application, log onto the appropriate directory using the DOS CD command (CD\INVMGR in this example). Run Paradox from that directory by entering the usual PARADOX2 command at the DOS prompt. From the Paradox Main menu, select Scripts, Play, and specify Inv as the script to play.

When instructed to enter a password, you can just press Enter to move directly to the inventory system main menu. This will bring you to the inventory system main menu options shown below:

Master Inventory   Sales   Purchases   Update   Leave

Below are some general tips on using the inventory system.

MANAGING THE MASTER INVENTORY TABLE

Any new item that is to be carried in the inventory system must be added to the Mastinv table before being entered on either the Sales or Purchase tables. Use the Add data option on the Master Inventory sub-menu to enter these new products. Each item must be assigned a unique part number (or product number). Duplicate part numbers will be rejected into a Keyviol table with the name Kv<number>, where <number> keeps track of multiple tables. For example, the first Key-viol table is named Kv1, the second is named Kv2, and so forth.

The Personal Programmer does not provide any built-in means for managing these Keyviol tables. As an applications developer, you have two choices for dealing with these:

- Teach users how to rectify key violations and use Tools, More, and Add to move the corrected key violations into the Mastinv table.

- Write a custom script to do this automatically.

If you use the second method, you can attach the custom script to the application menu so that users can access it from within the application.

You may enter the new item with an in-stock quantity of zero if you wish to use an entry on the Purchase table as the first items-received transaction for the new item. After updating, the master-inventory table will reflect the correct in-stock quantity.

You may change any information on the Mastinv table using the Change data option from the Master Inventory submenu. However, you should try to avoid changing part numbers once they've been assigned, as the same change will *not* be made on the Sales and Purchase tables. If you *must* change a part number on the Master Inventory table, do so *only* immediately after performing an update (using the Update option from the Inventory system main menu). That way, the Sales and Purchase tables will be empty when you make the change.

If you wish to keep track of orders as you place them, you can use the Change data option to alter the on-order quantities in the Mastinv table each time you place an order. For example, if you order 10 of product number 1002, and you already had 5 on order, enter 15 as the new quantity of items on order for that part number.

To locate information about a particular item in stock, select the Look up data option from the Master Inventory submenu. Enter the part number, or the part name, of the item to look up when instructed on the screen.

To bring the in-stock, on-order, and purchase price quantities up to date in the master inventory, select the Update and Proceed options from the inventory system main menu. Once you select this option, however, you cannot go back and make corrections to the Sales or Purchase table transactions, as those data will have been moved to the history tables. Instead, enter *adjustment transactions* into the Sales or Purchase tables, as discussed later in this section.

To print up-to-date reports of the status of the inventory, select the Reports option from the Master Inventory system submenu. Select either the Entire inventory or the Reorder report option, depending on which report you wish to print.

To leave the Master Inventory submenu and return to the main menu, press the Esc key.

MANAGING THE SALES TABLE

As items are sold, enter a record of the transaction of each sale into the Sales table, using the Add data option from the Sales submenu. You may only enter a part number for parts that have already been entered onto the Mastinv table. Any other part number will be rejected as invalid.

When entering sales transactions, you can press F1 while the cursor is in the Part No field to browse through valid part numbers and part names. You can use Zoom (Ctrl-Z) to look up the information if you wish. When you've located the appropriate part number, press F2 to copy those data to the Sales form. Optionally, press Esc to return to the Sales form without copying.

You can use the Change data option under the Sales submenu to edit or delete any *current* sales transaction (that is, any transaction which has not already been posted to the master inventory). To make corrections to sales transactions that have already been posted, use *adjustment transactions* instead, as discussed later in this section.

During editing of the Sales table, you can use F1 to browse through valid part numbers and names; you can also use the Zoom (Ctrl-Z) and Zoom Next (Alt-Z) keys to locate a particular record. You can, optionally, use the Look up data option under the Sales submenu to locate a particular current sales transaction.

Before performing an update, you should probably print a copy of all current Sales transactions, using the Reports option from the Sales submenu. Check for any obvious errors, and correct them using the Change data option from the Sales submenu, before performing the update.

To leave the Sales submenu and return to the main menu, press the Esc key.

MANAGING THE PURCHASES TABLE

The term "purchases" in this system refers to items that have actually been received. As items are delivered to you, enter transactions into the Purchase table using the Add data option from the Purchases submenu. While the cursor is on the Part No field of the Purchase data entry form, you can use the F1 key and Zoom to browse through part numbers and part names, if necessary.

The Change data, Look up data and Reports options from the Purchases submenu work in the same manner that they do on the Sales submenu. Before performing updates, you should probably print a report of all current purchases, and check it for any obvious errors. Any errors that are found should be corrected before performing an update.

To leave the Purchases menu and return to the main menu, just press Esc.

ENTERING ADJUSTMENT TRANSACTIONS

If an error on the Sales or Purchase table is discovered *after* the update has been performed, you can make corrections by entering adjustment transactions into either table. Use the usual Add Data option from either the Sales or Purchases submenu to enter adjustment transactions, and use the Remarks field to describe the adjustment. Doing so will correct any inaccurate values in the Mastinv table, and also provide an audit trail of the change.

Let's look at an example of an adjustment transaction. Suppose you enter a sales transaction of 100 of part number 1001, but actually only 10 of the items were sold. The Update procedure will delete 100 of part number 1001 from the Mastinv table In Stock quantity (as it should), but this is actually 90 too many items to subtract.

If the transaction has already been posted, you could enter a Sales transaction, using the usual Add data option from the Sales submenu, to enter an adjustment transaction. Enter part number 1001, and the quantity sold as − 90. Enter a descriptive remark such as "Adjustment to previous error" (or something more descriptive). Later, when you perform the update, − 90 will be subtracted from the In Stock quantity (which, if you remember your basic math, means that 90 will actually be added, because when you subtract a negative number, it actually gets added to the current value).

The same basic technique can be used for returned items. Either enter a Sales transaction with the appropriate part number, a negative quantity, and a remark, or enter a Purchase transaction with a positive quantity and the appropriate remark.

UPDATING

The *Update* option from the inventory main menu updates the in-stock and on-order quantities and the purchase price of the item. You can perform updates as often as you wish. When you opt to update, you'll be given the options to

Proceed   Cancel

Select Proceed to proceed with the update, or Cancel to cancel the update and return to the inventory system main menu.

LEAVING THE INVENTORY SYSTEM

To leave the inventory system and return to the Paradox Main menu, select Leave. Note that you can still use items from the Paradox Main menu to manage data in the Mastinv, Sales, and Purchase tables if you so desire.

MODIFYING AN APPLICATION

Developing an application is usually a trial-and-error process. You will probably find that after you initially create an application, there are more features that you want to add, or existing features that you'd like to change or delete. You can modify your application at any time by using the Personal Programmer. To do so, just log onto the same directory that the application is stored on, run the Personal Programmer in the usual manner, and select Modify from the Personal Programmer Main menu.

The Modify menu presents the options below:

Tables   MenuAction   NotDefined   SplashScreen   DO-IT!
Cancel

These options can be summarized as follows:

OPTION	EFFECT
Tables	Changes the tables that are used by the application
MenuAction	Changes a menu item, or the action assigned to an item
NotDefined	Moves directly to the first undefined menu action
SplashScreen	Develops a SplashScreen for the application
DO-IT!	Saves all current modifications
Cancel	Abandons all current modifications

From this point on, the submenus are virtually identical to the submenus you use to create an application. In fact, if you took the break when suggested earlier in this chapter, you were actually editing an existing application! Just select menu items and follow the instructions as they appear on the screen to modify your application to your liking.

The inventory application we developed in this chapter is somewhat rudimentary, because space simply does not permit us to develop a huge sample application. But if you are willing to experiment, you can use the Modify option from the Personal Programmer main menu to add new features, reports, tables, and anything else that comes to mind to tailor the inventory system to your own needs.

MORE PERSONAL PROGRAMMER FEATURES

The sample inventory application used in this chapter provided a useful tool for demonstrating some of the major features of the Personal Programmer, as well as some basic techniques for designing and developing applications. In this next section, we'll discuss some features of the Paradox Personal Programmer in a more general context.

ADDING CUSTOM HELP SCREENS

You can add custom help screens to your own applications using the Help option from the Action menu. When you select this option, you'll see a blank screen for designing your own help screen. Designing a help screen is very much like designing a form. You can manipulate the cursor and type in text using the usual arrow, Insert, Delete, and Backspace keys. You can also press F10 to bring up a menu with the following options on it:

OPTION	EFFECT
Area	Moves or deletes an area on the screen
Border	Draws a border on any area of the screen
DO-IT!	Saves the completed help screen
Cancel	Abandons the current help screen

The help screens that you develop for your application are unlike the Paradox help screens in that they do not ''pop up'' whenever the user presses F1. Instead, the help screen must be attached to a specific menu item. The best way to add help screens to your application is to define an item named Help on the application menu, and to assign Help as the action to that one item.

SPLASH SCREENS

A *splash screen* is an introductory screen that appears whenever a user runs your application. For example, when you first run Paradox itself, you see its splash screen before the Paradox Main menu appears.

Whenever you create or modify an application with the Personal Programmer, you'll be given the options below before the application is created and saved:

SplashScreen   NoSplashScreen

If you select SplashScreen, you can design a splash screen for your own application. The process for designing a splash screen is identical to the process of designing a help screen, as described above. Just design the screen to your liking, call up the menu, and select DO-IT! Then proceed with other menu items, as instructed on the screen, to save your application.

SUMMARIZING AN APPLICATION

The Summarize option from the Personal Programmer prints a report which describes how your application is structured and which files it uses. To use Summarize, you must run the Personal Programmer from the same directory that your application is stored on. Select Summarize from the Personal Programmer Main menu, and enter the application name when prompted. You'll be given the options

Menu   File   Tree   All

These options provide the following reports:

OPTION	*REPORT*
Menu	The application's menu options and their actions
File	A list of all files used by the application
Tree	A tree-structured diagram of the menus
All	All of the above reports

You'll then be given the option to send the report or reports to the printer, the screen, or a file. If you select File, you'll be prompted to enter a name for the file. Enter a valid DOS file name (eight letters maximum, no spaces or punctuation). The report will be stored with the file-name extension .RPT added to the file name you supply. The report is a standard ASCII file that can be viewed or printed with any word processor or text editor.

Figure 20.24 shows a partial example of the Menu summary for the Inv application. The Selection Name column lists the menu option, and the Selection Action column lists the action assigned to the menu option. The Source Table and Map Table columns show the names of any MultiTable views used in the application (the Personal Programmer assigns these names). The Tables Used column lists the names of tables used for the menu option, and the Query, Help, or User Script column lists the names of any of query forms, help screens, or custom scripts (developed outside the Personal Programmer) that the menu item accesses.

Figure 20.25 shows the simple File list for the Inv application. Most of the file names assigned are created by the Personal Programmer, though you should recognize the names of tables and custom scripts within that list. Figure 20.26 shows the menu tree for the Inv application.

TESTING THE MENU STRUCTURE

The Review option on the Personal Programmer allows you to test the menu structure of your application, without actually performing

```
11/11/87                Inv Menu Structure                    Page   1

Menu Path:
/Main/

Script containing this menu: Inv1
Library containing the procedures for this menu: Inv1          Query,
                                                              Help, or
    Selection            Selection     Source    Map      Tables   User
    Name                 Action        Table     Table    Used     Script
    ------------------   -----------   --------  -------- -------- --------
    Master Inventory     Menu
    Sales                Menu
    Purchases            Menu
    Update               Script
    Leave                Leave                                     Updater


Menu Path:
/Main/Master Inventory/

Script containing this menu: Inv2
Library containing the procedures for this menu: Inv1          Query,
                                                              Help, or
    Selection            Selection     Source    Map      Tables   User
    Name                 Action        Table     Table    Used     Script
    ------------------   -----------   --------  -------- -------- --------
    Add data             DataEntry                        Mastinv
    Change data          Edit                             Mastinv  Invq1
    Look up              View                             Mastinv  Invq2
    Reports              Menu

Menu Path:
/Main/Master Inventory/Reports/

Script containing this menu: Inv5
Library containing the procedures for this menu: Inv2          Query,
                                                              Help, or
    Selection            Selection     Source    Map      Tables   User
    Name                 Action        Table     Table    Used     Script
    ------------------   -----------   --------  -------- -------- --------
    Entire inventory     Report                           Mastinv
    Reorder report       Script                                    Reorder
```

Figure 20.24: A partial example of a menu summary for the Inv application

any of the actions associated with each menu item. This feature lets you experiment with your menu structure to decide if there is anything you want to change.

To work backwards through your menu structure at any time, press Esc. To actually modify the menu structure, you'll need to select the Modify option from the Personal Programmer Main menu and MenuAction from the submenu.

```
11/11/87            Application Scripts and Tables         Page   1

Libs:

      Name
      --------
      Inv1
      Inv2


Scripts:

      Name
      --------
      Reorder
      Updater
      Inv
      Inv1
      Inv2
      Inv3
      Inv4
      Inv5
      Invcp
      Invq1
      Invq2
      Invq3
      Invq4
      Invq5
      Invq6
      Invutl


Tables:

      Name
      --------
      Invm1
      Invm2
      Invs1
      Invs2
      Mastinv
      Purchase
      Sales
```

Figure 20.25: Files used by the Inv application

GENERAL APPLICATION MANAGEMENT

The Tools option on the Personal Programmer Main menu provides several useful tools for managing an application. These can be summarized as follows:

OPTION	*EFFECT*
Copy	Copies the entire application from the current directory to another directory or disk

OPTION	EFFECT
Delete	Deletes the entire application from the current directory
Rename	Changes the name of the application
Settings	Allows you to modify various settings in the application, as discussed below
Directory	Allows you to change to a new directory without exiting to DOS. (Never use this option while actually creating or modifying an application; use it only to switch to a new directory before creating a new application.)

The Settings option on the Tools menu offers the following options:

OPTION	EFFECT
PrinterSetup	Lets you change printer characteristics for the application
HelpMode	Removes or replaces the help screens that the Personal Programmer normally displays. Only old pros will want to switch from the helpful Verbose mode to the Terse mode that this option offers.
LibrariesOnly	Erases the files that allow you to modify an existing application, without erasing the application itself. Again, strictly for old pros.
Version	Lets you determine whether or not the application runs under the earlier version 1.1 of Paradox (will still run under version 2.0 as well)

OUTER JOINS

One of the more advanced features of the Personal Programmer is its ability to perform an *outer join*. This is a query that displays records from multiple tables so that all rows are displayed, even if there is not

```
11/12/87              Application Menu Tree:           Page  1.1
                      =====================

  Main --
      |--- Master Inventory --
      |                       |--- Add data  [ DataEntry ]
      |                       |--- Change data  [ Edit ]
      |                       |--- Look up  [ View ]
      |                       ---- Reports --
      |                                      |--- Entire inventory  [Report]
      |                                      ---- Reorder report  [Script]
      |--- Sales --
      |           |--- Add data  [ DataEntry ]
      |           |--- Change data  [ Edit ]
      |           |--- Look up  [ View ]
      |           ---- Reports  [ Report ]
      |--- Purchases --
      |               |--- Add data  [ DataEntry ]
      |               |--- Change data  [ Edit ]
      |               |--- Look up  [ View ]
      |               ---- Report  [ Report ]
      |--- Update  [ Script ]
      ---- Leave  [ Leave ]

  Note:  "...<Menu Selection>"  means that <Menu Selection> is not defined.
  ====
```

Figure 20.26: The menu tree for the Inv application

a matching key field on one of the tables. For example, suppose you wish to see a list of all the parts in the master inventory, along with individual sales transactions for each part. Furthermore, assume that the master inventory table includes part number 1003, Cherries, but no sales transactions exist for this table on the sales table.

If you use a conventional query to see such a list, as shown in Figure 20.27, the query displays only master inventory items for which sales transactions exist, as in Figure 20.28. (Part number 1003 is not displayed on the list, because there are no related sales transactions.)

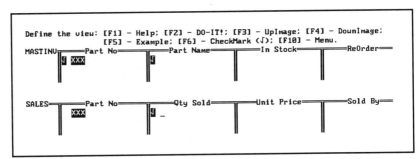

Figure 20.27: A conventional query of two tables

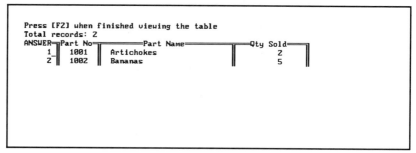

Figure 20.28: Results of the conventional query

When filling in query forms with the personal programmer, you can place an exclamation point (!) to the right of the example that links the two tables to perform an outer join, as shown in the top query form in Figure 20.29.

When you perform the query, part numbers which have no sales transactions associated with them are still displayed in the resulting query table. As shown in Figure 20.30, part number 1003 is displayed in the Answer table, even though there are no sales transactions associated with it.

CONFIGURING THE PERSONAL PROGRAMMER

You can configure many features of the Personal Programmer to your own liking using the Paradox Custom Configuration program. To do so, log onto the Paradox2 directory, and enter PPROG to run

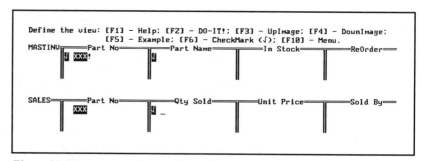

Figure 20.29: A query of two tables using an outer join

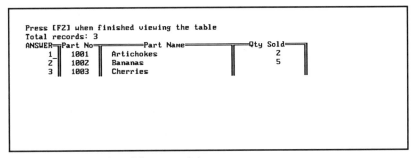

```
Press [F2] when finished viewing the table
Total records: 3
ANSWER┬Part No┐        ┌Part Name┐        ┬Qty Sold┐
    1 ║   1001 ║    Artichokes           ║      2
    2 ║   1002 ║    Bananas              ║      5
    3 ║   1003 ║    Cherries             ║
```

Figure 20.30: Results of the outer-join query

the Personal Programmer. Select Play from the Main menu, and specify Custom as the script to play.

Because you played the Custom script from within the Personal Programmer, any changes you make will affect only the Personal Programmer, and not Paradox in general.

SUMMARY

- The Personal Programmer lets you develop applications without programming. It asks you questions about the application, and writes programs automatically based on your answers.

- The Personal Programmer requires a hard disk, and must be installed on a subdirectory named \PARADOX2\PPROG.

- Before building an application, it is best to create all the tables used in the application, and to draw a diagram of the *menu tree* for the application.

- Each application that you develop should be stored on its own directory.

- To start the Personal Programmer, log onto the directory for the application, and enter the command PPROG at the DOS prompt.

- When the Paradox Personal Programmer Main menu appears, select Create to create a new application, or Modify to modify an existing application.

- Once the Paradox Personal Programmer is running, follow the instructions on the screen, making menu selections to develop the application to your liking.

- To run an completed application, log on to the application directory, run Paradox in the usual manner, and select Scripts, Play, and the application name. (Optionally, just enter the command PARADOX2 followed by the application name at the DOS prompt.)

THE DATA ENTRY TOOLKIT

THE DATA ENTRY TOOLKIT IS A FEATURE THAT
helps PAL programmers build sophisticated forms for data entry.
The Toolkit is entirely optional, and many of the features it offers can
be more easily achieved using the HelpAndFill option (discussed in
Chapter 12) and the Personal Programmer's MultiTable views
(Chapter 20).

Features that the Data Entry Toolkit offers that are not available
elsewhere include the following:

- Sophisticated form design with intersecting borders and
  menu-selected graphics characters

- Automatic script execution as soon as the cursor enters or
  leaves a field on the data-entry form

- The assignment of special keys that, when pressed, immediately play a script

- Pop-up menus that temporarily overwrite a small portion of
  the form currently on the screen and allow a user to select
  valid data from a field in a separate table

- Multiple rows of data for a single table on one screen. (For
  example, when filling in an order form, several rows of
  orders can be filled in for a single customer.)

The Data Entry Toolkit is a very advanced tool, and requires considerable knowledge of PAL and PAL programming techniques,
including procedure libraries. In this chapter, we'll develop a sample
application to demonstrate basic techniques for creating data-entry
forms with the Toolkit. But be forewarned: To take full advantage of
Toolkit's capabilities, you'll need to go beyond the scope of this book
and learn more advanced PAL programming techniques. You can

do so using the *PAL User's Guide* that comes with your Paradox package or other books that focus on PAL programming.

INSTALLING THE DATA ENTRY TOOLKIT

To use the Data Entry Toolkit, you must have a computer with a hard disk. (To install the Data Entry Toolkit on a network, see the *Network Administrator's Guide* that comes with your Paradox package.) The automatic installation procedure creates a subdirectory named \paradox2\detool on your hard disk, and stores the Toolkit there. Follow these steps to install the Toolkit on your own computer:

1. Log onto the directory that Paradox is stored on. (On most computers, enter the command CD\PARADOX2 next to the DOS prompt.)

2. Insert the Paradox disk labeled *Sample Application/Data Entry Toolkit* in drive A of your computer.

3. At the DOS prompt, enter the command A:DINSTALL and press Enter.

The installation program will provide additional instructions for completing the installation procedure.

ACCESSING THE TOOLKIT

To access the Toolkit, log onto the directory that Paradox is stored on (usually \PARADOX2) and run Paradox in the usual manner. When the Paradox Main menu appears, switch to the \PARADOX2\detool subdirectory by selecting Tools, More, and Directory from the Main menu. Change the current directory to

    C:\PARADOX2\detool

and press Enter. You'll be given the options to Cancel the selection or choose Ok to proceed. Select Ok.

When the Paradox Main menu appears, select Scripts and Play, and specify Toolkit as the name of the script to play. There will be a brief pause as the Toolkit script creates two procedure libraries named DemoApp and Toolkit. Then you'll see the Data Entry Toolkit Main menu:

Demonstration   FieldDefine   KeyDefine   HelpForm
PrepareFinal   Quit

For an introduction to the capabilities of the Toolkit, you may want to try the Demonstration option first, which is discussed below.

THE DATA-ENTRY DEMONSTRATION

The Demonstration option on the Toolkit Main menu allows you to experiment with a sample data entry form for entering orders. When you select this option, there will be a brief pause as the computer prepares the demonstration. Then you'll see the sample data-entry form, as shown in Figure 21.1.

Now, to experiment with the form, type in an invoice number, such as 123, and press Enter. The cursor moves to the field named

```
Entering invoice information.
Press [F1] for help, [F2] when done, [F10] for menu.

 Invoice #: _         ◀ Ship Via:            Date:

 Cust. ID:              Last Name:          First Name:
                        Address:
                        City:               State:    Zip:
 Discount:         %    Phone:

 Quantity     Part        Description        Price    Ext'd Price




 Subtotal    Discount    Freight     Tax        Total
                         60.00

                       paradox fig21-1
```

Figure 21.1: The Demonstration data-entry form

Ship Via, and waits for your entry. Press the F1 key to see a pop-up menu of valid selections. On this small pop-up menu you can use ↑, ↓, PgUp, PgDn, Home, and End to move the highlighter to any of the various postal carriers listed. Highlight any one of the options and press Enter. Your selection is automatically copied into the Ship Via field on the data-entry form.

After you've entered a valid carrier, you'll notice another feature of the Toolkit. It automatically fills in the Date field with the current date, and the cursor moves to the next field. (This is much like the ValCheck Default option, except that the Toolkit takes it a step further by moving the cursor out of the field after filling it in.)

Next, the cursor waits for you to fill in a customer number. Here, you can again press F1 to call up a table of valid customer numbers. When that table appears, you can move the highlight to any customer number and press F2. The look-up table will disappear, and the name and address for that customer will be filled in on the form automatically. Optionally, you can also type in a new customer number, and the form will then allow you to enter additional information for the new customer directly into the table of customer names and addresses.

When the cursor is in the Quantity field, you can type in a number and press Enter. When the cursor is in the Part field, you can type in a valid part number, or press F1 to see a list of valid part numbers. When the list appears, move the cursor to the part number you need, and press F2. You'll be returned to the data-entry form, and the appropriate information for the part number will automatically be copied to the form. At the bottom of the screen, you'll see the calculations for the order.

You can enter more orders for this customer by filling in the Qty field again, and pressing F1 to select from valid part numbers once again. You can enter up to eight orders for this single customer. As you add more orders, the calculations at the bottom of the screen are updated automatically.

You can move the cursor freely about the data entry form and make any changes as required. All the automatic fill-in fields, and calculations, will be updated accordingly. When done, press F2 to save the data. When the menu appears, select DO-IT!. You'll be returned to the Paradox workspace. (In your own applications, of course, you'd return the user to a menu within the application.)

Don't forget that \PARADOX2\detool is still the working directory. Use Tools, More, and Directory to log onto a different directory, if necessary.

DEVELOPING YOUR OWN DATA-ENTRY FORMS

Every data-entry form that you create with the Toolkit will consist of the following components:

- Tables that contain data, look-up information for pop-up screens, and a *source table* that contains fields from multiple tables. Use the usual Paradox Create menu option to create these tables (or optionally, use existing tables).

- A data-entry form that the user sees on the screen to enter data. The HelpForm option on the Toolkit Main menu lets you do this.

- Procedures that define what to do in the various fields on the form. Use the Scripts editor, or a word processor, to define these as you would any other PAL script.

- A table that defines which procedures are executed in which fields, and the circumstances under which the procedure should be played. The FieldDefine option on the Data Entry Toolkit Main menu helps you with this step.

- A table describing the effects of various keys, particularly special keys like F1 (Help) and F10 (Menu). The KeyDefine option on the Toolkit Main menu helps you with this step.

- The actual application scripts that integrate all of the above components into a complete application. You create these scripts on your own using the PAL editor.

Each of the steps described above is discussed in more detail in the sections that follow.

CREATING THE TABLES

The first step to using the Data Entry Toolkit is to create some tables to store the entered data and to provide look-up information. In this chapter, we'll store these tables on a new directory named \ToolTest, so that they do not become confused with sample tables on the \PARA-DOX2\detool directory. To create this new directory, and then log onto it, start from the DOS prompt at the root directory of your hard disk and use the MD command to make the new directory. The exact commands you enter at the DOS prompt are

```
CD\
MD\ToolTest
CD\ToolTest
```

Press Enter after typing in each command. (If you have not done so already, you might also want to enter the command

```
PROMPT $P$G
```

at the DOS prompt so the directory name is displayed with the DOS prompt.)

Next, run Paradox from the current directory by entering the command

```
PARADOX2
```

at the DOS prompt. (If Paradox won't run from this directory, you have not set the appropriate PATH command in your AUTOEX-EC.BAT file yet. You can enter the command PATH C:\PARA-DOX2 at the DOS prompt now, then reenter the PARADOX2 command to run Paradox. Later, take a look at the section on installing the Personal Programmer in Chapter 20 for instructions on setting up an AutoExec file with the appropriate PATH or SET PATH command.)

The sample tables used in this data entry form will be named Orders, Customer, Mastinv, OrdEntry, and Carriers. Use the usual Create option from the Paradox Main menu to create these tables. Their structures are shown in Figures 21.2 through 21.6. If you've already created the Mastinv table, you can use the Paradox Tools, Copy, and Table options to copy it from

```
\PARADOX2\Mastinv
```

to

```
\tooltest\Mastinv
```

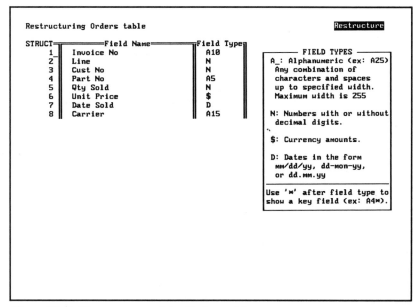

Figure 21.2: The structure of the Orders table

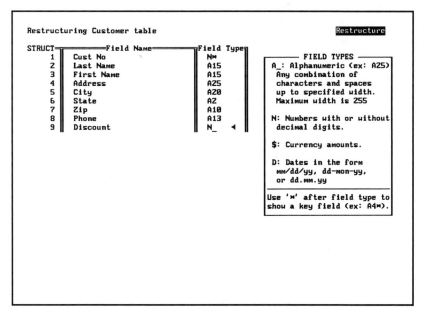

Figure 21.3: The structure of the Customer table

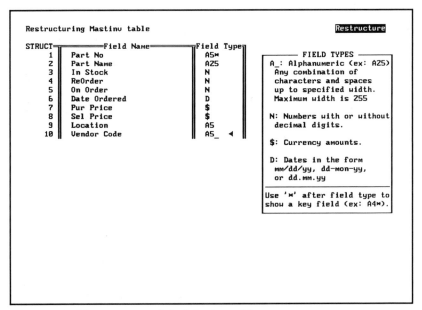

Figure 21.4: The structure of the Mastinv table

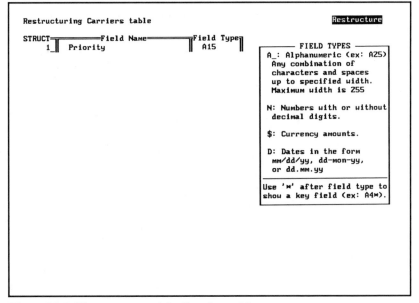

Figure 21.5: The structure of the Carriers table

```
STRUCT            Field Name          Field Type
     1    Invoice No                  A10
     2    Order Date                  D
     3    Carrier                     A15
     4    Cust No                     N
     5    Last Name                   A15
     6    First Name                  A15
     7    Address                     A25
     8    City                        A20
     9    State                       A2
    10    Zip                         A10
    11    Discount                    N
    12    Part1                       A5
    13    PartName1                   A15
    14    Qty1                        N
    15    Price1                      $
    16    ExtPrice1                   $
    17    Part2                       A5
    18    PartName2                   A15
    19    Qty2                        N
    20    Price2                      $
    21    ExtPrice2                   $
    22    Part3                       A5
    23    PartName3                   A15
    24    Qty3                        N
    25    Price3                      $
    26    ExtPrice3                   $
    27    Part4                       A5
    28    PartName4                   A15
    29    Qty4                        N
    30    Price4                      $
    31    ExtPrice4                   $
    32    Part5                       A5
    33    PartName5                   A15
    34    Qty5                        N
    35    Price5                      $
    36    ExtPrice5                   $
    37    Part6                       A5
    38    PartName6                   A15
    39    Qty6                        N
    40    Price6                      $
    41    ExtPrice6                   $
    42    SubTotal                    $
    43    Discount $                  $
    44    Tax                         $
    45    Total                       $
```

Figure 21.6: The structure of the OrdEntry table

Change the name of the Order Date field to Date Ordered as shown in Figure 21.4. We'll be using Order Date as a field name in the OrdEntry and Orders table to refer to the customer's order date, rather than the date that the business ordered an item from a vendor.

Enter some sample data to experiment with in the Customer, Mastinv, and Carriers tables. Use Modify and DataEntry to enter a couple of customers into the Customer table, with customer numbers 1001 and 1002. Use the same Paradox menu selections to enter some sample data into the Mastinv table (unless you've already done so in a previous chapter). Finally, enter a few shipping options into the Carriers table, as listed below:

> 1st Class Mail
> Federal Express
> Airborne
> Parcel Post
> Express Mail
> Ocean Freight
> UPS Blue Label
> 2nd Day Air

Most of the tables we've developed simply store data for the given application. The one exception is OrdEntry, which exists *only* to accept data into the data-entry form we'll develop in this chapter. As you can see, OrdEntry contains some fields that are identical to fields in other tables, such as Last Name, Cust No, Discount, Invoice No, and others. It also contains some ''numbered'' fields like Part1, Part2, Qty1, Qty2, and so forth. These special fields will allow you to enter multiple orders for a single invoice, as you'll soon see.

CREATING THE DATA ENTRY FORM

The next step is to create the form for entering data on the screen. You can use the Toolkit HelpForm option for this, or the usual Form and Design options from the Paradox Main menu. The Toolkit HelpForm option has a couple of advantages: it allows joining of single- and double-bar boxes, and lets you easily place graphics characters on the form.

Now, remember that the sample tables are on the \ToolTest directory, and the Toolkit is on the \PARADOX2\detool directory. To use the Data Entry Toolkit from the \ToolTest directory, stay logged on to the \ToolTest directory, select the Scripts and Play options from the Paradox Main menu, and enter

```
\PARADOX2\detool\toolkit
```

as the name of the script to play.

When the Data Entry Toolkit Main menu appears, select Help-Form and Design, and specify OrdEntry as the name of the table. Select option 1, and enter a form description such as *Order Entry*.

The basic techniques for designing a form with HelpForm are identical to those for creating forms under the Forms option of the Paradox Main menu. The only differences are that borders can intersect and overlap automatically, and that you can place the cursor anywhere on the form and type Alt-F1 to see a menu of special graphics characters. To select a graphics character, use the arrow keys to highlight it, and press Enter to select it. (Because HelpForm must figure out how to overlap borders, there is often a slight delay when you place a border before it appears on the screen. Be patient.)

Figure 21.7 shows the form for the current sample data entry form. No graphics characters were used on this form; all the borders were drawn with the Border and Place options from the menu (which you call up by pressing the usual F10 key).

Note that only those fields that are actually stored in the Orders table are placed with the Field, Place, and Regular options from the menu. All other fields are placed with the Field, Place, and DisplayOnly or

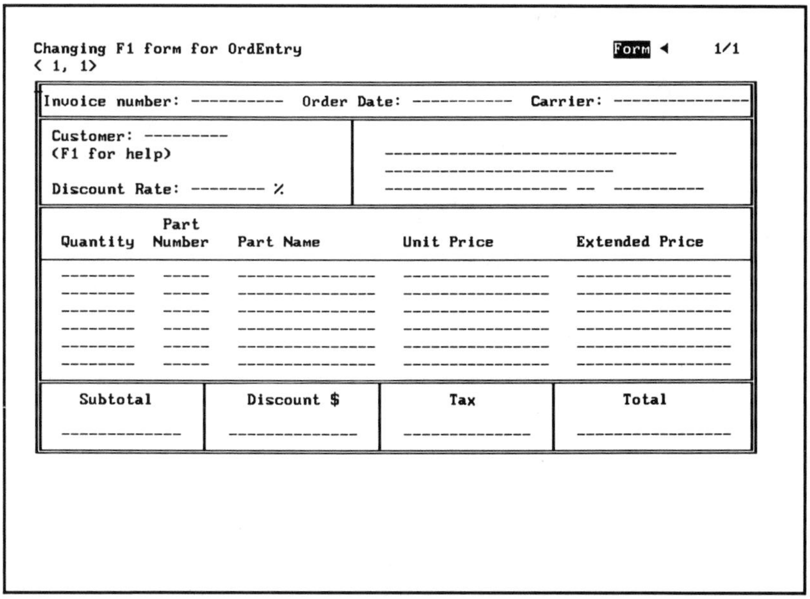

Figure 21.7: The form for the Data Entry Toolkit example

Field, Place, and Calculated options to prevent editing of separate tables. Table 21.1 lists the column and row positions of all fields placed on the sample screen. In the middle column, *Regular* indicates that the field is placed using the Field, Place, and Regular options, *DisplayOnly* indicates that the field is placed using the Field, Place, and DisplayOnly options, and *Calculated* means that the field expression is placed with the Field, Place, and Calculated menu options.

POSITION	PLACEMENT OPTION	FIELD NAME
< 2,18 >	Regular	Invoice No
< 2,42 >	Regular	Order Date
< 2,64 >	Regular	Carrier
< 4,13 >	Regular	Cust No
< 5,39 >	Calculated	[First Name] + "" + [Last Name]
< 6,39 >	DisplayOnly	Address
< 7,18 >	Regular	Discount
< 7,39 >	DisplayOnly	City
< 7,60 >	DisplayOnly	State
< 7,64 >	DisplayOnly	Zip
<12, 4 >	Regular	Qty1
<12,15 >	Regular	Part1
<12,23 >	DisplayOnly	PartName1
<12,41 >	DisplayOnly	Price1
<12,60 >	DisplayOnly	ExtPrice1
<13, 4 >	Regular	Qty2
<13,15 >	Regular	Part2
<13,23 >	DisplayOnly	PartName2

Table 21.1: Locations of fields on the sample form

POSITION	PLACEMENT OPTION	FIELD NAME
<13,41>	DisplayOnly	Price2
<13,60>	DisplayOnly	ExtPrice2
<14, 4>	Regular	Qty3
<14,15>	Regular	Part3
<14,23>	DisplayOnly	PartName3
<14,41>	DisplayOnly	Price3
<14,60>	DisplayOnly	ExtPrice3
<15,4>	Regular	Qty4
<15,15>	Regular	Part4
<15,23>	DisplayOnly	PartName4
<15,41>	DisplayOnly	Price4
<15,60>	DisplayOnly	ExtPrice4
<16, 4>	Regular	Qty5
<16,15>	Regular	Part5
<16,23>	DisplayOnly	PartName5
<16,41>	DisplayOnly	Price5
<16,60>	DisplayOnly	ExtPrice5
<17, 4>	Regular	Qty6
<17,15>	Regular	Part6
<17,23>	DisplayOnly	PartName6
<17,41>	DisplayOnly	Price6
<17,60>	DisplayOnly	ExtPrice6
<21, 4>	DisplayOnly	Subtotal
<21,22>	DisplayOnly	Discount $
<21,41>	DisplayOnly	Tax
<21,60>	DisplayOnly	Total

Table 21.1: Locations of fields on the sample form (continued)

When you place fields on the form, Paradox will usually suggest field widths that are much too wide for such a full form. When prompted, you can use the ← key to reduce the width on any field that you place on the form. Use Figure 21.7 to help you determine field widths as you create a form of your own.

When you've finished designing the form to your liking, press F2 to save it, and then select Quit and Yes to leave the Data Entry Toolkit for the moment and return to the Paradox Main menu.

Because you are still logged onto the \ToolTest directory, your form is stored on that directory. The next step is to define the usual ValCheck settings for the form, including TableLookup and HelpAndFill (as discussed in Chapter 12). Remember that when using HelpForm, you defined OrdEntry as the table associated with that form. To change ValCheck settings, call up the Paradox Main menu (F10) and select View and then OrdEntry as the table to view. Press F9 to enter the Edit mode.

To bring up the form you just created with HelpForm, press F10 and select Image, PickForm, and 1. The form will appear on the screen. Now, define the various ValCheck settings for appropriate fields, using Table 21.2 as your guide. Note that the table suggests

FIELD NAME	MENU SELECTIONS
Order Date	Default *today*
Carrier	TableLookup/**Carriers**/JustCurrentField/HelpAndFill
Cust No	TableLookup/**Customer**/AllFields/HelpAndFill
Part1	TableLookup/**Mastinv**/AllFields/HelpAndFill
Part2	TableLookup/**Mastinv**/AllFields/HelpAndFill
Part3	TableLookup/**Mastinv**/AllFields/HelpAndFill
Part4	TableLookup/**Mastinv**/AllFields/HelpAndFill
Part5	TableLookup/**Mastinv**/AllFields/HelpAndFill
Part6	TableLookup/**Mastinv**/AllFields/HelpAndFill

Table 21.2: ValCheck settings for fields in the OrdEntry table

making the current date (*today*) the default value for the Order Date field. The Carriers field uses a TableLookup ValCheck to help locate and copy data from the Carriers table into the current form.

The Cust No and various Part Number fields (Part 1 through Part 6) all use TableLookup to help locate and copy data from the Customer and Mastinv tables into the current form.

When using Table 21.2, position the cursor to the Field Name listed in the left column of the table, and select the ValCheck and Define options from the menu. Then select the options listed in the right column from the submenus. Note that *today*, in the Order Date field, is typed in directly rather than selected from a menu. The AllFields option is actually the AllCorrespondingFields option from the menu. (If you need a review of these various menu selections, see Chapter 12.)

When you've finished defining the ValChecks for the OrdEntry form, press F2 to save them.

ASSIGNING PROCEDURES TO FIELDS

The next step in developing a data-entry form with the Toolkit is to assign scripts (actually, procedures) to individual fields on the data-entry form. It does not matter whether you actually create the procedures first, or attach procedures (by name) to individual fields, so in the next section we'll go ahead and use FieldDefine to link individual fields in the OrdEntry table to our currently nonexistent procedures.

USING FIELDDEFINE

The FieldDefine option on the Toolkit menu lets you assign procedures to individual fields in a table. Using the four options below, you can specify the procedures attached to a field, as well as when the procedure is activated.

OPTION	EFFECT
Arrive	Executes procedure as soon as the cursor arrives in the field on the form

OPTION	*EFFECT*
Good Depart	Executes procedure when user moves the cursor out of the field, and the entry passes a validity check (as defined by ValCheck)
Bad Depart	Executes procedure when user moves the cursor out of the field, and the entry does not pass a validity check (as defined by ValCheck)
Keystroke	Executes procedure when user presses a certain key while the cursor is in the field

For the sample form we'll develop in this chapter, we'll create procedures with the names listed below:

PROCEDURE	*EFFECT*
Reqd	Requires that the invoice number field not be left blank
TodaysDate	Enters today's date in the Order Date field, then automatically moves to the next field
CustDone	Fills in the customer information and skips to the Quantity field on the form
NewDisc	Adjusts all calculations if the customer discount rate is changed
GetCarrier	Displays a pop-up menu of valid shipping options
GetPart	Helps locate a particular part number and calculate totals
ChangeQty	Allows the Qty field to be changed, and adjusts all calculations accordingly

It is easiest to use FieldDefine directly from the \PARADOX2\detool directory, because the Toolkit creates backup files in case of future changes. First press Alt-F8 to clear the workspace. Then from the Paradox Main menu, select Tools, More, and Directory, and enter **\PARADOX2\detool** as the new directory. (Select Ok when Paradox double checks.)

Next, run the Toolkit by selecting Scripts, Play, and Toolkit. From the Toolkit menu, select FieldDefine. You'll be given a suggested name for the script that FieldDefine creates, as shown below:

Script: FldSpec
Enter the name of the script in which to store field specifications.

Press Backspace to erase the suggested name, and enter the new name **FldProcs**. If a script by that name already exists, you will be asked if you want to Modify or Replace it. If the script does not already exist, you'll be asked for the name of the table that the data-entry form serves, as below:

Table: TKEntry
Enter the name of the underlying data entry table.

In this example, the underlying table is called OrdEntry, but it is stored on the \ToolTest directory. So, you need to press Ctrl-Backspace to erase the suggested name, and enter

\ToolTest\OrdEntry

as the name of the table. When you press Enter, you'll see the field definition table.

The field definition table is like any other Paradox table in that you can freely move the cursor around the fields and enter or change data. You need to place the names of the procedures associated with a field in the appropriate column on the table. In this example, we will assign procedures as listed in Table 21.3.

Figure 21.8 shows a portion of the FieldDefine screen with data entered (you need to scroll down and put the GetPart and ChangeQty procedures in the Good Depart column for the various Part and Qty fields as well).

Within FieldDefine, you can press F10 to call up a menu of options, including Borrow (to borrow from an existing definition), Print (to print the definition table), Help, DO-IT! and Cancel. Note that you cannot delete fields from the form, or move them using the Rotate key. After you've filled in the entire form, press DO-IT! (F2).

FIELD NAME	COLUMN	PROCEDURE NAME
Invoice No	Good Depart	Reqd
Order Date	Arrive	TodaysDate
Carrier	Bad Depart	GetCarrier
Cust No	Good Depart	CustDone
Discount	Good Depart	NewDisc
Part1	Good Depart	GetPart
Qty1	Good Depart	ChangeQty
Part2	Good Depart	GetPart
Qty2	Good Depart	ChangeQty
Part3	Good Depart	GetPart
Qty3	Good Depart	ChangeQty
Part4	Good Depart	GetPart
Qty4	Good Depart	ChangeQty
Part5	Good Depart	GetPart
Qty5	Good Depart	ChangeQty
Part6	Good Depart	GetPart
Qty6	Good Depart	ChangeQty

Table 21.3: FieldDefine specifications for a sample data entry

DEFINING KEYS

The next step in the process is to assign any special status to the keys on the keyboard. You can place any keystroke into one of the following categories:

TYPE	DEFINITION
Regular	A regular key that does not move the cursor
Illegal	An unacceptable keystroke to be rejected by the form

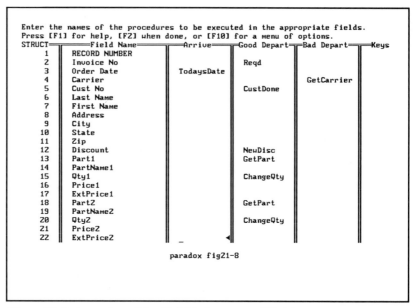

```
Enter the names of the procedures to be executed in the appropriate fields.
Press [F1] for help, [F2] when done, or [F10] for a menu of options.
STRUCT═══════════Field Name═════════Arrive══════Good Depart═╤═Bad Depart══════Keys
     1 ║ RECORD NUMBER
     2 ║ Invoice No                              Reqd
     3 ║ Order Date            TodaysDate
     4 ║ Carrier                                              GetCarrier
     5 ║ Cust No                                 CustDone
     6 ║ Last Name
     7 ║ First Name
     8 ║ Address
     9 ║ City
    10 ║ State
    11 ║ Zip
    12 ║ Discount                                NewDisc
    13 ║ Part1                                   GetPart
    14 ║ PartName1
    15 ║ Qty1                                    ChangeQty
    16 ║ Price1
    17 ║ ExtPrice1
    18 ║ Part2                                   GetPart
    19 ║ PartName2
    20 ║ Qty2                                    ChangeQty
    21 ║ Price2
    22 ║ ExtPrice2

                          paradox fig21-8
```

Figure 21.8: A portion of the FieldDefine screen filled in

TYPE	DEFINITION
Exit	A keystroke that exits the data-entry form
Special	A special key, handled by a procedure, that does not move the cursor

In addition, the Toolkit automatically assigns the status Depart-Special to Special keys that define a field, and Movement to Regular keys that depart a field. These categorizations are used internally by the Toolkit, and are not alterable.

In this example, we'll redefine the Menu (F10) and Help (F1) keys to Special status (and then later develop a script to handle these keys on the data-entry form). Select KeyDefine from the Toolkit menu. You'll be given the prompt

```
Script: KeySpec
Enter the name of the script to store key specification.
```

Type Backspace to erase the suggested name, and enter the new name **KeyProcs**. You'll see the key specification table with the following columns of information:

COLUMN	INFORMATION
Ascii Code	Contains the ASCII code assigned to the keystroke
Function	Contains the normal function of the key
Effect	Contains the status that you assign to the key (Regular, Special, Exit, and so forth)

The first two columns are for information only. The rightmost column is where you categorize the keystroke.

In this example, you want to locate the F10 and F1 keys (press PgDn a couple of times), and change their Effect settings to Special. Figure 21.9 shows this portion of the screen completed.

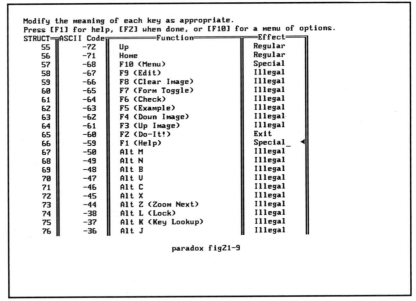

```
Modify the meaning of each key as appropriate.
Press [F1] for help, [F2] when done, or [F10] for a menu of options.
STRUCT═╦ASCII Code╦════════Function═══════╦════Effect═══
    55 ║   -72    ║ Up                     ║ Regular
    56 ║   -71    ║ Home                   ║ Regular
    57 ║   -68    ║ F10 (Menu)             ║ Special
    58 ║   -67    ║ F9 (Edit)              ║ Illegal
    59 ║   -66    ║ F8 (Clear Image)       ║ Illegal
    60 ║   -65    ║ F7 (Form Toggle)       ║ Illegal
    61 ║   -64    ║ F6 (Check)             ║ Illegal
    62 ║   -63    ║ F5 (Example)           ║ Illegal
    63 ║   -62    ║ F4 (Down Image)        ║ Illegal
    64 ║   -61    ║ F3 (Up Image)          ║ Illegal
    65 ║   -60    ║ F2 (Do-It!)            ║ Exit
    66 ║   -59    ║ F1 (Help)              ║ Special_   ◄
    67 ║   -50    ║ Alt M                  ║ Illegal
    68 ║   -49    ║ Alt N                  ║ Illegal
    69 ║   -48    ║ Alt B                  ║ Illegal
    70 ║   -47    ║ Alt V                  ║ Illegal
    71 ║   -46    ║ Alt C                  ║ Illegal
    72 ║   -45    ║ Alt X                  ║ Illegal
    73 ║   -44    ║ Alt Z (Zoom Next)      ║ Illegal
    74 ║   -38    ║ Alt L (Lock)           ║ Illegal
    75 ║   -37    ║ Alt K (Key Lookup)     ║ Illegal
    76 ║   -36    ║ Alt J                  ║ Illegal

                  paradox fig21-9
```

Figure 21.9: The Effect settings of the F1 and F10 keys changed to Special

Press F2 after finishing assigning the new effects to the F1 and F10 keys to save the definitions. The screen will present the prompt

Name of procedure to execute when 'Special' key is pressed: SpecialKey

Press Enter to accept the suggested name *SpecialKey*. You'll be returned to the Toolkit menu. For now, you've completed your work with the Toolkit, so select Quit and Yes to return to the Paradox Main menu.

COPYING THE GENERATED SCRIPTS

The FieldDefine and KeyDefine options from the Toolkit have created two scripts for you named FldProcs.SC and KeyProcs.SC, and those are still stored on the Toolkit directory. You'll need to copy these to the ToolTest directory, where the rest of the objects for the sample form are stored. To do so, select Tools, Copy, and Scripts from the Paradox main menu. Enter

\PARADOX2\detool\FldProcs

as the first script to copy, and

\tooltest\FldProcs

as the script to copy to. Select Tools, Copy, and Scripts again, and enter

\PARADOX2\detool\KeyProcs

as the script to copy, and

\tooltest\KeyProcs

as the script to copy it to.

Don't forget that you are still logged onto the \PARADOX2\detool directory. If you wish to start developing scripts for the data-entry form, use Tools, More, and Directory from the Main menu to log onto the \ToolTest directory.

DATA ENTRY TOOLKIT PROCEDURES AND VARIABLES

Before you begin developing custom procedures for a data-entry form, there are a number of things you need to know about the Toolkit and the features it offers. In particular, you need to know about the built-in procedures that it offers, accessed from your own custom procedures, and the special variables it uses.

The Toolkit offers 13 ready-to-use procedures that you can call from within your own procedure library when you use the Toolkit to develop data entry forms. These built-in procedures are in the file named Toolkit.lib, stored on the \PARADOX2\detool directory with the rest of the Data Entry Toolkit. When running your own applications, the Toolkit.lib file *must* be accessible on the computer.

The Toolkit also offers many specially defined variables, all beginning with the letters *TK*, which help you develop your own custom procedures. These variables indicate when some event has occurred. For example, the variable TKChanged is False until the data in some field has been changed, at which point it becomes True. The Toolkit procedures and variables are discussed in the sections below.

DATA ENTRY TOOLKIT VARIABLES

Your custom procedures can use any of the variables summarized below. The exact effect of the variables will depend on the type of activity involved (for example, Arrival, Good Depart, and so forth). Examples later in this chapter will demonstrate the use of some of these variables:

VARIABLE	DESCRIPTION
TKAccept	When set to false, tells the Toolkit to reject the users entry and keep the cursor in the current field
TKChanged	Sets to true automatically when the contents of a field are successfully changed
TKChar	Contains the value of the last key pressed

TKDebug	Calls a Toolkit debugging procedure from within a custom procedure
TKFieldVal	Contains the contents of the current field
TKHoldCanvas	When set to True in your custom procedure, suppresses display of the data-entry form
TKKeyType	Stores the type of keystroke as either M (movement), D (departure from a field), or E (exit from the form)
TKLibName	Contains the full name of the location of the Toolkit.LIB file (for example, \PARADOX2\DETOOL\toolkit.lib)
TKMessage	Displays any message stored in the variable on the screen until the user presses another key
TK<keyname>	Various keys are assigned names with the leading letters *TK*. For example, TKUnDo refers to the Undo (Ctrl-U) key, and TKDel refers to the Delete key. These are only active after the SetKeyCodes procedure is called

TOOLKIT BUILT-IN PROCEDURES

The Data Entry Toolkit offers 13 built-in procedures that can be accessed by your custom procedures. Let's look at each of these built-in procedures in turn.

ArriveField

The ArriveField procedure tells the DoWait or RecurseWait procedure (discussed below) that the cursor has moved to a new field, and activates an arrival procedure if one has been defined for the field. This procedure must be used when your custom procedure (rather than an actual keystroke) moves the cursor to a new field on the form.

DoWait

DoWait begins the entire data-entry procedure. It is used in place of WAIT when using the Data Entry Toolkit in an application. The DoWait procedure automatically plays your custom scripts and manages your special keys, according to the specifications defined in the FieldDefine and KeyDefine steps of the data-entry form development process.

DoWait can be used with a character string message that appears at the bottom of the screen when the procedure is called. For example, the call

DoWait("Enter data now.")

begins the data-entry process and displays the message

Enter data now.

in the bottom-right corner of the screen. The message is optional, and DoWait can be called using the syntax

DoWait("")

Like WAIT, DoWait remains in control until the user presses an Exit key. With DoWait, however, that Exit key is any key that has been categorized as Exit in the KeyDefine specifications. The PAL variable *Retval* stores the keystroke that is used to exit DoWait.

Before calling the DoWait procedure, you must call the InitWait procedure, discussed below.

EditMenu

The EditMenu procedure displays a simple Paradox-style editing menu at the top of the screen. The options available on this menu are

UnDo   Help   DO-IT!   Cancel

EditMenu can only be invoked in applications that categorize the F10 key as Special during the KeyDefine phase of the overall process.

GetFile

The GetFile procedure displays a list of file names in a Paradox-style menu, and lets the user select a file in the usual highlight-and-press-Enter fashion. The general syntax for this procedure is:

GetFile(*"mask"*,*"prompt"*,*"message"*,*"default"*,*required*)

The parameters can be summarized as follows:

PARAMETER	EFFECT
mask	A skeleton of the type of files to display (for example, *.DB displays table names)
prompt	The prompt to display on the top line of the screen
message	The message to display on the second line of the screen
default	The name of the default file name to display next to the prompt on the first line
required	*True* if the file must exist before being selected, *False* if the user can create a new file

GetFile returns the name of the selected file, which you can store in a variable.

In the example below, GetFile displays the names of all tables on the current directory in a menu, with no default file name. The user must select from the tables shown. The file name that the user selects is stored in a variable named FName:

FName = GetFile(*"*.DB"*,*"Table:"*,*"Select a table."*,*""*,True)

GetPassword

GetPassword works like ACCEPT to accept data typed in from the keyboard, but does not display the characters. The general syntax for GetPassword is

GetPassword(*length*,*"display"*)

where *length* is the maximum length of the entry, and *display* is a character to be displayed each time a key is pressed. (*Display* may be set to " " to prevent any message from being displayed.)

In the example below, GetPassword allows the user to type in a password of up to ten characters in length. A space is displayed with each keypress, and the password is stored in a variable named MagicWord:

```
MagicWord = GetPassword(10," ")
```

InitWait

The InitWait procedure sets up the entire data-entry process, and must be called before DoWait is called to begin data entry. The general syntax for InitWait is

```
InitWait("script1","script2")
```

where *script1* is the name of the script created during the FieldDefine process and *script2* is the name of the script created during the KeyDefine process.

For example, the InitWait call shown below initializes data entry using field and key definitions in scripts named FldProcs and KeyProcs:

```
InitWait("FldProcs","KeyProcs")
```

LookupSelect

LookupSelect activates the HelpAndFill capability assigned to a field on the form. It is necessary to use LookupSelect in cases where you've assigned Special status to the F1 key, because without its Regular status, F1 will not automatically perform the HelpAndFill when pressed.

LookupSelect returns the value of the key pressed to leave the look-up table—either TKDO_IT! or TKCancel.

In the example below, if the user presses DO-IT! to exit the look-up table, then the procedure presses the DO-IT! key to complete the HelpAndFill, otherwise it just erases the look-up table from the screen.

```
LookSelect()
IF RetVal = TKDO_IT! THEN
    DO_IT!
ELSE
    ESC
ENDIF
```

NewField

Like ArriveField, NewField tells DoWait or RecurseWait that the cursor has moved to a new field on the form. Unlike ArriveField, however, NewField does not automatically execute an arrival procedure for that field, even if one has been defined in FieldDefine.

Popup

Popup displays a pop-up menu that has been defined with SetPopup. The general syntax for Popup is

Popup(*row,column,number,length*)

where *row* and *column* are the screen coordinates of the upper-left corner of the pop-up menu, *number* is a number assigned by SetPopup, and *length* is the number of items that the pop-up menu displays. If the *length* is less than the number of rows in the look-up table, the user can scroll within the pop-up menu to view other values.

A pop-up menu can display only the leftmost column in a table. The user's selection from the pop-up menu is stored in the Retval variable.

In the example below, if the cursor is in the field named Carrier, pop-up menu number one is displayed at row 2, column 54 on the screen. Six rows from the table are displayed within the pop-up menu. If the user does not select a value, the TKAccept variable is set to False, so that the pop-up menu is removed but the actual keystroke is ignored. If the user does make a selection, that value is stored in the current field ([ ]):

```
CASE FIELD() = "Carrier":
    POPUP(2,54,1,6)
```

```
IF ISBLANK(Retval) THEN
    TKAccept = False    ;No selection made
ELSE
    [] = Retval
ENDIF
```

RecurseWait

RecurseWait lets you perform a DoWait within an already active DoWait. In other words, it allows the user to temporarily enter data on a separate table, and then return to the original table.

RecurseWait uses the general syntax

RecurseWait(*"message",procedure name*)

where *message* is a message to display when RecurseWait takes control, and *procedure name* is the name of a procedure containing commands for redefining FieldDefine and KeyDefine for the new table.

RecurseWait returns the keystroke that the user typed in to leave the second table. It stores this value in Retval.

In the example below, the procedure named ChangeSpecs contains instructions for loading a new set of FieldDefine and KeyDefine definitions. The RecurseWait call displays no message, but activates the ChangeSpecs procedure to assign new field and key definitions on the new table.

```
PROC ChangeSpecs()
    PLAY "FldProc2"
    PLAY "KeyProc2"
ENDPROC

RecurseWait("",ChangeSpecs)
```

SetKeyCodes

SetKeyCodes is the procedure that actually assigns the TK key names to various keys on the keyboard (for example, TKDO_IT! and TKEsc). This procedure must be called before using TK key names in your custom procedure. The procedure may be released immediately to regain some memory, leaving only the actual key-name assignments in memory.

SetPopup

SetPopup assigns numbers to tables used in pop-up menus, and performs behind-the-scenes tasks necessary to prepare the menus. The number assigned to a table is defined by the table's position in the list of table names. For example, the call below sets up two pop-up menus, one for the table named Carriers and another for the table named Parts (the Popup calls activate the appropriate pop-up menu):

```
SetPopup("Carriers","Parts")
Popup(5,5,1,10)  ;Pop up the Carriers menu (#1)
Popup(10,5,2,6)  ;Pop up the Parts menu (#2)
```

TKDebug

Most errors in developing custom procedures in the Data Entry Toolkit occur when DoWait has lost track of the cursor. The TKDebug procedure can be used as the first command in a custom procedure to determine whether or not DoWait is aware of the field that the cursor is currently in. If DoWait does not know what field the cursor is in when a custom procedure is called, TKDebug will display a warning to this effect.

TKDebug should only be used as a debugging tool. When all custom procedures are working as expected, the TKDebug calls should be removed, as they will slow down processing considerably. The PrepareFinal option on the Data Entry Toolkit Main menu can remove TKDebug calls from a procedure file automatically.

CUSTOM DATA-ENTRY PROCEDURES

To develop custom procedures for a data-entry form, you need to create a script that defines each procedure and writes that procedure to a pre-parsed procedure library. You can use the PAL Scripts editor to create the procedures, or a word processor with the ability to store DOS text (ASCII) files.

In the sample application we're developing in this chapter, the custom procedures must be stored on the \ToolTest directory. If you have not done so already, be sure to log onto the directory before creating any scripts. (In Paradox, use the Tools, More, and Directory options to log onto the \ToolTest directory.)

We'll discuss individual procedures in the sections below, and present a complete listing of the entire custom procedure file later in the chapter.

AN ARRIVAL PROCEDURE EXAMPLE

The only arrival procedure (that is, a procedure that is executed the moment the cursor enters a field) defined for the sample application is TodaysDate, which is executed as soon as the cursor enters the Order Date field.

As you may recall, we used a ValCheck Default setting to make the Order Date field default to the current date. To simplify data entry even more, we'll have the custom procedure automatically leave the field after the current date is filled in automatically. The TodaysDate procedure is shown in Figure 21.10.

```
; This procedure will automatically put today's date
; into the Date field.
; Called upon arrival into the Date field.
PROC TodaysDate()
    IF ISBLANK([]) THEN
        IF TKChar=TKReverseTab OR TKChar=TKLeft THEN
            LEFT  ;move left if came from right
        ELSE
            RIGHT ;otherwise, move right.
        ENDIF
        ArriveField()  ;Tell DoWait we're in a new field.
    ENDIF
ENDPROC
WRITELIB "NewDemo" TodaysDate
RELEASE PROCS TodaysDate
```

Figure 21.10: The custom TodaysDate procedure

The procedure uses the ISBLANK function to determine if the current field is blank. If the field is blank, and the user arrives in the field by moving backwards (that is, by pressing ← on Shift-Tab), then the procedure simply presses the ← key to keep moving the cursor to the left. If the user did not enter the field backwards, the procedure presses the → key to move the cursor right one field. The ValCheck Default option places the date into the field.

Note that the ArriveField procedure is called after the cursor is moved with the LEFT or RIGHT key command. This is to alert DoWait to the fact that the cursor has indeed moved, even though the user did not press any key.

If the date is not blank when the cursor arrives, the procedure does not move the cursor at all. Instead, it leaves the cursor in the field so the user can change the date if he wishes. There is no need to call ArriveField in this situation, because the user will have to press a key to move out of the field, and DoWait will be aware of this keypress.

The command

WRITELIB "NewDemo" TodaysDate

will later write the TodaysDate procedure to a library named NewDemo.LIB, which is the library that the data-entry process will use.

The command

RELEASE PROCS TodaysDate

releases the TodaysDate procedure from memory after it is stored in the NewDemo.LIB library, to regain memory for other procedures.

A BAD DEPART PROCEDURE EXAMPLE

The only Bad Depart procedure we've defined is GetCarrier, which is executed if the user tries to leave the Carriers field with an invalid entry in it. The GetCarrier procedure is shown in Figure 21.11.

```
; Reject invalid carrier, offer popup menu to help.

PROC GetCarrier()
    TKMessage="Invalid!  Press [F1] for help"
ENDPROC
WRITELIB "NewDemo" GetCarrier
RELEASE PROCS GetCarrier
```

Figure 21.11: The GetCarrier procedure

GetCarrier is a very simple procedure that uses TKMessage to display a warning message when there is a Bad Depart from the Carriers field. (By definition, the cursor stays in the field from which the bad departure is attempted.) There is, however, a procedure within SpecialKeys (defined later) that handles the press on the F1 key that the message suggests. That procedure is shown in Figure 21.12.

```
;-- Help for Carrier field
CASE FIELD()="Carrier":
     POPUP(2,54,1,6)
     IF ISBLANK(Retval) THEN
        TKAccept=False       ;No selection made
     ELSE
        []=Retval
        TKChar=TKRight
     ENDIF
```

Figure 21.12: The routine to display the Carriers field pop-up menu

The routine, which is embedded within a larger SWITCH-
...ENDSWITCH clause, detects an F1 keypress when the cursor is
in the Carriers field, and displays pop-up menu number 1. If the user
selects a value from the pop-up menu, that value is stored in Retval
(otherwise, Retval is left blank). This procedure sets TKAccept to
False if the user does not make a selection from the menu. In a Bad
Depart procedure, setting TKAccept to False does not display an
error message, and allows departure from the field.

If the user does select an option from the pop-up menu, then
Retval is not blank, so the routine stores that value in the current field
([] = Retval), moves the cursor to the next field, and sets the TKChar
variable to → (TKChar = TKRight). Setting TKChar explicitly like
this tells DoWait to ignore the key that is pressed to select the item
from the pop-up menu, and instead to respond to the movement to
the next field.

GOOD DEPART PROCEDURES

There are several Good Depart procedures in the custom application, including Reqd, CustDone, NewDisc, GetPart, and
ChangeQty.

The Reqd Procedure

The Reqd procedure works in a manner similar to the ValCheck
Required setting, but is more specific to the application. It is activated whenever the user attempts to leave the Invoice No field. As
shown in Figure 21.13, the procedure checks to see whether the field
has been left blank (ISBLANK[]) and some key other than Delete,

UnDo, or the Cancel option from the menu has been used to leave the field. If this is the case, the routine ignores the keypress (TK-Accept = False), and displays the message

An invoice number must be provided.

```
;-- Mimics "Required" ValCheck, but less restrictive.
PROC Reqd()
   IF ISBLANK([]) AND TKChar<>TKDel
                   AND TKChar<>TKUndo
                   AND TKChar<>TKCancel THEN
      TKAccept=False      ;Ignore keypress.
      TKMessage="An invoice number must be provided."
   ENDIF
ENDPROC
WRITELIB "NewDemo" Reqd
RELEASE PROCS Reqd
```

Figure 21.13: The Reqd procedure

Note that in Good Depart procedures, setting TKAccept to False tells DoWait not to accept the keypress or allow departure from the field.

The CustDone Procedure

When the cursor is in the Customer Number field, the user has complete HelpAndFill capabilities, because of the ValCheck Table-Lookup assigned to the field earlier. Whenever the cursor leaves the Customer Number field, the calculations on the screen need to be recalculated if the customer number has been changed and a new discount rate is on the screen. The CustDone procedure, shown in Figure 21.14, takes care of this situation.

First of all, if the value in the Cust No field has not been changed at all, then the procedure simply returns control to DoWait, and nothing is recalculated. If the customer number has been changed, then several operations take place. First, ECHO OFF and SYNCCURSOR are used to bring the PAL Canvas to the screen without disrupting the cursor position.

The original discount value is stored in a variable named OldDisc as a value to compare to the discount rate associated with the new customer number. Next, the procedure checks to see what key was pressed to depart the field. If that key was → or Tab (TKRight or TKTab), the MOVETO command moves the cursor to the first Qty

```
; Called when leaving Customer No field.
PROC CustDone()
   IF NOT TKChanged OR TKChar=TKCancel THEN
      RETURN  ;Customer number unchanged.
   ENDIF
   ECHO OFF
   SYNCCURSOR
   OldDisc=[Discount]   ;Store original discount.
   IF TKChar=TKEnter OR TKChar=TKRight
                    OR TKChar=TKTab THEN
      MOVETO [Qty1]   ;Skip over the Discount field.
   ELSE
      KEYPRESS TKChar ;Otherwise move where specified.
   ENDIF
   ;-- If Discount changed, recalculate.
   IF OldDisc<>[Discount] THEN
      CalcTotal()
   ENDIF
   ArriveField()      ;Tell DoWait we've moved.
ENDPROC
WRITELIB "NewDemo" CustDone
RELEASE PROCS CustDone
```

Figure 21.14: The CustDone procedure

field, skipping over the Discount field on the way. If some other key was pressed, the KEYPRESS command just presses that key.

Next, a routine checks to see whether the Discount rate has changed. If it has, the procedure calls another custom script, called CalcTotal, to recalculate all the values on the screen. Before the procedure ends, it calls ArriveField to tell DoWait that the cursor has moved to a new field.

The NewDisc Procedure

The NewDisc procedure is called whenever the cursor leaves the Discount field. It checks to see whether the Discount rate has been changed, and if so, calls the CalcTotal procedure to recalculate the screen. Again, ECHO OFF and SYNCCURSOR are used to keep control of the cursor as the new values are written into the calculated fields. Figure 21.15 shows the NewDisc procedure.

The GetPart Procedure

The GetPart procedure is called whenever the cursor leaves a Part field (that is, Part1, Part2, Part3, Part4, Part5, or Part6). This procedure uses some advanced, tricky PAL techniques that deserve some discussion. The basic problem is that there are six fields that call the GetPart procedure; Part1 through Part6. The procedure needs to perform some basic calculations for the current Part field.

```
; Update calculations if Discount % changes.
PROC NewDisc()
   IF TKChanged THEN
       ECHO OFF
       SYNCCURSOR
       CalcTotal()
   ENDIF
ENDPROC
WRITELIB "NewDemo" NewDisc
RELEASE PROCS NewDisc
```

Figure 21.15: The NewDisc procedure

Rather than use a large SWITCH...ENDSWITCH clause to handle each particular Part, the procedure creates the appropriate field name on the spot. It does so using the PAL SUBSTR function to determine the number, 1 through 6, for the current field, and the PAL EXECUTE command to perform the appropriate calculations.

The SUBSTR function copies a smaller substring from a larger character string. It uses the basic syntax

SUBSTR(*string, start position, number of characters*)

where *string* is the larger string, *start position* is the starting position for the substring within the larger string, and *number of characters* is the number of characters to include in the substring.

In this example, the command

FldNo = SUBSTR(FIELD(),5,1)

is used to store the number at the end of the field name in a variable named FldNo. For example, when the cursor is in the Part1 field, the command executed is

FldNo = SUBSTR("Part1",5,1)

A substring of Part1 starting at the fifth character, that is one character long, is 1. (When the cursor is in the Part5 field, this substring will be 5.)

The EXECUTE command assembles pieces of a command into a whole, and *then* executes the assembled command. For example, if FldNo contains 1, then the command

EXECUTE "Qty = [Qty" + Fldno + "] "

assembles the pieces of the command into the command

Qty = [Qty1]

It then executes this assembled command, which in turn stores the value in the Qty1 field in a variable named Qty. If FldNo equals 5 (because the cursor is on the Part5 field), then the EXECUTE command stores the value in the Qty5 field, in the variable named Qty.

The GetPart procedure uses the EXECUTE command with the value stored in FldNo to perform several calculations. Note that if the part number is left blank (ISBLANK[ ]), then the script performs calculations that store the BLANKNUM() value in several fields. BLANKNUM() is a PAL function that is equivalent to a numeric field that has been left blank.

Figure 21.16 shows the GetPart procedure. The basic functions that it performs involve first determining whether the part number

```
; Pull in data from the MastInv table, and
; recalculate subtotal, tax, discount, and total.
; Called upon departure from all Part No fields.
PROC GetPart()
    IF TKChanged THEN
        ECHO OFF
        SYNCCURSOR
        Fldno=SUBSTR(FIELD(),5,1)
        EXECUTE "Qty=[Qty"+Fldno+"] "
        EXECUTE "OldExt=[ExtPrice"+Fldno+"]"
        IF ISBLANK([]) THEN ;Part number blank?
            EXECUTE "[PartName"+Fldno+"]=\"\" [Price"+
            Fldno+"]=BLANKNUM() [ExtPrice"+Fldno+
            "]=BLANKNUM()"
            IF NOT ISBLANK(OldExt) THEN
                [Subtotal]=[Subtotal]-OldExt
                CalcTotal()
            ENDIF
        ELSE
            Part=[] ;Part number has been changed.
            HELP        ;Bring up lookup table
            LOCATE Part ;Find part in lookup table
            PartName=[Part Name]
            Price=[Sel Price]
            ESC          ;Remove lookup table
            EXECUTE "[PartName"+Fldno+"]=PartName"
            EXECUTE "[Price"+Fldno+"]=Price"
            IF NOT ISBLANK(Qty) THEN
                CalcSubtotal()
            ENDIF ;not isblank
        ENDIF ;not isblank
    ENDIF ;isblank
ENDPROC
WRITELIB "NewDemo" GetPart
RELEASE PROCS GetPart
```

Figure 21.16: The GetPart procedure

has changed. If the number has changed, the procedure recalculates various formulas on the form.

If the part number has not changed while the cursor is in the field, then the routine stores the new value in a variable named Part (Part = []), and looks up the new part number in the Mastinv table by pressing the Help key and using the PAL LOCATE command to find the new part number. It then stores the new Part Name and Sel Price values on variables that are used to recalculate formulas on the form. The CalcTotal procedure, which we'll develop later, is called to perform the actual calculations.

The ChangeQty Procedure

The ChangeQty procedure is similar to the GetPart procedure in that it figures out which quantity has been changed (Qty1 through Qty6), and recalculates values on the screen accordingly. Like Get-Part, it uses SUBSTR and EXECUTE to determine which fields to recalculate. Figure 21.17 shows the ChangeQty procedure.

```
; When leaving Qty fields, update calculations if necessary.
PROC ChangeQty()
    IF TKChanged THEN
        Fldno=SUBSTR(FIELD(),4,1)
        EXECUTE "Price=[Price"+Fldno+"]"
        EXECUTE "OldExt=[ExtPrice"+Fldno+"]"
        IF ISBLANK([]) THEN    ;Has Qty been removed?
            ECHO OFF
            SYNCCURSOR
            EXECUTE "[ExtPrice"+Fldno+"]=BLANKNUM()"
            IF NOT ISBLANK(OldExt) THEN
                [Subtotal]=[Subtotal]-OldExt
                CalcTotal()
            ENDIF
        ELSE
            IF NOT ISBLANK(Price) THEN
                ECHO OFF
                SYNCCURSOR
                Qty=[]
                CalcSubtotal()
            ENDIF
        ENDIF
    ENDIF
ENDPROC
WRITELIB "NewDemo" ChangeQty
RELEASE PROCS ChangeQty
```

Figure 21.17: The ChangeQty procedure

KEYSTROKE PROCEDURES

The SpecialKey procedure in the custom application is called whenever a special key, defined as F1 and F10 in this application, is

```
;-- Handle special keys F1 and F10.
PROC SpecialKey()
    SWITCH
    CASE TKChar=TKHelp:        ;Help key pressed.

        SWITCH
        ;-- Help for the Cust No field.
        CASE FIELD()="Cust No":
            OldDisc=[discount]
            HELP
            LookupSelect()
            IF Retval=TKDo_It! THEN
                Do_It!
                Moveto [Qty1]
                IF OldDisc<>[Discount] THEN
                    CalcTotal()
                ENDIF
                ArriveField()  ;New field.
            ELSE
                ESC
                TKAccept=False      ;No help allowed here.
            ENDIF
        ;-- Help for a part no field.
        CASE MATCH(FIELD(),"Part@",Fldno):
            HELP
            LookupSelect() ;Lookup MastInv data.
            IF Retval=TKDo_It! THEN
                Part=[Part No]
                PartName=[Part Name]
                Price=[Sel Price]
                ESC          ;Exit from lookup help
                EXECUTE "Qty=[Qty"+Fldno+"]"
                EXECUTE "OldExt=[ExtPrice"+Fldno+"]"
                EXECUTE "[Part"+Fldno+"]=Part"
                EXECUTE "[PartName"+Fldno+"]=PartName"
                EXECUTE "[Price"+Fldno+"]=Price"
                IF NOT ISBLANK(Qty) THEN
                    CalcSubtotal()
                ENDIF
                RIGHT                ;Move into next field
                ArriveField()     ;(Tell DoWait)
            ELSE
                ESC
                TKAccept=False    ;No help key here.
            ENDIF
        ;-- Help for Carrier field
        CASE FIELD()="Carrier":
            POPUP(2,54,1,6)
            IF ISBLANK(Retval) THEN
                TKAccept=False      ;No selection made
            ELSE
                []=Retval
                TKChar=TKRight
            ENDIF
        ENDSWITCH

    ;--- F10 key was pressed.
    CASE TKChar=TKMenu:
        EditMenu()        ;Display editing menu.
    ENDSWITCH
ENDPROC
WRITELIB "NewDemo" SpecialKey
RELEASE PROCS SpecialKey
```

Figure 21.18: The SpecialKey procedure

pressed. (These were designated as SpecialKeys during the KeyDefine phase of development.) The SpecialKey procedure is shown in Figure 21.18.

The SpecialKey procedure determines whether F10 or F1 is pressed. If F1 is pressed, a SWITCH...ENDSWITCH clause reacts accordingly, depending on which field the cursor is in when F1 is pressed.

If the cursor is in the Cust No field when F1 is pressed (CASE FIELD() = "Cust No"), then the LookupSelect function is called to allow the user to select a customer number from the Customer table. (The ValCheck TableLookup option sets up Customer as the look-up table for the Cust No field.)

If the cursor is in a Part field when F1 is pressed (CASE MATCH-(FIELD(),"Part@",Fldno)), then LookupSelect is called to let the user select a part number from the Mastinv table. Again, the Val-Check TableLookup options were selected earlier to assign Mastinv as the look-up table for the Part fields (Part1 through Part6).

Because there are six part fields, the CASE statement for this field uses the PAL MATCH function to determine if the cursor is in a Part field. MATCH returns True if the first argument matches the second argument, and also allows the wild-card characters .. and @, just as queries do. Arguments beyond the first two are variable names, in which MATCH will store elements that match any wild-card characters.

For example, if the cursor is in the field name Part6, then the expression

```
MATCH(FIELD(), "Part@", Fldno)
```

first of all returns True because *Part6* matches *Part@* (because @ matches *any* single character). Furthermore, the variable named FldNo receives the value 6, as this is the element that was matched by the @ wild-card character.

If the cursor is in the Carrier field when F1 is pressed, then the

```
CASE FIELD() = "Carrier"
```

routine displays a pop-up menu of carriers for the user to select from. (This routine was discussed earlier in the chapter—see Figure 21.12.)

If F10 (TKMenu) is pressed, the procedure simply calls the Edit-Menu function to display the edit menu.

MISCELLANEOUS PROCEDURES

There are two procedures in the custom procedure file that are not classified as either Arrival, Good Depart, Bad Depart, or even Keystroke procedures. Rather, these are general-purpose procedures to perform calculations. They are named CalcTotal and CalcSubtotal, and they serve to calculate values that are displayed on the screen. They are called by other procedures within the procedure file whenever some value changes, requiring formulas to be recalculated. These procedures are included in the NewDemo.SC script shown in Figure 21.19.

THE INITIALIZATION PROCEDURE

All Toolkit data-entry forms need to execute an initialization procedure to initialize the Toolkit. In the sample application in this chapter, this procedure is named DataEntry and is the first procedure listed in NewDemo.SC in Figure 21.19. The steps it performs are the same basic steps any application would use for initialization. First, it uses the PAL READLIB command to read in custom procedures from the custom library, and it also uses READLIB to read in procedures from the Toolkit.LIB file (whose name is automatically stored in a variable named TKLibName).

NewDemo.SC then empties the table that is used to store new records (OrdEntry.SC in this example) using the PAL EMPTY command, and puts the OrdEntry table into EDIT mode to begin adding data. In this example, the PICKFORM 1 command specifies the custom form we developed for data entry, the PROMPT command displays opening instructions, and then DoWait is called to initiate and oversee the entire data-entry process.

When data entry is complete (that is, when the user exits), DoWait gives up control, the PROMPT command erases the prompt on the screen, and the RELEASE PROCS command releases all the procedures stored in memory to make room for other operations.

Figure 21.19 shows the entire NewDemo.SC procedure. DataEntry is the first listed procedure. Once you have keyed in the entire NewDemo.SC procedure (on the \ToolTest directory in this example), you need to use the Paradox Scripts and Play options to play the procedure, so that it will create the NewDemo.LIB procedure file that the data entry is dependent on.

```
;---------------------------------------- NewDemo.SC
;------- Build procedure library for order entry form.

;-- New library is named NewDemo.LIB.
CREATELIB "NewDemo"

PROC DataEntry()
    READLIB "NewDemo" Reqd,TodaysDate,CustDone,NewDisc,
                      GetPart,ChangeQty,CalcTotal,
                      CalcSubtotal,GetCarrier,
                      SpecialKey
    READLIB TKLibName EditMenu,LookupSelect
    EMPTY "OrdEntry"
    EDIT "OrdEntry"

    PICKFORM "1"
    PROMPT "Entering invoice information.",
        "[F1] = Help, [F2] = Exit, [F10] = Menu."
    DoWait("")
    PROMPT          ;Clear the custom prompt.
    ;--- Release procedures when data entry complete.
    RELEASE PROCS Reqd,TodaysDate,CustDone,NewDisc,
                  GetPart,ChangeQty,CalcTotal,
                  CalcSubtotal,GetCarrier,
                  SpecialKey,EditMenu,LookupSelect
ENDPROC
WRITELIB "NewDemo" DataEntry
RELEASE PROCS DataEntry

;-- Mimics "Required" ValCheck, but less restrictive.
PROC Reqd()
    IF ISBLANK([]) AND TKChar<>TKDel
                    AND TKChar<>TKUndo
                    AND TKChar<>TKCancel THEN
        TKAccept=False      ;Ignore keypress.
        TKMessage="An invoice number must be provided."
    ENDIF
ENDPROC
WRITELIB "NewDemo" Reqd
RELEASE PROCS Reqd

; This procedure will automatically put today's date
; into the Date field.
; Called upon arrival into the Date field.
PROC TodaysDate()
    IF ISBLANK([]) THEN
        IF TKChar=TKReverseTab OR TKChar=TKLeft THEN
            LEFT  ;move left if came from right
        ELSE
            RIGHT ;otherwise, move right.
        ENDIF
        ArriveField()  ;Tell DoWait we're in a new field.
    ENDIF
ENDPROC
WRITELIB "NewDemo" TodaysDate
RELEASE PROCS TodaysDate

; Called when leaving Customer No field.
PROC CustDone()
    IF NOT TKChanged OR TKChar=TKCancel THEN
        RETURN  ;Customer number unchanged.
    ENDIF
    ECHO OFF
    SYNCCURSOR
    OldDisc=[Discount]    ;Store original discount.
    IF TKChar=TKEnter OR TKChar=TKRight
                       OR TKChar=TKTab THEN
        MOVETO [Qty1]  ;Skip over the Discount field.
    ELSE
        KEYPRESS TKChar ;Otherwise move where specified.
    ENDIF
    ;-- If Discount changed, recalculate.
```

Figure 21.19: The complete NewDemo.SC script

```
        IF OldDisc<>[Discount] THEN
           CalcTotal()
        ENDIF
        ArriveField()        ;Tell DoWait we've moved.
    ENDPROC
    WRITELIB "NewDemo" CustDone
    RELEASE PROCS CustDone

    ; Reject invalid carrier, offer popmenu to help.
    PROC GetCarrier()
        TKMessage="Invalid!  Press [F1] for help"
    ENDPROC
    WRITELIB "NewDemo" GetCarrier
    RELEASE PROCS GetCarrier

    ; Pull in data from the MastInv table, and
    ; recalculate subtotal, tax, discount, and total.
    ; Called upon departure from all Part No fields.
    PROC GetPart()
        IF TKChanged THEN
           ECHO OFF
           SYNCCURSOR
           Fldno=SUBSTR(FIELD(),5,1)
           EXECUTE "Qty=[Qty"+Fldno+"] "
           EXECUTE "OldExt=[ExtPrice"+Fldno+"]"
           IF ISBLANK([])  THEN ;Part number blank?
              EXECUTE "[PartName"+Fldno+"]=\"\" [Price"+
              Fldno+"]=BLANKNUM() [ExtPrice"+Fldno+
              "]=BLANKNUM()"
              IF NOT ISBLANK(OldExt)  THEN
                 [Subtotal]=[Subtotal]-OldExt
                 CalcTotal()
              ENDIF
           ELSE Part=[]  ;Part number has been changed.
              HELP         ;Bring up lookup table
              LOCATE Part ;Find part in lookup table
              PartName=[Part Name]
              Price=[Sel Price]
              ESC          ;Remove lookup table
              EXECUTE "[PartName"+Fldno+"]=PartName"
              EXECUTE "[Price"+Fldno+"]=Price"
              IF NOT ISBLANK(Qty) THEN
                 CalcSubtotal()
              ENDIF ;not isblank
           ENDIF ;not isblank
        ENDIF ;isblank
    ENDPROC
    WRITELIB "NewDemo" GetPart
    RELEASE PROCS GetPart

    ; When leaving Qty fields, update
    ; calculations if necessary.
    PROC ChangeQty()
        IF TKChanged THEN
           Fldno=SUBSTR(FIELD(),4,1)
           EXECUTE "Price=[Price"+Fldno+"]"
           EXECUTE "OldExt=[ExtPrice"+Fldno+"]"
           IF ISBLANK([]) THEN    ;Has Qty been removed?
              ECHO OFF
              SYNCCURSOR
              EXECUTE "[ExtPrice"+Fldno+"]=BLANKNUM()"
              IF NOT ISBLANK(OldExt) THEN
                 [Subtotal]=[Subtotal]-OldExt
                 CalcTotal()
              ENDIF
           ELSE
              IF NOT ISBLANK(Price) THEN
                 ECHO OFF
                 SYNCCURSOR
                 Qty=[]
                 CalcSubtotal()
              ENDIF
           ENDIF
        ENDIF
```

Figure 21.19: The complete NewDemo.SC script (continued)

```
ENDPROC
WRITELIB "NewDemo" ChangeQty
RELEASE PROCS ChangeQty
; This procedure updates tax and total information.
PROC CalcTotal()
    IF ISBLANK([Subtotal]) THEN
        [Subtotal]=0
    ENDIF
    IF ISBLANK([Discount]) THEN
        [Discount $]=0
    ELSE
        [Discount $]=[Subtotal]*([Discount]/100)
    ENDIF
    [Tax]=([Subtotal]-[Discount $])*TaxRate
    [Total]=[Subtotal]-[Discount $]+[Tax]
ENDPROC
WRITELIB "NewDemo" CalcTotal
RELEASE PROCS CalcTotal


; Fills in the extened price field with correct value.
; Called whenever Part No or Qty is changed.
PROC CalcSubtotal()
    IF ISBLANK([Subtotal]) THEN
        [Subtotal]=0
    ENDIF
    NewExt=Price*Qty
    EXECUTE "[ExtPrice"+Fldno+"]=NewExt"
    IF ISBLANK(OldExt) THEN
        [Subtotal]=[Subtotal]+NewExt
    ELSE
        [Subtotal]=[Subtotal]+NewExt-OldExt
    ENDIF
    CalcTotal()         ;Update calculations.
ENDPROC
WRITELIB "NewDemo" CalcSubtotal
RELEASE PROCS CalcSubtotal


; Update calculations if Discount % changes.
PROC NewDisc()
    IF TKChanged THEN
        ECHO OFF
        SYNCCURSOR
        CalcTotal()
    ENDIF
ENDPROC
WRITELIB "NewDemo" NewDisc
RELEASE PROCS NewDisc

;-- Handle special keys F1 and F10.
PROC SpecialKey()
    SWITCH
    CASE TKChar=TKHelp:     ;Help key pressed.
    SWITCH
    ;-- Help for the Cust No field.
    CASE FIELD()="Cust No":
        OldDisc=[discount]
        HELP
        LookupSelect()
        IF Retval=TKDo_It! THEN
            Do_It!
            Moveto [Qty1]
            IF OldDisc<>[Discount] THEN
                CalcTotal()
            ENDIF
            ArriveField()  ;New field.
        ELSE
            ESC
            TKAccept=False      ;No help allowed here.
        ENDIF
```

Figure 21.19: The complete NewDemo.SC script (continued)

```
;-- Help for a part no field.
CASE MATCH(FIELD(),"Part@",Fldno):
    HELP
    LookupSelect()  ;Lookup MastInv data.
    IF Retval=TKDo_It! THEN
        Part=[Part No]
        PartName=[Part Name]
        Price=[Sel Price]
        ESC          ;Exit from lookup help
        EXECUTE "Qty=[Qty"+Fldno+"]"
        EXECUTE "OldExt=[ExtPrice"+Fldno+"]"
        EXECUTE "[Part"+Fldno+"]=Part"
        EXECUTE "[PartName"+Fldno+"]=PartName"
        EXECUTE "[Price"+Fldno+"]=Price"
        IF NOT ISBLANK(Qty) THEN
            CalcSubtotal()
        ENDIF
        RIGHT              ;Move into next field
        ArriveField()     ;(Tell DoWait)
    ELSE
        ESC
        TKAccept=False    ;No help key here.
    ENDIF
;-- Help for Carrier field
CASE FIELD()="Carrier":
    POPUP(2,54,1,6)
    IF ISBLANK(Retval) THEN
        TKAccept=False      ;No selection made
    ELSE
        []=Retval
        TKChar=TKRight
    ENDIF
ENDSWITCH
;--- F10 key was pressed.
CASE TKChar=TKMenu:
EditMenu()         ;Display editing menu.
ENDSWITCH
ENDPROC
WRITELIB "NewDemo" SpecialKey
RELEASE PROCS SpecialKey
```

Figure 21.19: The complete NewDemo.SC script (continued)

A PROCEDURE TO RUN THE COMPLETED APPLICATION

After you have completed all other steps in the Data Entry Toolkit development cycle, you can create another script to try out the finished product. The procedure that actually presents the data entry to the user needs to have access to both the custom .LIB file you created and the Toolkit.LIB file. In the sample application, I have developed a script named RunDemo.SC on the \ToolTest directory to run the entire data-entry process. The script is shown in Figure 21.20.

```
;------------------------------------- RunDemo.SC
; Begin by initializing DOWAIT command.
READLIB "Toolkit" InitWait,SetKeycodes,SetPopup

;---Play definition scripts.
InitWait("FldProcs","KeyProcs")
SetKeycodes() ;-- Set up key codes.
SetPopup("Carriers")

;- Initialization procedures no longer needed.
RELEASE PROCS InitWait,SetKeycodes,SetPopup

TaxRate=.06    ;Current sales tax rate is 6%)

;----- Begin data entry.
READLIB "NewDemo" DataEntry
DataEntry()    ;-- Play the data entry script.

;----- Done entering data.
DO_IT!
CLEAR
CLEARALL

;-- Post from OrdEntry to Orders table.
STYLE BLINK,REVERSE
@ 10,22
?? "Posting newly added transactions..."
PLAY "OrdPost"
DO_IT!
CLEARALL
;-- Delete blank posted records.
PLAY "CleanUp"
DO_IT!
STYLE
CLEARALL
;- SORT below helps you see the results more clearly.
SORT "Orders"
VIEW "Orders"
```

Figure 21.20: The RunDemo.SC script

RunDemo.SC begins by initializing the Data Entry Toolkit, as your own applications must. It does this by reading the necessary built-in procedures into the memory using the READLIB command. It then calls the InitWait procedure to activate FldProcs and KeyProcs, the scripts we developed with the FieldDefine and KeyDefine options on the Toolkit menu.

Next, it plays the SetKeyCodes script, which loads the TK keynames into memory, and the SetPopup script to define Carriers as the table for the pop-up menu. Once these basic initialization procedures are complete, the RELEASE PROCS command releases them from memory, as they are no longer needed; only the data they leave behind in memory is needed.

A variable named TaxRate is created in the RunDemo script to define the tax rate for calculations on the screen. Then a READLIB command reads in the DataEntry procedure from the custom procedure library. The DataEntry procedure is called, allowing the user to enter data until he selects Exit. This single call to DataEntry is all that is required at this point to run the entire data-entry process, including all calculations, pop-up menus, and custom procedures, and everything else that has been previously defined throughout the development process.

POSTING THE ENTERED DATA

One last step that usually needs to be completed concerns storing the entered data on the appropriate tables. In this example, the OrdEntry table is used for entering data, but this table exists only to support the complicated data-entry form. The Orders table actually stores orders in this sample application, so a routine to copy records from OrdEntry into Orders is necessary when data entry is complete.

Two QuerySaves are used to perform the Posting process. You can create these by running Paradox in the usual manner, and using Tools, More, and Directory to log onto the \ToolTest directory. From the Main menu, select Ask to query the OrdEntry table, and place examples (using the F5 key) into the fields to be copied. Table 21.4 shows which example to put into which field on the query forms. (Don't forget to press F5 before typing in each example.)

After entering the examples in the OrdEntry query form, call up the menu (F10), select Ask, and query the Orders table. Enter the numbers 1 through 6 into six different rows of the Line field in the query form, and the command **Insert** in the left column of each row. Then enter examples, as shown in the bottom query form in Figure 21.21, using the Example (F5) key.

The Insert command in the left column of the Orders query form causes records from the OrdEntry form to be inserted into the Orders table. When you've filled out the two query forms, call up the menu once again, select Scripts and QuerySave, and specify **OrdPost** as the name of the file to save. Then press DO-IT! to complete the query. (There will probably be no result at this stage, because the OrdEntry table is probably empty.)

The one drawback to the OrdPost query form is that it inserts blank records (such as records for Part5 and Part 6 when only four parts were entered) into the Orders form. These can easily be deleted using a delete query. To create the deletion query, call up the menu, select Ask, and specify Orders as the table to query. Place the command **Delete** in the leftmost column, and the command **Blank** in the Part No column (don't use the Example key in either case). Figure 21.22 shows the completed query form.

FIELD	EXAMPLE
Invoice No	Inv
Order Date	ODate
Carrier	Carry
Cust No	CustNo
Part1	Part1
Qty1	Qty1
Price1	Price1
Part2	Part2
Qty2	Qty2
Price2	Price2
Part3	Part3
Qty3	Qty3
Price3	Price3
Part4	Part4
Qty4	Qty4
Price4	Price4
Part5	Part5
Qty5	Qty5
Price5	Price5
Part6	Part6
Qty6	Qty6
Price6	Price6

Table 21.4: Examples entered into the OrdEntry query form

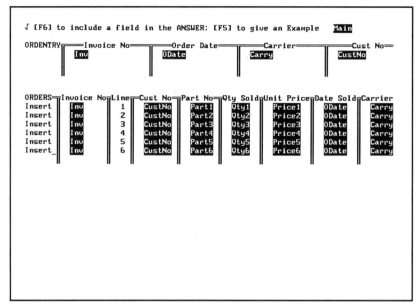

Figure 21.21: Query forms for posting order

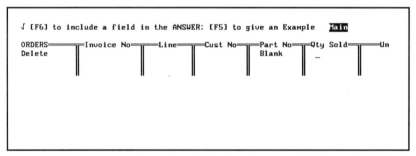

Figure 21.22: The query form for deleting blank records

After filling in the query form, call up the menu, select Scripts and QuerySave, and enter the file name **Cleanup** when prompted. Then you can press DO-IT! to clear the query form from the screen.

The RunDemo.SC script plays these two query forms automatically when data entry is completed. It is also set up to displays the Orders table automatically, sorted by invoice number, so you can verify that all the records that you entered through the custom form were eventually added to the Orders table.

RUNNING THE NEW DEMO PROGRAM

To experiment with the Data Entry application we've developed in this chapter, run Paradox in the usual manner, and select Tools, More, and Directory from the Main menu. Specify ToolTest as the new directory. Then, select Scripts and Play from the Main menu, and RunDemo as the name of the application to play. If you've successfully completed every step in the process, you'll see the data-entry form appear on the screen, as in Figure 21.23.

Many of the same basic techniques that work with the Demonstration table discussed earlier in this chapter will work here, such as automatic date fill-in, a pop-up menu for the Carriers field, HelpAndFill on the Customer Number and Part Number fields, and all of the various calculations. (This example does not, however, allow new records to be added to the Customer table on the fly. The MakeDemo.SC script, on the \PARADOX2\detool subdirectory, has several procedures that demonstrate how to add that feature to a data-entry form.)

```
Entering invoice information.
[F1] = Help, [F2] = Exit, [F10] = Menu.
┌─────────────────────────────────────────────────────────────────┐
│ Invoice number: _        ◄ Order Date:         Carrier:          │
├─────────────────────────────┬───────────────────────────────────┤
│ Customer:                   │                                   │
│ (F1 for help)               │                                   │
│                             │                                   │
│ Discount Rate:        %     │                                   │
├─────────────────────────────┴───────────────────────────────────┤
│          Part                                                    │
│ Quantity  Number   Part Name      Unit Price     Extended Price  │
│                                                                  │
│                                                                  │
│                                                                  │
│                                                                  │
├──────────────┬──────────────┬──────────────┬────────────────────┤
│  Subtotal    │  Discount $   │    Tax       │      Total         │
└──────────────┴──────────────┴──────────────┴────────────────────┘
```

Figure 21.23: The custom data-entry form

When you've finished entering one record, and are ready to enter another, you can just press Return or ↓ to scroll past the last field on the form. When you've finished entering records altogether, press the DO-IT! key.

You'll see a flashing message as the posting process takes place. Then you'll see the Orders table, sorted by Invoice Number, which displays any records you have added using the data-entry form.

MORE ADVANCED DATA ENTRY TOOLKIT EXAMPLES

The examples in this chapter are patterned after the examples presented in the MakeDemo.SC script, which creates the Demonstration data-entry form that you run from the Data Entry Toolkit Main menu. You can use the PAL Scripts editor or any word processor to print a copy of \PARADOX2\detool\MakeDemo.SC. Hopefully the examples in this chapter will make it easier for you to understand the more complex examples presented in MakeDemo.SC. Also, Chapter 22 of the *PAL User's Guide* that comes with your Paradox package discusses the Data Entry Toolkit.

SUMMARY

This chapter discusses the Data Entry Toolkit, which is perhaps the most advanced feature in the entire Paradox/PAL package. The Toolkit lets experienced PAL programmers develop highly sophisticated forms for entering data. The general steps for using the Data Entry Toolkit are summarized below:

- Create tables for the Toolkit using the usual Create option from the Paradox Main menu. These tables include the usual data tables, plus any special tables for look-ups and a source table for the data-entry form.

- Use the ValCheck option on the Paradox Edit menu to assign validity checks to tables, particularly the source table that the data-entry form is to be attached to.

- You can use the HelpForm option on the Data Entry Toolkit menu to design a data-entry form with overlapping borders and special graphics characters.

- Use the Data Entry Toolkit FieldDefine option to assign names of custom procedures to any of four types of events that occur in any field on the form: Arrival, Good Departure, Bad Departure, and Keystroke.

- Use the Data Entry Toolkit KeyDefine option to categorize keys as Regular, Special, Exit, or Illegal.

- Develop custom procedures to handle events on the data-entry form, using procedure names defined during FieldDefine.

- Include with your custom procedures a procedure to handle any keys that you've categorized as Special in KeyDefine.

- Your custom procedures may also access any of 13 Toolkit built-in procedures, and a number of special TK variables.

- Assemble your custom scripts into a procedure library using the PAL CREATLIB and WRITELIB commands.

- Write a script to access the Toolkit and custom procedures to activate the data-entry form.

APPENDICES

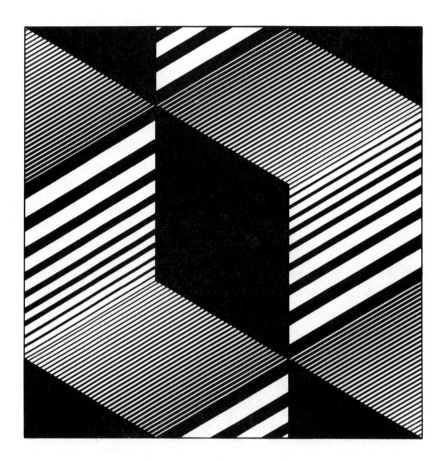

KEYS USED IN TABLE VIEW

Up one record
First record of table
Up one screen
Right one field
Right one screen
Down one screen
Down one record
Delete record
Insert new record
Last field of record
Last record of table
Left one screen
Left one field
First field of record

7 8 9
Home ↑ PgUp
Ctrl-Home
4 5 6
← →
Ctrl-← Ctrl-→
1 2 3
End ↓ PgDn
Ctrl-End
0 .
Ins Del

FUNCTION	*KEY*
First record of table	Home
First field of record	Ctrl-Home

Left one field	←
Left one screen	Ctrl-←
Last record of table	End
Last field of record	Ctrl-End
Right one field	→
Right one screen	Ctrl-→
Up one record	↑
Up one screen	PgUp
Down one record	↓
Down one screen	PgDn
Insert new record	Ins
Delete record	Del

APPENDIX B

KEYS USED IN FORM VIEW

First record of table
First field of current record
Previous field (left or up)
Last record of table
Last field of current record
Next field (right or down)
Up one field
Down one field
Previous page or record
Same field of previous record
Next page or record
Same field of next record
Insert new record
Delete record

7 8 9
Home ↑ PgUp
Ctrl-Home Ctrl-PgUp
4 5 6
← →
1 2 3
End ↓ PgDn
Ctrl-End Ctrl-PgDn
0 .
Ins Del

FUNCTION	*KEY*
First record of table	Home
First field of current record	Ctrl-Home
Previous field (left or up)	←

Last record of table	End
Last field of current record	Ctrl-End
Next field (right or down)	→
Up one field	↑
Down one field	↓
Previous page or record	PgUp
Same field of previous record	Ctrl-PgUp
Next page or record	PgDn
Same field of next record	Ctrl-PgDn
Insert new record	Ins
Delete record	Del

APPENDIX *C*

KEYS USED IN FIELD VIEW

Left one word
Right one word
First character of field
Last character of field
Left one character
Right one character
Delete character at cursor
Up one line on wrapped fields
Down one line on wrapped fields
Turn Insert mode on/off

```
7 8 9
Home ↑ PgUp
4 5 6
← →
1 2 3
End ↓ PgDn
0 .
Ins Del
Ctrl-←
Ctrl-→
```

FUNCTION	*KEY*
First character of field	Home
Last character of field	End
Left one character	←
Right one character	→
Delete character at cursor	Del
Left one word	Ctrl-←

Right one word	Ctrl-→
Up one line	↑
Down one line	↓
Insert mode on/off	Ins

KEYS USED IN REPORT/FORM/SCRIPT EDITOR

First line
Beginning of line
Left one character
Left one-half screen
Last line
End of line
Right one character
Right one-half screen
Up one line
Up one screen
Down one line
Down one screen
Begin or end Insert mode
Delete character at cursor

```
7  8  9
Home ↑ PgUp
Ctrl-Home
4  5  6
←  →
Ctrl-←  Ctrl-→
1  2  3
End ↓ PgDn
Ctrl-End
0  .
Ins  Del
```

FUNCTION	KEY
First line	Home
Beginning of line	Ctrl-Home

Left one character	←
Left one-half screen	Ctrl-←
Last line	End
End of line	Ctrl-End
Right one character	→
Right one-half screen	Ctrl-→
Up one line	↑
Up one screen	PgUp
Down one line	↓
Down one screen	PgDn
Begin or end Insert mode	Ins
Delete character at cursor	Del

INDEX

Selections from The SYBEX Library

* Indicates forthcoming titles.

Mastering Reflex
Robert Ericson/Ann Moskol
336pp. Ref. 348-1
A complete introduction to Reflex: The Analyst, with hands-on tutorials and sample applications for management, finance, and technical uses. Special emphasis on its unique capabilities for crosstabbing, graphics, reporting, and more.

dBASE III PLUS Programmer's Reference Guide
(SYBEX Ready Reference Series)
Alan Simpson
1056pp. Ref. 382-1
Programmers will save untold hours and effort using this comprehensive, well-organized dBASE encyclopedia. Complete technical details on commands and functions, plus scores of often-needed algorithms.

The ABC's of dBASE III PLUS
Robert Cowart
264pp. Ref. 379-1
The most efficient way to get beginners up and running with dBASE. Every 'how' and 'why' of database management is demonstrated through tutorials and practical dBASE III PLUS applications.

Mastering dBASE III PLUS:
A Structured Approach
Carl Townsend
342pp. Ref. 372-4
In-depth treatment of structured programming for custom dBASE solutions. An ideal study and reference guide for applications developers, new and experienced users with an interest in efficient programming.

Also:
Mastering dBASE III: A Structured Approach
Carl Townsend
338pp. Ref. 301-5

Understanding dBASE III PLUS
Alan Simpson
415pp. Ref. 349-X
A solid sourcebook of training and ongoing support. Everything from creating a first database to command file programming is presented in working examples, with tips and techniques you won't find anywhere else.

Also:
Understanding dBASE III
Alan Simpson
300pp. Ref. 267-1

Understanding dBASE II
Alan Simpson
260pp. Ref. 147-0

Advanced Techniques in dBASE III PLUS
Alan Simpson
454pp. Ref. 369-4
A full course in database design and structured programming, with routines for inventory control, accounts receivable, system management, and integrated databases.

Also:
Advanced Techniques in dBASE III
Alan Simpson
505pp. Ref.282-5

Advanced Techniques in dBASE II
Alan Simpson
395pp. Ref. 228-0

Simpson's dBASE Tips and Tricks (For dBASE III PLUS)
Alan Simpson
420pp. Ref. 383-X
A unique library of techniques and programs shows how creative use of built-in features can solve all your needs – without expensive add-on products or external languages. Spreadsheet functions, graphics, and much more.

Simpsons's dBASE III Library
Alan Simpson
362pp. Ref. 300-7
A goldmine of techniques and ready-made programs to expand the off-the-shelf power of dBASE. Includes tutorials on command file programming, plus routines for finance, statistics, graphics, screens, oversize databases, and much more.

Expert dBASE III PLUS
Judd Robbins/Ken Braly
423pp. Ref. 404-6
Experienced dBASE programmers learn scores of advanced techniques for maximizing performance and efficiency in program design, development and testing, database design, indexing, input and output, using compilers, and much more.

Understanding R:BASE System V
Alan Simpson
499pp. Ref. 394-5
This complete tutorial guide covers every R:BASE function, while exploring and illustrating the principles of efficient database design. Examples include inventory management, mailing list handling, and much more.

Also:

Understanding R:BASE 5000
Alan Simpson
413pp. Ref. 302-3

Power User's Guide to R:BASE System V*
Alan Simpson
350pp. Ref. 354-6

A tutorial guide to structured programming in R:BASE, including system design, procedure files, performance issues and managing multiple data tables. With complete working systems for mailing list, inventory and accounts receivable.

SPREADSHEETS AND INTEGRATED SOFTWARE

The ABC's of 1-2-3 (Second Edition)
Chris Gilbert/Laurie Williams
245pp. Ref. 355-4
Online Today recommends it as "an easy and comfortable way to get started with the program." An essential tutorial for novices, it will remain on your desk as a valuable source of ongoing reference and support. For Release 2.

Mastering 1-2-3
Carolyn Jorgensen
466pp. Ref. 337-6
Get the most from 1-2-3 Release 2 with this step-by-step guide emphasizing advanced features and practical uses. Topics include data sharing, macros, spreadsheet security, expanded memory, and graphics enhancements.

Lotus 1-2-3 Desktop Companion (SYBEX Ready Reference Series)
Greg Harvey
976pp. Ref. 385-6
A full-time consultant, right on your desk. Hundreds of self-contained entries cover every 1-2-3 feature, organized by topic, indexed and cross-referenced, and supplemented by tips, macros and working examples. For Release 2.

Power User's Guide to Lotus 1-2-3*
Pete Antoniak/E. Michael Lunsford
400pp. Ref. 421-6
This guide for experienced users focuses on advanced functions, and techniques for designing menu-driven applications using macros and the Release 2 command

language. Interfacing techniques and add-on products are also considered.

Lotus 1-2-3 Book of Style*
Tim K. Nguyen
350pp. Ref. 454-2

For users of 1-2-3 who want a definite and comprehensive guide to writing 1-2-3 spreadsheets in a stylistically correct and acceptable way. Lots of examples show how to create models that are powerful and efficient, yet easily understandable.

Also:
Advanced Techniques in dBASE III
Alan Simpson
505pp. Ref.282-5

Advanced Techniques in dBASE II
Alan Simpson
395pp. Ref. 228-0

Simpson's dBASE Tips and Tricks (For dBASE III PLUS)
Alan Simpson
420pp. Ref. 383-X

A unique library of techniques and programs shows how creative use of built-in features can solve all your needs—without expensive add-on products or external languages. Spreadsheet functions, graphics, and much more.

Simpsons's dBASE III Library
Alan Simpson
362pp. Ref. 300-7

A goldmine of techniques and ready-made programs to expand the off-the-shelf power of dBASE. Includes tutorials on command file programming, plus routines for finance, statistics, graphics, screens, oversize databases, and much more.

Expert dBASE III PLUS
Judd Robbins/Ken Braly
423pp. Ref. 404-6

Experienced dBASE programmers learn scores of advanced techniques for maximizing performance and efficiency in program design, development and testing, database design, indexing, input and output, using compilers, and much more.

Understanding R:BASE System V
Alan Simpson
499pp. Ref. 394-5

This complete tutorial guide covers every R:BASE function, while exploring and illustrating the principles of efficient database design. Examples include inventory management, mailing list handling, and much more.

Also:
Understanding R:BASE 5000
Alan Simpson
413pp. Ref. 302-3

Power User's Guide to R:BASE System V*
Alan Simpson
350pp. Ref. 354-6

A tutorial guide to structured programming in R:BASE, including system design, procedure files, performance issues and managing multiple data tables. With complete working systems for mailing list, inventory and accounts receivable.

Mastering Lotus HAL
Mary V. Campbell
342pp. Ref. 422-4

A complete guide to using HAL "natural language" requests to communicate with 1-2-3—for new and experienced users. Covers all the basics, plus advanced HAL features such as worksheet linking and auditing, macro recording, and more.

Simpson's 1-2-3 Macro Library
Alan Simpson
298pp. Ref. 314-7

Increase productivity instantly with macros for custom menus, graphics, consolidating worksheets, interfacing with mainframes and more. With a tutorial on macro creation and details on Release 2 commands.

Data Sharing with 1-2-3 and Symphony: Including Mainframe Links
Dick Andersen
262pp. Ref. 283-3

The complete guide to data transfer between Lotus products (1-2-3 and Symphony) and other popular software. With an introduction to microcomputer data formats, plus specifics on data sharing with dBASE, Framework, and mainframe computers.

Mastering Symphony (Third Edition)
Douglas Cobb
840pp. Ref. 470-4
A complex program explained in detail. Includes version 1.2 with the new Macro Library Manager. "This reference book is the bible for every Symphony user I know...If you can buy only one book, this is definitely the one to buy." —IPCO Info

Focus on Symphony Macros
Alan Simpson
239pp. Ref. 351-1
An in-depth tutorial guide to creating, using, and debugging Symphony macros, including developing custom menus and automated systems, with an extensive library of useful ready-made macros for every Symphony module.

Focus on Symphony Databases
Alan Simpson/Donna M. Mosich
398pp. Ref. 336-8
Master every feature of this complex system by building real-life applications from the ground up—for mailing lists, inventory and accounts receivable. Everything from creating a first database to reporting, macros, and custom menus.

Better Symphony Spreadsheets
Carl Townsend
287pp. Ref. 339-2
Complete, in-depth treatment of the Symphony spreadsheet, stressing maximum power and efficiency. Topics include installation, worksheet design, data entry, formatting and printing, graphics, windows, and macros.

WORD PROCESSING

The ABC's of WordPerfect
Alan R. Neibauer
239pp. Ref. 425-9
This basic introduction to WordPefect consists of short, step-by-step lessons—for new users who want to get going fast. Topics range from simple editing and formatting, to merging, sorting, macros, and more. Includes version 4.2

Mastering WordPerfect
Susan Baake Kelly
435pp. Ref. 332-5
Step-by-step training from startup to mastery, featuring practical uses (form letters, newsletters and more), plus advanced topics such as document security and macro creation, sorting and columnar math. Includes Version 4.2.

Advanced Techniques in WordPerfect
Kay Yarborough Nelson
400pp. Ref. 431-3
Exact details are presented on how to accomplish complex tasks including special sorts, layered indexing, and statistical typing. Includes details on laser printing operations.

WordPerfect Desktop Companion (SYBEX Ready Reference Series)
Greg Harvey/Kay Yarborough Nelson
663pp. Ref. 402-X
This compact encyclopedia offers detailed, cross-referenced entries on every software feature, organized for fast, convenient on-the-job help. Includes self-contained enrichment material with tips, techniques and macros. For Version 4.2.

WordPerfect Tips and Tricks
Alan R. Neibauer
441pp. Ref. 360-0
Expert on-the-job guidance and creative new uses for WordPerfect Version 4.1. Topics include technical typing, multi-column printing, macros, and even database, spreadsheet and graphics techniques.

Mastering SAMNA
Ann McFarland Draper
503pp. Ref. 376-7
Word-processing professionals learn not just how, but also when and why to use SAMNA's many powerful features. Master the basics, gain power-user skills, return again and again for reference and expert tips.

Mastering Microsoft WORD (Second Edition)
Matthew Holtz
479pp. Ref. 410-0
This comprehensive, step-by-step guide includes Version 3.1. Hands-on tutorials treat everything from word processing basics to the fundamentals of desktop publishing, stressing business applications throughout.

Advanced Techinques in Microsoft WORD*
Alan R. Neibauer
431pp. Ref. 416-X
The book starts with a brief overview, but the main focus is on practical applications using advanced features. Topics include customization, forms, style sheets, columns, tables, financial documents, graphics and data management.

Mastering DisplayWrite 3
Michael E. McCarthy
447pp. Ref. 340-6
Total training, reference and support for users at all levels—in plain, non-technical language. Novices will be up and running in an hour's time; everyone will gain complete word-processing and document-management skills.

Mastering MultiMate Advantage
Charles Ackerman
349pp. Ref. 380-5
Master much more than simple word processing by making the most of your software. Sample applications include creating expense reports, maintaining customer lists, merge-printing complex documents and more.

The Complete Guide to MultiMate
Carol Holcomb Dreger
208pp. Ref. 229-9
This step-by-step tutorial is also an excellent reference guide to MultiMate features and uses. Topics include search/replace, library and merge functions, repagination, document defaults and more.

Advanced Techniques in MultiMate
Chris Gilbert
275pp. Ref. 412-7
A textbook on efficient use of MultiMate for business applications, in a series of self-contained lessons on such topics as multiple columns, high-speed merging, mailing-list printing and Key Procedures.

Introduction to WordStar (Second Edition)
Arthur Naiman
208pp. Ref. 134-9
This all time bestseller is an engaging first-time introduction to word processing as well as a complete guide to using Word-Star—from basic editing to blocks, global searches, formatting, dot commands, SpellStar and MailMerge.

Introduction to WordStar Release 4 (For IBM PC's and Compatibles)
Arthur Naiman
250pp. Ref. 461-5
WordStar's latest release is now introduced by the bestselling author of the original WordStar tutorial. All the new features are explained to help you get the most out of the advanced word processing package.

Mastering Wordstar on the IBM PC (Second Edition)
Arthur Naiman
200pp. Ref. 392-9
A specially revised and expanded introduction to Wordstar with SpellStar and MailMerge. Reviewers call it "clearly written, conveniently organized, generously

illustrated and definitely designed from the user's point of view."

Practical WordStar Uses
Julie Anne Arca
303pp. Ref. 107-1
A hands-on guide to WordStar and MailMerge applications, with solutions to comon problems and "recipes" for day-to-day tasks. Formatting, merge-printing and much more; plus a quick-reference command chart and notes on CP/M and PC-DOS.

Practical Techniques in WordStar Release 4*
Julie Anne Arca
300pp. Ref. 365-8
A task oriented approach to WordStar Release 4 and the DOS operating system. Special applications are covered in detail with summaries of important commands and step-by-step instructions.

WordStar Tips and Traps
Dick Andersen/Cynthia Cooper/Janet McBeen
239pp. Ref. 261-2
A real time-saver. Hundreds of self-contained entries, arranged by topic, cover everything from customization to dealing with the DISK FULL error to keystroke programming. Includes MailMerge and CorrectStar.

Mastering WordStar Release 4
Greg Harvey
375pp. Ref. 399-6
Practical training and reference for the latest WordStar release – from startup to advanced featues. Experienced users will find new features highlighted and illustrated with hands-on examples. Covers math, macros, laser printers and more.

Introduction to WordStar 2000
David Kolodney/Thomas Blackadar
292pp. Ref. 270-1
This engaging, fast-paced series of tutorials covers everything from moving the cursor to print enhancements, format files, key glossaries, windows and MailMerge. With practical examples, and notes for former WordStar users.

Advanced Techniques in WordStar 2000
John Donovan
350pp. Ref. 418-6
This task-oriented guide to Release 2 builds advanced skills by developing practical applications. Tutorials cover everything from simple printing to macro creation and complex merging. With MailList, StarIndex and TelMerge.

DESKTOP PUBLISHING

Mastering Ventura*
Matthew Holtz
400pp. Ref. 427-5
A complete, step-by-step guide to IBM PC desktop publishing with Xerox Ventura Publisher. Practical examples show how to use style sheets, format pages, cut and paste, enhance layouts, import material from other programs, and more.

Mastering PageMaker on the IBM PC
Antonia Stacy Jolles
287pp. Ref. 393-7
A guide to every aspect of desktop publishing with PageMaker: the vocabulary and basics of page design, layout, graphics and typography, plus instructions for creating finished typeset publications of all kinds.

Understanding PostScript Programming
David A. Holzgang
450pp. Ref. 396-1
In-depth treatment of PostScript for programmers and advanced users working on custom desktop publishing tasks. Hands-on development of programs for font creation, integrating graphics, printer implementations and more.

SYBEX Computer Books are different.

Here is why . . .

At SYBEX, each book is designed with you in mind. Every manuscript is carefully selected and supervised by our editors, who are themselves computer experts. We publish the best authors, whose technical expertise is matched by an ability to write clearly and to communicate effectively. Programs are thoroughly tested for accuracy by our technical staff. Our computerized production department goes to great lengths to make sure that each book is well-designed.

In the pursuit of timeliness, SYBEX has achieved many publishing firsts. SYBEX was among the first to integrate personal computers used by authors and staff into the publishing process. SYBEX was the first to publish books on the CP/M operating system, microprocessor interfacing techniques, word processing, and many more topics.

Expertise in computers and dedication to the highest quality product have made SYBEX a world leader in computer book publishing. Translated into fourteen languages, SYBEX books have helped millions of people around the world to get the most from their computers. We hope we have helped you, too.

For a complete catalog of our publications:

SYBEX, Inc. 2021 Challenger Drive, #100, Alameda, CA 94501
Tel: (415) 523-8233/(800) 227-2346   Telex: 336311
Fax: (415) 523-2373

MASTERING PARADOX (Version 2)

Available on Disk

If you'd like to use the sample databases, reports, and scripts in this book but don't want to type them in yourself, you can send for a disk containing all the examples. To obtain this disk, complete the order form and return it along with a check or money order for $30.00. California residents add 6 percent sales tax.

SMS Software

P.O. Box 2802

La Jolla, CA 92038-2802

Name _____

Address _____

City/State/ZIP _____

Enclosed is my check or money order.
(Make check payable to SMS Software.)
Mastering Paradox—Version 2

Sybex is not affiliated with SMS Software and assumes no responsibility for any defect in the disk or program.

SUMMARY OF PARADOX OPERATIONS

OPERATIONS	MENU OPTIONS OR KEY	PAGE
Queries (calculations)	Ask *Calc* option	263
Queries (multiple tables)	Ask	253
Queries (saving)	Scripts/Querysave	278
Queries (speedup)	Tools/QuerySpeedup	382
Queries (subtotals)	Ask	265
Queries (unique items)	Ask	103
Queries (updating)	Ask	357
Rename an object	Tools/Rename	369
Reports (blank lines)	BLANKLINE	306
Reports (calculations)	Report/Field/Place/Calculated	292
Reports (column format)	Report/Field/Reformat	288
Reports (column justification)	Report/Field/Justify	303
Reports (copy a column)	Report/Tabular/TableBand/Copy	287
Reports (copy format)	Tools/Copy/Report	155
Reports (create)	Report/Design	134
Reports (date and time)	Report/Field/Place/Date or Time	170
Reports (delete columns)	Report/Tabular/TableBand/Erase	286
Reports (delete fields)	Report/Field/Erase	158
Reports (export)	Report/Output/File	389
Reports (group headings)	Report/Tabular/Group/Headings	321
Reports (grouping)	Report/Tabular/Group	312
Reports (insert column)	Report/Tabular/TableBand/Insert	285
Reports (margins)	Report/Setting/Margin	153
Reports (modify format)	Report/Change	150
Reports (move column)	Report/Tabular/TableBand/Move	287
Reports (multiple tables)	Tools/Copy/JustFamily	326
Reports (number formats)	Report/Field/Reformat	171
Reports (page breaks)	PAGEBREAK	164
Reports (page length)	Report/Setting/PageLayout/Length	153
Reports (page numbers)	Report/Field/Place/Page	171
Reports (page width)	Report/Setting/PageLayout/Width	153
Reports (place fields)	Report/Field/Place/Regular	138
Reports (print)	Report/Output	149
Reports (print size)	Report/Setting/Setup	173, 297

DOS and OS/2

Mastering DOS

Judd Robbins
$19.95
7½" x 9"
600 pp.
ISBN: 0-89588-400-3

The ABC's of MS-DOS

Alan R. Miller
$17.95
7½" x 9"
224 pp.
ISBN: 0-89588-395-3
also available:
**The ABC's of
PC-DOS**
Alan R. Miller

MS-DOS Power User's Guide, Volume I (Second Edition)

Jonathan Kamin
$19.95
7½" x 9"
500 pp.
ISBN: 0-89588-473-9
also available:
**MS-DOS Power
User's Guide,
Volume II**
Martin Waterhouse

Essential OS/2

Judd Robbins
$22.95
7½" x 9"
400 pp.
ISBN: 0-89588-478-X

DATABASES

dBASE III PLUS Programmer's Reference Guide

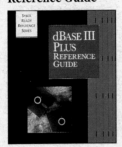

**(SYBEX
Ready Reference
Series)**
Alan Simpson
$26.95 (H/c)
7½" x 9"
1035 pp.
ISBN: 0-89588-382-1

The ABC's of dBASE III PLUS

Robert Cowart
$16.95
7½" x 9"
264 pp.
ISBN: 0-89588-379-1

Understanding dBASE III PLUS

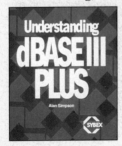

Alan Simpson
$19.95
7½" x 9"
415 pp.
ISBN: 0-89588-349-X

Understanding R:BASE System V

Alan Simpson
$19.95
7½" x 9"
499 pp.
ISBN: 0-89588-394-5

STAY ON THE LEADING EDGE WITH SYBEX BOOKS

**SYBEX publishes
best-selling
books on:**

New Software Versions
OS/2 and DOS
Business Software
Programming
and more...

Use the response card
to join our mailing list
or to order if your local
bookstore doesn't have
the SYBEX titles you
want. Or call
800-227-2346. Allow
21 days for delivery.

SYBEX titles can be
found at major book-
stores—ask your local
bookstore for their
selection.

On bestsellers lists for
the last decade, month
in and month out,
SYBEX titles continue
to receive praise from
readers and reviewers
alike. There are two
hundred titles to
choose from.

Prices are subject
to change.

SYBEX PUBLISHES THE BROADEST RANGE OF COMPUTER BOOKS

SYBEX publishes at every level:

ABCs series for new users
Mastering titles for general users
Advanced titles for special skills
Understanding titles for programmers
SYBEX Ready Reference Series for long-term value
SYBEX Prompter Series for an instant reminder
and more...

SYBEX publishes across the board:

1-2-3, SuperCalc, dBASE, R:BASE, WordPerfect, Word-Star, MS WORD, Pagemaker, Ventura, DOS, OS/2, Apple, Macintosh, 8088/80288/80386, Pascal, C, BASIC, and more...

Select your interest group on the reply card to ensure you receive the latest information on the subjects you need.

SPREADSHEETS

Lotus 1-2-3 Desktop Companion

(SYBEX Ready Reference Series)
Greg Harvey
7½" x 9" 976 pp.
$26.95 (H/c)
ISBN: 0-89588-385-6
$22.95 (S/c)
ISBN: 0-89588-501-8

The ABC's of 1-2-3 (Second Edition)

Chris Gilbert and Laurie Williams
$16.95
7½" x 9"
245 pp.
ISBN: 0-89588-355-4

Mastering 1-2-3

Carolyn Jorgensen
$19.95
7½" x 9"
466 pp.
ISBN: 0-89588-337-6

Mastering Symphony (Third Edition)

Douglas Cobb
$24.95
7½" x 9"
838 pp.
ISBN: 0-89588-470-4

WORD PROCESSING

WordPerfect Desktop Companion

(SYBEX Ready Reference Series)
Greg Harvey and Kay Yarborough Nelson
$26.95 (H/c)
7½" x 9"
663 pp.
ISBN: 0-89588-402-X

The ABC's of WordPerfect

Alan R. Neibauer
$16.95
7½" x 9"
239 pp.
ISBN: 0-89588-425-9

Mastering WordPerfect

Susan Baake Kelly
$19.95
7½" x 9"
435 pp.
ISBN: 0-89588-332-5

Mastering WordStar Release 4

Greg Harvey
$19.95
7½" x 9"
413 pp.
ISBN: 0-89588-399-6